MODERN CRIMINAL LAW

This book brings together leading scholars from the next generation of UK criminal lawyers to celebrate the work of GR Sullivan, Emeritus Professor at University College London, in the year of his retirement from writing *Simester and Sullivan's Criminal Law: Theory and Doctrine.*

The contributors examine many of the areas in which GR (Bob) Sullivan's own writing has been influential, ranging from general doctrines such as causation and culpability, across specific offences like theft and fraud, through defences including necessity and insanity; before turning, finally, to matters affecting the criminal process, notably challenges to the doctrine of precedent in criminal law.

Taken together, the essays are a powerful tribute to Bob's standing and influence upon modern criminal law. At the same time, individually they make sophisticated contributions to our understanding of some pressing issues in contemporary criminal law. The essays illustrate the increasing importance of theoretical argument in modern criminal law, as well as the manner in which doctrinal debates have become interwoven with arguments about criminalisation norms. The resulting collection is thus a tribute also to the character of modern academic criminal law, a character that Bob and the writers of his generation did so much to develop.

Modern Criminal Law

Essays in Honour of GR Sullivan

Edited by
AP Simester

•HART•
OXFORD • LONDON • NEW YORK • NEW DELHI • SYDNEY

HART PUBLISHING

Bloomsbury Publishing Plc

Kemp House, Chawley Park, Cumnor Hill, Oxford, OX2 9PH, UK

1385 Broadway, New York, NY 10018, USA

29 Earlsfort Terrace, Dublin 2, Ireland

HART PUBLISHING, the Hart/Stag logo, BLOOMSBURY and the Diana logo are trademarks of Bloomsbury Publishing Plc

First published in Great Britain 2024

A catalogue record for this book is available from the British Library.

A catalogue record for this book is available from the Library of Congress.

Library of Congress Control Number: 2023951829

ISBN: HB: 978-1-50995-614-2
ePDF: 978-1-50995-616-6
ePub: 978-1-50995-615-9

Typeset by Compuscript Ltd, Shannon

PREFACE

There are many troubling cases in the criminal law. Some are troubling because of a conundrum generated by the courts. What should the Court of Appeal do, for instance, when issued a directive from the Supreme Court on a matter that was freely acknowledged to be obiter dicta?[1] Other cases may challenge our moral intuitions whatever the law says about them. How should we judge, for example, Mr Kingston – a person who performed indecencies upon a fifteen-year-old victim, but did so only because he had, without his knowledge, been drugged by an enemy seeking to blackmail him?

I first met Bob Sullivan when he was a guest of ATH Smith in Cambridge. Bob had come over from Durham to give a paper on the Court of Appeal's decision in *Kingston*.[2] The Court's decision to allow the defendant an excuse seemed morally fair yet, as the House of Lords concluded,[3] not legally justiciable. Accepting the legal worries, Bob sought to show that there might nonetheless be space – sometimes – to recognise an out-of-character defence in the criminal law. It was a fascinating evening and, buttressed by a colliding (*Wales v New Zealand*) interest in rugby, it laid the foundations of a lifelong friendship.

The late Sir John Smith once described Bob as 'a first-rate lawyer, a very perceptive analyst of legal concepts and an original thinker'. These are qualities that any great criminal law academic must possess. He or she needs to be an excellent doctrinal lawyer, one able to reason by analogy, to identify and work constructively with legal rules, and to draw and defend persuasive distinctions. At the same time, rigorous analytical skills are not enough. The best academic work also demands creativity, an ability to see new ways of solving problems and of interpreting the law. Bob possesses all of these qualities. His essays are consistently interesting and important. Doubtless they are not always *right*: but nobody is, and Bob also scores highly on that count. Moreover, if everybody agrees that a given article is right, it is unlikely to be interesting. I mean this as praise when I say that Bob's writings are always worth disagreeing with.

Of course, not all of Bob's contributions to the development of our criminal law are by means of essays. He has written a well-known textbook;[4] there is also

[1] *Barton* [2020] EWCA Crim 575, [2021] QB 685, following *Ivey v Genting Casinos* [2017] UKSC 67, [2018] AC 391, noted (2020) 136 LQR 523 (Sullivan and Simester). See further the chapter by Grant Lamond in this volume.

[2] *Kingston* [1993] 4 All ER 373 (CA). Bob's paper saw the light of day as 'Making Excuses' in AP Simester and ATH Smith (eds), *Harm and Culpability* (Oxford, Oxford University Press, 1996) 131.

[3] *Kingston* [1995] 2 AC 355 (HL).

[4] AP Simester and GR Sullivan, *Criminal Law: Theory and Doctrine* (Oxford, Hart Publishing, 2000); Bob's last edition as author was the seventh (2019, also with JR Spencer, F Stark and GJ Virgo).

an edited collection.[5] In addition, there is much indirect influence. Bob's writings are widely referenced by leading criminal law academics, and have been cited in court judgments including judgments given in the Supreme Court of the United Kingdom, the House of Lords, the Court of Appeal of England and Wales, the Supreme Court of Canada and the High Court of Australia. His publications appear frequently, too, in the Reports of the Law Commission of England and Wales. Bob has also acted as consultant for the Serious Fraud Office of England and Wales and for other bodies including the OECD and the International Chamber of Commerce.

In closing, though, it is important to honour one other form of contribution. There is no doubt but that Bob has been a leading scholar in the development of a modern criminal law across the past forty years. This has been achieved, in part, through his own extensive writings. But he has also mentored and assisted many younger colleagues in the United Kingdom – the very colleagues who are now leading academic criminal law research in this country. Many of those younger colleagues are contributors to this book. Collectively, in many respects they represent the future of academic criminal law in England and Wales. This book is intended, thus, not only to honour Bob but to draw attention to our new generation of criminal law academics, academics whose own work has been influenced by the writings of Bob Sullivan and by that generation of great scholars with whom Bob has worked.

APS
August 2023

[5] GR Sullivan and Ian Dennis (eds), *Seeking Security: Pre-empting the Commission of Criminal Harms* (Oxford, Hart Publishing, 2012).

CONTENTS

PART IV
CRIMINAL JURISPRUDENCE

LIST OF CONTRIBUTORS

Antje du Bois-Pedain, Professor of Criminal Law and Philosophy, University of Cambridge, and Fellow of Magdalene College, Cambridge.

JJ Child, Professor of Criminal Law, University of Birmingham.

Jennifer Collins, Associate Professor in Law, University of Bristol.

Mark Dsouza, Associate Professor of Law, University College London.

Claire Hogg, Research Fellow, University College London.

Jeremy Horder, Professor of Criminal Law, London School of Economics.

Beatrice Krebs, Associate Professor in Criminal Law, University of Reading.

Grant Lamond, Associate Professor and University Lecturer in Legal Philosophy, University of Oxford, and Felix Frankfurter Fellow in Law, Balliol College, Oxford.

Henry Mares, Lecturer in Criminal Law, King's College London.

Paul Roberts, Professor of Criminal Jurisprudence, University of Nottingham.

AP Simester, Amaladass Professor of Criminal Justice, National University of Singapore.

John Stanton-Ife, Reader in Criminal Law, King's College London.

Findlay Stark, Professor of Criminal Law, University of Cambridge, and Fellow of Jesus College, Cambridge.

PART I

The General Part

1

Free, Deliberate and Informed?

AP SIMESTER*

The common law knows a principle that free, deliberate and informed (FDI) interventions by other human actors negate chains of causation in the criminal law. That principle was endorsed unanimously and unambiguously in 2007 by the House of Lords in *Kennedy (No 2)*.[1] More recently, however, the Court of Appeal has handed down a number of judgments that appear to disapply the FDI principle. This chapter begins by considering the decision in *Kennedy* and the extent to which it is compatible with those more recent cases. It then discusses the relationship between the FDI principle and other principles of causation, and contests the notion that there is a single legal test for tracing causal paths through the interventions of others. The causal path from D's conduct to a prohibited outcome cannot run *through* the FDI intervention of another person. Because there is a variety of causal paths, however, it does not follow that the presence of an FDI intervention makes it is *impossible* for D's conduct ever to be recognised as a (concurrent) cause of the outcome. Finally, the chapter re-evaluates the normative case for the FDI principle. An argument can indeed be made for restricting or even abandoning the FDI principle. However (and in this I concur with some of Bob Sullivan's writings[2]), I argue that doing so would be misguided. The FDI principle

* Grateful thanks are due to Jane Stapleton, Findlay Stark, Sandy Steel and Bob Sullivan for their very helpful comments on drafts of this chapter; also to members of the Cambridge Centre for Criminal Justice, at which an advanced version was presented.

[1] *Kennedy (No 2)* [2007] UKHL 38, [2008] 1 AC 269; overruling *Kennedy v R* [2005] EWCA Crim 685, [2005] 1 WLR 2159. A previous appeal had also been unsuccessful: *Kennedy* [1999] Crim LR 65 (CA). In what follows, references to '*Kennedy*' are to the 2007 House of Lords decision.

[2] In addition to numerous case notes, Bob has written on causation in a number of papers, including 'Causation, Fault and Responsibility' in A Reed, M Bohlander, B Simpson and V Adams (eds), *Fault in Criminal Law: Domestic and Comparative Perspectives* (Abingdon, Routledge, 2022; with AP Simester); 'Wrongs and Responsibility for Wrongs in Tort and Crime' in M Dyson (ed), *Unravelling Tort and Crime* (Cambridge, Cambridge University Press, 2014) 82; 'Causation without Limits: Causing Death While Driving Without a Licence, While Disqualified, or Without Insurance' [2012] *Crim LR* 753 (with AP Simester); 'Cause and Contemporaneity of Actus Reus and Mens Rea' (1993) 52 *CLJ* 487. An alternative take can be found in his 'Doing Without Complicity' (2012) 1 *Journal of Commonwealth Criminal Law* 199, where Bob suggests that the conduct of a voluntary agent can sometimes be caused not only by the agent but by other persons too.

is appropriate to the criminal law, notwithstanding that it sometimes results in what might be perceived as undeserved acquittals.

I. The Leading Case

It is 10 September 1996. A drug dealer, Simon Kennedy (SK), is asked for a dose of heroin. He prepares a syringe and gives it to Marco Bosque (MB). MB self-injects the heroin and returns the syringe to SK, who leaves. Subsequently, MB dies. His death is caused by a combination of heroin and alcohol: *Kennedy*.

As is well known, SK's conviction of manslaughter was ultimately quashed by the House of Lords for lack of proved causation. In supplying MB with the heroin, SK enabled MB to take it. But he did not cause MB to take the heroin; his contribution was, as is sometimes said, merely part of the historical 'setting' in which MB unintentionally killed himself.[3] As such, there was no unlawful act of causing MB to take a noxious substance contrary to section 23 of the Offences Against the Person Act 1861; and while there was an unlawful act of supplying heroin, *that* act did not cause MB's death.

Why not? It was eminently foreseeable that MB would self-inject. Moreover, the dangers of doing so, especially when drinking alcohol, are well known. Yet the power of the ruling in *Kennedy* is that a mere act of supply *cannot*, in law, be a cause of death if the drugs are then freely self-administered: 'D is not to be treated as causing V to act in a certain way if V makes a voluntary and informed decision to act in that way rather than another.'[4] At least for the purposes of the criminal law, MB's voluntary intervention supervenes over any causal chain that might otherwise have linked SK's actions to MB's death.

What makes an intervention voluntary in this way? The language of voluntariness is inherently ambiguous, and there is some variation in the judgment when it comes to characterising MB's intervention. Most often, the Court talks in terms of a voluntary and informed choice.[5] But there is also reference to a 'free and voluntary' action,[6] and to a 'free and informed' one.[7] A more complete answer can be derived from their Lordship's reply to the question that was certified by the Court of Appeal:

> When is it appropriate to find someone guilty of manslaughter where that person has been involved in the supply of a class A controlled drug, which is then freely and voluntarily self-administered by the person to whom it was supplied, and the administration of the drug then causes his death?[8]

[3] cp *Smith* [1959] 2 QB 35, 42–43 (C-MAC).
[4] *Kennedy* [14].
[5] See eg *Kennedy* [12], [14], 20]; also [16], [17] ('informed voluntary choice').
[6] ibid [18].
[7] ibid [22].
[8] ibid [2].

To which the response was, 'In the case of a fully-informed and responsible adult, never.'[9] Thus it is a free, fully informed and voluntary intervention by a responsible adult that counts in law as causally independent. 'Voluntary' here does not simply mean that MB had the physical capacity to act otherwise than he did. It means that his act was *volitional*;[10] that it was intentional or deliberate. As such, the gist of the principle is well captured by Hart and Honoré's formulation, which was itself quoted by their Lordships:

> The free, deliberate, and informed intervention of a second person, who intends to exploit the situation created by the first,[11] but is not acting in concert with him, is normally held to relieve the first actor of criminal responsibility.[12]

As noted, the courts have sometimes expressed the principle in terms of a *voluntary* intervention. However, given the ambiguity of that term, it is simpler to speak in terms of free, deliberate, and informed interventions, and indeed the courts have from time to time done just that. That is the convention adopted in this chapter.

Internal Limitations on the Principle

The FDI principle was said in *Kennedy* to be 'fundamental and not controversial'.[13] But it is not without limitations. Some of those limitations are *internal* to the principle, and were acknowledged in *Kennedy* itself:

> The law recognises certain exceptions, in the case of the young, those who for any reason are not fully responsible for their actions, and the vulnerable, and it acknowledges situations of duress and necessity, as also of deception and mistake.[14]

In scenarios like these, V's intervention will not be sufficiently free, responsible or informed to trigger the FDI principle and to count as causally independent. The fourth criterion, deliberateness, goes largely unexplored in the case, but it is significant for reasons that will be explored later. V's intervention must be intentional and not inadvertent, and it must be intentional *under the relevant description* of V's conduct. This mattered in *Kennedy* because it was clear that MB did not

[9] ibid [25].
[10] cp G Williams, '*Finis* for *Novus Actus*?' (1989) 48 *CLJ* 391, 392, quoted in *Kennedy*, [14].
[11] It is not clear what, if anything, is added by the reference to exploitation. Hart and Honoré remark that '[t]he intention of the intervening actor is, however, relevant in the sense that he must intend to exploit the situation created by the defendant, i.e. to treat it as providing the opportunity or occasion for a certain course of conduct' (ibid 136, n 23). They do not suggest that this 'exploitative' act must involve an independent wrong or even particular kinds of motivation. Indeed, it is hard to think of any interesting sense in *Kennedy* in which MB 'exploited' the situation that SK 'created'.
[12] HLA Hart and AM Honoré, *Causation in the Law*, 2nd edn (Oxford, Oxford University Press, 1985) 326; *Kennedy* [14].
[13] *Kennedy* [14]. cp *Pagett* (1983) 76 Cr App R 279, 289; *Latif* [1996] 1 WLR 104, 115; *Hughes* [2013] UKSC 56, [2013] 1 WLR 2461, [21].
[14] *Kennedy* [14].

intend *to kill himself*, even though that is what he did. Rather, he intended *to inject himself with heroin*, and he was held to be sufficiently informed about the nature and properties of the drug he was injecting. Causally speaking, matters might have been different if MB had died because the dose was adulterated with some other material.[15] In such a case, it could not be said that MB had 'voluntarily' chosen to take the substance that killed him. But there was no suggestion in *Kennedy* that what SK supplied was anything other than what MB requested. MB chose to inject himself, 'knowing what he was doing'.[16] As the House of Lords concluded: 'It was his act' – alone.[17]

These internal limitations are, as they should be, compatible with the informing idea behind the FDI principle. What makes V's action uncaused by D is not V's capacity for autonomous action as such. Rather, it is V's *exercise* of that capacity. If V's choice to act is sufficiently autonomous, ordinarily D is not directly responsible for that choice, however much D may have facilitated it. As Glanville Williams has pointed out, in a passage endorsed in *Kennedy*, D's responsibility, if any, for V's action falls to be evaluated within the doctrines of complicity:

> Indeed, it was because the instigator was not regarded as causing the crime that the notion of accessories had to be developed. This is the irrefragable argument for recognising the *novus actus* principle as one of the bases of our criminal law.[18]

Williams's point is both important and right. If I do no more than lend you a jemmy, I do not cause you to break and enter somebody else's house. Neither do I cause the damage you inflict upon the window frame. Those are wrongs that you do. They are your acts – alone. To be sure, depending on the facts, I may share legal responsibility for your wrongs. But not as principal. I am, if at all, liable as a secondary party. The legal requirements for my liability – especially, my mens rea – are distinct from yours, reflecting the truth that our contributions to your wrong differ. Even if I participate in your wrong, I don't perpetrate it.

Two Exclusions?

More on that later. What is more controversial, especially among academics, is the acknowledgement in *Kennedy* of *external* restrictions. External restrictions are those that exclude application of the FDI principle in contexts where the conditions for finding an FDI intervention are met (and where, I shall argue, the rationale behind the FDI principle still applies). One such exclusion was said by their Lordships to arise in *Environment Agency (formerly National Rivers Authority) v*

[15] cp *Kennedy* [18] ('knowing what it was'). Albeit the point was not argued, it was unclear whether the victim knew what drugs she was taking in *Broughton* [2020] EWCA Crim 1093, [2021] 1 WLR 543.

[16] ibid [19].

[17] ibid. (The pronoun refers to MB's act of taking the heroin.)

[18] Williams (n 10) 398; *Kennedy* [17].

Empress Car Co (Abertillery) Ltd.[19] In that case, E Ltd had attached an extension pipe to the tap on a diesel tank in its yard, thereby making it possible for overflows from the tap to drain into the nearby river. E's business was unpopular locally; one night, the tap was opened by an unknown person, causing the entire contents of the tank to overflow into the adjacent river. Significant environmental damage resulted. E's conviction of 'causing polluting matter to enter controlled waters'[20] was affirmed by the House of Lords.

Empress is incompatible with the FDI principle. Moreover, its reasoning is problematic. Giving the leading judgment in *Empress*, Lord Hoffmann relied specifically upon two precedents to undermine the fundamental nature of the FDI principle. The first was *Stansbie v Troman*,[21] in which a decorator, who was working alone in a client's house, left the door unlocked when he went out. According to Lord Hoffmann, 'for the purpose of attributing liability to the decorator, the loss was caused by his negligence because his duty was to take reasonable care to guard against thieves entering'.[22] That is right. But *Stansbie v Troman* is a civil case. The relevant purpose was to assign compensatory liability in respect of a loss, and the FDI principle is less deeply embedded in that context,[23] if it be embedded in tort law at all.[24] The FDI principle is paradigmatically a principle of the criminal law,[25] for reasons to which we come in section IV. As such, *Stansbie v Troman* was not a good precedent for *Empress*.

The second authority invoked was *Alphacell Ltd v Woodward*,[26] which was cited for the proposition that 'the *deliberate* act of a third party does not necessarily negative causal connection'.[27] The citation derives from Lord Wilberforce's obiter comments in *Alphacell* upon an earlier case, *Impress (Worcester) Ltd v Rees*,[28] in which the valve on I's fuel oil tank had been opened deliberately one night by an unknown person, with the consequence that the oil escaped and flowed ultimately into the river Severn. On appeal, the Divisional Court quashed I's conviction, holding that the opening of the valve was a novus actus:

> On general principles of causation, the question which the justices ought to have asked themselves was whether that intervening cause was of so powerful a nature that the

[19] *Environment Agency (formerly National Rivers Authority) v Empress Car Co (Abertillery) Ltd* [1999] 2 AC 22 (hereafter *Empress*); discussed in *Kennedy* [15].

[20] Contrary to the former s 85(1) of the Water Resources Act 1991.

[21] *Stansbie v Troman* [1948] 2 KB 48; see *Empress* (n 19) 31–32.

[22] ibid 31.

[23] cp Hart and Honoré (n 11) 194–200.

[24] Something denied, for example, by Jane Stapleton, who argues that 'the relevance of interventions is simply that they may be the materialisation of a risk that fell outside the scope of the risks in relation to which the defendant owed a duty to be careful'. *Three Essays on Torts* (Oxford, Oxford University Press, 2021) 93.

[25] cp *Commonwealth v Root* 170 A 2d 310, 311–13 (1961).

[26] *Alphacell Ltd v Woodward* [1972] AC 824; see *Empress* (n 19) 32–35.

[27] *Empress* (n 19) 33 (emphasis added); see *Alphacell* (n 26) 835 (below in the text). The comments were obiter because *Alphacell* did not involve a third-party intervention. The pollution in that case occurred when the defendant's pumps became blocked by vegetation.

[28] *Impress (Worcester) Ltd v Rees* [1971] 2 All ER 357 (DC).

conduct of the appellants was not a cause at all but was merely part of the surrounding circumstances. If the justices had asked themselves that question, it seems to me that it would have been susceptible of only one answer, namely that it was not the conduct of the appellants but the intervening act of the unauthorised person which caused the oil to enter the river.[29]

Discussing that decision in *Alphacell*, Lord Wilberforce said:

I do not desire to question this conclusion, but it should not be regarded as a decision that in every case the act of a third person necessarily interrupts the chain of causation initiated by the person who owns or operates the installation or plant from which the flow took place.[30]

Strictly speaking, this is not an assertion about the *deliberate* acts of interveners. Even so, Lord Hoffmann's stronger claim, that deliberate interventions do not always negate causation, is undoubtedly true. Yet it does not contradict the FDI principle. For one thing, as we noted earlier, the FDI principle admits of internal restrictions. A deliberate intervention is not causally independent unless it is also free and informed. More interesting is a possibility to be explored in section III, that the effects of an FDI actor's intervention sometimes operate *alongside* the defendant's contribution, rather than supervening over that contribution.[31] In such cases, it can be legitimate to hold the defendant causally responsible for an outcome notwithstanding that the outcome was *also* caused by the deliberate intervention of another person. But more on this later. It suffices for now that *Alphacell* does not deny the validity of the FDI principle.

Be all that as it may, *Empress* was distinguished rather than disapproved in *Kennedy*. It was distinguished on the grounds that, for the offence in question,

strict liability was imposed [by the legislature] in the interests of protecting controlled waters; and that in the situation under consideration the act of the defendant could properly be held to have caused the pollution even though an ordinary act of a third party was the immediate cause of the diesel oil flowing into the river. It is worth underlining that the relevant question was the cause of the pollution, not the cause of the third party's act.[32]

En passant, one may doubt the persuasiveness of this distinction. The fact that a crime involves strict liability is not by itself reason to adopt an expansive analysis of its actus reus.[33] If anything, a more restrictive approach might be thought desirable to prevent overreach. The potential for profound injustice is laid bare in *L(R) and F(J)*,[34] where members of an unincorporated golf club were in principle

[29] ibid 358.

[30] *Alphacell* (n 26) 835.

[31] cp *Blaue* [1975] 1 WLR 1411; *National Rivers Authority v Yorkshire Water Services Ltd* [1995] 1 AC 444 (HL). Both of these cases are discussed in section III.

[32] *Kennedy* [15].

[33] Contrast, for example, the approach in *Hughes* [2013] UKSC 56, [2013] 1 WLR 2461.

[34] *L(R) and F(J)* [2008] EWCA Crim 1970, [2009] 1 Cr App R 16.

criminally liable for the same offence as in *Empress*, after an underground pipe was carelessly fractured by independent building contractors and oil seeped into a nearby watercourse:

> By the time of the ruling by the Judge with which we are now concerned, the prosecution had abandoned any allegation that either defendant was personally culpable in any manner, nor was there any allegation that either had done anything to make him criminally liable beyond being a member of the club which maintained the tank and pipe. The club had 900 or so members. Any one or all of those members would have been in an identical legal position.[35]

Yet on a 'purposive' approach to causation, all were in principle guilty. Moreover, the limits of such an approach are opaque. One might think that the purpose of imposing homicide liability is to protect human life, yet even that purpose does not warrant abandoning the FDI principle. The statute at issue in *Empress* did not suggest that deviation from standard criminal law causation principles was envisaged by the legislature. It referred simply to 'causing' without qualification. Neither would a less expansive interpretation frustrate the legislative purpose. Admittedly, it would render the protection of controlled waters less stringent. But the FDI principle does that to most crimes; it is not clear why controlled waters should be special. The exceptionalism in *Empress* goes deeper than *Kennedy* admits, because it has the potential to render the FDI principle ad hoc, rather than the 'fundamental' principle it is said to be.

Nevertheless, for practical purposes *Empress* appears to be restricted to a narrow class of regulatory wrongs, especially those concerning the environment. By contrast, a second exclusion left open in *Kennedy* involves a more obviously stigmatic crime: manslaughter by gross negligence. It is to that exclusion, and to other attempts to bypass the FDI principle, that we now turn.

II. Avoiding the FDI Principle

According to the House of Lords, the appeal in *Kennedy* was 'concerned only with unlawful act manslaughter and nothing in this opinion should be understood as applying to manslaughter caused by gross negligence'.[36] On its face, this is a surprising qualification. In keeping with its characterisation as 'fundamental', the FDI principle endorsed by their Lordships seems equally applicable to other forms of homicide besides unlawful act manslaughter. Imagine, for example, that D unlawfully supplies P with a handgun. P, an FDI actor, then fatally shoots V. It is clear from *Kennedy* that D does not cause V's death for the purposes of the criminal law. To paraphrase the Court's quotation from *Dalby*, supplying

[35] ibid [2].
[36] *Kennedy* [6].

the weapon would have led to no harm unless P had subsequently used it in a manner that was dangerous.[37] Suppose, then, that it was grossly negligent for D to supply the gun to P, because of an obvious and serious risk that P would kill somebody.[38] (Perhaps P had been threatening to do just that.) The same reasoning surely applies: however irresponsible it was of D to supply the weapon, his doing so would have led to no harm unless P subsequently misused it. The shooting was P's act – alone.[39]

Their Lordship's denial that *Kennedy* has any application to gross negligence manslaughter was therefore too strong. Something similar can be said of the attempt to distinguish *Empress* by emphasising that 'the relevant question was the cause of the *pollution*, not the cause of the *third party's act*'.[40] In homicides, the relevant question is the cause of the death, not the cause of the killer's act: yet the FDI principle still applies. This truth tends to be obscured by the additional requirement in unlawful act manslaughter (the offence at issue in *Kennedy*) that, besides being a cause of death, D's act must have been unlawful – hence the Court's focus on section 23 of the 1861 Act. In terms of causation, however, that focus is a distraction. If, on a given set of facts, a mere act of supply cannot cause death for the purposes of unlawful act manslaughter, it cannot cause death for the purposes of homicide generally.

Read carefully, nothing in the subsequent Court of Appeal decision in *Evans* is inconsistent with that conclusion,[41] albeit *Kennedy* was sidelined as 'an authority expressly stated to have no application to gross negligence manslaughter'.[42] In truth, however, *Evans* did not turn on this. Rather, it turned on a crucial difference in the material facts. Unlike in *Kennedy*, the defendant, Gemma Evans (GE), had *remained on the premises* after supplying her half-sister, Carly Townsend (CT), with the heroin that CT self-injected. Because of this, the Court of Appeal was able to locate the actus reus at a later point in time, ie when GE did not summon medical assistance for CT. That omission was, it seems,[43] a cause of death – not the original act of supply.

[37] *Dalby* [1982] 1 WLR 425, 429; *Kennedy* [7]: 'the supply of drugs would itself have caused no harm unless the deceased had subsequently used the drugs in a form and quantity which was dangerous'. It is clear from the context of the relevant paragraph in *Dalby* that the language of 'caused' was deployed there in a non-legal sense, meaning something like 'led to' or 'occasioned'.

[38] Arguably, it was grossly negligent for SK to supply heroin to somebody who was also drinking: he had even told MB 'to take care that he did not go to sleep permanently'. See *Kennedy* [3].

[39] cp *Kennedy* [19]. Depending on the facts, D's liability would fall to be determined under s 2 of the Suicide Act 1961 or, were P to kill another person, under ordinary principles of complicity.

[40] ibid [15] (emphasis added).

[41] *Evans* [2009] EWCA Crim 650, [2009] 1 WLR 1999. GE bought heroin for CT, who self-injected. When CT became ill, GE and their mother decided not to seek medical help for fear that they may all 'get into trouble' (at [6]). CT later died. GE's conviction of manslaughter was upheld by the Court of Appeal.

[42] ibid [16].

[43] The point was uncontested before the Court of Appeal, but it would have been necessary to prove at trial that T would have survived had assistance been sought (cp *Morby* (1882) 8 QBD 571; *Broughton* [2020] EWCA Crim 1093, [2021] 1 WLR 543).

The decision in *Evans* is nonetheless problematic. It is well established in the criminal law of omissions that one may incur a duty to prevent harms the risk of which one has caused. As was said by Lord Diplock in the leading case of *Miller*, that duty is 'to take measures that lie within one's power to counteract a danger that one has oneself created'.[44] In *Miller*, however, that duty was circumscribed by, inter alia, insistence upon a causal relationship between the defendant's original conduct and the potential harm. Without explicitly acknowledging it had done so, the Court of Appeal appeared to extend the scope of that duty in *Evans*:

> [F]or the purposes of gross negligence manslaughter, when a person has created *or contributed to the creation of* a state of affairs which he knows, or ought reasonably to know, has become life threatening, a consequent duty on him to act by taking reasonable steps to save the other's life will normally arise.[45]

The difficulty with this extension is that it makes principals out of people whose conduct is, at most, in the nature of assistance or encouragement. *Kennedy* is unequivocal on this point: GE did not create the risks that followed CT's self-injection. She committed a supply offence but not manslaughter, because causal responsibility for CT's death lay with CT herself. While the facts of *Kennedy* can be differentiated on the basis of ongoing presence, in substance *Evans* is a significant incursion upon the FDI principle.

Unfortunately, a similar move is made in *Wallace*:

> [T]hough an assessment has to be made in the overall scheme of things of the causative significance of intervening acts or events, the all-important question on legal causation [in homicide cases] remains whether 'the accused's acts can fairly be said to have made *a* significant contribution to the victim's death'.[46]

This is simply incorrect. One can contribute to a result without causing it – a possibility that is very much in point for complicity law, and something that was central to the analysis in the case. Knowing that their relationship was failing, Berlinah Wallace (BW) poured sulphuric acid upon her boyfriend, Mark van Dongen (vD), while he was sleeping. vD sustained horrific and untreatable, but non-fatal, injuries. After relocating to hospital in Belgium, he underwent a medical euthanasia process in accordance with Belgian law. At the conclusion of that

[44] *Miller* [1983] 2 AC 161, 176; see also at 175. M fell asleep in a squat whilst smoking a cigarette. He awoke to find the mattress smouldering. Rather than extinguishing the fire, M simply moved to the next room and went back to sleep. The house itself caught fire; M's conviction of arson was upheld by the House of Lords.

[45] *Evans* [2009] EWCA Crim 650, [2009] 1 WLR 1999, [31] (emphasis added). James Manwaring has suggested to me that perhaps the Court meant 'created or contributed *causally* to the creation' of the risk, in which case the difficulty lies in the Court's application, rather than identification, of the legal principles governing *Miller*-type situations. That is a plausible analysis, and one that would explain why *Evans* has not been widely relied upon in subsequent cases. For the purposes of this discussion, however, I shall assume that the Court had in mind the broader test, that D 'created or contributed', not necessarily in a causal way, to the risk.

[46] *Wallace* [2018] EWCA Crim 690, [2018] 2 Cr App R 22, [64] (emphasis in original).

process, vD was killed by doctors who injected drugs directly into his heart, bringing about his immediate death.

At BW's first trial, May J dismissed a charge of murder on the ground that BW did not cause vD's death. The Court of Appeal demurred. Remitting the case for retrial, the Court endorsed a model direction that included a three-part test for causation. The jury needed to be sure about all three of the following criteria:[47]

(i) But for the injuries caused by the acid attack, vD would not have undergone voluntary euthanasia.
(ii) W's act of throwing acid upon vD must be a significant and operating cause of death; not necessarily the only cause of death but playing more than a minimal role.
(iii) At the time of the acid attack, it must have been reasonably foreseeable that the defendant would commit suicide or undergo voluntary euthanasia as a result of his injuries.[48]

But this test ignores the ruling in *Kennedy*. *Wallace* is not a case of suicide. It is a case of voluntary euthanasia. In terms of the FDI principle, that difference matters. The doctors who killed vD did so deliberately and with a full understanding of what was being done. Neither were they under any kind of compulsion to accede to vD's request. They chose freely to do so.[49] Even if we concede that vD's election to undergo voluntary euthanasia was reasonably foreseeable, that concession is not in point. MB's self-injection in *Kennedy* was entirely predictable, yet it was MB's act. Similarly, in *Wallace*, the killing of vD was the doctors' act.

A less blatant attempt to steer around *Kennedy* can be found in *Field*.[50] Benjamin Field (BF) ruthlessly preyed upon the affections of a vulnerable elderly man, Peter Farquhar (PF). BF moved into PF's home. A 'betrothal ceremony' followed and PF changed his will in BF's favour. Thereafter, BF embarked on an appalling, premeditated (and fully documented) campaign to destabilise his companion and to bring about his death in a manner that would appear self-inflicted. One evening, he plied PF with a bottle of 60 per cent proof whisky, pouring it out and handing the glasses to PF. PF died that night from acute alcohol poisoning, exacerbated by the effects of Dalmane.[51]

Once again, this is a supply case. PF drank the whisky freely and deliberately, knowing what it was. Unlike in *Wallace*, however, the Court engaged with *Kennedy*, which was acknowledged as the 'critical authority' for the purposes of the appeal.[52] Neither was the approach in *Evans* adopted, even though BF had remained on the

[47] ibid [86(3)].

[48] ibid [86(3b)]: suicide and voluntary euthanasia were not differentiated by the Court.

[49] The Court rightly observed (ibid [76]) that vD's choice to die was not free. But what matters for the FDI principle is whether the doctors' act of killing was free.

[50] *Field* [2021] EWCA Crim 380, [2021] 1 WLR 3543.

[51] In what follows, I disregard the Dalmane, a sleeping pill that was taken only in a therapeutic dose. There was no evidence that it was not voluntarily taken, or that PF was unaware of the dangers of mixing sleeping pills with alcohol.

[52] *Field* [2021] EWCA Crim 380, [2021] 1 WLR 3543, [58].

premises for at least some time.[53] Rather, the Court held that the FDI principle did not apply because its internal conditions went unmet – specifically, because PF was not fully informed:

> [He] would have believed that he was drinking 60% proof whisky in the company of someone who loved and would care for him, not someone who wished for his death. As a consequence, PF would not have had an informed appreciation of the truly perilous nature of what was occurring. … Engaging in this activity was not, as a consequence, the result of a free, voluntary and informed decision by PF. … The appellant's undisclosed homicidal purpose, in these circumstances, changed the nature of the act: PF was to a material extent unwittingly lured into a perilous drunken and drugged position by someone who feigned to be his loving partner.[54]

The difficulty with this analysis is that it modifies the description of PF's intervention so as to evade the FDI principle. If we look back to *Kennedy*, what counted in that case was whether MB's action was deliberate and informed under the description, 'inject himself with the syringe of heroin'; *not*, 'kill himself'.[55] Presumably MB understood the risks involved with taking heroin and alcohol. Despite that, it seems clear that MB did not realise that he *would* die. To that extent, MB lacked full information about the further consequences of his act of self-injection. Doubtless, like PF, MB would have refrained from injecting himself had he known what would happen next. But that didn't matter. He freely chose to take the heroin, knowing the drug's properties.

The same applies to PF. We can assume, for the prosecution did not disprove and the Court of Appeal accepted,[56] that he freely chose to drink the whisky knowing its strength.[57] Even if he was inebriated, a drunken intent to drink is still an intent to drink.[58] Thus PF deliberately chose to drink the very thing that caused his death, knowing what it was. What he didn't know was that his partner wouldn't help him; that, in fact, BF wanted him dead. But that was merely an ancillary mistake. Moreover, the lack of help was not a legally relevant cause of death, and the prosecution did not allege that it was.[59] Like the facts of *Kennedy*, PF was

[53] See eg ibid [39]. It seems that the possibility of an *Evans*-type duty was not pursued at trial, and it is unclear how long BF remained in the house after pouring the whisky.

[54] ibid [60].

[55] Contrast *Wallace*, where the facts were even stronger on this point than they were in *Kennedy*.

[56] *Field* [2021] EWCA Crim 380, [2021] 1 WLR 3543, [60]; quoted above in the text.

[57] In '*Novus Actus* and Beyond: Attributing Causal Responsibility in the Criminal Court' (2021) 80 CLJ (Supp) s61, s75, Antje du Bois-Pedain suggests that causation might be attributed because of the manner in which BF had manipulated PF – so that, in effect, PF's choice to drink was unfree and not his own. But this is speculative. The facts, as proved, did not allow the Court to reconceptualise the case in this way.

[58] cp *Sheehan* [1975] 2 All ER 960, 963 (CA): 'a drunken intent is still an intent'. See also *Bree* [2007] EWCA Crim 804, [2008] QB 131, [32], in the context of consent.

[59] Things might have been otherwise. The prosecution did not seek to argue that BF was under a duty to intervene *after* the whisky was drunk. Potentially, such a duty could have been grounded upon an assumption by BF of responsibility for PF's welfare, arising from the ostensibly caring relationship between BF and PF: cp *Sinclair, Johnson and Smith* [1998] EWCA Crim 2590, (1998) 148 NLJ 1353.

fully informed about the nature of the action that he chose to take and which directly brought about his death. BF had, of course, facilitated that action. But he didn't make it happen.

III. Understanding the FDI Principle in its Legal Context

In terms of standard doctrine, there are two main strategies for circumnavigating *Kennedy*. One strategy is to hold that D's earlier action remains a cause of the relevant outcome despite another person's intervention. The other strategy is to locate the actus reus in a later, duty-violating omission by D to prevent the outcome from occurring. Both strategies respond to the moral pull of what are often abhorrent facts, and are typically deployed in cases where it is not possible to convict D on the basis of complicity. It is in such cases that the law's causation doctrines, and the FDI principle in particular, come under the greatest pressure.

Hard cases of this kind can, of course, make for bad law. Yet before we turn to the merits of the FDI principle itself, we should acknowledge a related but distinct source of difficulty in this area. At least sometimes, there is a failure clearly to understand the FDI principle and its relationship to causation doctrines as a whole. Consider the following two theses, which offer possible interpretations of the FDI principle:

> *Sufficiency Thesis*: Interventions that are free, deliberate and informed *always* break the causal chain linking defendants and outcomes.
> *Necessity Thesis*: Interventions that are not free, deliberate and informed *never* break the causal chain linking defendants and outcomes. That is to say, an intervention must be free, deliberate and informed if it is to 'break' the causal chain.

The FDI principle makes neither of these claims. Moreover, both claims are false.[60] Yet their falsity is not always apparent. Consider, for example, the facts of *Rebelo*,[61] another supply case. Bernard Rebelo (BR) sold dinitrophenol (DNP) as a slimming pill to Eloise Parry (EP). DNP is a dangerous substance that is unlicensed as a food or medicine in the United Kingdom; it is illegal to sell DNP for human consumption. EP, who suffered from personality disorders and had developed bulimia nervosa, was aware of the risks of taking DNP but was unable to control

(Sinclair was a close friend of the victim and they lived together.) It may be that this route to conviction, which would have better reflected the causal sequence of events in *Field*, was not pursued because of the potential difficulties involved in sustaining findings of causation for omissions cases: difficulties well illustrated in *Broughton* [2020] EWCA Crim 1093, [2021] 1 WLR 543.

[60] To be clear, I reject the Sufficiency Thesis only because of the possibility of *Smith*-type concurrent causation, discussed below in this section.

[61] *Rebelo* [2021] EWCA Crim 306, [2021] 4 WLR 52.

her urges to do so. On 12 April 2015, she overdosed on eight of the pills and died. On a retrial, BR was convicted of manslaughter by gross negligence. With respect to causation, the main focus in the case concerned whether EP's taking an overdose was an FDI intervention. Doubtless the jury was entitled to find that it was not, on the grounds that BR was in an extreme state of psychological compulsion when she took the pills. But that does not conclude the question of causation. An unfree intervention might still be unforeseeable or, as was said in *Empress*, 'extraordinary'.[62] Yet that possibility was elided in the jury direction:

> If, on the other hand, you are sure that Eloise Parry did not make a fully free or fully voluntary or fully informed decision to take the DNP, then, if the defendant was in gross breach of his duty of care owed to her, his negligence remains a substantial and operative cause of her death, even if it was not the sole cause of her death. He is guilty of manslaughter.[63]

Not so. Suppose, as seems plausible, that EP died only because she took eight of the pills rather than the expected dose of one. In that case, the jury should also have been asked whether her doing so was reasonably foreseeable. Maybe overdoses of this order are indeed foreseeable – but that needs to be established, and established beyond reasonable doubt. The general point is that an unfree or unintentional intervention can still be a novus actus interveniens. Such interventions are, in terms of causal analysis, no different from the interventions of a non-human animal or a natural event. None of them engages the FDI principle: yet, when they are unforeseeable, they can sometimes defeat ascriptions of causation to the defendant.[64]

The quoted direction from *Rebelo* exemplifies the Necessity Thesis. Antje du Bois-Pedain, by contrast, rejects the FDI principle because she associates it with the Sufficiency Thesis.[65] For du Bois-Pedain,[66] the FDI principle sits uncomfortably with cases like *Blaue*,[67] in which Jacolyn Woodhead (JW) died from stab wounds inflicted by Ronald Blaue (RB). JW's death resulted only after she refused a blood transfusion that, as she knew, was essential to save her life. RB's conviction of manslaughter was rightly upheld by the Court of Appeal. Correctly understood, however, the FDI principle is not in tension with *Blaue*. Let us grant, for the sake of argument, that JW's rejecting the transfusion was an autonomous choice; her

[62] *Empress* (n 19) 34. A classic example is *Jordan* (1956) 40 Cr App R 152.

[63] *Rebelo* [2021] EWCA Crim 306, [2021] 4 WLR 52, [30].

[64] cp *Martin* (1827) 3 C & P 211, 172 ER 390 (M held not to have caused death after he offered his child a sip of gin, but the child seized and drank the entire glass). To vary the facts of *Hart* [1986] 2 NZLR 408, for example, suppose that D assaults V, leaving her lying unconscious on a beach. Later, a very large dog strays by and drags V below the high-water mark. If V subsequently drowns under the incoming tide, causation would not ordinarily lie. Similarly, in *Roberts* (1971) 56 Cr App R 95, 102, where V injured herself by throwing herself out of a moving car after being assaulted by D, the Court held that causal responsibility for V's injuries would not lie if V's reaction were 'daft'.

[65] du Bois-Pedain (n 57).

[66] ibid s 65.

[67] *Blaue* [1975] 1 WLR 1411.

doing so was a causal factor in her death. Yet it does not follow that RB's actions cannot *also* be a cause of death – for the Sufficiency Thesis is false, and it does not articulate the FDI principle.

To explain this, let's back up a bit. Historically, there is a tendency in the common law to treat the question of causation as a matter of 'common sense'. In practice, common sense is an unruly guide.[68] Yet, as Lord Hoffmann observed in *Empress*, its invocation does not mean that we lack legal principles when it comes to dealing with the interventions of other actors or natural forces.[69] (Indeed, the Court of Appeal in *Wallace* sought to capture some of those principles in its recommended jury direction.[70]) For Lord Hoffmann, at least regarding the crime at hand in *Empress*,[71] there was a single test for all such interventions: whether the intervention was 'abnormal and extraordinary'.[72]

There is much to be said for the language of extraordinariness, in as much as it emphasises the objective character of the more familiar inquiry into whether an intervention was 'unforeseeable'. One might, of course, deny that *any* unitary test for interventions is adequate, and part of the point of this chapter is to do just that. But the more immediate question is, where should we locate such tests within the overall analysis? Answer: not at the beginning. Rather, our causal analysis should start with the possibility that interventions are irrelevant. To put things differently, it should start by asking whether the case at hand is like *Smith*.[73]

Thomas Smith (TS) stabbed another soldier during a barracks fight. Nobody realised that the victim's lung was pierced. While being carried to the medical station, V was dropped twice by a fellow soldier. When he finally got there, V received 'thoroughly bad' treatment for someone with his injuries; had he been properly treated, V would very likely have survived. Nonetheless, TS's conviction of murder was upheld. Rightly so. There were certainly interventions by others – V's fellow soldier and the doctors – but, from the perspective of TS's causal responsibility, those interventions were irrelevant. They were irrelevant because TS's causal responsibility for V's death did not run through them. The wound that TS inflicted led directly to V's death: it was, as Lord Parker CJ put it,[74] still a substantial, 'operating' cause at the time of V's death. V died (inter alia) of the stab wound. TS inflicted that wound; it follows that his doing so was a cause of death *without more*.

[68] 'It is remarkable how many cases there are under this Act in which justices have attempted to apply common sense and found themselves reversed by the Divisional Court for error of law.' *Empress* (n 19) 29.

[69] ibid: 'The principles involved are not complicated or difficult to understand, but they do in my opinion call for some explanation.'

[70] *Wallace* [2018] EWCA Crim 690, [2018] 2 Cr App R 22, [86(3)]; summarised in the text above at n 47.

[71] *Empress* (n 19) 33: 'On what principle, therefore, will some acts of third parties (or natural events) negative causal connection for the purposes of section 85(1) and others not?'.

[72] ibid, 34.

[73] *Smith* [1959] 2 QB 35 (C-MAC).

[74] ibid 42.

This is an example of the 'common sense' part of causation that, save for the de minimis constraint, generally requires no guidance by legal principles. If each of E and F stabs V, and V dies of blood loss from the combined wounds, then both E and F cause V's death.[75] Unless negligible, it matters not that F's contribution was much less substantial than E's; that the wound inflicted by F would not have caused death on its own; that E's action was free, deliberate and informed; or that V would ultimately have died even had F not stabbed him at all. The so-called 'but for' test is irrelevant as well as unhelpful. The foreseeability test and the FDI principle are irrelevant too. The fact of the matter is that V died from a combination of the wounds; each was a significant and operating cause of death. Case closed.[76]

Some pollution cases are like *Smith*. In *National Rivers Authority v Yorkshire Water Services Ltd*,[77] for example, Y operated a treatment works that collected water from the drains, treated it, then discharged the neutralised effluent into Hunsworth Beck and thence into the River Spen. In May 1990, an unknown rogue unlawfully poured iso-octanol solvent into the drains. Unsurprisingly, it was collected and passed through the treatment works, entering the Spen in virtually undiluted form. Y's conviction, for causing the iso-octanol to enter the Spen, was upheld by the House of Lords. Appropriately so. The rogue was an FDI actor who also caused the pollution, but it was Y's treatment works that gathered the solvent and redirected it into Hunsworth Beck. Thus the operation of those works was a cause of the pollution too. Properly understood, the FDI principle is consistent with *Yorkshire* because it was not engaged by the facts of that case.

At the level of principle, interventions become important *only when we do not have* Smith-*type causation*. In the absence of a direct causal relationship of that kind, our challenge is to *construct* a causal path that runs through the interventions of others (or nature). In this, more common, type of case, D's action becomes a cause only by intersecting in various ways with the agencies of other persons and events. Necessarily, there are legal principles – interlocking principles – to guide that construction.[78] It is not simply a matter of common sense.

The Importance of Not Mixing Up the Criteria

Blaue is like *Smith*. The fact that JW's refusal of treatment may have been free, deliberate and informed is neither here nor there, because the original wound remained an operating cause of her death. Contrast, for example, *Roberts*,[79] in

[75] cp *People v Lewis* 57 P 470 (1899).

[76] At least in the criminal law. Apportionment may be relevant in tort.

[77] *National Rivers Authority v Yorkshire Water Services Ltd* [1995] 1 AC 444 (HL).

[78] For a sketch map of the relevant principles, see AP Simester, JR Spencer, F Stark, GR Sullivan and GJ Virgo, *Simester and Sullivan's Criminal Law: Theory and Doctrine*, 7th edn (Oxford, Hart Publishing, 2019) 113–14.

[79] *Roberts* (1972) 56 Cr App R 95.

which Kenneth Roberts made sexual advances to V while driving a car. V jumped out of the car and was thereby injured. KR's conviction of assault occasioning actual bodily harm was rightly upheld by the Court of Appeal, but the case is not like *Smith*. It was V's act of throwing herself out of the car that was the direct cause of her injuries. Yet that act was not free; and it was foreseeable:

> The test is: Was it the natural result of what the alleged assailant said and did, in the sense that it was something that could reasonably have been foreseen as the consequence of what he was saying or doing? As it was put in one of the old cases, it had got to be shown to be his act, and if of course the victim does something so 'daft', in the words of the Appellant in this case, or so unexpected, not that this particular assailant did actually foresee it but that no reasonable man could be expected to foresee it, then it is only in a very remote and unreal sense a consequence of his assault, it is really the result of a voluntary act on the part of the victim which could not reasonably be foreseen and which breaks the chain of causation between the assault and the harm or injury.[80]

In terms of the facts of *Roberts*, this passage is unobjectionable. But it harbours a potential conflation. An unforeseeable response by V need not be 'voluntary' in the sense associated with the FDI principle. The FDI principle is quite separate from the principle that an unforeseeable intervention is not attributed to the defendant. They cut across each other: both principles, or neither, may apply in a given case.

Frequently, the courts do not see all these differences clearly. *Blaue* supplies an example. The Court of Appeal correctly drew an analogy to *Smith*, observing that 'The physical cause of death … was the bleeding into the pleural cavity arising from the penetration of the lung. This had not been brought about by any decision made by the deceased but by the stab wound.'[81] Pressed by counsel, however, it felt obliged to over-egg the causal pudding with a digression into the reasonableness of JW's refusal:

> It has long been the policy of the law that those who use violence on other people must take their victims as they find them. … It does not lie in the mouth of the assailant to say that his victim's religious beliefs which inhibited him from accepting certain kinds of treatment were unreasonable.[82]

Taking victims as one finds them is a maxim about pre-existing susceptibilities: it does not apply to the victim's subsequent actions. *Roberts* is clear authority to that effect. We should not be surprised that, immediately following the quoted passage, the Court continued: 'The question for decision is what caused her death. The answer is the stab wound. The fact that the victim refused to stop this end coming about did not break the causal connection between the act and death.' In

[80] ibid 102.
[81] *Blaue* [1975] 1 WLR 1411, 1415.
[82] ibid.

other words, the foreseeability of her refusal was irrelevant. Like *Smith*, the case was already closed.

An à la carte approach can also be seen in the Court of Appeal's model direction for *Wallace*.[83] As we saw earlier, the Court required BW's action to be a significant and operating cause of his death. In terms of the criteria laid down in *Smith*, however, it was not an operating cause. vD did not die of his injuries. The operating cause of his death was the injection of drugs into his heart. In setting up 'operating cause' as a criterion of causation, the Court effectively trivialised it, turning it into a conclusion rather than a sufficient (albeit not necessary) condition.

The real question in *Wallace*, of course, was whether a causal path could be constructed *through* the medical intervention. To address that question, the Court offered only the so-called 'but for test' and the requirement of foreseeability. Yet the 'but for test' is irrelevant here. In general, counterfactual speculations are relevant only to causation via omission. Who knows how vD's life would have gone had BW not thrown acid on him? We cannot say for sure – and it doesn't matter. What matters is the actual, not counterfactual, chain of events that BW initiated. Undoubtedly, she set in motion events that led vD to be killed by the doctors. But can their intervention be attributed to BW? Here, at least, the foreseeability test is relevant. But so too is the FDI principle, which got left off the menu altogether.

IV. Interventions and the FDI Principle

It is easy to see why foreseeability (or extraordinariness) is an important criterion of causal ascriptions for intervention cases. The effects of our actions can intersect with a myriad of other events, and a requirement of foreseeability helps to filter those ramifications. It allows us to hold defendants responsible for outcomes they have been involved in but have not directly caused, without unduly expanding their liability to embrace all the vagaries of the world. Foreseeability thus puts a partial cap on moral luck.[84] Outcomes *can* be laid at D's door notwithstanding that they resulted from causal processes that D did not initiate. But not always.

The case for the FDI principle is less straightforward. It begins with the point that convictions, unlike adverse tort verdicts, are deeply personal. They are intrinsically significant and not merely gateways to sanctions. The conviction condemns D publicly as a wrongdoer and affixes her with a criminal record,

[83] Summarised earlier in the text at n 47.

[84] Only a partial cap. In addition to the possibility mentioned earlier of *Smith*-type causation, it is also plausible that causal responsibility may be ascribed for the effects of interventions that were actually foreseen or sought by D: cp *Quinn v Leatham* [1901] AC 495, 537; *Hart and Honoré*, 170–72. For the purposes of this chapter, it is unnecessary to pursue those supplementary grounds.

with all the implications that can have for her future life. The conviction is inherently censorious. Even more to the point: it is inherently censorious *of the person convicted*. It is not merely an acknowledgement that something has gone wrong, something for which, as it happens, D must pay. This is part of the problem with decisions like *L(R) and F(J)*, mentioned earlier.[85] Even if the golf club members were to receive a nominal punishment, their lives and their membership of the community would still be tainted by their being labelled, publicly, as criminals. That label cannot be defrayed or passed to anybody else.[86] It belongs to the person convicted.

By contrast, the finding of liability in tort operates as a licence to move money around, but it normally lacks the censorious nature of a criminal conviction.[87] The defendant in *Stansbie v Troman* should pay for the thefts albeit he stole nothing.[88] Tort verdicts are, in this sense, instrumental and largely *impersonal* – something reflected in the fact that damages awards are transferable and can be offset by insurance; and in the fact that liability can be incurred on a vicarious basis. Sometimes in private law, even though D herself did no wrong, the risk of liability may justly fall on her. Similar liability would be unjust in the criminal law.[89]

This is not to deny that one may be held criminally liable for the acts of deliberate interveners. But such liability is properly governed by the more nuanced rules of complicity, as both Williams and Sandy Kadish have argued.[90] There is no possibility that the defendant in *Empress* could have been guilty of aiding or abetting pollution of the river; yet the constraints that complicity law imposes were rendered irrelevant by the simple expedient of convicting D as a principal. At the level of principle, this is problematic, however efficacious it may be in reducing pollution. When a secondary party (S) lends P the knife that P later uses to stab V, we may, depending on S's mens rea, hold S responsible for V's injury on the basis that she participated in the causing of that injury. Yet we should deny, as the law denies,[91] that S caused V's injury. That would make S a principal.

[85] See the text at n 34.

[86] Neither can the punishment. The conviction may sometimes become spent – even then, however, it is not spent for all purposes. It must be disclosed in England, for example, when applying for a judicial appointment.

[87] Punitive damage awards may be an exception, but are problematic in as much as they lack the procedural safeguards embedded in criminal law. See too F Stark, 'Tort Law, Expression, and Duplicative Wrongs' in J Oberdiek and P Miller (eds), *Civil Wrongs and Justice in Private Law* (Oxford, Oxford University Press, 2020) 441.

[88] See above in the text at n 21.

[89] This is the key point that was missed by Lord Hoffmann in *Empress*. His Lordship made much of the claim that causation doctrines depend upon the purpose of the relevant legal rule (cp *Hughes* [2013] UKSC 56, [2013] 1 WLR 2461, [20]). I have already questioned in the text whether this is a convincing basis upon which to distinguish pollution from homicide laws. Yet there is a much deeper division at work here, pointed to earlier, between the basic purpose of criminal law and that of tort. The criminal law is condemnatory and punitive; tort law is primarily compensatory.

[90] Williams (n 10); SH Kadish, 'Complicity, Cause and Blame: A Study in the Interpretation of Doctrine' (1985) 73 *California Law Review* 323.

[91] See too Hart and Honoré (n 11) 377–88; J Gardner, 'Complicity and Causality' (2007) 1 *Criminal Law and Philosophy* 127.

Let's think about the disutility of that. A constraint of foreseeability cannot reliably save us from the implication that S would be liable as a principal. Doubtless, P's use of the knife will on occasion be unforeseeable. Often, though, it will be foreseeable or even foreseen – wherefore convictions for crimes of recklessness or negligence *as a principal* may be in play. Were V to die, for example, S could become guilty of gross negligence manslaughter without having foreseen P's actions. Part of the point of the FDI principle is to avoid such possibilities by respecting the difference between S and P, and shielding S from being a joint principal alongside P.

The temptation to convict of murder is understandable in extreme cases such as *Wallace*.[92] But the FDI principle is much bigger than that. It plays a key role in allowing the law to recognise the distinctive ways in which secondary parties are complicit in crimes that *they do not themselves perpetrate*. It is not open, and should not be open, to the courts to abandon the FDI principle on a selective basis; and we should not sacrifice a whole field of doctrine for the sake of ad hoc retribution. Admittedly, the FDI principle has some potential to generate undeserved acquittals. In general, however, D will be guilty of a predicate offence, such as supplying heroin (*Kennedy*, with three years' imprisonment) or applying a corrosive substance with intent (*Wallace*, with imprisonment for life and a minimum tariff of twelve years). Rare will be the case where D's action constitutes no predicate crime at all: we should not respond to such cases by modifying general rules. Where necessary, we should regulate them with specific crimes.

Consider, on the other hand, what abandoning the principle might entail for conduct that should *not* be a predicate crime. Doubtless, in some parts of England and Wales, it is foreseeable, when a shopkeeper sells baseball bats or Japanese cooking knives, that they may be used as weapons. A bartender may see one of her regulars start a fight in a burst of drink-fuelled aggression.[93] The FDI principle helps to protect such persons from liability for causing harm. Without it, the net of criminalisation is spread much wider and threatens to deter all kinds of activities that might facilitate wrongdoing by others, activities that are quotidian and not apt for proscription. Sometimes, of course, such activities *should* generate criminal liability – but that is the very point of complicity doctrines. Extending criminal responsibility for the acts of another is a complex matter, one that demands a considered trade-off of interests and freedoms. It requires specialist mens rea rules that are sensitive to the contributions of both S and P. Above all, it is a matter that is unsuitable for the kind of blunt treatment that abandoning the FDI principle implies.

Implicit in this argument is that the FDI principle is as much a principle about legal responsibility and autonomy as it is about causation. The perpetrator is not

[92] With that said, we should not lose sight of the fact that, even when directed at the retrial in terms of foreseeability, the jury refused to find that BW caused vD's death.

[93] See too the examples collected in Kadish (n 90) 404, nn 259–60.

a mere cipher or an unthinking drone.[94] In treating P with the respect due to a 'voluntary', autonomous actor, we also help to preserve S's freedom. To illustrate this point, consider the well-known case of *Beatty v Gillbanks*.[95] The Salvation Army was banned by local magistrates from marching in the town of Weston-super-Mare. The ban arose because their marches against alcohol had come to attract opposition from a self-styled 'Skeleton Army', who sought to disrupt the marches by violent means, resulting in numerous injuries and even some deaths. The violence and the injuries were, thus, predictable. Rightly, however, the Divisional Court quashed the ban. The injuries were not caused by the Salvation Army, and should not be laid at their door. People should not lose their liberties to do what is otherwise entirely lawful, merely because exercising those liberties can generate the opportunity for others to misbehave.

Beatty v Gillbanks shows the inadequacy of making causal ascriptions purely on the basis of foreseeability. The Salvation Army did not cause the injuries that their opponents inflicted, and to hold otherwise would be wrongly to restrict their freedom to assemble. At the same time, the case also has rule-of-law implications. To uphold a ban would have confirmed that the Skeleton Army were empowered to change the Salvationists' legal position. It would have imposed upon the Salvationists a conditional duty not to assemble in public, where the triggering of that duty lay in their opponents' hands. As such, the FDI principle not only protects S – the Salvationist; the shopkeeper; the bartender – from unwarranted exposure to criminal liability as principals: it also restricts the powers that P has over S, by reducing P's opportunities to make of S a criminal.[96]

The rule of law demands that my criminal liability should not be determined by the whims of a fellow citizen.[97] This is part of the problem with vicarious criminal liability too. Besides generating convictions of the blameless, vicarious liability puts the defendant at the mercy of, say, a disgruntled employee. An analogous worry applies to *Empress*, where the opening of the tap was clearly malicious and may well have been done with the aim of making D guilty of a crime. D's conviction in *Empress* thus infringes principles of equality as well as fairness. It subordinates D's status in the community to the will of a stranger. Of course, sometimes D's liability does lie in the hands of another – but once again, this is properly the domain of complicity law. As a secondary party, S must sign up to P's project, by aiding or abetting it with the requisite mens rea. In such cases, S deliberately puts her liability in P's hands: something that cannot be said of the shopkeeper or bartender. Nor of the Salvation Army in Weston-super-Mare.

[94] There will, of course, be exceptional cases. But those are ones to which the FDI principle does not apply.

[95] *Beatty v Gillbanks* (1882) 9 QBD 308; noted in Williams (n 10) 397.

[96] Elsewhere, I have called this the principle of personal control over criminal liability: AP Simester, *Fundamentals of Criminal Law: Responsibility, Culpability, and Wrongdoing* (Oxford, Oxford University Press, 2021) § 5.3.5.

[97] Or even the police: this is one of the central worries about *Larsonneur* (1933) 24 Cr App R 74 and *Winzar v Chief Constable of Kent* (1983) The Times, 28 March.

V. Conclusion

The FDI principle is sometimes characterised as a doctrine of *novus actus interveniens*.[98] There is an important sense in which that is misleading. An FDI intervention is not truly described as a *novus actus* that 'breaks' a causal chain, because, typically, *there was no* direct, *Smith*-type causal chain running from D's action that, but for another person's intervention, would have led to the outcome. By itself, as the House of Lords in *Kennedy* saw, SK's act of passing heroin to MB had no causal potential to kill. It played no operating role in MB's death. There was, in other words, *no causal chain* linking SK to MB's death *there to be broken* by a so-called *novus actus*. Instead, the issue in *Kennedy* was the other way around. The Court was considering whether to *construct* a chain to link the defendant's act to the consequences of another's intervention. Unlike *Smith*-type causation, that is an intrinsically normative exercise. And the FDI principle is simply one normative limitation upon such constructions. Which is why, as I said earlier, the FDI principle is about legal responsibility and autonomy, and not just about causation.

Alas, and in the teeth of precedent, the Court of Appeal has sometimes been propelled by the awful facts of cases such as *Wallace* and *Field* to restrict or even disregard the FDI principle. Partly, this reflects the kind of judicial reluctance seen in *Empress*, to embrace a more complex, multi-threaded yet principled analysis of causation. Frequently, too, the courts have failed to acknowledge the crucial difference between criminal and civil verdicts. At the same time, *Kennedy* itself created ammunition for gunning down the very principle that it so clearly endorsed. It allowed that *Empress* and, potentially, *Evans* were compatible decisions. In truth they are not. The justification of (external) restrictions on the FDI principle depends upon a claim that the reasons for endorsing that principle in the criminal law are overridden by other ad hoc factors. That case has not been made.

[98] See eg Williams (n 10); du Bois-Pedain (n 57) s64.

2

Against Knowledge (in the Criminal Law)

FINDLAY STARK*

Those leafing through the mens rea chapter in an English criminal law textbook are greeted by a wide variety of fault terms. Amongst his other achievements, Bob Sullivan has markedly improved our understanding of several mens rea concepts. Now that the legal meaning of most of the relevant concepts is more settled, the following question can sensibly be posed: how many fault elements does English criminal law need?

In recent decades, the courts have begun to address that question indirectly through whittling fault elements down. For example, malice and wilful neglect are now translated into intention and ('subjective') recklessness.[1] This chapter contends that the fault element of knowledge – a term that Sullivan has illuminated significantly[2] – should similarly be consigned to history.[3]

There are three main ways in which English criminal law employs knowledge, analysed in Parts I–III below: (I) as a stand-alone fault element, typically in relation to circumstantial elements of crimes; (II) as an alternative to other fault elements such as belief and reasonable cause to suspect, again typically in relation to circumstantial elements of crimes; and (III) as a covert substitute for intention as a fault element in (at least some) consequence-based crimes. It will be argued that, in each context, knowledge does more harm than good. Knowledge's particular problems can be avoided by focusing simply on the defendant's *beliefs*

* Thanks are due to Rachel Clement Tolley, Mark Dsouza, Alexander Greenberg, Tom Hawker-Dawson, Bob Sullivan and participants at seminars at the University of Cambridge, King's College London, and the University of Surrey for comments on earlier drafts. I am grateful, in particular, to Andrew Simester for his patience as editor and his comments on multiple versions of this paper.

[1] *Cunningham* [1957] 2 QB 396 (malice); *Sheppard* [1981] AC 394 (wilful neglect).

[2] GR Sullivan, 'Knowledge, Belief and Culpability' in S Shute and AP Simester (eds), *Criminal Law Theory: Doctrines of the General Part* (Oxford, Oxford University Press, 2005).

[3] Some uses of knowledge appear to be 'indirect', forming aspects of other fault elements: S Shute, 'Knowledge and Belief in the Criminal Law' in S Shute and AP Simester (eds), *Criminal Law Theory: Doctrines of the General Part* (Oxford, Oxford University Press, 2005) 179–82. As Shute recognises, it is *belief* that more readily plays this role.

and amending actus reus requirements if the 'truth' of a certain matter is of importance to the crime's definition.

I. Intention, Knowledge and Circumstances

To understand the deployment of knowledge as a fault element in relation to circumstance elements, one must first understand the limitations of intention in this context.

Intending, Knowing, Believing and Suspecting

The English courts have generally preferred not to define intention, viewing it as an ordinary word that jurors can typically comprehend.[4] There is, however, widespread agreement amongst theorists that intention has necessary elements. Two of these components of intention are problematic regarding circumstance elements, and apparently necessitate recourse to knowledge (and, in turn, the differentiation of knowledge and belief).[5]

First, there is a close connection between intention and one's motivations for actions.[6] Circumstantial elements of crimes frequently play no role in D's motivations for acting as he did; D is unlikely to view his action as a failure if the relevant circumstance does not exist (or come to exist). Circumstances are more typically the surrounding context in which behaviours and their consequences operate.[7] Of course, circumstances *can* (atypically) play a motivational role: D, for the thrill of being involved in illegal activity, places an advertisement for stolen goods online. D goes to extravagant lengths to question those who respond to the advert regarding the provenance of the offered goods. Here, D places the relevant advertisement *because* he believes that it will bring it about that he is offered goods for purchase that are stolen.

A second feature of intention is nevertheless likely to be absent in D's case: to intend to bring about *X* one must believe that it is at least possible to influence *X*'s occurrence through one's behaviour.[8] Additionally, such control must be

[4] *Moloney* [1985] AC 905, 926; *R (Charles) v CCRC* [2017] EWHC 1219 (Admin), [2017] 2 Cr App R 14, [57]–[59]. See, however, section III, below.

[5] Indeed, that these requirements of intention cannot typically be satisfied in relation to *X* is a strong indication that *X is* a circumstantial element.

[6] AP Simester, JR Spencer, F Stark, GR Sullivan and GJ Virgo, *Simester and Sullivan's Criminal Law: Theory and Doctrine*, 7th edn (Oxford, Hart Publishing, 2019) 150; RA Duff, *Intention, Agency and Criminal Liability* (Oxford, Basil Blackwell, 1990) 61.

[7] Duff (n 6) 42, 88.

[8] ibid 17, 55–57; AP Simester, *Fundamentals of Criminal Law* (Oxford, Oxford University Press, 2020) 357–59; Simester et al (n 6) 141; L Zaibert, *Five Ways Patricia Can Kill Her Husband* (Chicago, Open Court, 2005) 188–89.

suitably direct if an ascription of intention is to be appropriate.[9] Control of this kind will often be absent in relation to circumstantial elements. In the example above, D ultimately has no control over the provenance of the goods offered to him – either they are illicit, or they are not, and nothing he can do can alter that fact. Accordingly, talk of D's 'intending' that the goods be illicit is inappropriate.

To avoid the problems identified above, where the criminal law claims to require intention regarding circumstances, this is typically translated into other terms – most relevantly,[10] knowledge and belief.[11]

Like intention, knowledge has often been thought to be 'a straightforward word which does not need judicial exegesis'.[12] When the courts have attempted to define knowledge, however, 'it is scarcely an exaggeration to say that any true belief held with conviction' will do.[13] The English courts' definitions of knowledge have almost always contained the ingredients of belief that a relevant proposition (*p*) is true and that *p* is, in fact, true.[14]

To understand the criminal law's concept of knowledge, then, one must additionally grasp belief. English criminal law is also unclear regarding what constitutes a *belief* that *p* is true. I have argued elsewhere that the best understanding of belief for the criminal law's purposes is one that focuses on a person's dispositions relative to the truth of *p*.[15] Are D's dispositions such that D will have the relevant mental experience that *p* is true,[16] and will plan, act and react based on the truth of *p* in appropriate conditions? So long as D possesses a suitable number of these relevant dispositions, an ascription of a belief that *p* is appropriate.

[9] Whether we can be *held responsible* for circumstances that are beyond our control is another matter. See Simester (n 8) 197–200.

[10] Sometimes, intention in relation to circumstances is translated into 'hoping' or 'desiring' that the relevant circumstance exists: Simester et al (n 6) 150; D Ormerod and K Laird, *Smith, Hogan and Ormerod's Criminal Law*, 16th edn (Oxford, Oxford University Press, 2021) 101. But the law is often (too) quick to claim that desire is irrelevant to culpability (eg *Mohan* [1976] QB 1, 11), and no real effort – judicial or academic – has been spent on establishing the limits of these terms. See, too, Model Penal Code, § 2.02(2)(a)(ii), defining purpose in relation to circumstances in terms of awareness, belief or hope.

[11] AP Simester, 'The *Mens Rea* of Criminal Attempts' (2015) 131 *LQR* 169, 171; Simester et al (n 6) 150; Ormerod and Laird (n 10) 101. Some authors explain things simply in terms of knowledge: G Williams, *Textbook of Criminal Law*, 2nd edn (London, Stevens, 1983) 116.

[12] *Afalabi* [2009] EWCA Crim 2879, [29].

[13] Sullivan (n 2) 207. See: *Saik* [2006] UKHL 18, [2007] 1 AC 18, [26]; *Montila* [2004] UKHL 50, [2004] 1 WLR 3141, [27]. The famous (if contested) tripartite understanding of knowledge from philosophy as *justified* true belief has not been adopted judicially. This avoids various problems with the justification requirement explained in F Stark, *Culpable Carelessness: Recklessness and Negligence in the Criminal Law* (Cambridge, Cambridge University Press, 2016) 151–63. Although it is *possible* for a word to mean different things in different contexts in the criminal law, this is unwise in terms of fostering public understanding of the law, and constraining adjudicators' discretion adequately – see ibid, ch 3.

[14] An arguable exception is found in section II, below.

[15] See: Stark (n 13) ch 4. See, further, E Schwitzgebel, 'A Phenomenal, Dispositional Account of Belief' (2002) 36 *Noûs* 249. cf J Quilty-Dunn and E Mandelbaum, 'Against Dispositionalism: Belief in Cognitive Science' (2018) 175 *Philosophical Studies* 2353.

[16] This is perhaps what is meant by 'acceptance' – eg *Forsyth* [1997] 2 Cr App R 299, 320. The role of 'acceptance' in this context is discussed below in section II.

Several features of this conception of belief are noteworthy. First, and most crucially in terms of distinguishing knowledge and belief, beliefs can be false. Secondly, beliefs can be non-occurrent, insofar as D might not be thinking consciously about *p* yet still believe that *p* if she is disposed to act and react as if *p* were true; this opens up the possibility of non-occurrent knowledge. Thirdly, this conception of belief allows for D to be *somewhat* inconsistent in her dispositions regarding the truth of *p* whilst still ascribing to her the belief that *p*. *Some* degree of doubt that *p*, as manifested in one's dispositions, is compatible with a belief that *p*, and consequently (legal) knowledge that *p*.[17] It is only where the doubts become more significant – when one's dispositions diverge more significantly from the relevant 'dispositional stereotype'[18] – that this ascription is no longer warranted. For instance, if a person only *sometimes* has the relevant mental experience, or only *sometimes* acts and reacts as though the wiring is faulty, they do not believe that the wiring is faulty. They may, of course, believe that the wiring *might* be faulty, etc, a point to which I will return below.

Further clarity on the criminal law's understanding of belief can be achieved by examining briefly a concept that is frequently juxtaposed with it, and indeed with knowledge: suspicion. *Suspicion* begins where belief runs out,[19] but there is no clarity in the case law regarding precisely where this line is to be drawn.

Dictionary definitions of suspicion tend to emphasise the low level of confidence placed by the agent in the truth of *p*.[20] Suspicion finds its kin amongst 'doubts, qualms, … misgivings, and the like',[21] even if, as the courts have suggested, it requires more than a sense of unease,[22] an 'inkling' or a 'fleeting' thought'.[23] A suspicion that *p* can, accordingly, be conceptualised as a probabilistic belief about *p*:[24] 'by no means to believe [*p*] to be so [but] to believe only that it may be so';[25] to 'think that there is a possibility, which is more than fanciful' that [*p*] exists[26] or, if one prefers, a belief that there is a risk that *p*.[27] On this view,

[17] Compare the 'virtual certainty (barring some unforeseen intervention)' test from *Nedrick* [1986] 1 WLR 1025, 1028. Although ostensibly about *intention*, *Nedrick* is best viewed as endorsing a standard of knowledge – see section III, below.

[18] A term coined in Schwitzgebel (n 15).

[19] See eg: *Dunn* [2021] EWCA Crim 439, [44]; *Forsyth* [1997] 2 Cr App R 299, 321.

[20] See eg https://dictionary.cambridge.org/dictionary/english/suspicion. See also E Griew, 'Consistency, Communication and Codification – Reflections on Two *Mens Rea* Words' in PR Glazebrook (ed), *Reshaping the Criminal Law* (London, Stevens, 1978) 71.

[21] G Graham, 'Russell's Deceptive Desires' (1986) 36 *Philosophical Quarterly* 223, 226.

[22] *Da Silva* [2006] EWCA Crim 1654, [2007] 1 WLR 303, [16].

[23] ibid [19].

[24] Sometimes called a 'belief-first' view of the matter. See further EG Jackson, 'The Relationship between Belief and Credence' (2020) 15 *Philosophical Compass* 1, 3.

[25] *Saik* [2006] UKHL 18, [2007] 1 AC 18, [120]. See further S Edwards, 'Nondoxasticism about Self-deception' (2013) 67 *Dialectica* 265, 272–73.

[26] *Da Silva* [2006] EWCA Crim 1654, [2007] 1 WLR 303, [16].

[27] Compare A Sarch, *Criminally Ignorant: Why the Criminal Law Pretends We Know What We Don't* (Oxford, Oxford University Press, 2019) 19. Granted, matters *can* be made more complex, ontologically, for instance by distinguishing 'partial' and 'all-out beliefs' that *p*: R Holton, 'Intention as a Model for

suspicion forms an important component of ('subjective') recklessness, a point that will be revisited below.[28] And, if knowledge of what *may* or *might* be the case is deployed by the criminal law (and, as will be seen below, it is), this again looks like a probabilistic belief that *p*, and accordingly – when D's assessment of the probability that *p* is low enough – suspicion that *p*.

With these understandings of knowledge, belief and suspicion in hand, attention can turn to the problems of requiring knowledge in relation to circumstance elements. The first major problem concerns cases in which the relevant circumstances are yet to materialise.[29]

Knowing the Future?

If knowledge, in law, requires a *true* belief about *p*, then the truth of *p* must be ascertainable at the time that it is claimed that D possessed knowledge that *p*. There is a view that there can be *no* knowledge of matters that will only be determined in the future – sometimes called 'future contingents'. If this sceptical position is right, then D's knowledge of future facts and circumstances *cannot* be proved to have existed at the time it must be proved to have existed – D's performance of the behavioural aspects of the actus reus.

It is helpful to distinguish between two types of scepticism about future contingents that are relevant to the criminal law:

> *Logical scepticism*: it is logically impossible for a proposition regarding a future contingent (PRFC) to have a truth value; and
> *Epistemological scepticism*: even if it is logically possible for a PRFC to have a truth value, the criminal law often requires proof that D knew the relevant PRFC *before* the stage where it is plausible that D could have grasped the truth of the relevant PRFC.

One argument for *logical scepticism* is that, if representations about future events are true today, then those events are either necessarily going to happen or necessarily not going to happen. This position is typically rejected by those who see it as incompatible with free will. Accordingly, a common tactic in philosophy is

Belief' in M Vargas and G Yaffe (eds), *Rational and Social Agency: The Philosophy of Michael Bratman* (Oxford, Oxford University Press, 2014) 26–28. I am unconvinced that it is *necessary* for the criminal law to do this.

[28] The other component of recklessness being that it is 'objectively' unreasonable/unjustified for D to run the risk that she believes to exist.

[29] Child and Hunt argue that this debate is misconceived, because it assumes that mens rea questions must be asked at t_1 relative to later t_2 using t_1 mens rea concepts: J Child and A Hunt, 'Beyond the Present Fault Paradigm: Expanding *Mens Rea* Definitions in the General Part' (2022) 42 *OJLS* 438. I do not have space to engage fully with their impressive alternative approach here, but Child and Hunt are responding, in the main, to problems that arise because of the law's overprivileging of intention and knowledge – the same difficulty being addressed (in a different way) in this paper.

simply to deny that representations and statements regarding future contingents can have a truth value until the contingent matters are resolved.[30] In consequence, one cannot know about the existence of a particular circumstance in the future because its truth is simply not determined yet. If knowledge is required by the criminal law in such situations, the prosecution's task is, on this view, logically impossible.

Some theorists have doubted this conclusion, but it will be argued that, even if they can cast doubt on *logical scepticism*, the concerns of *epistemological scepticism* can rarely be overcome.

Non-sceptical Responses

One line of argument is advanced by Stephen Shute. For him, the belief that there will be daylight in New York tomorrow seems an apt candidate for knowledge.[31] This reflects a natural usage of the term knowledge, at least about things that have only an infinitesimal chance of not occurring. A hitherto-undiscovered asteroid might block out the sunlight (hence the logical problem), but those possibilities can rationally be excluded when ascribing knowledge.

It is difficult, however, to extrapolate this insight to the kinds of future contingent with which the criminal law concerns itself.[32] Contrast Shute's daylight example with a requirement to prove that, at the time of D's handing P a baseball bat, it was sufficiently clear that P would assault someone else with it. *Epistemological scepticism* arises in relation to such examples because of the variables (most prominently, the choices of free, independent agents) involved.

It might be countered that *some* statements about others' future conduct are appropriate candidates for ascriptions of knowledge, again at least conventionally. Consider Andrea Iocana's example of a man who always goes for a walk at 10am. That man's neighbour is waiting by the window at 9.50am one day, and says 'In about 10 minutes, he will go out'.[33] It is at least colloquially plausible to say that the neighbour *knows* that the man will appear at 10am. But, again, having *knowledge* here seems to require a tremendous amount of uniformity in the man's habits, and such uniformity is unlikely to be relevant in criminal cases. One can imagine examples (an overnight security guard who is particularly fastidious about when he takes his tea break), but there is no clear utility in employing a mens rea term such as knowledge if it is virtually never applicable in legal practice.

[30] See, classically, Aristotle, *On Interpretation* ([350 BCE] Oxford, Clarendon, 1928, trans EM Edghill) part 9.

[31] Shute (n 3) 187.

[32] D Ormerod, 'Making Sense of *Mens Rea* in Statutory Conspiracies' (2006) 59 *Current Legal Problens* 185, 209–10.

[33] A Iocana, 'Knowledge of Future Contingents' (2022) 179 *Philosophical Studies* 447–67, 448.

A contrast is sometimes drawn with one's *own* future conduct in this regard.[34] I know, whilst typing, how this sentence will end. Here, knowledge of one's future conduct seems, however, to collapse into a statement of one's intentions and beliefs regarding such conduct, and again seems to exclude only extremely unlikely variables, such as temporary paralysis. It is less clear, at 2.14pm, that I can *know* that I will cycle home at 4pm. Too much may readily intervene. Additionally, as my *own* conduct is at issue, and I can control that, there is no need to place this weight on knowledge – I *intend* to cycle home at 4pm, even if I realise that this is optimistic.

An alternative line of argument against *logical scepticism* is to point out the oddity of claiming that the truth or falsity of present statements is determined only once contingent matters are resolved. For instance, at the time of writing (late 2023), it is plausibly either true or false that Russia will occupy parts of Ukraine. It does seem odd to claim that this statement only *becomes* true or false in the event of Russia's occupying those regions.[35]

But even if this response is along the right lines, *epistemological scepticism* looms large. The main reason for this is the criminal law's requirement of contemporaneity of mens rea and actus reus.[36] The court cannot say that D knew at t_1 that *X* would later occur at t_2 on the basis that, t_2 now having passed, *the court* knows that *X* in fact occurred; that would *not* be to find a point in time where actus reus and mens rea coincided. D must be proved to have known about *X* at t_1, when he satisfied the behavioural elements of the actus reus. The difficulty here is that human beings cannot usually hope to know the relevant truth until the relevant conditions are at least closer to being resolved.[37]

Even though it ignores the question of justification of one's beliefs (normally the problem here, in epistemology), English and Welsh criminal law does not typically define its actus reus elements such that the truth of the relevant proposition about future facts or circumstances will be graspable at the moment that mens rea must be proved to have existed.

For instance, the parties to a conspiracy are liable at the stage of agreeing to commit a crime, even if the plan is never put into action.[38] Despite this, the conspirators must apparently 'intend or know that [any particular fact or circumstance necessary for the commission of the offence] shall or will exist at the time when the conduct constituting the offence is to take place'.[39] It has already been

[34] See S Hampshire, *Freedom of the Individual* (Princeton, NJ, Princeton University Press, 1975) ch 3.

[35] Sullivan (n 2) 214.

[36] See, generally, *Simester and Sullivan*, § 5.8. It might be argued that this is not the only, or best, account of the relationship between actus reus and mens rea, but it is certainly the one prevailing in English law.

[37] See AR White, *Grounds of Liability* (Oxford, Oxford University Press, 1985), ch 8.

[38] eg *Walker* [1962] Crim LR 458.

[39] Criminal Law Act 1977, s 1(2).

explained why talk of intention here is problematic.[40] Knowledge also founders. Taking into account the discussion above, if there is any likelihood of a circumstance's not occurring or existing at the relevant time, knowledge about it will be out of the defendants' grasp at the time of the agreement, and this must mean that the defendants are not guilty.[41] This difficulty has given rise to the view that conspirators would only be liable if the relevant circumstances were verifiable at the time of the agreement; where they are 'existing facts'.[42] Even here, however, there is a problem: D1 and D2 agree at t_1 to deal with money later at t_2. Perhaps, it might be thought, D1 and D2 can – in terms of logic and epistemology – know that the money *shall* be the proceeds of crime at t_2 if there is no way the money can become legitimate in the interim. If D1 and D2 are arrested at t_1, though, how is the prosecution to prove that the money shall even be available to D1 and D2 at t_2?[43] Indeed, if the conspirators did not agree a precise time and place for committing an offence (which is entirely compatible with their being liable for conspiracy), it is possible even the court trying D1 and D2 will not know whether the relevant fact or circumstance exists, has existed, or will exist, despite the benefit of hindsight.

Far from supporting a general thesis about knowledge of the future's being possible, in a way that would warrant retaining knowledge as a fault element, this provision regarding conspiracies merely indicates how unfit for purpose the offence of conspiracy is, if read strictly.[44] The courts have been clear that the relevant statutory provision is to be read strictly to require intention or a true belief regarding the relevant circumstance.[45] The only way conspiracy must function in practice is by fudging these concepts, by convicting conspirators who *believed*, at the point of agreement, that the relevant circumstance element *would* exist when necessary for the commission of the agreed offence. Truth is quietly ignored.

Similar problems infect complicity law. The defendant must intend to provide encouragement or assistance to the principal, *knowing* the essential elements (broadly, the actus reus and mens rea) of the principal's future crime.[46] Talk of 'intending' that the principal's crime will take a particular form meets problems regarding control: accessories ordinarily do not control the principal's conduct in any meaningful sense. This worry is particularly acute when one considers that, at the time of supplying the assistance or encouragement, the defendant must satisfy a mens rea requirement with regard to the principal's state of mind at the time of

[40] This is the case whether one looks directly at an intention regarding the relevant fact or circumstance (using ibid, s 1(2)) or the intentions of the party regarding carrying out the agreement (using s 1(1)).

[41] Sullivan, 'Knowledge, Belief and Culpability', 215.

[42] See, also, in the context of complicity, *Jogee* [2016] UKSC 8, [2017] AC 387, [9].

[43] Compare JC Smith, 'Conspiracy under the Criminal Law Act 1977' [1977] *Crim LR* 598, 603.

[44] ibid, 604.

[45] *Saik* [2006] UKHL 18, [2007] 1 AC 18.

[46] *Johnson v Youden* [1950] 1 KB 544.

committing the offence.[47] Another person's future mental state is not usually an apt candidate for the kind of control generally thought to be essential to intention. Granted, one can imagine cases where an accessory does have sufficient influence over the principal's behaviour and attendant mental states to count as having adequate control: in this sense, procurers may be in a different position from assisters and encouragers.[48] But such cases are comparatively rare. Assisters and encouragers may hope, or desire, or believe that the principal will have the relevant mens rea for the offence at the time the actus reus is performed. But they typically cannot *intend* that.[49] Furthermore, such a view is impossible to reconcile with the long-established point that D need not intend *that P commits the relevant offence* in order to be an accessory to it.[50]

The leading case of *Jogee* does not require us to speak in such ways. Consider the Supreme Court's view that, '[i]f the crime requires a particular intent, [the accessory] must intend to assist or encourage [the principal] to act with such intent'.[51] One way of reading this sentence is to hold that complicitly requires that 'the defendant intended that the principal would have the mens rea required for the offence. Intention is now what is required.'[52] That analysis would render complicity typically impossible to prove.[53] Many accessories are presumably indifferent to the ultimate offence's commission.[54]

The better reading might accordingly be thought to be that secondary parties must intend to offer encouragement or assistance to P, *knowing* what P will do and with what mental state P will do it.[55] But this reading's resort to knowledge is ultimately unhelpful, too, unless D *can know*, at the time of providing the encouragement or assistance, what P's precise mental state will later be. Too many variables are involved in even the most standard cases.[56] Again, this must be

[47] *Jogee* [2016] UKSC 8, [2017] AC 387, [10], [90].

[48] Indeed, the courts sometimes suggest procurement exceptionally requires 'causation' of the principal's offending: eg *Attorney-General's Reference (No 1 of 1975)* [1975] QB 773, 780.

[49] One might query whether this statement applies to 'indirect' intention. Indirect intention is still a form of *intention*, and must still relate to things that one can control adequately by one's behaviour. It is, thus, usually inapposite when considering future circumstance elements.

[50] Eg *NCB v Gamble* [1959] 1 QB 11; *Jogee* [2016] UKSC 8, [2017] AC 387, [90].

[51] *Jogee* [2016] UKSC 8, [2017] AC 387, [10]. See, also, [90].

[52] D Ormerod and K Laird, '*Jogee*: Not the End of a Legal Saga but the Start of One?' [2016] *Crim LR* 539, 540.

[53] Much depends on what 'conditional intention' requires, in practice, post-*Jogee*. For criticisms of the comments about this concept in *Jogee*, see: AP Simester, 'Accessory Liability and Common Unlawful Purpose' (2017) 133 *LQR* 73, 84–86; J Child, 'Understanding Ulterior *Mens Rea*: Future Conduct Intention is Conditional Intention' (2017) 76 *CLJ* 311, 316, 318–319.

[54] There is no requirement that an accessory intends that P *will* commit the crime – see, eg, *Jogee* [2016] UKSC 8, [2017] AC 387, [90]. Any such requirement would seem impossible to satisfy in most cases for the reasons mentioned above.

[55] See the account presented in Simester et al (n 6) § 7.4(iv).

[56] Child and Hunt think that truth claims go beyond knowledge and infect future recklessness due to the requirement that – 'objectively' – the principal's subsequent risk-taking is unjustified. This requires (they contend) an assessment of future facts that are, ex ante, unknowable: (n 29) 449. D can, however, believe, at the point of giving assistance or encouragement to P, that: (1) P *will* do the relevant action in

fudged in practice, such that defendants are convicted on the basis of their hopes and settled beliefs, not their intentions or knowledge.

The logical and epistemological objections discussed above arise because the word 'knowledge' is being read literally, as the courts have insisted. An alternative approach would be to read knowledge more loosely, such that it concerns knowledge of the *probability* of future circumstances. It will be contended below that this proposal ultimately fails.

Knowledge and Probabilities

Whether there is a *probability* that something will happen in the future is, in principle, ascertainable now, even if the actual occurrence of that future event is not.[57] Putative accessories and conspirators can know, ahead of time, that there is a probability (even a 'high' probability)[58] that something will happen in the future. Could, then, the law avoid the logical and epistemological problems mentioned in the previous section by interpreting knowledge that *p* to mean knowledge of some probability of *p*'s future occurrence?[59]

This proposal fails to explain the law concerning knowledge at present and would require an overhaul of its rules.[60] First, it goes against the statutory language regarding conspiracies noted above: D must know that the relevant circumstances 'shall or will exist', not that there is some probability that they will exist. This is not to say that doctrinal deployments of knowledge in the criminal law are *always* inconsistent with reading knowledge that *p* to require knowledge of a present probability that *p* will exist in the future. For instance, a defence of duress will fail 'where [D] knows … that he may be the subject of compulsion by' those he voluntarily associates with, or their associates.[61] Similarly, D commits an offence if he intends to use an item to damage or destroy property knowing it is *likely* to endanger life.[62]

the future, with P believing that the relevant risk(s) exist; and (2) P's action *will*, in the light of P's beliefs and reasons, be unjustified. That should be sufficient for secondary liability unless P's actual risk-taking is markedly different from what P believed would occur.

[57] We may of course often lack the information required to make this assessment in many cases. The epistemological worries are, however, far less significant in this context than in the ones discussed above.

[58] See Model Penal Code, § 2.02(7).

[59] One aspect of this proposal that cannot be discussed further here is the extent to which such a probabilistic assessment would rely on 'predictive' evidence, such as that about P's propensities, the employment of which might be thought to be inconsistent with the criminal law's commitment to free will. For discussion of this sort of tension, see A Pundik, 'Predictive Evidence and Unpredictable Freedom' (2020) 40 *OJLS* 238.

[60] See, too, Shute (n 3) 196.

[61] *Hasan* [2005] UKHL 22, [2005] 2 AC 467, [38]. D will also be barred from pleading duress if he *ought to have known* there was a risk of being coerced in the future.

[62] Criminal Damage Act 1971, s 3(b).

This use of knowledge is, in doctrine, unusual.[63] Furthermore, it risks a slide into other familiar mens rea states. It is not clear how knowledge of what *may* happen differs from foresight of a risk that that thing *may* happen, the hallmark of recklessness; or indeed how it differs from bare suspicion. Tellingly, when setting out the above rule on duress, Lord Bingham vacillated between the language of foresight of future coercion, and the language of knowledge of that possibility.[64] The proposal under discussion lends itself naturally to this type of slippage.

Some clear water might be visible in theory, depending on what level of probability were to be settled upon. Knowing that *p may* occur excludes knowledge of lower probabilities – knowing that *p has a remote chance* of occurring, for instance. Such lower degrees of foresight could still form part of recklessness, provided it was unjustified for D to take the relevant risk, or be classed properly as suspicion. There is even more significant space, in theory, between knowledge that *p* will *probably* (ie is more likely than not to) be the case and recklessness regarding *p*. How sustainable this distance would be in practice is, however, debatable, and it would be desirable for the sake of consistency and certainty that one standard be settled upon.[65]

A second problem with a probability-based approach to knowledge is that knowledge of an existing fact would become distinct in kind from knowledge of future facts, contrary to what appears to be the law's general approach. To say that I know these goods before me are stolen is not simply to make a claim about probabilities; it is to assert the truth of the relevant proposition.[66] A prosecution for handling that sought to prove that D believed the goods were *probably* stolen should fail. Granted, knowledge of the present and the future could be disaggregated. This would, however, add to the law's complexity if *both* were called 'knowledge', and unnecessarily so if, as contended below, belief would be a satisfactory alternative when pertaining to future circumstances.[67]

Alternatives to Knowledge

In summary, it is often logically impossible for knowledge of the types of future contingents with which the criminal law deals to exist at the point when the prosecution is required to prove that it existed. Even where this logical bar appears to be overcome, it is highly unlikely, given the limitations of proof, and the variables

[63] Another example involves fraud – see section II, below.

[64] *Hasan* [2005] UKHL 22, [2005] 2 AC 467, [37]–[38].

[65] cf *Director of Public Prosecution's Reference No 1 of 2019* [2021] HCA 26.

[66] Iocana (n 33) 453–54.

[67] The question of whether knowledge is a sensible mens rea concept for *present* circumstances raises two issues that cannot be resolved here. First, it might be more natural for laypersons to understand an offence of *knowing* that *p*, rather than having an actus reus requirement that *p* and requiring that D must have a corresponding belief that *p*. Secondly, there is the difficult question of whether the facts *ought* to matter to one's liability (and to what extent).

involved, for such knowledge of future facts and circumstances to be grasped by human beings at the time it must be proved to have been grasped (the time of the performance of the behavioural aspects of the actus reus). Furthermore, it is not clear why knowledge should be required, in any event. One might have some sympathy with a requirement that the truth of a certain proposition be proved beyond reasonable doubt as a barrier to overcriminalisation. As noted above, no conduct in pursuit of the agreement in a conspiracy need be undertaken: it is thus perhaps understandable that knowledge might be adopted in relation to relevant future facts or circumstances, even if it renders the offence virtually incapable of being prosecuted successfully unless the words 'intention' and 'knowledge' are in practice read contrary to the way the senior courts have read them (which must be what is happening, as conspiracies are routinely prosecuted successfully). The overcriminalisation worry could, however, be addressed through requiring conspirators to take concrete steps towards committing the offence,[68] rather than necessitating proof of intention or knowledge regarding things that cannot generally be intended or known at the relevant time.

The clearest way of avoiding all of this – and perhaps what happens in practice – is to translate intention regarding circumstances into belief that those circumstances will materialise, bypassing talk of knowledge altogether.

Statutory endorsement of such a move can be alleged. Section 1(3) of the Criminal Attempts Act 1981 provides that: 'if the facts of the case had been as [D] believed them to be, his intention would be [regarded as having amounted to an intent to commit an offence], then … he shall be regarded as having had an intent to commit that offence'.[69] Andrew Simester's explanation of this provision is that it 'affirms' what he sees as a more general principle of the common law, 'that an intention requirement, when applied to circumstance elements, is satisfied by proof of D's knowledge or settled belief regarding those circumstances'.[70] The history of section 1(3) in the Law Commission, Parliament and the courts suggests that it was designed exclusively for cases where D believes, incorrectly, that it is factually possible to commit an offence,[71] but Simester's more general principle is one that *should* be endorsed, shorn of reference to the problematic concept of knowledge. Where a requirement of intention is (unwisely) applied to circumstance elements, belief that that element exists or will exist is a better substitute than knowledge.

Granted, various of the concerns of *epistemological scepticism* will bite with regard to belief, as well: D might credibly be able to argue that she did not believe

[68] Compare Model Penal Code, § 5.03(5).

[69] Criminal Attempts Act 1981, s 1(3)(b).

[70] AP Simester, 'The *Mens Rea* of Criminal Attempts' (2015) 131 *LQR* 169, 172.

[71] Law Commission, *Attempt and Impossibility in Relation to Attempt, Conspiracy and Incitement* (Law Com No 120, 1980) para 2.93; HC Deb 19 January 1981 vol 997 c 21; HL Deb 13 April 1981 vol 419 cc 766–67, 780. See also: *Anderton v Ryan* [1985] AC 560, 572; *Shivpuri* [1985] QB 1029, 1036; *Shivpuri* [1987] AC 1, 22–23; *Pace and Rogers* [2014] EWCA Crim 186, [2014] 1 WLR 2867, [39].

that X would exist, because of everything that could get in the way of X's existence. If this is viewed (on some basis) as being too 'narrow', then an alternative fault element will need to be found. But that is a separate debate.

The discussion of knowledge in this part arose from the fact that knowledge is sometimes required as an alternative to the 'higher' fault element of intention. The next section argues that knowledge is equally problematic and unnecessary when twinned with 'lower' fault elements, and explores further this hierarchical model of fault.

II. Knowledge, Circumstances and Other Fault Elements

It is sensible to begin with the twinning of knowledge and belief, given their close relationship. Consider the offence of handling stolen goods:

> A person handles stolen goods if (otherwise than in the course of the stealing) knowing or believing them to be stolen goods he dishonestly receives the goods, or dishonestly undertakes or assists in their retention, removal, disposal or realisation by or for the benefit of another person, or if he arranges to do so.[72]

'A person handles stolen goods' has been interpreted to require that the goods in fact be stolen. If D believes that the goods are stolen, he is not liable for the full offence (as opposed to an attempt) unless that belief is true.[73] And, because his belief is true, D would *know* – at least according to English criminal law's definition – that the goods are stolen. The offence could, therefore, be reformed to remove the reference to belief (or, indeed, knowledge) without making any difference.[74]

Shute rejects this conclusion, and posits that the dual mens rea requirement of handling may indicate that the law views proceeding in the face of one's 'acceptance' that *p* to be just as culpable as proceeding in the face of one's belief that *p*.[75] On this view, to 'accept' that *p* stands in for believing that *p*; belief – the mens rea mentioned in the offence – is not itself present. This does not appear to be quite what the courts say. For instance, the view has been expressed judicially that '[t]he ordinary meaning of belief is the mental acceptance of a fact as true or existing'.[76] This appears to say that belief *is* acceptance (and vice versa). If that is right, and knowledge in law is simply a true belief, then a true acceptance *is* knowledge (in law), despite Shute's claim.

[72] Theft Act 1968, s 22.
[73] *Haughton v Smith* [1975] AC 476, 490, 497–98, 503–04.
[74] The distinction between knowledge and belief is not mentioned in the relevant sentencing guidelines: https://www.sentencingcouncil.org.uk/offences/crown-court/item/handling-stolen-goods-2/.
[75] Shute (n 3) 194.
[76] *Forsyth* [1997] 2 Cr App R 299, 320.

Maybe the courts are wrong about this, and acceptance is a legally sanctioned *substitute for* belief. The law arguably deploys such equivalence mechanisms in other contexts – wilful blindness is the most famous example.[77] But what remains problematic is Shute's next step – that this equivalence of acceptance and belief does not transfer to knowledge that *p*.[78] If the mental states of acceptance and belief are equally culpable, and the only additional ingredient for *legal* knowledge is, as the courts have repeatedly told us, factual accuracy, why should the law not allow the relevant transfer from acceptance to knowledge? Culpability for wrongdoing ought to turn on the defendant's beliefs, not the facts.

It remains unclear, then, why handling needs to be drafted this way. For those interested in understanding the relationship between knowledge and belief, however, the inclusion of both fault elements in handling has proved useful. The courts have attempted to distinguish between them, in ways that are not parasitic on truth.

Knowledge Without Truth?

In *Hall*, the distinctions between knowledge, belief and suspicion were famously explained in the following fashion:

> A man may be said to know that goods are stolen when he is told by someone with first hand knowledge (someone such as the thief or the burglar) that such is the case. Belief, of course, is something short of knowledge. It may be said to be the state of mind of a person who says to himself: 'I cannot say I know for certain that these goods are stolen, but there can be no other reasonable conclusion in the light of all the circumstances, in the light of all that I have heard and seen.' [Belief] is enough … even if the defendant says to himself: 'Despite all that I have seen and all that I have heard, I refuse to believe what my brain tells me is obvious.' What is not enough, of course, is mere suspicion. 'I suspect that these goods may be stolen, but it may be on the other hand that they are not.' That state of mind, of course, does not fall within the words 'knowing or believing'.[79]

One reading of this distinction between knowing that *p* and believing that *p* turns on the source of the evidence that *p*: if from the person who committed the initial offence, knowledge; if not, (potentially) belief.[80] A similar view was expressed in *Saik*, to the effect that one could only 'know' that money was the proceeds of crime if one had been involved in that initial crime.[81] It is not clear, however, that the source of the information should have this effect.[82] I know that the earth is round

[77] See, generally, Sarch (n 27).
[78] Shute (n 3) 191–95.
[79] *Hall* (1985) 81 Cr App R 260, 264.
[80] This was how the trial judge had explained matters in *Hall*.
[81] *Saik* [2006] UKHL 18, [2007] 1 AC 18, [25].
[82] Ormerod and Laird (n 10) 1089.

because of the overwhelming evidence available to me from multiple second-hand sources, founding a justified belief about the earth's roundness; and because it is in fact round. I believe that the cat is in the garden because I let him out earlier (first-hand experience), but in the interim my wife has let him back in, rendering my belief false.

The distinction drawn *in Hall* is more plausibly interpreted as one concerning D's confidence in the truth of *p*. At a certain level of confidence that the goods are stolen, D goes from suspecting the goods to be stolen (or being reckless regarding that same matter) to believing them to be stolen. At a greater level of confidence still – perhaps when 'absolutely sure'[83] – D knows that they are stolen. The source of the information may be operating as a proxy for D's level of confidence in the provenance of the goods, which itself may be thought of as a proxy for the culpability of D's choice to deal with the property, something that increases with D's confidence that it is illicit.[84]

Shorn of a connection to the truth of *p*, however, even being 'absolutely sure' that *p* is no guarantee of knowledge that *p*. I can be as sure as can be that Venus is a star, but I cannot *know* that. Furthermore, the statutory requirement in handling is that the defendant believes that the goods *are* stolen. If one does not have full confidence in the truth of that proposition, does one not believe merely that they are *probably* stolen? That would seem again to begin a slip into recklessness or bare suspicion, and not be sufficient for the offence, as drafted.

Handling demonstrates some of the ways in which knowledge proves problematic. It also illustrates how an actus reus can be amended, if required, to necessitate that the relevant circumstance in fact exists. That allows the law to distinguish between attempted and completed handling, without having to vary the fault element from a belief that the goods are illicit. If the goods are stolen, the defendant has committed handling. If they are not, then the defendant will necessarily have the mens rea for an attempt.[85] In other words, knowledge is not *necessary* to accommodate a 'truth' requirement, and a distinction between choate and inchoate wrongs, within the criminal law. Furthermore, it is not clear that mixing and matching actus reus and mens rea elements via a knowledge requirement is, in fact, helpful, even if it is more efficient in terms of wording.[86]

Additionally, the law does not always draw such distinctions between results in reality and D's beliefs. Famously, fraud is now defined in the 'inchoate mode':[87] if D dishonestly makes a false representation and intends thereby to make a

[83] *Godir* [2018] EWCA Crim 2294, [15].

[84] See Sarch (n 27) 88. The courts began to regret the guidance in *Hall* except where, exceptionally, a discussion of suspicion had arisen on the facts: eg *Toor* (1987) 85 Cr App R 116. This meant that clarity on the *Hall* guidance was never achieved.

[85] By virtue of Criminal Attempts Act 1981, s 1(3) (discussed above).

[86] K Simons, 'The Willful Blindness Doctrine: Justifiable in Principle, Problematic in Practice' (2021) 53 *Arizona State Law Journal* 655, 662.

[87] J Horder, *Ashworth's Principles of Criminal Law*, 8th edn (Oxford, Oxford University Press 2016) 418.

gain or expose another to a loss/risk of loss, then D is guilty, even if nobody is influenced.[88] For a representation to be false, D must know that the statement 'is, or might be, untrue of misleading'.[89] This requirement is noteworthy in two respects. First, it merely requires that there is knowledge that *p might* be the case. But, as noted already, knowledge that *p might* be the case overlaps significantly with recklessness (or even suspicion). Recklessness, of course, covers 'a very wide spectrum of culpable behaviour from the venial to the depraved',[90] meaning that not requiring knowledge *that p* broadens the offence significantly. But the advantage of recklessness is that it requires the prosecution to prove that the defendant's action was unreasonable in the light of its social costs.[91] No such protection exists in relation to this aspect of fraud, as drafted.

Secondly, presumably the prosecution must prove that it was indeed the case that D's statement *might* be untrue or misleading. In theory, D should be acquitted if he thought it might be untrue or misleading, but in fact if there is a reasonable doubt over that fact. But, if the new fraud offence is one premised almost entirely on D's culpability, and not results, why not simply require that the defendant *believes* that it might be misleading? It is once again hard to see what the knowledge requirement in fraud *adds*.

Knowledge is similarly problematic in relation to a range of other combinations of fault elements.[92]

Knowledge and the Hierarchy of Fault Elements

Some statutory offences require proof that D knew that *p* or had 'reasonable cause to suspect' that *p*.[93] The invocation of knowledge in this context is, on a culpability-centred view, puzzling. There should be no need to state anything other than the 'lower'/'lowest' form of culpability – as demonstrated by a particular type of mens rea – that suffices for an offence. It should be no defence to argue that one had a mens rea state that involved a 'higher' level of culpability – for instance, that one was not reckless (as the prosecution alleges), but instead *intended* to bring about the relevant result.

The basis for such a hierarchical principle is not logical entailment.[94] Knowing actors are usually also reckless, insofar as they have maximal foresight of the relevant circumstance or consequence and, ceteris paribus, they will be unjustified

[88] Fraud Act 2006, s 2(1).

[89] ibid s 2(2).

[90] GR Sullivan, 'Intent, Subjective Recklessness and Culpability' (1992) 12 *OJLS* 380, 389.

[91] *G* [2003] UKHL 50, [2004] 1 AC 1034, [41], endorsing *A Criminal Code for England and Wales* (Law Com No 177, 1989) vol 1, cl 18(c).

[92] See, further, Shute (n 3) 173–78.

[93] eg Terrorism Act 2000, s 17A(1).

[94] DN Husak, 'The Sequential Principle of Relative Culpability' (1995) 1 *Legal Theory* 493, 506–11.

in proceeding.[95] But not all actors who intend a consequence will have knowledge that it will come about: the purposeful actor may think that the relevant consequence is very unlikely (yet still possible) to come about, and thus fail to meet the standard of knowledge.[96] Instead, such a hierarchical principle of culpability recognises that – ceteris paribus – 'higher' fault elements demonstrate *at least an equivalent level of* culpability to 'lower' fault elements, and, as such, in proving the 'higher' element, the prosecution has proven sufficient fault to warrant conviction.[97]

Indeed, it is plausible that 'higher' fault elements demonstrate *more* culpability – in the sense of insufficient concern for the interests of others[98] – than 'lower' fault elements, again ceteris paribus (although that claim is not necessary to defend a hierarchical fault principle). For instance, *intentionally* causing damage to another's property (without an adequate justification or excuse) demonstrates particularly clearly one's insufficient concern for others' property rights in a way that is distinctive from cases of reckless damage. The actor who intended damage sets the relevant criminal harm as her goal. This particularly clear demonstration of her agency explains why she is more culpable for the relevant result than if she had been reckless.[99] On the same basis, it can be understood why knowledge and belief are often thought to be 'higher' fault elements than recklessness: if one knows or believe *that* harm will follow one's acts (and has no adequate justification or excuse), one's choice to proceed demonstrates a greater disregard for others' interests than where one advertently takes lower risk of them without justification. Similarly, one can understand why negligence is thought to be 'lower', in culpability terms, than recklessness. The absence of a belief that harm might follow in negligence means that there is a less clear demonstration of insufficient regard for others' rights than in cases where the defendant was undeterred by her belief that the relevant risk existed (in both cases, the risk-taking will need to be unjustified if culpable wrongdoing is to be found).[100]

The importance of the ceteris paribus requirement mentioned above cannot be overstated.[101] It is trite to note that intentionally stealing a chocolate bar demonstrates a 'lower' level of insufficient concern for others than recklessly burning down a building. Similarly, one must be careful not to build in defences (whether recognised by the law or not) into supposed counterexamples. A reluctant decision to kill a consenting, terminally ill relative plausibly demonstrates more regard for others' interests than a decision to set fire to a building, being reckless regarding

[95] See, similarly, L Alexander, KK Ferzan and S Morse, *Crime and Culpability* (Cambridge, Cambridge University Press, 2009) 32–35.

[96] See Simester et al (n 6) 140.

[97] American Law Institute, *Model Penal Code and Commentaries* (Philadelphia, American Law Institute, 1985) 228, 247; Sarch (n 27) 140–41.

[98] A now common way of explaining criminal culpability. For useful analysis, see Sarch (n 27) ch 2.

[99] See, similarly, Duff (n 6) 99, 102.

[100] See, further, Stark (n 13) 176.

[101] See, further, Husak (n 94) 494–95.

the risk of killing any occupants. But such counterexamples do not embarrass defenders of a principle of hierarchical fault, due to its ceteris paribus constraint.

The principle of hierarchical fault is defensible in theory. There is, however, no formal statement of this rule in English criminal law, presumably because, without a code,[102] there has been no occasion to state the rule: no competent lawyer would advise a client to attempt to argue that they were *more* culpable than the prosecution alleges. The American Law Institute's Model Penal Code, by contrast, explicitly endorses a principle that 'higher' mental states can fulfil the requirements of 'lower' mental states.[103] The order, from 'highest' to 'lowest', is purpose, knowledge, recklessness, negligence. In the Model Penal Code, it is accordingly no defence to an offence based on recklessness to argue that one knowingly or purposefully brought about the relevant harm.

In principle, then, there is no reason to use knowledge (or any other fault element) in any criminal offence unless it is the *bare minimum* acceptable fault element for that offence. The legislature could simply mention, for instance, 'reasonable cause to suspect' that *p* and be assured that a person who intended that *p*, 'knew' that *p*, believed that *p*, was reckless that *p*, etc, would be guilty.

A further puzzle remains, however, if the concern here is relative culpability. The level of concern demonstrated by one's culpable wrongdoing is not determined by the external facts; it is determined relative to one's beliefs and choices (or, in the case of negligence, the beliefs that one ought to have had at the relevant time). Accordingly, in a hierarchical system of mens rea, defended in terms of *at least equivalent* culpability, it is not knowledge, but belief, that can, and should, satisfy the requirements of 'lower' mental states such as recklessness, suspicion and negligence. There is, thus, no *need* for the legislature ever to use knowledge as a fault requirement. Once again, belief better fits the bill.

A similar issue arises in relation to some statutory defences. For instance, section 58 of the Terrorism Act 2000 prohibits the collection, recording, possession or accessing of information of the kind likely to be useful in the planning or commission of terrorism. One defence available to someone charged with this offence, which places an evidential burden on the defendant,[104] is that she 'did not know, and had no reason to believe, that the document or record … contained, or was likely to contain, information' of that kind.[105] This defence only operates where the defendant *has* collected, etc, information of the relevant kind. What this provision means, then – if knowledge is simply true belief in the criminal law – is that D must raise the credible possibility that she did not *believe* that the material was of the relevant form. But, more pertinently, she will have to raise the credible possibility that she had *no reason to hold such a belief*, or else a conviction is likely

[102] Notably, the Law Commission included a similar principle in its draft code: *A Criminal Code for England and Wales* (Law Com No 177, 1989) vol 1, cl 19 and vol 2, para 8.22.

[103] Model Penal Code, § 2.02(5).

[104] Terrorism Act 2000, s 118.

[105] ibid s 58(3A).

to be returned. Here, once again it is the 'lower' mental state that sets the actual boundary of the defence (and, accordingly, the offence). Knowledge that *p* (or, indeed, anything 'higher' than having a reason to believe that *p*) need not be an express element.

The conclusion is once again that the criminal law could tolerably live without knowledge and rely simply on belief and other mens rea elements.[106] If the best argument for retaining pairings of knowledge and other mens rea elements is that doing so does no harm in practice, that is insufficient.[107]

The next section expands this argument against knowledge to the context of consequence elements.

III. Knowledge and Consequences

One can often exercise adequate control over consequences to intend their occurrence, making them distinct from circumstances. That means less pressure has been placed on knowledge and belief in the context of consequence elements. But the motivational requirement of intention still creates problems in cases where the defendant's purpose in acting as he did was to bring about *X*, but he realised that *Y* was likely to occur. Such cases do not involve intention in its core sense. In such cases, knowledge once again enters the frame.[108]

This clear picture is muddied by the courts' insistence, in this context, that they are always discussing *intention*, not 'knowledge'. It is therefore necessary to explain why knowledge *is* what is being discussed by the courts.

Unmasking Knowledge

As mentioned above, juries are typically given no assistance regarding the meaning of intention. *Nedrick*[109] and *Woollin*[110] nevertheless authorize the trial judge to tell the jury deciding a murder case that it can 'find' an intention to kill or cause grievous bodily harm where:

(a) it was virtually certain that one of those outcomes would occur as a result of D's acting as he did; and
(b) D appreciated, at the time of so acting, that it was virtually certain that one of these outcomes would result.

[106] See, similarly, Shute (n 3) 195.

[107] cf Law Commission, *A Criminal Code for England and Wales* (Law Com No 177, 1989) vol 2, para 16.14.

[108] The discussion below centres on murder, for reasons of space and because this is where the doctrinal discussion has occurred most prominently.

[109] *Nedrick* [1986] 1 WLR 1025.

[110] *Woollin* [1999] 1 AC 82.

Technically, *Nedrick* and *Woollin* were limited to (completed) murder, but the same approach to intention and consequences has been taken in attempted murder,[111] and is assumed to exist elsewhere.[112]

Element (b) requires the defendant to believe that death or serious injury is virtually certain to occur if D acts as he does. A belief that death or serious injury could, may, or might result is insufficient.[113] D must have a strong dispositional commitment to the truth of *p* before a finding of intention is competent.

Element (a) requires that belief to be true. Accordingly, if D believes that death or serious injury are virtually certain to result from his acting as he does, but this is not proven as 'objective' fact, then D is not guilty of murder. Note that the fact that death occurs does not imply that death was necessarily *virtually certain* to occur: it could, from the relevant ex ante perspective, in fact have been highly unlikely to occur.

If *Nedrick* and *Woollin* require a true belief that death or serious injury are virtually certain to occur, they require what English criminal law would distinctively call knowledge of the same.

This requirement of knowledge in the context of murder has rightly been criticised on culpability grounds.[114] Consider: D is in a gang, and pushes suspected police informant V, who tells D (honestly) that he cannot swim, into a river.[115] D intends to terrify V and others who might interfere with the gang's activities. D would be perfectly satisfied if V survived, and could tell other would-be informants of his ordeal, but D believes that it is virtually certain that V will suffer at least serious injury. V drowns. Expert evidence at trial nevertheless suggests that it was not virtually certain that death or serious injury would occur, but 'only' very likely, given the height from which V was pushed, the depth of the water, the speed of its flow, etc. D's decision to push V into the river, in the face of his belief that this would be virtually certain to cause at least serious harm, demonstrates the same level of insufficient concern for V's life as it would in a case where it *was* proved to be virtually certain that serious injury would follow. Accordingly, D's culpability is identical in both instances. Why should the jury be entitled to convict D of murder in the latter case, but not the former?

The problem is one of moral luck: the extent of D's liability depends upon the extraneous circumstances surrounding D's action, not upon D's culpability. Although moral luck cannot be jettisoned entirely from the criminal law, a compelling case must be given for its impact, particularly when it makes such a stark difference to the extent of D's liability. None is presented in *Nedrick* or

[111] *Pearman* (1985) 80 Cr App R 259.

[112] In the context of complicity, see: Simester (n 53) 83–84; Ormerod and Laird (n 52) 545–48. See also *Thacker* [2021] EWCA Crim 97, [2021] QB 644.

[113] cf *Thacker* [2021] EWCA Crim 97, [2021] QB 644, [86], where the Court of Appeal appears to entertain a lower standard of foresight than virtual certainty, in direct conflict with *Woollin*.

[114] Simester et al (n 6) 149.

[115] An example based loosely on *Matthews and Alleyn* [2003] EWCA Crim 192, [2003] 2 Cr App R 30.

Woollin, and accordingly a case can be made for their *over*privileging moral luck. The truth requirement in those cases is certainly not required to differentiate between attempted and completed murder, given the requirement that, for the completed offence, D must in fact and law cause V's death. Any worries about non-insane defendants being convicted on the basis of highly unusual beliefs could be addressed through a requirement that D's beliefs about the likelihood of death or serious injury must be proved to be *reasonable* ones to hold.[116]

The justification for the truth requirement might, however, arise outside of concerns of culpability.

Beyond Culpability

For instance, one argument for the truth requirement in *Nedrick* and *Woollin* is that it helps to keep the law of murder as narrow as possible, distinguishing it from manslaughter. There are two problems with this view. First, it is usually thought that what distinguishes murder from manslaughter is simply D's culpability, and – as noted above – that is best understood to depend on D's beliefs, not the facts. If that is so, and the truth requirement is irrelevant to culpability, it is not clear why it would be doing any work in differentiating these offences. And yet, as a matter of doctrine, it apparently does so.

It is likely that, instead of any principled reason for the truth requirement, the mandatory life sentence for murder is the most plausible explanation for its existence. The courts are justifiably wary of allowing that sanction to be applied liberally, and the truth requirement limits (albeit minimally) the number of culpable defendants who can be subjected to it, through keeping the legal category of 'indirect' intention narrow. Moulding the law's understanding of mens rea terms around such practicalities nevertheless incurs a cost. Despite the efforts of the courts to try and limit mens rea decisions to specific contexts (including in *Woollin*),[117] the courts tend to apply them elsewhere. Again, this is understandable: uniform definitions of mens rea terms can advance rule of law values and minimise the risk of adjudicators wielding too much discretion.[118]

Rather than create a rule regarding murder that is likely to migrate, there are two obvious alternative ways to resolve the difficulty caused by *Nedrick* and *Woollin*. First, intention could be limited to the ends sought by a person and the means to those ends; 'indirect intention' could on this score be eliminated from the law on murder. Given the slim moral distance between 'directly' intended and *Nedrick*- and *Woollin*-type 'knowing' killings in most instances, however, this option would inevitably require legislation. Parliament could, for example, make

[116] Compare, in the context of endangerment offences, F Stark, 'The Reasonableness in Recklessness' (2020) 14 *Criminal Law and Philosophy* 9.
[117] *Woollin* [1999] 1 AC 82, 90.
[118] See Stark (n 13) ch 3.

clear that intention is limited to purpose, and/or allow belief that the relevant result would occur to also be sufficient mens rea.[119]

Second, the truth requirement in *Nedrick* and *Woollin* could be jettisoned as inappropriate, so that the jury can find the relevant fault existed where the defendant *believed* that it was virtually certain that *X* would result from acting as he did. This step would have the effect of expanding the reach of the offence of murder, perhaps in a way that is not readily predictable, in the light of the present lack of explanation for the truth requirement. Given the mandatory life sentence, one could further understand the courts' reluctance to countenance this step. It is, on that score, again one that probably requires the intervention of Parliament. In the absence of a criminal code's being enacted, such intervention is presumably highly unlikely, meaning the unsatisfactory nature of *Nedrick* and *Woollin* will remain. Thankfully, situations where juries will be directed in their terms are rare.

IV. Conclusion

Knowledge should be excised from English criminal law's arsenal of fault elements. In relation to circumstances, knowledge is highly problematic when it is required in relation to future contingents. In relation to *existing* circumstances, it is not clear why it is a mens rea term that must carry the weight of the 'objective' facts of the defendant's wrongdoing, when the actus reus can necessitate this if required. Furthermore, given the hierarchical nature of fault, it is unclear why it is thought necessary to include knowledge alongside the mens rea terms with which it tends to be paired. In relation to consequences, a requirement of knowledge overprivileges moral luck and is unnecessary to curb overcriminalisation. Belief can better perform the roles for which knowledge is employed, avoiding almost all of knowledge's problems. Granted, belief *that p* may sometimes itself be too demanding a standard to require of prosecutors in certain contexts, but, again, that is a different debate.[120]

[119] cp Serious Crime Act 2007, s 44(2).

[120] Alexander famously argues that ('subjective') recklessness is the only necessary fault element: L Alexander, 'Insufficient Concern: A Unified Conception of Criminal Culpability' (2000) 88(3) *California Law Review* 931. But requiring proof of a positive belief that *p*, rather than simply a belief that a risk that *p* exists, 'preserves a desirable zone of liberty': K Cole, 'Knowledge and Belief as Criminal Law Mental States' (2019) 16 *Ohio State Journal of Criminal Law* 441, 448. That liberty should not be withdrawn lightly.

3

Why Outcomes Matter (And How They Do)

ANTJE DU BOIS-PEDAIN

I. Introduction

The problem of outcome responsibility in criminal law is the problem of providing a normative foundation for criminal law practices that make outcomes relevant to criminal liability and sentencing (practices I summarily refer to as the criminal law's 'outcome responsiveness'). The central feature of an outcome-responsive criminal law is the presence of result-based crimes, where in the absence of a bad outcome, criminal liability is either completely absent or only arises for a different and less serious offence. Similarly striking are the differences between the result-based liability regimes that exist for intended as contrasted with negligent wrongdoing. Negligent conduct is only occasionally criminalised in the absence of bad results, and where such conduct is criminalised in a freestanding, result-independent offence, it is typically categorised as a minor offence. By contrast, for result-based crimes of intent, in the absence of the bad result liability typically arises for a criminal attempt to commit the substantive result-based crime, and the available maximum sentence is often the same as for the completed offence.[1] It is also noteworthy that result-based crimes of negligence frequently attract substantially less grave punishment than do result-based crimes of intent in respect of the same bad result.[2]

[1] In England and Wales, the maximum sentence available for an attempted crime is the same as for the completed crime although in practice attempts are usually punished less severely (Criminal Attempts Act 1981, s 1). The same pattern obtains in German law (Strafgesetzbuch (StGB), s 23(2) read in conjunction with s 49(1) (providing that an attempted offence may, but need not, be punished more mildly than the completed offence)). By contrast, careless driving (Road Traffic Act (RTA) 1988, s 3), which can be treated as a proxy for negligent driving, can in the absence of bad results only be punished with a fine, whereas significant periods of imprisonment are available when injury or death are caused as a result of such driving (RTA 1988, s 2C (injury): up to two years; RTA 1988, s 2B (death): increased, in 2022, from a maximum of fourteen years' imprisonment to a maximum of life imprisonment).

[2] A particularly clear example is provided by German law, where intended killings (StGB, s 212) attract (in the absence of further factors which qualify the intended killing as murder under German law)

Whether an outcome-responsive criminal law is justified is a question our honorand put on the table when responding to an invitation to consider 'legacies and modern challenges to criminal law reform' arising from the experience of the Indian Penal Code – an early and still instructive effort to cast criminal law into ideal, codified form.[3] In that context, Bob Sullivan asks what would constitute an appropriate framing in general terms of the conduct element of a criminal offence. Starting with the 'basic question: why causation at all?' (a question one can rephrase, for the purposes of this chapter, as 'why outcome responsivity at all?'), he points out that 'it would be perfectly possible to draft a criminal code where causation in the sense of bringing about physical effects going beyond bodily movements carried out in specified circumstances is dispensed with',[4] something that might appear defensible provided that 'the reasoning supportive of this "results don't matter to morality" thesis is sound'.[5] While Sullivan remains equivocal on this moral question, he proceeds to reject a result-insensitive criminal law due to 'enormous doubts concerning the public acceptability of a criminal code taking a radically, non-causal turn'.[6] The reasons he gives for this are threefold: first, '[r]esults matter enormously in terms of psychological/emotional reactions to harmful events'; secondly, '[m]ere causal agency in itself imposes social duties to express regret and offer condolence'; and, thirdly, '[w]here the causal agency is additionally accompanied by a blameworthy state of mind, the damaging results of the conduct will intensify the anger and resentment of those adversely affected and will play a potent part in the negative public perception of the person responsible for the bad outcome'. Since these reactions are 'in no sense discreditable feelings … they must be given institutional recognition in a criminal code'.[7]

I fully agree with these institutional reasons in favour of an outcome-responsive criminal law. The question I want to pursue in this chapter, however, is whether even before one considers such institutional reasons, the criminal law would need to commit itself to outcome responsivity.[8] In addressing this question, I draw

a *minimum* sentence of five years' imprisonment and a maximum of life imprisonment, whereas negligent killings (StGB, s 222) attract a *maximum* sentence of five years' imprisonment and a minimum sentence of a fine. In English law, murder attracts a mandatory life sentence whereas gross negligence manslaughter, while in principle also punishable with imprisonment up to life, usually attracts a lesser punishment than life.

[3] WC Chan, B Wright and S Yeo (eds), *Codification, Macaulay and the Indian Penal Code: The Legacies and Modern Challenges of Criminal Law Reform* (Abingdon, Routledge, 2011).

[4] GR Sullivan, 'The Conduct Element of Offences' in Chan, Wright and Yeo, ibid, 90, 101.

[5] ibid, 102. Sullivan mentions Larry Alexander and Kim Kessler Ferzan as the main criminal law proponents of this moral thesis. See L Alexander and K Kessler Ferzan (with contributions by SJ Morse), *Crime and Culpability: A Theory of Criminal Law* (Cambridge, Cambridge University Press, 2009) esp ch 5.

[6] Sullivan (n 4) 102.

[7] ibid.

[8] See eg J Edwards and AP Simester, 'Crime, Blameworthiness, and Outcomes' (2019) 39 *OJLS* 50, who approach this issue as a question about an agent's blameworthiness for outcomes on the assumption that the criminal law should be committed (at least in principle) to tracking blameworthiness of agents.

on a tradition of criminal law theorising that treats this as an issue to be grappled with through an understanding of structure(s) of responsible agency and of norm-violation which, in turn, undergird the criminal law's construction of the elements of crime.[9] I start from an understanding of human agency that allows us to appreciate why producing an outcome (either as an intended or as a negligently unintended one) makes a difference: so long as the outcome can be imputed to the agent, it qualifies what the agent is responsible for.[10] The object of assessment ('what the agent has done') changes from 'X activity' (minus the outcome) to 'X activity with outcome Y'[11] – a difference which is, in ordinary language, often marked by a new description (the agent 'has done Z') being applicable to the agent's conduct once the outcome has occurred.

This observation about a change in the object of assessment may well hold true for *all* outcomes, even outcomes that were neither intended by the agent nor negligently produced. In the words of a US tort laywer: 'Faultless agency is not morally the same as misfortune.'[12] Whether or not one accepts this point, it calls for a second observation: non-faultless agency is not morally the same as faultless agency. My concern in this chapter is with the specific significance for us, as agents, of the outcomes of our *faulty* agency. How, and why, do these outcomes matter?

Here, many philosophers and legal scholars adopt a unitary position. The outcomes of our faulty agency matter in the same way, whether the fault in question lay with our culpable inattention or with our culpable choice of aim (or, for that matter, with other markers of culpable agency such as indifference, knowledge or belief). In what follows, I am going to challenge this position. Adopting a two-step process, I will first introduce a particular account of the connection between agents and outcomes that follows, and builds upon, the work of seventeenth-century scholar Samuel Pufendorf. Pufendorf's doctrine of imputation allows me to trace an agent's responsibility for an outcome through any marker

[9] The key terms in the German literature are *allgemeine Handlungslehre* (general theory of agency) and *allgemeine Verbrechenslehre* (general theory of criminal norm-violation).

[10] Some criminal law theorists reject this starting point. Alexander and Ferzan are on record as denying that results should feature as offence elements, arguing instead that the culpable unleashing of unjustified risk is the unified criterion of criminal responsibility-ascription as well as of culpable agency (see eg Alexander and Ferzan (n 5) 197). For a brief discussion, see section III below.

[11] See eg Edwards and Simester (n 8) 54 (arguing that 'those who try and those who succeed commit different wrongs'). The 'different wrong' argument is the standard view in the German theoretical literature which has long distinguished between the wrongness that resides in the activity itself (*Handlungsunrecht*) and the wrongness that resides in the imputable result (*Erfolgsunrecht*). For a good introduction to these concepts, see H Kudlich, 'Handlungs- und Erfolgsunrecht sowie Gesinnungsunwert der Tat' in E Hilgendorf, H Kudlich and B Valerius (eds), *Handbuch des Strafrechts*, vol 2: *Strafrecht Allgemeiner Teil I* (Heidelberg, CF Müller, 2020) ch 29. For a German criminal lawyer's attempt to evaluate the doctrines of the general part in light of the Anglo-American literature on outcome luck, see B Burghardt, *Zufall und Kontrolle. Eine Untersuchung zu den Grundlagen der moralphilosophischen und strafrechtlichen Zurechnung* (Tübingen, Mohr Siebeck, 2018).

[12] GC Keating, 'Recovering *Rylands*: An Essay for Bob Rabin' (2012) 61 *DePaul Law Review* 543, 573. The author continues with the observation: 'It is a source of responsibility as well as regret.'

of faulty agency, excluding only such occurrences that bear no traces of an agent's personal agency. From this perspective it makes good sense for the outcomes of faulty agency to matter for criminal liability. However, that still leaves unexplained the extent to which the criminal law subjects intended and negligently produced unintended outcomes to different liability regimes. This is why I turn, next, to the work of Alan Brudner, who draws on Hegel's theory of agency to develop a version of imputation which generates the important upshot that outcomes may matter differently depending on whether they were intended by the agent, or whether they were brought about by the agent in some other culpable way.

My first aim, then, is general in nature: to show that the answers to the questions how and why the outcome matters for our responsibility are affected by whether the outcome is the product of our intentions, or whether it is the product of unintended negligently created risks. Having done so, I then turn to the implications of this analysis for central features of the criminal law. If accepted as sound, this analysis explains and potentially justifies many of the outcome-responsive practices highlighted earlier: the much heavier punishment that attaches to crimes of intended harm-causation compared with crimes of negligent harm-causation; the restriction of attempts liability to crimes of intent; and the heavier punishment for completed crimes compared with attempted crimes. At the same time, it puts pressure on the justification of outcome-dependent crimes of negligence. For how can the criminal law's practice of making the occurrence of the outcome the linchpin for most offences of criminal negligence be defended, if it is indeed correct that – as Brudner's analogy of outcome responsibility to ownership suggests – we have a more divestible connection to the negligently produced unintended outcomes of our agency than to those we intended to bring about?

To defend this final feature of an outcome-responsive criminal law, I shall return to my earlier discussion of the concept of imputation as originally introduced by Pufendorf. Pufendorf's account allows us to appreciate that the questions, whether an agent is responsible for an outcome – whether the outcome is something the agent did – and whether merit or demerit arises for the agent in respect of his deed thus constituted, are questions that need to be kept distinct. Combined with the major insight from the discussion of Brudner's work on imputation – that the harmful consequence qualifies the negligent deed in a different way from how it qualifies a deed where the outcome was intended – this permits me to show that it is appropriate for the criminal law to cast crimes of negligence as result-crimes, but also to treat such crimes as far less serious offences than the equivalent intent-based result-crimes.

Throughout this chapter, the phrase 'intended outcomes' refers only to outcomes brought about purposively or knowingly. These outcomes are contrasted with negligently produced unintended outcomes. The latter, apart from their not being motivating for the agent or correctly anticipated by him as certain to occur, are outcomes in respect of which the agent fails to act with the degree of prudence that could and should be expected of that agent. This failure to meet subjectivised expectations of prudence obtains not only when the agent, if prudent, would have perceived risks he in fact failed to perceive, but also when the agent perceived risks that he, if prudent, would not have taken. In other words, for the notion of negligently produced unintended outcomes employed in this chapter, actual risk perception by the agent is not the central question: what matters is the agent's imprudence in running the risk that leads to unintended consequences.[13]

I employ these stipulations to maximally sharpen the contrast between these two pathways leading to bad outcomes – intended or negligent harm-doing – hoping to avoid, as far as possible, the terrain at the confluence of *dolus eventualis* and recklessness. I take no view in this chapter about how best to categorise and treat outcomes which are not intended in the sense defined above but which the agent realises are likely to occur while demonstrating an attitude of indifference or uncaringness towards their possible occurrence that goes beyond mere imprudence. Which liability frameworks should apply in such scenarios must be left to separate investigations not pursued in this chapter.

II. Agency and Imputation: Conceptualising Action for the Purposes of the Criminal Law

I start with two issues that are central for any discussion of human action. The first pertains to the individuation of actions: what counts as part of an action and what is separable from it. The second pertains to the ascriptive (or authorial) dimension of actions: what counts as an action by a human agent and what as a mere happening involving a human source. These issues are to some extent interconnected. Depending on how we identify the relevant components of an action, ascription to a human agent may be more or less difficult.

'Human action', Bebhinn Donnelly-Lazarov writes, 'is constituted by the unified exercise of mental and (at least sometimes) physical capacities. When human beings are responsible for their actions, they are responsible for actions so constituted.'[14] This notion of action is used by Donnelly-Lazarov to explain when, and on what grounds, omissions constitute actions. In encompassing omissions, this is a wide notion of what constitutes human action. But as regards the

[13] cf RL Rabin, 'The Fault of Not Knowing: A Comment' (2003) 4 *Theoretical Inquiries in Law* 427, 429: '[T]his moral equivalency between knowledge and what is often referred to as constructive knowledge – ie, what the defendant should have known – seems so unexceptionable as to require little comment. Indeed, it is the foundation for treating deviation from custom as evidence of negligence. As Clarence Morris put it in his classic article on the subject, "Sub-conformity tends to show that the defendant either heedlessly failed to look about for safeguards or consciously refused to take precautions which he knows others think essential."'.

[14] B Donnelly-Lazarov, 'The Unified Constitution of Action in Understanding Responsibility for "Omissions"', Criminal Justice Theory Blog Post, 21 October 2021, available at https://criminaljusticetheoryblog.wordpress.com/2021/10/29/the-unified-constitution-of-action-in-understanding-responsibility-for-omissions/.

components of an action that it recognises, it can at first blush appear rather limited, in that the suggestion that actions are 'constituted … by the unified exercise of mental and … physical capacities' does not (yet) advert to the possibility that human actions may have a more complex constitution, in that certain other features may be partly constitutive of them. However, as Donnelly-Lazarov clarifies, her concern is precisely to

> seek to understand action as a composite of desires, reasons, motivations, knowledge, movements, foresight, evaluations, senses … contrary to any enterprise that divorces a single, physical, capacity from the others, setting it up as the essence of action, to be understood as such via the role of these others in producing it.[15]

A first additional feature of actions is the goal or objective of the agent. Considering a human action in light of its goal or objective gets us to the realisation that this particular instance of a unified exercise of mental and physical capacities is deemed by the agent a suitable means to his end. It also allows us to pose the further question whether the action – given external facts – is, or can be, such a means. We can call this the 'instrumentality' of the action – considered by some theorists the central constitutive feature of an action.[16]

A second additional feature is the possible impact of an action on its surroundings, its potential to bring about benefits or harms. This can be termed the 'riskiness' or 'potentiality' of the action.[17]

Attention to these two additional features also allows for the observation that the goal or objective of an action is for the agent only sometimes connected to its riskiness. Put differently: the instrumentality which the action has for the agent can reside in its riskiness but the two can also diverge.[18] Consider the following example:

Deliberate Shooting: Adam fires a gun. The bullet hits and kills Victoria.

If Adam fires the gun after taking aim at Victoria in order to hit and kill her, instrumentality and riskiness are united. Firing the gun is the instrumentality by which

[15] ibid. Regarding individuation and appropriate action-description, Donnelly-Lazarov observes that, if Jim raises his arm to make a point, '[t]he mental parts of this action are … integral to the thing done [such that] the statement, "Jim is raising his arm" is a poor description of the action. The statement, "Jim is trying to prove a point" is a better one, even though it excludes the physical entirely' (ibid).

[16] These theorists adopt what has been labelled a 'finalistic' concept of agency. See esp H Welzel, *Das neue Bild des Strafrechtssystems. Eine Einführung in die finale Handlungslehre*, 3rd edn (Göttingen, Otto Schwartz, 1957).

[17] It is a difficult question whether potentiality constitutes a feature of agency regardless of its perceptibility or perception by the agent. In this chapter, this question is addressed (indirectly) in my discussion of Pufendorf's and Brudner's views on responsibility-ascription for outcomes.

[18] In other unpublished work by Donnelly-Lazarov (on 'Criminal Law, Omissions and the Absence of Action') she brings what she calls the 'ontological complexity' of actions into view. In oral discussion of that work, Donnelly-Lazarov pertinently observed that we tend to prioritise intentional act descriptions as primary over secondary act descriptions in terms of matters risked or inadvertently done but that in respect of certain events the secondary act description may well come to the fore.

Adam wants to kill Victoria, and the relevant instrumental risk that firing the gun creates is the risk of hitting and killing Victoria.

Now consider the following modification:

> *Wedding Celebration*: Adam fires the gun without aiming at anyone or anything in order to produce a loud noise. The bullet he discharges hits and kills Victoria who stood some metres away.

Here, instrumentality and riskiness come apart. The act that was Adam's chosen instrument to produce a loud noise was an act that created an incidental risk to Victoria's life which materialised.

To get a better grip on the complexity of human action, and particularly on the extent to which actions encompass their outcomes, I now turn to the notion of *imputation* central to the concept of agency developed in the seventeenth century by Samuel Pufendorf.[19] This conception of agency provided the foundation for subsequent philosophical engagement in a genuinely pan-European conversation.[20] It also exerted significant influence on continental criminal law theory.[21] My exposition follows the extended explication and discussion by Joachim Hruschka of Pufendorf's insights and that subsequent philosophical debate.[22]

[19] Pufendorf's theory of imputation is developed in S Pufendorf, *Elementorum jurisprudentiae universalis libri duo* (The Hague, Adriani Vlacq, 1660) and in S Pufendorf, *De Jure Naturae et Gentium, Libri Octo* (Lund, Junghans, 1672). A concise summary can be found in W Hardwig, *Die Zurechnung. Ein Zentralproblem des Strafrechts* (Hamburg, Cram, de Gruyter & Co, 1957) 35–45.

[20] On Pufendorf's reception and influence, see eg I Hunter, 'The Invention of Human Nature: The Intention and Reception of Pufendorf's *Entia Moralia* Doctrine', (2019) 45 *History of European Ideas* 933; C Heydt, *Moral Philosophy in Eighteenth-Century Britain: God, Self, and Other* (Cambridge, Cambridge University Press, 2018) ch 1 (discussing what he calls 'the Pufendorfian shift in moral philosophy'). On Pufendorf's lasting significance for moral philosophy, see esp JB Schneewind, *The Invention of Autonomy. A History of Moral Philosophy* (Cambridge, Cambridge University Press, 1997) ch 7 (with the telltale title: 'The Central Synthesis: Pufendorf'). Pufendorf's writings also significantly influenced constitutional theory and the theorisation of public authority, see esp T Behme, *Samuel von Pufendorf, Naturrecht und Staat: Eine Analyse und Interpretation seiner Theorie, ihrer Grundlagen und Probleme* (Göttingen, Vandenhoeck & Ruprecht, 1995). On the influence of Pufendorf's conceptions of agency and imputation, see esp M Auer, 'Die Substanz der Freiheit: Pufendorfs Begriff der moralischen Person' in R Gröschner, S Kirste and OW Lembcke (eds), *Person und Rechtsperson. Zur Ideengeschichte der Personalität* (Tübingen, Mohr Siebeck, 2015) 81 and J Hruschka, 'Zurechnung seit Pufendorf. Insbesondere die Unterscheidungen des 18. Jahrhunderts' in M Kaufmann and J Renzikowski (eds), *Zurechnung als Operationalisierung von Verantwortung* (Frankfurt, Peter Lang, 2004) 17.

[21] For the historical development, see esp S Stübinger, 'Von der alten Imputationen-Lehre zum klassischen Verbrechensbegriff – Ein Beitrag zur Geschichte des strafrechtlichen Zurechnungsbegriffs' (2011) 2 *Rechtswissenschaft* 154. Pufendorf's concept of imputation was first retrieved by the influential criminal law theorist Hans Welzel, in his doctoral dissertation dating from 1928 which Welzel later reissued in an updated form (H Welzel, *Die Naturrechtslehre Samuel Pufendorfs. Ein Beitrag zur Ideengeschichte des 17. und 18. Jahrhunderts* (Berlin/New York, De Gruyter, 1958)). Welzel's own finalistic theory of agency, while similar to Pufendorf's in its selection of the ontologically relevant aspects of human behaviour, differs importantly, however, in its theoretical approach to action as a given structure of ontological reality, whereas Pufendorf's own understanding of agency, due to its inbuilt normative dimension, is closer to a normative conception of agency.

[22] J Hruschka, 'Imputation' (1986) 50 *Brigham Young University Law Review* 669. In present-day theoretical usage, the concept of imputation has been narrowed so that it is now mainly employed

As Hruschka notes, Pufendorf introduced the concept of imputation to address the ascriptive dimension of agency – that is, to settle the conditions under which some happening involving a human source qualifies as a human action.[23] For Pufendorf (and for the philosophical tradition in which he writes[24]), these conditions are identical to those that make the happening in question properly subject to moral evaluation.[25] They require that the happening can be 'traced to a person as their author, whose decisive characteristic consists of being the free cause thereof'.[26] As Kant put it: 'We impute something when it … is assigned to a person, ie when it is conceived of *as having originated in freedom*.'[27] The notion of freedom invoked by these authors was not especially exacting (and by and large unaffected by deterministic concerns[28]). These authors took it as given that there was a relevant difference between, on the one hand, happenings – including some involving a human source – that were compelled in a naturalistic-physicalist sense and, on the other hand, happenings that were not so compelled.[29] The latter have

to address the ascription of responsibility for outcomes; its close link to a theory of human agency (which was its historical hallmark and function) has thereby been lost. For the present-day usage, see F Zieschang, 'Kausalität und objektive Zurechnung' in Hilgendorf, Kudlich and Valerius (n 11) ch 33. Its original broader function – ascription of an event to a human being as its author and not merely its source – lives on in the terminology of criminal responsibility in concepts such as *Zurechnungsfähigkeit* (capacity) but without the older doctrine doing any further theoretical work in that context. Hruschka's valiant attempts to revive Pufendorf's original doctrine of imputation for criminal-law theory have (in my view, regrettably) not had much uptake in the theoretical mainstream. For a laudable exception, see P Sánchez-Ostiz, 'Auswirkungen der Zurechnungslehre in den aktuellen Verbrechenslehren' (2005) 13 *Jahrbuch für Recht und Ethik* 669.

[23] Hruschka (n 22) 670.

[24] See esp T Pink, 'Reason and Obligation in Suárez' in B Hill and H Lagerlund (eds), *The Philosophy of Francisco Suárez* (Oxford, Oxford University Press, 2012) 175 (for the connections between Pufendorf and scholastic writings) and Hardwig (n 19) (for roots in Aristotelian thought).

[25] See A Aichele, 'Zurechnungsmetaphysik? Samuel Pufendorfs Begriff der *imputatio* als Realitätsgrund von Moralität' (2011) 19 *Jahrbuch für Recht und Ethik* 325.

[26] Hruschka (n 22) 674. As Aichele explains, for Kant, 'The possibility of freedom concerning free causation just says that a natural cause can do nothing but bring about its adequate effect, whereas the cause which is the subject of imputation is capable of refraining from bringing about a certain effect' (A Aichele, 'Causation to Culpability: Why Imputation Matters' in B Kahmen and M Stepanians (eds), *Critical Essays on Causation and Responsibility* (Berlin, De Gruyter, 2013) 311, 326).

[27] I Kant, 'Imputatio facti' in Preussiche Akademie der Wissenschaften (ed), *Kant's Gesammelte Schriften*, vol 19: *Kant's handschriftlicher Nachlass VI: Moralphilosophie, Rechtsphilosophie und Religionsphilosophie* (Berlin, De Gruyter, 1934) 157, quoted and translated by Hruschka (n 22) 674 (emphasis Hruschka's). The affinities between Kant's and Pufendorf's conceptions of responsibility, including the possibility that responsibility may therefore come in degrees, are helpfully brought out in Blöser's interpretation of Kant (C Blöser, 'Degrees of Responsibility in Kant's Practical Philosophy' (2015) 20 *Kantian Review* 67. See also C Blöser, *Zurechnung bei Kant. Zum Zusammenhang von Person und Handlung in Kants praktischer Philosophie* (Berlin, De Gruyter, 2014)).

[28] Kant is to some extent an exception in that he grounded the possibility of moral philosophy in a transcendental methodology and was thereby able to split off deterministic concerns as insignificant due to their pertaining to the empirical realm. On Kant's method, see esp PW Franks, 'Nineteenth-Century and Early Twentieth-Century Post-Kantian Philosophy' in H Cappelen, T Szabó Gendler and J Hawthorne (eds), *The Oxford Handbook of Philosophical Methodology* (Oxford, Oxford University Press, 2016) ch 4.

[29] For an interesting introduction, see K Hammacher, 'Freiheit im Recht. Kritische Betrachtungen zur Entwicklung des Freiheitsbegriffs' in MV d'Alfonso et al (eds), *Fichte und seine Zeit: Streitfragen*

the features that humans are familiar with when they take themselves to be acting; essentially, they consist of self-directed behaviour which is experienced by its human originator as his choice. Behaviour in the latter category can be 'imputed' to its human originator as his deed; the significance of this classification being that the event then is an appropriate object for moral evaluation; that is, for the application of moral laws formulating standards and expectations for what is morally right to do.[30] That an event can be imputed to its human originator as his deed is therefore presupposed by any application of the moral law to it.[31]

This imputation of an event to a person as his deed is, however, only the first aspect or 'level' of imputation. As Hruschka explains, 'the judgment that the event to which the law is applied is to be traced to a (particular) person as its free cause' – that it therefore counts as this person's deed – is, as such, neutral.[32] It does not yet tell us whether what is imputed to the person is morally good or bad. The moral quality of a human deed comes into focus only on the second level of imputation, which concerns the question whether merit or demerit arises from the deed.[33] Hruschka explains Pufendorf's starting point as follows:

> Pufendorf distinguished between good actions, profitable and not owed; actions the performance of which is owed (*debitum*); and bad actions. The 'material effect' of the first kind of action is merit (*meritum*) and the material effect of the third kind is demerit (*demeritum*), while the second kind of action has no 'material effect'.[34]

What is meant in this quotation by 'material effect' is the praiseworthiness or blameworthiness of the agent, as the case may be. Performance of one's duty attracts, on this view, neither praise nor blame. Only supererogatory action attracts praise; only action contrary to duty attracts blame.[35] Performance of one's duty here is to be understood as compliance with a behavioural expectation imposed by a moral or legal norm.

As Hruschka highlights, the distinction between these two levels of imputation matters for another reason as well. First-level imputation (the identification of a happening as a human action and thus as a suitable object of moral evaluation) 'precedes the application of a [moral] law to the deed [whereas] second-level

(Leiden, Brill, 2017) 209. See also Auer (n 20) and HE Allison, *Kant's Conception of Freedom. A Developmental and Critical Analysis* (Cambridge, Cambridge University Press, 2019).

[30] For references pertaining to the works of Christian Wolff, Pufendorf, Francis Hutcheson and Kant on this point, see Hruschka (n 22) 672–76.

[31] It is a further question, to which we turn in the next section, when and on what basis results are imputable to an agent as part of his deed. This discussion, which in part falls into the territory of the appropriate individuation of human actions, complements the discussion in the present section.

[32] Hruschka (n 22) 674.

[33] Hruschka credits the philosopher Joachim Georg Daries (sometimes spelled Darjes) as having been the first to distinguish the two levels of imputation in his explication of Pufendorf's approach. See JG Daries, *Institutiones Jurisprudentiae Universalis, Introductionis ad Jus Naturae et Gentium Pars Generalis* (Jena, Cuno, 1740) quoted by Hruschka (n 22) 677, n 30 and 679, nn 37–39.

[34] Hruschka (n 22) 669, n 33 with reference to Pufendorf, *Elementorum* (n 19) Lib I Def XIX.

[35] cf ibid 680.

imputation, ie, the "judgment as to the merit of the deed", succeeds the application of the [moral] law'.[36] He proceeds to explain that:

> This sequence implies that the judgment as to the merit or demerit of a deed, ie, second level imputation, is logically different from the application of the law to that deed and its possible result (supererogation, fulfilment of duty, or violation of duty). Consequently, the supererogatory nature of an act may be a necessary, but is not a sufficient, condition for the assumption of merit, and an act being contrary to duty may be a necessary, but is not a sufficient, condition for the assumption of demerit.[37]

According to Hruschka, the fact that it is possible to judge a human deed in terms of its compliance with prescriptive standards of behaviour (ie norms), and to separate the outcome of this judgement from the question how the performance of the deed morally reflects on its doer, is of fundamental importance for the criminal law. He illustrates its significance with the example of a person who is forced at gunpoint to perform a supererogatory action (say, to save a drowning swimmer at grave risk to his or her own life). We impute the action to the saviour as his deed (he chose to jump into the waters and attempt the dangerous rescue rather than try and dodge the bullet, and in that sense he was a 'free cause' of the rescue in Pufendorfian/Kantian terms), and this action is clearly supererogatory due to the grave risk to the rescuer's own life; but it does not necessarily follow from this that we should *praise* the rescuer for his rescue. As Hruschka puts it, if he was forced at gunpoint to attempt the dangerous rescue '[a]t least there would seem to be no particular reason for praising the actor's "heroism"'.[38]

The flipside of this, as Hruschka also stresses, is that if an agent is forced at gunpoint to kill his victim, 'then, although the act is clearly in violation of duty, doubt exists as to its demerit'.[39] That such doubt exists should not be taken to mean that the finding of a violation of duty would, in this scheme, somehow remain morally neutral. The finding that an action is contrary to duty is never neutral; it already constitutes criticism. The important point is, though, that the extent to which that criticism rebounds on the agent is subject to separate consideration at the second level of imputation.

The distinction between first-level and second-level imputation thus allows not only for a clear differentiation between norm-violating agency and blameworthiness which is fundamental to criminal law; it also allows us to understand the contingent connection which blameworthiness has to norm-violating agency (and why this is so). We will return to this important insight later. Before we do so, however, we need to address an issue that pertains to the individuation of

[36] ibid 679 (with the quote within the quote going to Daries's treatise quoted at n 33 above). This means that 'the application of the moral law to the deed' becomes an intermediate step for the evaluator-observer.

[37] ibid 679.

[38] ibid 680.

[39] ibid.

actions to be ascribed to a person at the first level of imputation. This is the extent to which – and the grounds on which – results form part of the deed ascribed to a human agent. This question has also long been treated as a problem of imputation. Indeed, the term 'imputation' has, in German criminal law doctrine, come to replace the notion of 'legal causation' as the framework for the attribution of responsibility for outcomes in the criminal law.[40] That said, the two concepts are not completely equivalent[41] and my concern here is with the imputation of outcomes.

III. Imputable Outcomes

As explained in section II, for Pufendorf, some happening involving a human source qualifies as a human action when the happening (as Kant would later put it) 'originated in freedom'.[42] But when is that judgement warranted in respect of an occurrence that flowed from what was consciously done? Put differently, when, if ever, is it the case that a change in the world that was brought about by an instance of deliberate human behaviour, 'originated in freedom'?

In this section, I will first consider two extreme modern positions on an agent's responsibility for the outcomes of his action. I will then argue that these views are problematic for the same reason: they do not rest on an adequate conception of human agency. This will bring me back to Pufendorf's conception of agency, which I will then use to address the question when, and on what grounds, consequences are imputable to agents.

When is an agent responsible for the consequences of her action? Two extreme answers can be given to this question: 'always', and 'never'. The first answer arises from Bernard Williams's and Thomas Nagel's discussion of moral luck.[43] Both writers contend (with different nuances) that our moral reactions to what a person has done are inescapably affected by how the thing she did turned out. While they view this as indicative of a deep-seated tension, possibly even a contradiction, in our practices of moral evaluation, I want to focus here on one particular implication of the view that consequences always, necessarily, and without any restriction or qualification, affect the moral quality of the act from which they stem. This view – if taken to mean that the moral quality of our actions depends on their

[40] See generally Zieschang (n 22).

[41] See further M Zalewska, 'Causality and Imputation (Kelsen)' in M Sellers and S Kirste (eds), *Encyclopedia of the Philosophy of Law and Social Philosophy* (Dordrecht, Springer, entry first published online 2017) and A Walen and B Weißer, 'Causation and Responsibility for Outcomes' in K Ambos et al (eds), *Core Concepts in Criminal Law and Criminal Justice*, vol 2 (Cambridge, Cambridge University Press, 2022) ch 3.

[42] Kant (n 27).

[43] B Williams, 'Moral Luck' (1976) Suppl Vol 50 *Proceedings of the Aristotelian Society*, 115 and T Nagel, 'Moral Luck' (1976) Suppl Vol 50 *Proceedings of the Aristotelian Society* 137.

outcome(s) even if we had no meaningful control over these outcomes – invites an understanding of human agency that is perhaps best described as 'tragic': while we can choose to act, we cannot control what happens when we act but can only act regardless; and for this very reason we are responsible for *everything* that flows from our engagement with the world.[44]

The contrasting extreme position is taken by Larry Alexander and Kim Ferzan. They also start from the assumption that we have no control over what happens once we have acted and thereby 'unleashed' a risk.[45] But the conclusion they draw from this is radically different: they contend that moral assessment of a person's conduct therefore always, and necessarily, has to stop short of weighing in the consequences of what that person has done. Their challenge to '[d]efenders of the claim that "results matter"' consists in asking whether an agent's 'positive moral ledger' is enhanced by completely unforeseen and unforeseeable further consequences of an initial well-intended action, such as the saving of 1,000 lives brought about by helping an old lady across the street.[46] The implication is that other situations are not fundamentally different in that the occurrence or non-occurrence of consequences is always down to luck.[47]

Both of these positions draw their diametrically opposed conclusions from the same diagnosis of the human condition: that we lack control over what we bring about. But it must be doubted that either view reaches the right conclusion about how moral luck should affect moral evaluation. To see this, let us turn to Margaret Urban-Walker's discussion of moral luck. As Urban-Walker argues, moral luck is 'a fact of our moral situation and our human kind of agency' which human agents have to '*grasp*' as '[p]art of [their] normal and required self-understanding'.[48] What follows from this, as Urban-Walker explains, is that the

> 'moral luck problem' is one about conceptions of agency and responsibility of the sort that morality requires [with] agency situated within the causal order in such ways as to be variably conditioned by and conditioning parts of that order, without our being able to draw for *all* purposes a *unitary* boundary to its exercise at either end, nor always for *particular* purposes a *sharp* one.[49]

This observation allows us to identify the extreme positions' shared weakness: they do not respond adequately to how humans are situated in a causal world

[44] This is merely one possible reading of the 'moral luck' problem. I do not wish to suggest that it is the best possible reading; there is a vast debate on what exactly the 'moral luck' problem is. Nor do I wish to suggest that either Williams or Nagel are committed to precisely this view of human agency. They take their respective discussions of moral luck into other directions.

[45] Alexander and Ferzan (n 5) 198.

[46] ibid 179 (their example).

[47] Alexander and Ferzan express their position as a claim that results are not relevant to 'culpability' but translated into the context of the present discussion their view is one about the imputability of results.

[48] M Urban-Walker, 'Moral Luck and the Virtues of Impure Agency' (1991) 22 *Metaphilosophy* 14, 19 (original emphasis).

[49] ibid 22.

in a way that gives them some influence. What the human condition calls for is a position on the ascription of responsibility for outcomes that proceeds from a nuanced understanding of human agency as being, in Urban-Walker's words, 'situated within the causal order in such ways as to be variably conditioned by and conditioning parts of that order'.

Urban-Walker does not tell us *which* structures of responsibility ascription and blame *are* appropriate for changes brought about by the exercise of our agency. But one important implication of her view is that the observation that a particular instance of human behaviour led to a certain change in the world can only be a starting point for further differentiation. Even assuming that we stand in a special relationship to *any* change in the world connected to our behaviour, the question arises whether that relation is the same whatever our mental link to the outcome, or whether it differs depending on the precise configuration of that link.

It is this question that I want to address through Pufendorf's conception of agency. For Pufendorf, human agency is inherently both goal-oriented and rule-oriented. The human activities of setting and pursuing goals require mental engagement with a normative orientation. The rules with which the agent engages are not just practical rules of experience (eg the agent's understanding of causal connections) but also practical rules of ethics (eg the agent's understanding of the normative expectations and standards that apply to him).[50] This truth has relevance for the conceptualisation of human action. It is inherent to human action that the agent applies or orients himself towards rules in acting, and it follows from this inherence that human action is underdescribed, phenomenally, by those who merely look at it in terms of a willed bodily movement or willed bodily motionlessness. Moreover, the ascription of responsibility that Pufendorf argues for rests crucially on *this* orientation feature of human agency.[51] Some animals can engage in complex planning behaviour in pursuit of a goal (such as to get to a difficult-to-reach source of food); what is distinctly human is that the appropriateness of pursuing the goal is evaluated, by the agent no less than by a later judge, in terms such as whether the food belongs to someone else, whether the amount taken exceeds a fair share of a scarce resource, etc. It is this dimension of agency which explains why 'agency' (imputation) is genuinely an *ascription* of responsibility, an interpretive scheme that builds on ontological observations and assumptions, rather than a label for an ontological constellation of facts. To impute a happening to a human being as his deed necessarily reflects a choice or practice to import a moral significance to behaviour thus constituted.[52]

[50] For this dimension of the classical scheme of imputation, see esp J Hruschka, *Strukturen der Zurechnung* (Berlin, De Gruyter, 1976) 12–40 and esp 36–39.

[51] On this point, compare T Pink (n 24) 198–201.

[52] See Hruschka, *Strukturen* (n 50) 39 (stressing that free will, act/deed and culpability/guilt are not 'ontic categories' but 'ascriptions', in that they posit their human source as free and thus as the author of a deed, which is in turn necessary for moral evaluation to be coherently possible).

My specific concern in this section is with outcomes of actions that were not 'entirely unpredictable' and in respect of which this very fact may serve to explain why they form part of an agent's deed. The key question in respect of such outcomes is whether predictability or foreseeability as such provides sufficient grounds for responsibility attribution. This, at least, is how we ask the question today. Pufendorf approached the matter from a different direction. As Hruschka sets out Pufendorf's position:

> Pufendorf distinguished between 'what in itself was in the power of an individual to do or not to do', 'what in itself was not in the power of an individual but in its cause was in his power', and 'what neither in itself nor in its cause was in the power of an individual'.[53]

What falls into the first and the second category is imputed to the agent; what falls into the third category is not.

It is unlikely that, when construing these categories, Pufendorf took himself to be addressing the outcomes of human negligence. Pufendorf wrote at a time when the framing of the problem of responsibility for foreseeable and thus avoidable unintended consequences as 'responsibility for negligence' lay still in the future.[54] Instead, discussions of scenarios that would later come to be taken to raise a problem of negligence (although the factual overlap is incomplete) proceeded in terms of a doctrine developed in canon law, of *versari in re illicita* – any bad consequence arising from an illicit (unlawful) act was taken to rebound on the agent.[55] As late as 1793, Immanuel Kant insisted that 'the consequences of [a human being's] former free but unlawful actions can also be imputed to him; by saying this, one will say only: one need not … agree on whether the latter may be free or not because already in the admittedly free action that was the cause of these later actions there is sufficient reason for imputation',[56] while vacillating on the question whether it was possible to impute *any* event that had occurred where the actor had been the free cause of his later 'impotence to act or not act'.[57] In these discussions, what the agent could or should have foreseen at the time of his earlier (free) action was not usually addressed.

That said, once responsibility for negligence is raised as a problem, it is possible to conceive of it as a problem to which Pufendorf's second basis for responsibility ascription provides an answer. This is clear from the Scottish philosopher Francis Hutcheson's reading of Pufendorf's text. Hutcheson had little choice but to read (and teach) Pufendorf since Pufendorf's main works were standardly used as

[53] Hruschka (n 22) 688 with reference to Pufendorf, *Elementorum* (n 19) Lib II, Axioma I.

[54] See Hardwig (n 19) 45.

[55] See ibid 25 and H Kollmann, 'Die Lehre vom versari in re illicita im Rahmen des corpus juris canonici' (1914) 35 *Zeitschrift für die gesamte Strafrechtswissenschaft* 46.

[56] I Kant, *Religion within the Boundaries of Reason* (1793); quoted in J Hruschka, 'On the Logic of Imputation in the Vigilantius Lecture Notes' in L Denis and O Sensen (eds), *Kant's Lectures on Ethics: A Critical Guide* (Cambridge, Cambridge University Press, 2015) 170, 180.

[57] See Hruschka, ibid 180.

textbooks in Scottish (and other Protestant) universities.[58] This, as the editor of a twenty-first-century edition of Hutcheson's *Philosophiae moralis institutio compendiaria* remarks, put 'Hutcheson … in the difficult position of having to instruct his students in the principles and subtleties of natural and civil law even though he was a keen critic and severe judge of one of the most important systems of such law, that of Pufendorf.'[59] Hutcheson connects what Pufendorf says of an event's (or its cause's) being 'within the power' of an agent to the criteria of avoidability and voluntariness:

> These alone are the … unimputable events which neither any present desire or action of ours can prevent, nor could they have been prevented by any prior diligence or care which we ought to have had about such matters. Such as prior forethought and care could have prevented, tho' they be now unavoidable, are in some measure voluntary and imputable.[60]

This position, however, was not unchallenged. Pufendorf's second ground of imputation (that producing 'the cause was within the agent's power') was rejected by another Scottish philosopher, Thomas Reid, on the basis that, here, admittedly the agent is not in a position to avoid the outcome when he performs the decisive action.[61] This was taken to violate the maxim that no one can be obliged to do the impossible[62] and more broadly to disregard the requirement of free agency for imputation; or, to put this differently, the necessary connection between imputable agency and the will.

To address this challenge, we need to return to Pufendorf's conception of human agency as not merely goal- but also rule-oriented. This conception offers a basis for arguing that Hutcheson is right to include the consequences of negligently performed actions in Pufendorf's second category of imputable actions. Pufendorf deduces the specificity of human agency – as well as the possibility of morality – from human beings' embeddedness in a cultural realm.[63] It is in that realm, where human interaction occurs, that specific 'objects' of human cognition arise: these are what Pufendorf calls 'entia moralia', moral entities (which one can loosely translate as moral facts, or moral truths).[64] Human beings are active in that

[58] See eg G Carmichael, *Observationes et Supplementa ad Cl Puffendorfii libros duos De Officio Hominis et Civis* (1718).

[59] L Turco, 'Introduction' in F Hutcheson, *Philosophiae moralis institutio compendiaria with a Short Introduction to Moral Philosophy*, ed L Turco (Indianapolis, Liberty Fund, 2007).

[60] F Hutcheson, *A System of Moral Philosophy* (posthumous, London 1755) in B Fabian (ed), *The Collected Works of Francis Hutcheson*, vol 5 (Hildesheim, Olms, 1969) 229, quoted by Hruschka (n 22) 689, n 58. Hutcheson clarifies that this includes 'omissions of actions now impossible … when they might have been possible, had that previous diligence been exerted which becomes a good man'. See ibid.

[61] T Reid, *The Works of Thomas Reid*, ed W Hamilton, 5th edn (Edinburgh, 1858) 27, quoted by Hruschka (n 22) 691–92.

[62] Hruschka, ibid.

[63] See Welzel (n 21) 21–22.

[64] On 'entia moralia', see esp Hartwig (n 19) 35–39. As Hardwig (ibid, 36–37) explains, 'The effect of the entia moralia does not consist in a physical effect … but they are directed towards a human being's

realm when they engage in goal-directed behaviour. Such behaviour is possible by their use of reason. Reason draws not merely on the ability to identify goals, and means to ends, but also on knowledge of the moral worth of these goals and of the moral law.[65] Reasoning without such normative orientation is unthinkable. Because of this normative dimension of human agency, it can be morally evaluated and judged – by the agent and by others. We can therefore see why, for Pufendorf, someone who is driving faster than at a safe speed to get to the theatre in time for the start of a performance is also engaging with the norm that says, 'do not endanger others unreasonably' and chooses to disregard that norm or to put it second behind his reasons for attending the performance from the start. This is also why, even were it the case that, at a later time when an accident occurs, it was (due to his excessive speed) not within the power of the driver to brake on time, Pufendorf would consider it significant that this later (unfree) act – say, running over a child who has suddenly darted out onto the road – had its cause in the prior free action of speeding.[66] The imputed action of running over the child is, on this account, traceable to the agent's will – notwithstanding the fact that the agent might protest, 'But I didn't want *that* to happen!'

IV. Imputation of Negligently Produced Outcomes and the Will

What, then, shall we do about the cry, 'But I didn't want *that* to happen!'

While Pufendorf helps us to identify a basis for responsibility ascription for negligently produced outcomes, his writings do not provide us with the resources to address the further question whether responsibility for these outcomes arises to the same extent as it arises for intended outcomes. In the above quotation he appears to be treating both pathways as equivalent. In this section, I want to pursue the question whether there could be a relevant difference between an agent's responsibility for intended and for negligently produced unintended outcomes. I will do so by drawing on a philosopher for whom the question whether a human being was the free cause of an event is similarly central. That philosopher is GWF Hegel, whose theory of imputation connects agency and responsibility through of the concept of the will.[67]

free reason … such that the entia morality enable him to guide his own actions through practical reasoning and to affect the actions of other reasonable beings in like manner' (my translation).

[65] See esp Welzel (n 21) 23.

[66] From a modern theoretical vantage point, one could raise the question whether this Pufendorfian argument constitutes a tracing or a non-tracing view of responsibility for negligence. I will not pursue the question here.

[67] See esp W Schild, 'Der strafrechtsdogmatische Begriff der Zurechnung in der Rechtsphilosophie Hegels' (1981) 35 *Zeitschrift für philosophische Forschung* 445 and K Seelmann, 'Ebenen der Zurechnung bei Hegel' in Kaufmann and Renzikowski (n 20) 85.

For Hegel, what matters for free agency is that there are – or, more precisely, that we experience the world such that we take there to be – courses of action open to us. These courses of action are open to us in a meaningful way only because we are also embodied beings located in a physical world. Our freedom is thus also linked to the awareness we develop that (and how) we can shape our surroundings in certain ways through our behaviour. This awareness, developed from experience, makes it possible for us to engage in projects, in courses of action that are directed at achieving certain changes in the world. Hegel therefore maintains that our freedom is concrete (or 'real') only when we *do* something, when we actualise our possible agency. It remains no more than abstract so long as we merely think of doing something, imagine ourselves doing it, but do not yet do it and thereby live it. So, in the Hegelian analysis, freedom is not abstract possibility in the sense of having a range of options. (If we think that this matters at all for free agency, it could only be as a precondition.) Freedom consists in engaging self-directedly in object-directed behaviour in the world.[68] Pufendorf's rule-oriented dimension of agency reappears in Hegel's conceptualisation of agency when Hegel insists that what the agent 'wills' is not just the action in light of its agent-defined goal (A drives his car to reach his destination on time), but also in light of its general quality (A drives dangerously because the weather conditions are such that he would not be able to brake in time if, as might well happen, the traffic suddenly slows down).[69]

Drawing on Hegel's conception of agency, Alan Brudner conceives of the relationship between actors and the outcomes of their actions as a form of 'ownership', a concept he understands in Hegelian terms through its connection to human agency.[70] Hegel's conception of ownership signifies a distinctive kind of relation of a person to an object based on that object's relation to a human will. As we shall see, it allows us to appreciate how a teleological understanding of action weaves the changes in the world that result from the action into the concept of action.[71]

For our projects to be implementable, Hegel sees, we need to use things. Our free agency thus necessarily subjects objects in the world to our use. As Hegel describes this phenomenon, we place our will in objects in the world, we 'invest' ourselves in objects. This relationship of will-investment in a thing is what Hegel calls ownership.[72]

[68] On Hegel's conception of agency, see esp C Yeomans, *Freedom and Reflection: Hegel and the Logic of Agency* (Oxford, Oxford University Press, 2012). See also S Houlgate, 'Action, Right and Morality in Hegel's Philosophy of Right' in A Laitinen and C Sandis (eds), *Hegel on Action* (Basingstoke, Palgrave Macmillan, 2010) 155.

[69] On this point, see esp G Jakobs, '"Recht des Willens" – "Schuld des Willens". Schuldzurechnung bei Hegel' in T Fischer and E Hoven (eds), *Schuld* (Baden-Baden, Nomos, 2017) 111, 113–18. See also AW Wood, 'Hegel on Responsibility for Actions and Consequences' in Laitinen and Sandis (n 68) 119, 125.

[70] A Brudner, 'Owning Outcomes: On Intervening Causes, Thin Skulls, and Fault-undifferentiated Crimes' (1998) 11 *Canadian Journal of Law and Jurisprudence* 89.

[71] For details, see Wood (n 69) 123–30; Houlgate (n 68) 162–69.

[72] GWF Hegel, *Elements of the Philosophy of Right* [1821], ed AW Wood, trans HB Nisbet (Cambridge, Cambridge University Press, 1991) §§ 44–45; see also §§ 46–64 for a fuller development. The translation

This notion of ownership is then connected to an agent's responsibility for outcomes in the following way: when we invest our will in an object by using it for our purposes, we recruit it into the realisation of our projects and thereby constitute the object as 'what it is now' by assigning and enacting its purpose for us – a quotidian and ubiquitous process, as mundane as picking up fallen fruit and starting to eat it, which constitutes the apple as 'food' in the same moment as it is constituted as 'mine'. That very relationship of will-investment is also what turns the outcomes of my agency into 'my outcomes', what justifies attributing them to me as 'mine'. According to Brudner, this is the link philosophers have traditionally rendered as 'imputation', which Brudner defines as 'a factual judgment indicating the person to whom an event belongs'.[73]

Assuming Brudner is right about this, then – based on the analogy with ownership – we can also begin to appreciate differences in the connection between an agent and the various outcomes by which his freedom manifests itself in the world. Brudner's starting point is that, 'The more intelligible the outcome in light of the agent's reasons for acting, the more its facticity is raised into the teleological relation, the less of it is left to the impact of blind causal forces.'[74] This 'raising' of the outcome 'into the teleological relation' is a matter of normative evaluation rather than brute fact. Brudner explains: '[O]nce we see a project that the outcome reflects, we no longer comprehend the outcome as the effect of a cause. Rather, we view it as the realization *of* a purpose within a set of facilitating preconditions.'[75] Note that this is not so because the materialisation of an intended outcome leaves 'less to chance' empirically than the materialisation of an unintended outcome, but because evaluatively the intended outcomes constitute our projects, such that we cannot disassociate ourselves from these. The idea is, thus, that 'a purposive account of the outcome acquires an epistemological primacy over causal explanations without, however, rendering the latter superfluous'.[76] Indeed, Brudner states explicitly that 'since an intended outcome is perfectly transparent in light of the agent's goal, there is no remainder attributable to causes as distinct from purposes'.[77]

When an outcome 'cannot be fully explained by [the agent's] purpose in acting', however, 'it has a residual existence outside the teleological relation, and so … it

uses 'property' for the German *Eigentum* but the term 'ownership' is preferable since it captures the relational aspect of the concept. For a fuller account of the connection between personhood and property in Hegel's theory of agency, see D Hüning, 'Die "Härte des abstracten Rechts", Person und Eigentum in Hegels Rechtsphilosophie' in D Hüning, G Stiening and U Vogel, *Societas rationis. Festschrift für Burkhard Tuschling zum 65. Geburtstag* (Berlin, Duncker & Humblot, 2002) 235.

[73] Brudner (n 70) 107.

[74] ibid 105.

[75] ibid 103 (original emphasis). These facilitating conditions are simply the state of the world in which the agent acts, which includes such outcome-enabling states as 'no one at home' for the burglar, etc.

[76] ibid.

[77] ibid 104.

is partially a chance effect of causes'.[78] Again, it is important to bear in mind that this is not a reference to the epistemic probability of the outcome's occurrence (which may indeed be lower in the case of an intended outcome than in the case of a negligently unintended one) but to the extent to which agency, on an evaluative level, claims 'explanatory priority' over the brute forces of nature in moral evaluation.

Specifically in respect of negligently produced outcomes, Brudner traces the extent to which they originate with their human originator's agency (and hence attract responsibility) through the fact that agency involves, and invokes, 'a capacity for … surveying the network of interconnected forces within which my action occurs, and for anticipating the action's probable effects'.[79] He argues that:

> Because I as an agent … cannot disown this capacity, I must acknowledge partial authorship not only of the effects that I as *this* individual foresaw but also of those that the reasonably circumspect agent would have foreseen as a serious possibility.[80]

To illustrate, recall the scenarios involving Adam's firing a gun from section II. In *Deliberate Shooting*, where Adam fires the gun at Victoria in order to hit and kill her, Victoria's death is (as Brudner puts it) 'perfectly transparent' in light of Adam's goal, such that her death is fully 'owned' by Adam. Given the explanatory priority of the action's teleological dimension over its natural-force situatedness, explanatory components pertaining to chance, such as the likelihood of Adam's bullet hitting its target, remain by-the-by.[81] Since Victoria's death *can be* 'fully explained by [Adam's] purpose in acting', it has *no* 'residual existence outside the teleological relation'.[82]

Matters are different in *Wedding Celebration*, where Adam fires the gun without aiming at anyone. Reference to Adam's goal in acting – making a loud noise – provides no explanation, on its own, for Victoria's death. It lifts into the 'teleological relation' only the noise produced by the discharge of the gun, not anything else about the lethal risk to Victoria that Adam's firing of the gun in this precise setting created. On Brudner's Hegelian-inspired analysis, then, there is a massive explanatory remainder left by the teleological account of Victoria's death.

[78] ibid.

[79] ibid. This feature is also stressed by Hegel, see Wood (n 69) 127–30.

[80] Brudner (n 70) 104 (original emphasis). I part company with Brudner, however, in respect of his further contention, that therefore negligent outcomes bear 'no trace of my specific agency' (ibid), and also more generally in respect of his argument against criminal liability for negligence, which he develops in A Brudner, *Punishment and Freedom* (Oxford, Oxford University Press, 2009).

[81] Brudner illustrates this point by giving an example of, on the one hand, the result of a top-notch professional basket-player's difficult but successful shot, and on the other hand, the result of a third-rate basketball player's wild shot that hits the target. In both cases, Brudner suggests, 'the intentionality of the outcome somehow makes the outcome his, we no longer attribute it to chance' (Brudner (n 70) 101).

[82] Incidentally, this supports the view that the (un)likelihood of the occurrence of an intended outcome, and/or the fact that it occurs through a freaky causal chain, does not block the attribution of responsibility for that outcome to the agent who intended by his action to bring this very outcome about.

That gap needs to be filled by an account of misfortune suffered in consequence of negligent creation of risk.[83] This is the reason why, in this account, the likelihood of the unfortunate outcome matters for the attribution of responsibility. If the outcome was extremely unlikely to occur, it must be doubted that the agent's failure to exercise his 'capacity for … surveying the network of interconnected forces within which [his] action occurs, and for anticipating the action's probable effects', has (on an evaluative, not only a factual level) any explanatory significance for the occurrence of the outcome.

Brudner's Hegelian approach thus not only provides an explanation for why the outcomes of our negligent agency are attributable to us as agents – our (unexercised) capacity for prudential agency is reflected in them, in that it provides part of the explanation for why the outcome occurred – but also for why the connection between the act and the outcome is different, and less tight, for negligently produced compared with intended outcomes. The negligently produced outcome cannot, as such, be understood in terms of 'a project that the outcome reflects'. It is connected to an agent's project aimed at a different outcome (such as Adam's shot being aimed at making a loud noise), and what is therefore reflected in the negligently produced unintended outcome (the bullet's hitting Victoria and killing her) is not only Adam's original project, in terms of the risks he created in pursuing it, but also his bad luck in having Victoria standing where the bullet hit her, and for the external conditions being such that the discharged bullet takes this trajectory and no other.

Based on the analogy Brudner draws between imputation and ownership, we can therefore appreciate differences in the connection between an agent and the intended outcomes of the manifestations of his freedom in the world. Brudner renders these differences as differences in degree. 'An outcome is more or less imputable to an agent depending on the degree of clarity with which it reflects the agent's purpose in acting.'[84] In particular, negligently produced outcomes are 'not fully intelligible in light of the agent's purpose in acting'.[85] This is why it is perfectly coherent for Adam to say both 'I wanted to fire the gun' and 'I didn't want to injure Victoria', and why we morally treat this as relevant: such that we are prepared to acknowledge that Adam's responsibility for Victoria's death is partly his own misfortune.

[83] Brudner (n 70) suggests that 'the materialized risk belongs less to chance and more to agency if the agent foresaw the risk than if he was simply negligent, because we think that objects attain their own reality to the degree that they are related to a purpose' (105). Brudner's argument here must be doubted as an interpretation of Hegel's view. For Hegel, the matter of A's responsibility for the outcome turns on the general quality of A's action as a 'dangerous' action – a quality which follows from the obviousness of the risk and which the standard, sane adult agent is therefore taken to have understood whether or not he 'thought of' the risk (see Houlgate (n 68) 165–66). For present purposes I leave open whether Brudner is nevertheless right to suggest that an agent's connection to an unintended is necessarily less tight when the agent failed to advert to an obvious risk (and hence was oblivious of it when she acted) than when she ignored a risk that had crossed her mind.

[84] Brudner (n 70) 105.

[85] ibid.

V. Explaining and Justifying an Outcome-Responsive Criminal Law

So that gets me to the big criminal law question: if we accept this analysis of agency and imputation, what implication does it have for the criminal law?

To start with, this perspective explains why outcomes should be relevant to an agent's criminal responsibility; why an agent's responsibility extends to them. Provided the agent's activity meets the requirements that make it imputable (in Pufendorf's sense[86]) to the agent as his deed, that deed extends to alterations of the world which the agent brought about. The moral connection between an agent's action and its outcome is structurally identical to the connection that obtains between an agent's action and any bodily motions the agent performs. Imputable outcomes are appropriately objects of responsibility.

Taken in combination, Pufendorf's and Hegel's/Brudner's views also allow us to understand the true differences between intended and negligently produced (unintended) outcomes. Intended outcomes define the project of the agent in a manner different from negligently unintended outcomes. An intended outcome qualifies the agent's action as being of a particular sort even before the outcome's occurrence, whereas an unintended possible outcome does not (before its occurrence) qualify the agent's action in a comparable manner. The difference is highlighted by the fact that one can coherently consider a negligent actor who produces an unintended outcome by his negligence as having become a 'victim' of his own actions, whereas it is impossible for an agent who produces an intended outcome to distance himself from that outcome in a similar way.

What we can see now, however, is also that this distancing – while possible – is only partial. It cannot preclude the attribution of responsibility for the negligently produced outcome. The criteria which enable imputation on the first level of imputation – that the agent engaged self-directedly in the relevant behaviour, and that this behaviour violated norms of prudential behaviour that applied to him – are made out. But, importantly, the negligent production of an outcome affects the ascription of demerit for that outcome. This is what Pufendorf's conception of imputation helps us to see.

Recall that Pufendorf insisted that the questions whether an agent is responsible for an outcome – whether the outcome is something the agent did, and whether merit or demerit arises for the agent in respect of his deed thus constituted – need

[86] I take this to permit imputation at both levels, ie including merit/demerit-imputation. Note that Pufendorf does not see any asymmetry between merit-imputation and demerit-imputation. He does, however, hold that merit only arises from supererogatory actions whereas actions in accordance with duty are in this respect neutral (they do not give rise to merit). Whether this position allows him to deal adequately with the unfortunate consequences of an action done in accordance with duty is a question I cannot address here. It seems that such conduct – including its consequences – would attract first-level imputation. If that is so, it is unclear whether Pufendorf would be able to coherently avoid imputing merit or demerit on the grounds he offers. For a discussion of these difficulties in connection with Kant's reading of Pufendorf, see Hruschka (n 56) 171–72.

to be kept distinct. If we combine this insight with the important insight from the philosophy of agency which Alan Brudner developed out of Hegel's theory of agency – that the harmful consequence qualifies the negligent deed in a different way from an intended outcome – we can see how we might explain the puzzle of criminal liability for negligently produced outcomes: that these outcomes are, on the one hand, typically preconditions of criminal liability arising for the negligent conduct at all, and that, on the other hand, those result-based crimes of negligence attract substantially much less punishment than result-based crimes of intent (of the same result).

As regards the first part of the puzzle, in the case of negligent harm-doing, it is not merely the case that (as it does with intended outcomes) the 'activity plus outcome' constitutes a different and more serious wrong compared with the same activity short of its intended outcome. Rather, the harmful outcome of a negligent act is a necessary component of the agent's wrong. Whereas the actor who intends to bring about a criminally prohibited outcome already wrongs (in the sense of victimises) his victim when he takes steps to bring that outcome about, the negligent actor wrongs (or victimises) his victim only when he harms him through his negligence. That the outcome is imputable to the agent's negligence is what qualifies an agent's 'activity plus its unintended negligent outcome' as a crime. It is therefore entirely appropriate for the criminal law to cast crimes of negligence as result-crimes.[87]

As regards the second part of the puzzle, we need to remind ourselves of the need to attend to the second level of imputation – the extent to which merit or demerit arises for the agent from his performance of the deed. It is in respect of *this* question that it matters that the connection of the negligent agent to the outcome is *weaker* than the connection that obtains between an agent and his intended outcomes – both in terms of responsibility (the agent can in some sense also be described as a victim of his own negligence) and in terms of wrongfulness (this was no attack on the victim; the agent did not negate the victim's rights when engaging in the behaviour although he ended up violating the victim's rights when he negligently brought the outcome about).

The partial disassociation of the negligent actor from the outcome occurs on this second level of imputation. The negligent actor cannot (on the first level of imputation) deny that his activity-plus-outcome constitutes an attributable deed contrary to duty, but he can point to the extent to which the bad outcome is explained by chance – is not 'raised into the teleological relation', ie explained by the goals he set himself in his action – when we ask how badly the action reflects on him. It is at this point that we acknowledge the important general truth about negligently unintended outcomes: that the action itself pursued a harmless or even a worthy goal and, when considered under that description (which was the one at

[87] I take no view here on whether it is appropriate for the criminal law to criminalise certain typified dangerous behaviours, such as careless driving, in the absence of bad results. My argument in the text pertains to a comparison of victimising crimes of intent with victimising crimes of negligence.

the forefront of the agent's mind), cannot give rise to demerit. What is to the agent's demerit is the agent's failure to exercise his capacity for prudent behaviour, and a person assessing the extent of that demerit will therefore rightly have regard to the extent to which that capacity was developed, to the presence or absence of reasons of understandable human weakness why that capacity remained unexercised, etc. But this is a different, and less grave, demerit than the demerit that arises from the pursuit of evil goals. This explains why, despite the fact that the negligently produced outcome rightly constitutes a precondition of criminal liability, result-crimes of negligence should attract substantially less blame than result-crimes of intent which generate the same result.

VI. Final Remarks

Bob Sullivan has always shown great interest in questions that concern the structure and nature of a criminal offence at the most abstract and general level. In the tradition of criminal law thought I have drawn upon in this chapter, these issues have long had pride of place. My aim in this chapter has been to show how the classical doctrine of imputation – lost in present-day Anglo-American theorising, and buried under multiple layers of subsequent doctrinal discussion in German criminal law theory – can, when read together with modern interpretations of Hegel's theory of agency, help to resolve the question left open by Sullivan: whether 'the reasoning supportive of this "results don't matter to morality" thesis is sound'.[88] By demonstrating that, and how, results indeed matter to morality, the classical doctrine of imputation thereby provides a firm theoretical underpinning for the criminal law's complex, and differentiated, outcome-responsive practices that a modern criminal law should preserve.

[88] Sullivan (n 4) 102.

4

Why *Ivey* was a Mistake (aka Two Times I Flirted with Theft)

MARK DSOUZA*

I have learned a tremendous amount about the criminal law from Bob Sullivan's work, and so I am delighted to contribute to this collection of essays to mark his retirement from *Simester and Sullivan's Criminal Law*. Having never studied English criminal law as an undergraduate student, it was the fourth edition of the Simester and Sullivan textbook that became my first and main criminal law teacher when, as a PhD student, I frantically read up on the subject in order to lead undergraduate criminal law supervisions. I do not exaggerate when I say that the Simester and Sullivan textbook has shaped my entire approach to, and understanding of, not just English criminal law, but also key concepts in the theory and philosophy of law. In this chapter, I want to focus on one area of law to which Sullivan has returned time and again, even in his work outside the textbook – the law of theft. In particular, I want to focus on the test for determining whether some conduct has been performed dishonestly.

For decades, the test set out in *R v Ghosh*[1] was used to determine whether a person had behaved dishonestly for the purposes of the criminal law. According to that test, the jury was required to decide the following questions:

1. Was what was done dishonest according to the ordinary standards of reasonable and honest people? And if so,
2. Did the defendant (D) realise that reasonable and honest people would regard what he did as dishonest?[2]

The Court of Appeal illustrated how it thought this this test should apply with the example of the *Visitor on the Bus*: a man who, hailing from a country in which

* I am extremely grateful to Andrew Simester, Bob Sullivan, and Findlay Stark for their detailed comments and suggestions on various drafts of this essay. My thanks also to Ian Williams, Matt Gibson, Flora Page, David Ormerod, John Stanton-Ife, Alex Sarch, and Rory Kelly for their inputs in relation to an early draft.

[1] *R v Ghosh* [1982] QB 1053, 1064.

[2] ibid 1064.

public transport is free, assumes the same is true in England, and does not pay for bus travel. It said of the visitor, 'His mind is clearly honest; but his conduct, judged objectively by what he has done, is dishonest.'[3] In other words, the Court of Appeal thought that first limb of the test would be satisfied. However, it went on to affirm that the second limb of its test prevented the visitor from being found to have acted dishonestly, on the basis that he would not realise that reasonable and honest people would regard what he did as dishonest.[4]

The Court of Appeal's explanation of the *Visitor on the Bus* example swiftly came in for criticism. Campbell argued that,

> on any reasonable interpretation, [the first limb] would ask: was it dishonest by common standards for the accused to travel on British public transport without paying when he genuinely believed, albeit erroneously, that British public transport is, like that of his own country, free? And the answer to that will surely be 'No.' So this reason given by the court for including limb (2) turns out, on inspection, to be no reason at all. Properly interpreted, limb (1) by itself gives the answer to this example which the court believed could be obtained only by including limb (2).[5]

So, Campbell argued that in applying the first limb of the *Ghosh* test, account should be taken of the visitor's beliefs regarding the norms applicable in society, including, apparently, the legal norms that govern travel on public transport. Presumably, though, the visitor's beliefs as to what constitutes behaving dishonestly would have to be excluded, since that limb of the test refers to the standards of reasonable and honest people, not of D herself. In sum, what I shall call 'Campbell's Gloss' on the *Ghosh* test asks in the first limb of the test, whether the reasonable and honest observer would judge D to have acted dishonestly, taking account of D's knowledge and beliefs about the facts relevant to D's actions. The second limb of the test remains unchanged.

If Campbell is correct that there is no reasonable interpretation of the *Ghosh* test that would treat the *Visitor on the Bus* as satisfying the first, but not the second, limb of the test, then the Court of Appeal erred in its discussion of the *Visitor on the Bus* example, and we have no realistic choice but to reject that part of its judgment. But in the case law, we do find one suggestion about how the Court of Appeal wanted us to understand its test that is consistent with its explanation of the *Visitor on the Bus* example. The Supreme Court has suggested that the Court of Appeal meant for us to consider 'only the [defendant's] actions and not the state of knowledge or belief as to the facts in which they were performed' in the first limb of its test.[6] Let us call this reading of the *Ghosh* test the 'Simplistic View'. If the Simplistic View or any other reading of the *Ghosh* test that is consistent

[3] ibid 1063.
[4] ibid 1064.
[5] K Campbell, 'The Test of Dishonesty in *Ghosh*' (1984) 43 *CLJ* 349, 354.
[6] *Ivey v Genting Casinos* [2017] UKSC 67, [60]. It then went on to say that this was a mistake on the part of the Court of Appeal.

with the Court of Appeal's analysis of the *Visitor on the Bus* example proves to be reasonable, then we do not *need* to reject the Court of Appeal's construction of its own test in favour of Campbell's Gloss. There has been no case in which the court was required to decide between Campbell's Gloss and the Simplistic View (or indeed any other reading of the first limb of the *Ghosh* test), but most commentators have coalesced around Campbell's Gloss.[7]

While the *Ghosh* test was proposed in the context of charges under sections 15(1) and 20(2) of the Theft Act 1968, it came to be applied more broadly, both to other offences in that Act and to offences of dishonesty under other statutes. However, in October 2017, the Supreme Court, in the civil case of *Ivey v Genting Casinos*,[8] decided that the *Ghosh* test was incorrect and resolved authoritatively to state the test for determining dishonesty in both civil and criminal law contexts. According to the *Ivey* test, the jury must ask the following questions:

1. What was D's actual state of knowledge or beliefs as to the facts? And
2. In light of that knowledge or those beliefs, was D's conduct dishonest by the standards of ordinary decent people?[9]

Along the way, the Supreme Court explicitly endorsed Campbell's Gloss as a general principle, stating that, 'in order to determine the honesty or otherwise of a person's conduct, one must ask what he knew or believed about the facts affecting the area of activity in which he was engaging'.[10] This suggests that, for the *Ivey* test too, in identifying D's actual state of knowledge or beliefs about the facts, we should be mindful of all of D's beliefs, including beliefs as to the norms governing conduct,[11] but not including beliefs as to what constitutes behaving dishonestly.[12] We should then ask whether ordinary decent people would judge D's chosen conduct to be dishonest in the light of her beliefs about the facts (including facts about norms).

[7] See eg: E Griew, 'Dishonesty: The Objections to Feely and Ghosh' [1985] *Crim LR* 341, 352–53; M Dyson and P Jarvis, 'Poison Ivey or Herbal Leaf Tea?' (2018) 134 *LQR* 198. There is also some oblique support for this view in *R v Hancock* [1990] 2 QB 242, 252–53.

[8] *Ivey* (n 6). The Court of Appeal (Criminal Division) (henceforth 'CA(CD)'), in *Barton and Booth v R* [2020] EWCA Crim 575, has subsequently confirmed that even though it was strictly obiter dicta, the test set out in *Ivey* should also be applied by criminal courts.

[9] *Ivey* (n 6) [74].

[10] ibid [60].

[11] See also the CA(CD) in *Barton* [2020] EWCA Crim 575, which confirmed that for the purposes of the first question in the *Ivey* test, '[a]ll matters that lead an accused to act as he or she did will form part of the subjective mental state, thereby forming a part of the fact-finding exercise before applying the objective standard'.

[12] cf D Ormerod and K Laird, 'The Future of Dishonesty – Some Practical Considerations' (2020) 6 *Archbold Review* 8, 9; D Ormerod and K Laird, *Smith, Hogan, & Ormerod's Criminal Law*, 16th edn (Oxford, Oxford University Press, 2021) 917. Ormerod and Laird suggest that D's belief as to whether others would see her conduct as dishonest is relevant to the first limb of the *Ivey* test, but does not determine the outcome in the second limb of the test. If so, then the test tells us nothing about *when* these beliefs make any difference under the *Ivey* test. Besides, D's belief as to how others would see her conduct is not, strictly speaking, a belief as to what constitutes behaving dishonestly.

The change in the law brought about by *Ivey* has been criticised trenchantly by most, including Fortson,[13] Dyson and Jarvis,[14] Virgo,[15] and Spencer.[16] Sullivan, writing with Simester, recently added his own voice to the chorus of criticism.[17] Sullivan and Simester argue that differentiating between the standards applied in civil and criminal law on the question of dishonesty is, *pace* the Supreme Court in *Ivey*, entirely defensible; and that the *Ghosh* test (which they read in line with the Campbell Gloss) was both preferable on the merits and better suited to complying with the fair notice standards required by Article 7 of the European Convention on Human Rights.[18] To a large extent, I agree. In this piece, I want to offer two further reasons to think that the Supreme Court's ruling in *Ivey* was a step backwards for English criminal law. I propose a slightly different reconstruction of the *Ghosh* test, one that I think coheres better with the words of the Court of Appeal in *Ghosh* and the law relating to offences of dishonesty as it stood when *Ivey* was decided.

The first reason to think that the ruling in *Ivey* was a mistake is that, perhaps surprisingly, there is a respect in which the *Ivey* test over-subjectivises the law of dishonesty, such that offences like theft become, in extreme cases, almost entirely thought crimes. The second reason is that the *Ivey* test is overinclusive. It is not as good as the *Ghosh* test was at capturing the right sort, *and only the right sort*, of culpability. Not only does the *Ghosh* test do better in each of these respects but, I argue, the substantive normative criticisms of the test fail to land. In terms of identifying the sort of culpability that should be captured by a subjective mens rea element such as dishonesty, (a plausible reconstruction of) the *Ghosh* test gets things essentially right.

I. Over-subjectivisation and *Ivey*

My first close encounter with the English law of theft came within days of my first coming to England from India in September 2008. I spent a few days in London before taking up my place at university. Travelling everywhere by tube, I took in both the imposing architecture in central London and the habits of the people. In respect of the latter, I was struck by the contrast between the relative order in things such as riding escalators and boarding and alighting from trains on the one hand, and the blatant and shameless routine theft of newspapers from just outside tube stations on the other. One after another, a stream of well-dressed and

[13] R Fortson, 'Making Dishonesty Fit the Crime' Queen Mary University of London, School of Law Legal Studies Research Paper No 292/2018, https://ssrn.com/abstract=3299369.

[14] Dyson and Jarvis (n 7).

[15] G Virgo, 'Cheating and Dishonesty' (2018) 77 *CLJ* 18.

[16] J Spencer, 'Two Cases on the Law of Theft: A Concertina Movement?' (2018) 8 *Archbold Review* 4.

[17] GR Sullivan and AP Simester, 'Judging Dishonesty' (2020) 136 *LQR* 523.

[18] ibid 525–26.

respectable looking people of all ages, genders, and ethnicities would walk up to an unguarded newspaper stand and, without so much as a quick glance to see if they were being observed, pick up a newspaper and just walk off, without even trying to pay! In those days, I was not a criminal law specialist, and I knew little of the details of English criminal law. I didn't know, for instance, that theft is defined as dishonestly appropriating property belonging to another with the intention of permanently depriving the other of it.[19] But I was certain that I was witnessing widespread criminality. I confess that, seeing the impunity enjoyed by all comers, I was tempted to get in on the act myself. However, since these newspapers were regularly abandoned in the tube, and therefore freely accessible anyway, the temptation did not quite overcome me. It was only months later, on a subsequent visit to London, that I realised that the *Metro* is a free newspaper, distributed at tube stations in open newspaper stands.

But what if, during my first stay in London, I too had grabbed a newspaper from the stand, and hurried into the crowd at Euston station? Would I have committed theft? A newspaper is property. And even if I acquired ownership of it by picking it up, it would, for the purposes of the law of theft, belong to another[20] – the persons whose agents placed it at the station for distribution. I could not have done as I pleased with the newspapers – I could not, for instance, have picked them all up and dumped them in an adjacent rubbish bin. By picking up a newspaper, I would appropriate it, and since I would not be planning to return it to the stand, I would intend permanently to deprive the then owner of it. It would not even matter that the owner of the newspaper consented to my picking up the paper.[21] Everything would turn on whether, in picking up the *Metro*, I was acting dishonestly.

At the time, the *Ghosh* test was the relevant authority on the question of dishonesty.[22] On the Simplistic View of that test, a prosecution against me would fall at the first hurdle. My conduct – picking up a free newspaper in the manner meant for its distribution – would not be dishonest according to the ordinary standards of reasonable and honest people, and so I would not be dishonest irrespective of how I judged my own conduct. Today, however, the *Ivey* test would apply. An investigation of my actual state of knowledge or beliefs as to the facts (including about the norms governing newspaper distribution outside tube stations in London) would show that I genuinely believed that the newspapers were offered for sale, and that one could only take a newspaper if one paid for it. In light of those beliefs, my taking a newspaper without even trying to make payment would surely be dishonest by the standards of ordinary decent people.

I fear that, under the *Ivey* test, I would have been in trouble had I picked up the *Metro* in September 2008 – I would have been guilty of stealing a free newspaper!

[19] Theft Act 1968, s 2.
[20] *R v Hinks* [2001] 2 AC 241.
[21] ibid.
[22] The Theft Act 1968, s 2 does not apply on these facts.

Given that the *Ivey* test was meant to correct the supposed over-subjectivity of the *Ghosh* test, it must surely be a surprise that it enables people, by their subjective beliefs, to convert objectively innocuous events into crimes. Something seems to have gone wrong here.

Perhaps the error is in the way I set up this apparent oddity. You might think that this problem is not unique to the *Ivey* test – in fact, the same result would also follow under the *Ghosh* test if we applied Campbell's Gloss. But recall that Campbell's Gloss was not how the Court of Appeal in *Ghosh* itself thought that its test should operate, and in criticising the *Ghosh* test, the Supreme Court also tacitly suggested that the Court of Appeal's view was how the *Ghosh* test had been understood during the thirty-five years for which it was law.[23]

So, if we read the *Ghosh* test in terms of the Simplistic View, it seems to deliver the intuitively correct outcome in the *Free Newspaper* example, whereas the *Ivey* test seems to deliver an intuitively troubling outcome. But perhaps you disagree with my intuitions. Why shouldn't we bite the bullet and convict in the *Free Newspaper* example?[24] Recall that had I taken the newspaper back in September 2008, I would deliberately have been setting out to do something that I believed was dishonest. There is no doubt that in doing so, I would have demonstrated substantial subjective culpability. In some respects, convicting me would align with the logic of the ruling in *Hinks*,[25] in which, despite D's being taken to have received perfectly good legal title to property from V, she was held to have stolen it because of the dishonesty of her means of appropriating that property. Here too, although I would unknowingly have obtained perfectly good title to the newspaper upon picking it up, you might think that given my dishonesty in picking it up, I deserve to be convicted of theft.

There are, however, a few problems with this line of thinking. The most obvious one is that the decision in *Hinks* is itself far from uncontroversial. Simester and Sullivan have argued that 'theft is concerned directly and primarily with protecting the legal structure of proprietary entitlements',[26] such that 'the harm of theft is the misappropriation of a person's property and the wrong of theft is to take property without claim of right to it and intending to keep or dispose of it'.[27] For them, in treating as criminal receipts of property that are valid in the civil law,

[23] *Ivey* (n 6) [60].

[24] A more drastic alternative is to accept that that if I picked up the newspaper, I would be acting dishonestly, but argue that since by picking up the newspaper, I would obtain full, unimpeachable ownership of it, I cannot be convicted of theft. This would entail rejecting the House of Lords' ruling in *Hinks* [2001] 2 AC 241. I cannot consider that alternative in this chapter, since my aim here is to consider whether it was a mistake for *Ivey* to overturn *Ghosh*, and that matter is best considered against the backdrop of the law (including the ruling in *Hinks)* as it stood when *Ivey* was decided.

[25] *Hinks*, ibid.

[26] AP Simester and GR Sullivan, 'On the Nature and Rationale of Property Offences' in RA Duff and SP Green (eds), *Defining Crimes: Essays on the Special Part of the Criminal Law* (Oxford, Oxford University Press, 2005) 168, 174.

[27] ibid 179.

the rule in *Hinks* destabilises the foundations of the civil proprietary regime that the criminal law was meant to protect.[28] They add that it is 'undesirable for rule of law reasons that [the] amorphous and vague concept [of dishonesty] should bear [the] very significant weight [of segregating non-criminal from criminal transactions]'.[29]

To the extent that this critique of the rule in *Hinks* is persuasive, it is persuasive also against biting the bullet and supporting a conviction in the *Free Newspaper* example. But not everyone shares the concern expressed by Simester and Sullivan. Bogg and Stanton-Ife have argued that that the ruling in *Hinks* allows the law to protect the vulnerable against exploitation, and that although rule of law considerations could militate against using the law of theft in this way, in fact they do not.[30] Notice, however, that even if we agree with Bogg and Stanton-Ife, we may still validly object to convicting someone of 'stealing' a free newspaper. In *Hinks*, there was at least someone we could plausibly describe as having been victimised – Mr Dolphin was *wronged* by Mrs Hinks' dishonest and exploitative conduct, even though, technically, none of his proprietary interests was harmed. In the *Free Newspaper* example, though, there is no plausible victim in sight. Not only has nobody suffered any harm to their proprietary interests, nobody has been the target of any wrong – exploitation or otherwise – either. On the surface, we have perfectly legitimate and quotidian behaviour. The only thing that would seem to make this behaviour a crime is what was in the mind of the agent.[31] Effectively, and especially given how even mundane conduct can satisfy the actus reus of theft, we would have a thought crime. A person happy to bite *this* bullet is a braver person than I.

II. Overinclusiveness

The second criticism of the *Ivey* test is more tentative. My worry is that the test in *Ivey* is potentially overinclusive (even more so than is suggested by my previous criticism). Furthermore, the *Ghosh* test was arguably better at capturing the right sort, *and only the right sort*, of culpability. To see this, consider briefly the statutory indications about the sort of culpability that the test should be capturing, and how the courts in *Ghosh* and *Ivey* built upon them.

[28] ibid 179–81.

[29] ibid 180.

[30] A Bogg and J Stanton-Ife, 'Protecting the Vulnerable: Legality, Harm and Theft' (2003) 23 *Legal Studies* 402.

[31] Elsewhere, I have argued that we should read the conduct element of each offence such that it is not triggered by objectively unremarkable behaviour such as, in this case, picking up a free newspaper from a newsstand. See M Dsouza, 'Beyond Acts and Omissions: Remark-able Criminal Conduct' (2021) 41 *Legal Studies* 1. But as currently understood, '[p]rovided that D does anything whatsoever in connection with property belonging to another person, the actus reus [of theft] is made out'. See AP Simester et al, *Simester and Sullivan's Criminal Law*, 7th edn (Oxford, Hart Publishing, 2019) 559.

For convenience, let us focus on the offence of theft under section 1 of the Theft Act 1968, which identifies culpability in *dishonestly* appropriating property belonging to another with *intention* to permanently deprive the other of the property. In that context, the *Ivey* test focuses on when someone appropriates dishonestly.

The first thing to note is that the Theft Act 1968 gives us no definition of what it is to do something 'dishonestly'. This suggests that Parliament expected ordinary people – society at large – to recognise dishonesty when they saw it. The courts too have consistently expected the same; in *Ghosh* they expected 'reasonable and honest' persons to recognise dishonesty, and in *Ivey* they expected the same of 'ordinary decent' persons.

Instead of a definition, section 2 offers a non-exhaustive list of three instances in which a person does not behave dishonestly, and singles out one factor that is emphatically not sufficient by itself to disprove dishonesty (although neither does its absence establish dishonesty). Each of these provisions refers expressly to D's subjective beliefs (and implicitly, motivations).[32]

But *how* do D's motivations and beliefs matter? This is the nub of the disagreement between the courts in *Ghosh* and *Ivey*. The Court of Appeal in *Ghosh* was clear that D did not get to set, and be judged by reference to, her own standards.[33] A person who professes certain standards but does not live up to them is, amongst other things, a hypocrite. But the various offences that require conduct to have been performed dishonestly in the Theft Act do not also require it to have been performed hypocritically. Instead, the Court of Appeal devised a test according to which D's dishonesty stems from her *knowing* contravention of the standards of honestly of the reasonable and honest person.

It was swiftly pointed out that, since the Court of Appeal had insisted on knowing contravention, a person who was mistaken about the standards of honesty of a reasonable and honest person may well not *knowingly* contravene those standards. In fact, the more deluded D was about the standards of the reasonable and honest person, the more likely she would be to evade conviction. And, critics asked, 'How can that be right?'[34]

[32] Section 2(1) states:

> A person's appropriation of property belonging to another is not dishonest –
>
> (a) if he appropriates the property *in the belief that* he has in law the right to deprive the other of it, on behalf of himself or of a third person; or
>
> (b) if he appropriates the property *in the belief that* he would have the other's consent if the other knew of the appropriation and the circumstances of it; or
>
> (c) (except where the property came to him as trustee or personal representative) if he appropriates the property *in the belief that* the person to whom the property belongs cannot be discovered by taking reasonable steps. (emphasis added).

Section 2(2) adds that 'A person's appropriation of property belonging to another may be dishonest notwithstanding that *he is willing to* pay for the property.'

[33] As was suggested by the Court of Appeal in *R v Gilks* [1972] 3 All ER 281, 283.

[34] *Ivey* (n 6) [59]; D Ormerod, DH Williams, *Smith's Law of Theft*, 9th edn (Oxford, Oxford University Press, 2007) para 2.296; Griew (n 7) 353; B Hale, 'Dishonesty' (2019) 48 *Common Law World Review* 5, 11.

Permit me a brief interlude at this point. When this argument is made in classrooms across the country, the question in which it culminates is meant to be a rhetorical one. I am reminded of a friend and classmate on the LLM degree who was a rather quirky character. Amongst his many quirks was a tendency to puncture the sophic silence that followed rhetorical questions asked by professors in the Cambridge Law Faculty's cavernous lecture theatres (the one I recall was, 'If someone cleaned your windscreen at a traffic light and then demanded a pound for their service, would you feel obliged to pay?') by loudly volunteering an answer all the way from his seat in the very last row ('Yes!'). This prompted much mirth from the gathered masses … but after we settled down, those who took my friend's answer seriously ended up reflecting much more deeply on the issue at hand than even the somewhat nonplussed professor at the lectern had hoped. In much the same vein, Sullivan and Simester recently took seriously the question with which I ended the previous paragraph, and argued that, 'if D is genuinely unaware that others would disapprove of D's conduct, it becomes less clear that society should condemn D with the full force of the criminal law'.[35] The Court of Appeal in *Ghosh* hinted that we could go even further. It recognised that, in borderline cases, if the jury thought that 'the defendant may have believed what he was doing was in accordance with the ordinary man's idea of honesty … [it may have to conclude] that the defendant … was *disobedient or impudent, but not dishonest* in what he did'.[36] Accordingly, it should not convict D of an offence requiring dishonesty.

There is something in these suggestions – and I propose to explore that presently. But for now I note that, unfortunately, not enough people took it upon themselves to answer the rhetorical question I identified previously. So, relatively unquestioned, over the years the concern implicit in that question worked its way up to the Supreme Court in *Ivey*. It was this concern, principally,[37] that motivated the Supreme Court's rejection of the *Ghosh* test.

The Court in *Ivey* took a very different approach to D's state of mind in the test for dishonesty. It built as much as possible of what D knew and believed into the background of D's conduct, and required D's conduct to be judged objectively by reference to this background. Thus, if D deludedly believed that payment was not expected in the *Visitor on the Bus* example, then D's conduct travelling without payment would not be judged objectively dishonest in light of that belief. But if D deludedly believed that it is not dishonest to fail to pay for bus travel even where payment is required, then D would be judged objectively to be dishonest, despite his own contrary belief. Moreover, some parts of the Supreme Court's judgment seem to suggest that a belief *must genuinely be held* if it is to be relevant to the test. For instance, immediately after stating that 'the fact-finding tribunal must first

[35] Sullivan and Simester (n 17) 526.
[36] *Ghosh* [1982] QB 1053, 1064 (emphasis added.).
[37] *Ivey* (n 6) [58]; Hale (n 34) 11.

ascertain (subjectively) the actual state of the individual's knowledge or belief as to the facts', the Supreme Court explains that the 'reasonableness or otherwise of his belief is a matter of evidence … going to *whether he held the belief*, but it is not an additional requirement that his belief must be reasonable; *the question is whether it is genuinely held*'.[38]

If this is true, then the *Ivey* test is overinclusive. Under it, consideration of D's motivations drops out entirely; the *Ivey* test treats falling short of the objective standards of dishonesty applicable to a person with D's knowledge and beliefs as being, by definition, dishonest. In a sense, it is true that the *conduct* is dishonest. But, as I will illustrate presently, it is not necessarily true that the agent performs the conduct *for dishonest reasons*, such that it becomes appropriate to say that she conducted herself dishonest*ly*. That is, our adverse judgement of the conduct does not necessarily translate into an adverse judgement – of the sort we can make when subjective fault is present – of D.

Another way of making this point is to compare the source of culpability in the *Ghosh* and *Ivey* tests. The second limb of the *Ghosh* test identifies the source of D's culpability: D's culpability stems from a volitional act, ie her *choice* to conduct herself in a manner that she (correctly) believed would be seen as dishonest by reasonable and honest people. This choice reveals something about the D's values. It reveals, prima facie, that she is the sort of person who wilfully disregards the social conventions of dishonesty – D seems content to be seen as dishonest. And so, prima facie, she is.[39] But another person who chose to perform the very same conduct and did not, for whatever reason,[40] believe that it would be seen as dishonest by reasonable and honest people would not be dishonest, since her choice would not reveal that she is the sort of person who wilfully disregards the social conventions of dishonesty. The *Ghosh* test therefore identifies D's culpability in what her *choice* of conduct reveals about her.

Assuming that only genuinely held beliefs and knowledge are relevant to the *Ivey* test, culpability under that test flows from D's (absent) cognitive state, ie the absence of any knowledge of or belief in propositions that, if true, would prevent her conduct (given that it was performed in light of those propositions) from being objectively dishonest. Nothing would turn on her reasons for choosing to perform her conduct. But notice that here D's cognitive state by itself says nothing especially damning about D's standards of honesty. The main thing the test

[38] *Ivey* (n 6) [74] (emphasis added).

[39] For more detail on how D's choices can allow us to draw valid conclusions about D's personal blameworthiness, see AP Simester, *Fundamentals of Criminal Law* (Oxford, Oxford University Press, 2021) 244–45; M Dsouza, 'Criminal Culpability After the Act' (2015) 26 *King's Law Journal* 440, 444, 449–50.

[40] See eg *R v Hayes* [2015] EWCA Crim 1944, [15], [28] and [33], where the CA(CD) was open to the possibility of a jury's finding that D was dishonest because he did not realise that reasonable and honest people would regard his conduct as dishonest, even if his reasons for so thinking included that D believed his actions to be in line with acceptable industry practices in the specialised field of LIBOR trading.

seems to reveal is whether, given the knowledge and beliefs that D had, the *conduct* that D chose to perform deserves the label 'dishonest'. The same conduct, performed by anyone with the same set of beliefs and knowledge, would always be judged the same way, irrespective of why a particular agent chose to perform the conduct. And although it will sometimes be true that the agent who performed such conduct was motivated by a disregard for social conventions of honesty, this is not inevitable.

Let me illustrate this point with my second close encounter with the English law of theft. In August 2018, well after *Ivey* was decided, I moved to Highgate in London. Near my house was a small take-away that, I discovered, did excellent piri-piri chicken. One day, feeling too lazy to cook, I placed an order over the phone and walked over to collect it. I got there a few minutes before my order was ready, and spent that time chatting with the proprietor. He told me that he was from Pakistan, and I reminisced with him about the one time I had visited his country, telling him how much I loved the food there, and how welcome I had been made to feel. As he handed me my order, the proprietor said he looked forward to seeing me again and, smiling, I promised that he would. Neither of us realised how soon. It was only 45 seconds later that I heard him calling down the street to me. It transpired that, caught up in our friendly chit-chat, neither of us realised that I had not paid.

What if I had been charged with theft?[41] The chicken I had taken was property and, at the relevant time, it belonged to the proprietor. I had undoubtedly appropriated it, and I had every intention of permanently depriving the proprietor of that very chicken. But had I acted dishonestly? None of the exceptions in section 2 of the Theft Act 1968 applied to me, and so the question falls to be decided by reference to the *Ivey* test. I certainly knew that I was meant to pay for the food. I also knew that I had the food as I walked out of the establishment. I did not subjectively believe that I had paid – in truth, the payment stage of our transaction had simply slipped my mind. In fact, if by 'beliefs' we mean dispositional beliefs (as surely we must – if only occurrent beliefs could exculpate, the *Ivey* test would be wildly overinclusive), then one might even say that I believed that I had not paid; no doubt, had I been asked, I would have confirmed that proposition, as indeed I did when the proprietor called out to me.[42] So if my conduct – walking

[41] Absent-minded defendants have been charged with theft before: *R v Clarke* (1972) 56 Cr App R 225, usually considered in the context of the insanity defence, was actually a case in which D was charged with shoplifting. D had put some supermarket grocery items into her carrier bag rather than the supermarket's wire basket, and walked out without paying for them. She later explained that she had recently been feeling depressed and overwhelmed, and had been acting absent-mindedly. She claimed to have no recollection of having picked up the concerned items, some of which were items that she never consumed. Perhaps in that case, given D's absent-mindedness, in addition to the dishonesty issue, there is some doubt about whether D had the intention to permanently deprive the supermarket of the concerned items. No such complications arose in my case.

[42] See F Stark, *Culpable Carelessness* (Cambridge, Cambridge University Press, 2007) 94–111 for an extended explanation of the dispositional account of what it is to believe a proposition, and an explanation of why this account is apt for criminal law purposes.

away with the chicken – stood to be judged objectively in light of the beliefs that I confess I held, I would seemingly be found to have acted dishonestly according to the test in *Ivey*.

Perhaps one might dispute this conclusion on the basis that the *Ivey* test's reference to 'D's actual *state of* knowledge or beliefs as to the facts'[43] somehow means that I am exculpated by fact that I had *no occurrent* belief that I had not paid. For this to be true, it would have to be the case under the *Ivey* test, first, that my not having an occurrent belief that I had not paid is *ex*culpating, and second, that my dispositional belief that I had not paid is not *in*culpating (or at least, that if it is inculpating, its effect is trumped by the exculpation supplied by my having no occurrent belief as to the same proposition). But it is far from obvious that these claims are plausible. Nothing in the Supreme Court's judgment suggests anything quite so complicated. In fact, parts of the judgment seem to indicate that, in the Court's view, a belief has to be held 'subjectively' and 'genuinely' if it is to be relevant to the test. This suggests that the *absence* of an occurrent belief, inculpating or otherwise, is not relevant. Neither is it clear that such an absence should be relevant, let alone have such a decisive effect, on the determination of D's actual state of knowledge or beliefs as to the facts. Why should someone who would willingly affirm the truth of a proposition if asked be found not to believe the proposition simply because she happened not, at the time of acting, to call that proposition to mind? Furthermore, treating the absence of an occurrent inculpating belief as exculpating would run contrary to the criminal law's approach in relation to the closely allied notion of awareness. In that context, the courts have unambiguously treated the dispositional awareness of a risk to be sufficiently inculpating, notwithstanding the absence of an occurrent awareness of the risk.[44] There seems little, either doctrinally or normatively, to commend adopting the opposite approach in the context of beliefs in dishonesty.

At the least, if it is indeed the position that the absence of occurrent inculpating beliefs is relevant to, and overrides even the presence of, dispositional inculpating beliefs when determining D's actual state of knowledge or beliefs as to the facts, a judicial clarification to this effect would be welcome. Until then, there is at least the suspicion that the *Ivey* test is so overinclusive that it cannot distinguish people who display a wilful disregard for the social conventions of dishonesty from absent-minded (associate) professors.

[43] *Ivey* (n 6) [74].

[44] See *R v Parker* [1977] 1 WLR 600. D argued that so frustrated was he with how his evening had been going that 'It did not occur to [him] that [slamming the handset of a phone down onto the cradle] might damage [the phone].' In other words, he denied occurrent knowledge of the risk of damaging the phone by his actions. However, the court ruled that the relevant knowledge could be attributed to D given that he 'was plainly fully aware of all the circumstances of the case. He was fully aware that what he was handling was a telephone handset made of Bakelite or some such material. He was well aware that the cradle on to which he admittedly brought down the handset was made of similar material. He was well aware, of course, of the degree of force which he was using.' In other words, it allowed dispositional awareness to trump occurrent unawareness.

Moreover, even if such a clarification were forthcoming, the *Ivey* test would still be overinclusive. To see this, recall that while the *Ivey* test is generally sensitive to D's beliefs about the (general) normative standards applicable in society, D's beliefs specifically about what society would consider to be dishonest behaviour do not determine whether she behaved dishonestly. For this test, the concept of 'behaving dishonestly' is objective, in the sense that it is weakly mind-independent:[45] the fact of what constitutes dishonest behaviour transcends the beliefs or attitudes of any given individual (and, in particular, D), and derives instead from the beliefs and attitudes shared by individuals who interact as a group (for our purposes, the set of ordinary decent people in our society).

Now consider cases in which D behaves in a manner that is considered dishonest in this weakly mind-independent sense because she is genuinely unaware that others would judge her conduct to be dishonest. Perhaps in some such cases, the reason that D is unaware that others would judge her conduct to be dishonest is that she is so dishonest that she is also morally warped. There could be no serious objection to assigning the morally condemnatory label 'dishonest' to D in such cases. The problem is that a lack of awareness of societal moral standards may also be explicable by reference to factors that do not suggest that D is a dishonest person. For instance, some people on the autism spectrum find it especially difficult to pick up and correctly interpret social cues, and may therefore form incorrect beliefs about whether ordinary decent people would consider certain types of conduct dishonest.[46] Imagine someone with an undiagnosed autism spectrum disorder watching *Oliver!* together with a trusted companion, and missing the sarcasm in the latter's declaration of Fagan as a paragon of virtue. This person may genuinely come to believe that 'You've got to pick a pocket or two' – or at least that it is appropriate to take something you really want from someone who is much better off. But this mistake about societal standards is not attributable to any factor that justifies our labelling her dishonest. It is not just that 'if D is genuinely unaware that others would disapprove of D's conduct, it [is] less clear that society should condemn D with the full force of the criminal law';[47] in fact, it is not

[45] MH Kramer, *Objectivity and the Rule of Law* (Cambridge, Cambridge University Press, 2007) 3–4 and MH Kramer, 'Is Law's Conventionality Consistent with Law's Objectivity?' (2008) 14 *Res Publica* 241, 242–43.

[46] In *Barton* [2020] EWCA Crim 575, the CA(CD) held that:

> All matters that lead an accused to act as he or she did will form part of the subjective mental state, thereby forming a part of the fact-finding exercise before applying the objective standard. That will include consideration, where relevant, of the experience and intelligence of an accused.

But the relationship between intelligence and being on the autism spectrum are complicated; the CA(CD)'s reference to considering the accused's intelligence does not obviously apply to autistic defendants. Moreover, courts have refused to subjectivise *other* objective tests by considering the defendant's autism spectrum disorder (see *R v B(MA)* [2013] EWCA Crim 3); it is far from certain that they would do so for the *Ivey* test. Neither is being on the autism spectrum per se enough to trigger an insanity defence. If a defendant on the autism spectrum is unable to point to their disorder to deny mens rea, she will usually have no defensive plea available at all.

[47] Sullivan and Simester (n 17) 526.

clear that D has *any* of the sort of culpability needed to establish that she has even prima facie committed an offence involving dishonesty.[48]

In short, the *Ivey* test makes an unsubstantiated logical leap in treating a lack of awareness about societal standards of dishonesty as conclusive proof that D is a dishonest person. Even if making this logical leap would not lead to persons being unfairly labelled 'dishonest' in most cases (and to the best of my knowledge, there is no empirical basis for thinking that this is the case), it will do so in some cases. And being on the autism spectrum is just one example of an explanation for being unaware of societal standards of dishonesty that does not suggest that the unaware person deserves to be called dishonest; there may well be others. In treating what is, at best, a moderately good proxy for dishonesty as being constitutive of dishonesty, the *Ivey* test is overinclusive.

III. Why *Ghosh* Does Better

It is all well and good criticising the *Ivey* test, but given that statute does not define the term 'dishonestly', we need something with which to replace it. There are two broad possibilities – either we return to (some version of) the *Ghosh* test, or we come up with something new. My own view is that we do not need to devise a new test. This is not just because, as has been pointed out by others,[49] the Supreme Court's doctrinal criticisms of the *Ghosh* test were largely unfounded or not of a magnitude that called for its being jettisoned. I think that on its own merits, the *Ghosh* test, or at least a plausible reconstruction of it, actually does a very good job of identifying the sort of culpability that we want to target with the requirement of dishonesty in performing certain conduct. What's more, on close inspection, the various substantive objections that commentators have, over the years, made to the *Ghosh* test fail to land. Consider first, this latter claim.

[48] In fact, in *Hayes* [2015] EWCA Crim 1944, which was a case involving an offence of dishonesty, D was, during his trial, diagnosed with an autism spectrum disorder. However, the medical evidence in that case was that D's condition was mild and was therefore 'unlikely to have affected his ability to determine if an action was potentially illegal or fraudulent, unless this was communicated by subtle social means' [104]–[105]. Therefore, the CA(CD) was satisfied that in that case, there was nothing objectionable about the finding that D acted dishonestly [107]. *Hayes* was decided before the *Ivey* test replaced the *Ghosh* test, and the CA(CD)'s apparent openness in principle to the proposition that D's autism spectrum disorder might influence the finding on dishonesty must be read in that light. But one can easily imagine a case involving a more severe autism spectrum disorder, and/or more subtle communications about the potential dishonesty of some course of conduct, in which D's ability to determine if an action was dishonest was significantly compromised. Under the *Ivey* test, which is unconcerned with *why* D's conduct fell short of the standards of honesty of ordinary decent people, such a person would inevitably be deemed to have acted dishonestly.

[49] See eg: Sullivan and Simester (n 17); Fortson (n 13); Dyson and Jarvis (n 7); Virgo (n 15); D Ormerod and K Laird, '*Ivey v Genting Casinos* – Much Ado About Nothing?' (2017–18) 9 *UK Supreme Court Yearbook* 380, 388–91; and Spencer (n 16).

Substantive Normative Criticisms of the *Ghosh* Test

The most comprehensive and sustained critique of the *Ghosh* test was made by Griew;[50] most subsequent critiques of the test essentially restate the points that he made.[51] Therefore, I focus here on Griew's criticisms and, more specifically, on those of his criticisms that addressed the *Ghosh* test on substantive normative grounds.

Griew took it that Campbell's Gloss provided the correct reading of the *Ghosh* test[52] and focused his criticisms on that reading of the test, although most of his arguments can apply equally to the Simplistic View. He divided up his criticisms based on which limb of the *Ghosh* test they addressed. His substantive normative criticisms of the first limb of the *Ghosh* test – the requirement that the jury decide whether what was done was dishonest according to the ordinary standards of reasonable and honest people – are all connected. With some paraphrasing, they are that:

(a) the notion that there are community norms of dishonesty is a fiction,[53]
(b) the test lets the standard for dishonesty be set by jurors, whereas these should be dictated by the law,[54] and
(c) the test licenses jurors to reach verdicts that, though inconsistent, are not technically perverse.[55]

It is worth noting that insofar as the *Ivey* test requires essentially the same thing as Campbell's Gloss on the first limb of the *Ghosh* test – the jury must decide by reference to what would be seen as 'dishonest by the standards of ordinary decent people' – these criticisms could equally be made of the *Ivey* test. I think they would be equally unconvincing in that context too.

Consider Griew's first objection. That there isn't perfect unanimity in any given legal community about what constitutes dishonesty is hardly surprising. There will always be some outliers. But if that is Griew's objection, it is extremely weak. The criminal law has never needed unanimity in order to refer sensibly to a community standard; all it requires is adequate consensus. Reliance on community norms established by adequate consensus is ubiquitous in the criminal law. We find it in the test for whether an omission satisfies the conduct element of an offence,[56] the

[50] Griew (n 7).
[51] See eg: *Fraud and Deception* (Law Com Consultation Paper No 155) paras 5.11–5.20; *Simester and Sullivan's Criminal Law* (n 31) 584–85; *Smith, Hogan, & Ormerod* (n 12) 912–14.
[52] Griew (n 7) 352–53.
[53] ibid 344, 345.
[54] ibid 346, 347.
[55] ibid 346, 346–47.
[56] It does so when the omission was in breach of a duty to act, and a duty to act typically requires the duty holder to take only *reasonable* steps. See eg: *R v Miller* [1983] 2 AC 161; *R v Evans* [2009] EWCA Crim 650. Therefore, it is always necessary to determine whether a defendant's omission amounted to a failure to take reasonable steps. This determination depends on the existence of some community norm as to what steps were reasonable to take in a given context.

definition of recklessness,[57] the mens rea standard for serious sexual offences,[58] the test for gross negligence manslaughter,[59] and in most any other place we care to look for it.

If the claim is that there is something especially obscure about dishonesty that means there is inadequate consensus on this specific norm, then that claim needs to be supported with empirical evidence. Griew supplies none.

When the Law Commission considered the same issue, it too, without empirical evidence, agreed that there was especial uncertainty as to the norms of dishonesty. One reason it cited was that while, traditionally, fact-finders are required to evaluate D's conduct by reference to objectively defined legal standards, dishonesty is a *moral* standard.[60] It is not clear why the characterisation of a standard as 'moral' or otherwise matters. From a practical perspective, all we should care about is whether a given standard (be it moral or otherwise) provides enough guidance to the fact-finder. And, as previously mentioned, there was no evidence to suggest that the standard of dishonestly does not. Besides, it is not clear that the various standards other than dishonesty to which the criminal law refers routinely and uncontroversially are not also moral standards. For instance, the criminal law regularly asks fact-finders to evaluate the reasonableness of conduct and beliefs. It seems to me that the standard underlying such evaluations is a moral one. Surely, 'How much should we care about the interests of those affected by our conduct or beliefs?' is a moral question. And yet, this does not make the test of reasonableness too obscure or difficult to apply in the criminal context. Why should dishonesty be any different?

The Law Commission suggested another reason to think that norms of dishonesty are too uncertain to establish a suitable criminal law standard. Contrasting the evaluation required in the *Ghosh* test with the one that fact-finders make when deciding whether negligence resulting in death was gross enough to merit a conviction for gross negligence manslaughter, it argued that the latter

[57] *R v G and R* [2004] 1 AC 1034. The test asks whether it was reasonable to take a foreseen risk, and the jury decides this by asking what a hypothetical reasonable person would do. This is essentially a proxy for referring to community norms of reasonableness relating to particular instances of risk-taking.

[58] The mens rea in each of the offences in ss 1–4 of the Sexual Offences Act 2003 includes the absence of a reasonable belief as to consent. The determination of whether a belief as to consent was reasonable relies on there being some community norm as to what beliefs about consent are reasonable to form in a given set of circumstances.

[59] Determinations of the level of risk high enough to amount to a *serious* and *obvious* risk of death (see *R v Misra* [2004] EWCA 2375; *R v Rudling* [2016] EWCA Crim 741) depend on there being normative consensus on these matters within the relevant community or subcommunity of persons that might be expected to respond to such risks. Likewise, to determine whether a defendant's negligence was bad enough to amount to *gross* negligence, we must ask whether the negligence was so bad as to merit a criminal conviction. See *R v Adomako* [1995] 1 AC 171. This test depends upon there being adequate community consensus as to when negligence is so bad as to merit a criminal conviction.

[60] Law Com No 155 (n 51) 5.11.

evaluation 'is more objective, because the riskiness of a person's conduct is more quantifiable than its dishonesty [which] … is not quantifiable, even in theory'.[61] With respect, even granting the debatable claim that the riskiness of conduct is easier to quantify than its dishonesty, nothing in that claim supports the Law Commission's conclusion that there is inadequate consensus on dishonesty to use it as a criminal law standard. First, nothing in the key cases setting out the grossness element of the test for gross negligence manslaughter[62] says that the jury must determine whether the risk of death crosses some numerical threshold. And if a numerical quantification of risk is not required, then the supposed ease with which the degree of risk could, had it been necessary, have been quantified seems unconnected with whether the community standard to which the test for grossness refers is fit for purpose. Second, even if the quantity of risk is a relevant consideration when evaluating the grossness of negligence, nothing in the *Ghosh* test requires the jury to quantify the degree of D's dishonesty. The jury need only decide a binary question: 'Did D behave dishonestly: yes or no?' The supposed comparative difficulty in quantifying dishonesty does not imply that there is insufficient consensus on dishonesty for it to offer adequate guidance on this binary question. In all respects that matter, it seems that the Law Commission was actually correct in its initial hypothesis, namely that the *Ghosh* test was 'no different in principle'[63] from the test for grossness in gross negligence manslaughter.

Griew's second criticism can be divided into two subclaims: first, that the jury must set the standards for dishonesty; second, that the standard in the *Ghosh* test is not dictated by law. The first subclaim assumes that asking the jury to decide whether something was dishonest according to the ordinary standards of reasonable and honest people is the same as asking it to decide whether something was dishonest according to the jurors' own standards. Despite the fact that it is regularly made,[64] this claim is simply false. The *Ghosh* test does not authorise the jury to set the standard for what amounts to dishonesty by reference to its own (shared) beliefs and attitudes, any more than it authorises D to do so. Instead, the jury is required to tap into a standard that exists independently of any given jury – one that refers to the beliefs and attitudes shared by society as a whole. And while it is true that (much like D) the twelve people in any given jury room may have their own individual or shared esoteric conception of

[61] ibid 5.13. The Law Commission added that a '30% risk of death is greater than a 10% risk'. But there is nothing extraordinary about making similar comparative assessments of levels of dishonesty ('Boris is even more dishonest than Dominic'), and the fact that we do not assign numerical values when doing so need not necessarily undermine the confidence with which we can make such claims.

[62] *R v Adomako* [1995] 1 AC 171; *R v Misra* [2004] EWCA 2375.

[63] Law Com No 155 (n 51) 5.13.

[64] See eg ibid 5.11, 5.13; JR Spencer, 'Dishonesty: What the jury Thinks the Defendant Thought the Jury Would Have Thought' (1982) 41 *CLJ* 222, 224; Ormerod and Laird (n 49) 382, 397; *Smith, Hogan, & Ormerod* (n 12) 911.

what amounts to dishonesty, if they applied that esoteric conception of dishonesty in their appraisal of D's conduct, they would not be applying the *Ghosh* test correctly.[65]

Now consider Griew's second subclaim, namely that the standard in the *Ghosh* test is not dictated by law. The Law Commission found this objection persuasive: it considered that, unlike the standards applicable in the offences of careless driving and dangerous driving, the standard for dishonesty under *Ghosh* was not legally defined and was left to the jury to decide.[66] I have already addressed the latter proposition, but consider now the former. According to the Law Commission, when fact-finders are required to determine whether some instance of driving was bad enough to make it careless or dangerous, they refer to standards that are legally defined. The standard of what constitutes dangerous driving is set out in statute, and the standard of what constitutes careless driving was, at the time, defined in case law.[67] But the statutory test for dangerousness in driving to which the Law Commission referred[68] is replete with terms that call for reference to community standards: a person's driving is dangerous when it 'falls far below what would be expected of a competent and careful driver', and when 'it would be obvious to a competent and careful driver that driving in that way would be dangerous'. The same is true of the common law tests for carelessness in driving, which the Law Commission identified as coming from *Taylor v Rogers*[69] and *Scott v Warren.*[70] The test in *Taylor v Rogers* asks whether 'the defendant [was] exercising *that degree of care and attention which a reasonable and prudent driver would exercise in the circumstances*'.[71] The test in *Scott v Warren* asks whether D 'acted with the alertness, skill and judgment *reasonably to be expected in the circumstances of any emergency which disclosed itself*'.[72] It appears, then, that by the Law Commission's lights, standards are considered legally defined when statute and case law refer to community standards. By that yardstick, the standard applicable under the *Ghosh* test too is legally defined.

Griew's third criticism of the first limb of the Ghosh test fares no better. True, different juries may reach different conclusions regarding whether the same conduct performed with the same state of mind is dishonest. But since this can happen with respect to *any* evaluative element that different juries are asked to decide, it is only an especial problem if, as Griew suggests, none of the conflicting

[65] Notice that exactly the same is true also of the test for 'grossness' in gross negligence manslaughter. The jury is required to apply a standard of grossness that refers to beliefs and attitudes shared by society as a whole; a standard that exists independently of any given jury.

[66] Law Com No 155 (n 51) 5.12.

[67] Although now see Road Traffic Act 1988, s 3ZA, which was inserted by the Road Safety Act 2006, s 30.

[68] Road Traffic Act 1988, s 2A.

[69] *Taylor v Rogers* (1960) 124 JP 217.

[70] *Scott v Warren* [1974] RTR 104.

[71] *Taylor* (n 69) 218 (emphasis added).

[72] *Scott* (n 70) 107 (emphasis added).

juries acts perversely.[73] Griew's thought seems to be that each jury can legitimately choose to identify different community norms relating to the honesty of D's conduct, and can therefore reach different verdicts on exactly the same facts without acting perversely. But insofar as the community norms of dishonesty exist independently of any given jury's determination of what those norms are, it is not true that each jury can *legitimately* choose to identify different community norms relating to the honesty of D's conduct. A jury that chose to identify norms that it knew to be different from the community norms of dishonesty would indeed be acting perversely.[74]

Now consider Griew's substantive normative criticisms of the second limb of the *Ghosh* test – the requirement that D have realised that reasonable and honest people would regard what she did as dishonest. Griew argues that exonerating D based on her mistaken beliefs as to the societal standards of honesty is akin to allowing her to raise a mistake of law defence.[75] Furthermore, he says, doing so would lead to the 'remarkable' result that the more ignorant and deluded D was as to the standards of the reasonable and honest person, the more likely she would be to escape a conviction.[76]

Griew is right that, in a sense, the *Ghosh* test lets D raise something like a mistake of law defence. But of course, section 2 of the Theft Act 1968 is exceptional in precisely that respect – section 2(1)(a) expressly says that a person's appropriation of property belonging to another should not be regarded as dishonest if she appropriates it *in the belief that she has a legal right to deprive the other of it*. It expressly allows a mistake of law-based response to an accusation of dishonesty. If anything, the *Ghosh* test is in keeping with the statutory scheme for dishonesty. And as to Griew's second point, I have already argued that it makes perfect sense to say that when D chooses to conduct herself in a manner that she (correctly) believes would be seen as dishonest by reasonable and honest people, she reveals herself to be dishonest. Conversely, when she makes no such choice, she does not reveal herself to be dishonest.

Culpability under the *Ghosh* Test

So Griew's criticisms of the *Ghosh* test fail to convince. But before we rush to endorse the *Ghosh* test, we need to settle the controversy about whether the first

[73] Griew (n 7) 346. See also DW Elliott, 'Law and Fact in Theft Act Cases' [1976] *Crim LR* 707, 711; DW Elliott, 'Dishonesty in Theft: A Dispensable Concept' [1982] *Crim LR* 395, 408–09; Law Com No 155 (n 51) 5.18.

[74] There is a separate concern about whether local community norms may differ across the jurisdiction, but this is not a concern especially for the norms of dishonesty – it may arise in respect of any reference to a community standard.

[75] Griew (n 7) 353.

[76] ibid.

limb of that test is best read in line with the Simplistic View, or Campbell's Gloss, or in some other way.

Recall that the first limb of the *Ghosh* test required the jury to decide whether 'what was done' was dishonest according to the ordinary standards of reasonable and honest people. Unfortunately, the Court of Appeal in *Ghosh* did not specify how rich a conception of 'what was done' we should adopt. Confusion over this issue founds much of the criticism of the test. On the Simplistic View, which the Supreme Court in *Ivey* attributed[77] to the Court of Appeal in *Ghosh*, we could read that phrase to refer to what the reasonable and honest observer, with no special insight into D's mind, would judge D to have done based solely on appearances. However, the Supreme Court ultimately agreed with Campbell[78] that under 'the (objective) first leg of the *Ghosh* test … in order to determine the honesty or otherwise of a person's conduct, one must ask what he knew or believed about the facts affecting the area of activity in which he was engaging'.[79] In other words, it believed that we should adopt a much richer reading of what was done – a reading that is sensitive to D's own understanding of what was being done within the context of the rules that D believed governed his activity.

Although these readings of 'what was done' reach the same finding on the issue of dishonesty in the *Visitor on the Bus* example, they do so by different routes. Unlike Campbell's Gloss, the Simplistic View does not need to insist that the Court of Appeal erred in its discussion of the Visitor on the Bus example. This is one reason to prefer the Simplistic View over Campbell's Gloss. Furthermore, while Campbell's Gloss would support a finding of dishonesty (leading to a conviction for theft) in the *Free Newspaper* example, the Simplistic View would not. I take it that this is a desirable outcome, and for this reason too, we should prefer the Simplistic View to Campbell's Gloss. But before we embrace it, we need to address one worry about the Simplistic View. There is one respect in which the Simplistic View seems to be underspecified. To see this, consider the following example:

> *Casual Carjacker:* Aruna is seen casually accepting car keys from a valet, and driving off with a car. Unknown to the observer (and the valet), Aruna does not own the car; she is a carjacker with chutzpah.

When setting out the Simplistic View, the Supreme Court in *Ivey* did not specify whether the observer judging the defendant's actions has access to the objective situational facts about the deed done. If the observer does not, then she would not know, for instance, who owned the car. Therefore, given how confidently Aruna picks up the keys and drives away, the observer, considering only Aruna's actions and not her state of knowledge or belief as to the facts when

[77] *Ivey* (n 6) [60].
[78] Campbell (n 5) 353. See also Griew (n 7) 352–53; Dyson and Jarvis (n 7) 202.
[79] *Ivey* (n 6) [60].

performing them, would have no reason to think that what was done in *Casual Carjacker* was dishonest. The first limb of the test would therefore rule out a finding of dishonesty, despite the fact that on any sensible understanding of *Casual Carjacker*, Aruna is dishonest. This is clearly not what was contemplated in *Ghosh*. What's more, in requiring D's conduct to be judged based solely on appearances, this reading of the Simplistic View would throw open the door for the jury to make snap judgements based on all sorts of preconceptions about what sorts of people and behaviours are 'dodgy'. In sum, this reading of the Simplistic View is so obviously flawed that it is not a realistic option – we can discard it without further ado.

So the better reconstruction of the Simplistic View is that the observer does have access to, and can take account of, the objective situational facts about the deed done. On this reconstruction, the phrase 'what was done' in the first limb of the *Ghosh* test refers to what the reasonable and honest observer would judge D to have done, taking account of all objective situational facts about the deed done, but not any matters that reside solely in D's subjectivity (such as D's beliefs, plans, or motivations). Call this the 'Proposed Reconstruction'. The Proposed Reconstruction is consistent with how the *Ghosh* test has been understood and applied by some courts.[80] To see how adopting it affects the analysis, consider also the following additional examples:

> *Bicycle Version 1:* Ayesha is seen cutting the lock on a bicycle by a reasonable and honest observer who has no special awareness of Ayesha's mental state. The bicycle belongs to Ayesha, but she has lost her keys.
> *Bicycle Version 2:* Same facts as above, but this time Ayesha (wrongly) believes the bicycle belongs to her and, puzzled that her key has stopped working, has decided to cut the lock.

The reasonable and honest observer described here would characterise what D did by taking account of all relevant objective situational facts, but not the agents' beliefs, intentions, or motivations. Accordingly, she would characterise what was done by considering, in both versions of the *Bicycle* example, who actually owned the bicycle. Similarly, in *Casual Carjacker*, she would consider who owned the car; and in *Free Newspaper*, that the newspaper was distributed free of charge. On this basis, she would conclude in *Bicycle Version 1* and in *Free Newspaper* that what was done was not dishonest, and that the first limb of the *Ghosh* test was not satisfied. Although in principle, the second limb of the test would apply differently to these two agents, we would never get to the point of applying it. She would also conclude that what was done *was* objectively dishonest in *Bicycle Version 2* and *Casual Carjacker*. But, in *Bicycle Version 2*, Ayesha would not realise that the reasonable and honest observer would regard what

[80] See *General Medical Council v Krishnan* [2017] EWHC 2892 (Admin) [25]; *Hayes* [2015] EWCA Crim 1944, [18] and [20] read with [33].

she did as dishonest, not least because, given that she believed that the bicycle belonged to her, Ayesha would have a different characterisation of the deed done than that of the reasonable and honest observer. Accordingly, the second limb of the *Ghosh* test would preclude a finding of dishonesty in that case. It would not, however, similarly protect Aruna, who would realise that reasonable and honest persons, knowing that the car was not hers, would regard her impersonating the owner and taking the car as dishonest conduct. The Proposed Reconstruction then, supports a finding of dishonesty in *Casual Carjacker*, but not in either version of *Bicycle*. I take these to be desirable liability outcomes, and indeed they are the same liability outcomes that both the *Ivey* test and Campbell's Gloss would generate. Additionally, and unlike either the *Ivey* test or Campbell's Gloss, the Proposed Reconstruction accommodates the analysis of the Court of Appeal in *Ghosh* in relation to *Visitor on the Bus* example, and blocks a finding of dishonesty (leading to a conviction for theft) in the *Free Newspaper* example. For these reasons, we should prefer the Proposed Reconstruction to Campbell's Gloss.

One cannot be certain whether the Proposed Reconstruction was the Court of Appeal's intended reading of the *Ghosh* test, but it is the most charitable of the compatible interpretations canvassed. This, coupled with its greater precision in identifying subjective culpability, means that this reading of the *Ghosh* test is clearly a better test for dishonesty than the *Ivey* test. In fact, given its pedigree and familiarity in the English criminal law, there is no reason to look beyond it for a test for dishonesty in criminal law.

IV. Conclusion

The Supreme Court's decision in *Ivey* to cast aside the *Ghosh* test took many criminal lawyers and commentators by surprise, not least because it did so in a civil case, away from the watchful eye of criminal lawyers. The unorthodox circumstances in which a well-established rule in the criminal law came to be discarded may have contributed to the generally negative reaction to *Ivey*. But set aside for the moment the criticisms relating to how the change was made, whether it was really needed, and whether the Supreme Court's critiques of the *Ghosh* test were compelling.[81] As a practical matter, not everyone was convinced that the change in the law was especially significant. Indeed, some suggested that, actually, 'the Supreme Court's judgment may have less practical impact for the vast majority of cases than might be imagined'.[82] One might even have thought that, in normative terms, there is little to choose between *Ghosh* and *Ivey*.

[81] These are set out in great detail in Fortson (n 13). See also Sullivan and Simester (n 17), Dyson and Jarvis (n 7), Virgo (n 15), and Spencer (n 16).

[82] K Laird, 'Dishonesty: *Ivey v Genting Casinos UK Ltd*' [2018] *Crim LR* 395, 396.

I have argued here that, actually, the move from *Ghosh* to *Ivey* was normatively significant and that it was unfortunate. The *Ivey* test supports convictions in respect of perfectly quotidian behaviour that neither harms nor wrongs anybody, based purely on D's (false) belief in matters, in light of which her chosen conduct would be dishonest. Effectively, on certain facts, it turns offences of dishonesty into thought crimes. Moreover, even where D holds no false beliefs, the *Ivey* test is overinclusive. It assumes that persons who conduct themselves in a manner that is objectively dishonest in light of their knowledge and beliefs are dishonest. While unobjectionable at first glance, this standard also arguably treats people who were merely absent-minded as having been dishonest. Moreover, it deems 'dishonest' people who have mistaken beliefs about the societal standards of dishonesty for reasons that do not undermine their personal integrity. The *Ghosh* test, as reconstructed here, is superior in comparison to the *Ivey* test in each of these respects. Moreover, in terms of identifying the sort of subjective culpability that we would expect from a subjective criminal law mens rea element, the *Ghosh* test arguably gets it essentially right. There is every reason to reconsider the *Ivey* test insofar as it applies to the criminal law. If and when that happens, I have argued that the best course of action would be to revert to the *Ghosh* test, as reconstructed here.

PART II

Substantive Offences

5

Criminal Fraud and the Toleration of False Political Speech

JEREMY HORDER

I. Introduction

Not every fraud (the intentional or reckless use of false statements[1]) falls within the scope of a criminal wrong, even when harm is done by it. In itself, that is not controversial. After all, not every instance of harm done by intentional physical contact falls within the scope of a criminal wrong.[2] In the case of fraud, though, any harm done thereby is done through the medium of communication. In liberal democracies, this fact is in itself liable to make problematic the criminalisation of some (harm-causing) frauds. That is because, in some circumstances, people's Article 10 rights to freedom of expression may be unduly restricted or undermined if the threat of coercion – should harm come from their (fraudulent) speech – is allowed to deter them from speaking.[3] In that regard, my concern will be a particular kind of political fraud that is frequently subject to criminalisation world-wide, including in liberal democracies.[4] This is 'political viewpoint' fraud, fraud concerning facts about – for example – candidates for political office and their policies.[5]

[1] This definition is focused on the knowledge that a false statement is (or may indeed be) false. It thus differs somewhat from GR Sullivan's definition, which is focused on a particular kind of economic wrong: the intention to (or knowledge that one might) cause loss or make a gain through dishonest conduct. See GR Sullivan, 'Framing an Acceptable General Offence of Fraud' (1989) 53 *Journal of Criminal Law* 92.

[2] See the discussion in *Collins v Willcock* [1984] 3 All ER 374. So far as fraud is concerned, frauds committed without dishonesty may not warrant criminalisation: see Law Com No 276, *Fraud* (London, HMSO, 2002) part V.

[3] The opening words of Art 10(1) read: 'Everyone has the right to freedom of expression. This right shall include freedom to hold opinions and to receive and impart information and ideas without interference by public authority and regardless of frontiers.'

[4] For a general discussion, see J Horder, *Criminal Fraud and Election Disinformation: Law and Politics* (Oxford, Oxford University Press, 2022).

[5] By contrast, I will not be concerned with 'electoral participation' fraud, fraud committed to gain an advantage or impose a disadvantage in the voting process (such as falsely telling someone they are not eligible to vote). For a full discussion, see Horder, ibid, ch 1. Further, I will not be concerned with

The dissemination of such frauds is very commonly unjustified and inexcusable,[6] in some instances as a violation of someone's right to their reputation: an interest protected, in so far as it is as an aspect of private life, under Article 8.[7] Societies have developed a number of means by which to deter the perpetration and spread of false political viewpoint claims;[8] but my aim here will be to make the case for protecting the dissemination of false political viewpoint claims from one means in particular: criminalisation.

This will not simply be an individual rights-based argument narrowly concerned with the requirements of Article 10. It is also a claim about the republican limits, in a democratic state, of the rights of officials' and election candidates to use coercion to dictate the terms on which other people describe and evaluate their fitness for office, the nature and merits of the policies they endorse and reject, and so on. As Shauer and Pildes put it:

> Rights were not designed to protect individuals in their atomistic interests in, for example self-expressiveness; rather, rights were designed to sustain a political culture in which public liberty was enhanced by recognising certain domains as relatively autonomous. This conception meant defining certain domains as off limits to state action that rested on particular impermissible purposes.[9]

It might come as a surprise to discover that the criminal law becomes involved at all in seeking to deter and punish political viewpoint fraud directed at officials or election candidates, but it commonly does so. In some jurisdictions, an example is provided by criminal defamation cases involving statements it is known are or may be false. In German law, Article 188 of the Criminal Code creates an offence of defaming, 'a person involved in popular political life [in a way that] may make [the person's] public activities substantially more difficult'.[10] Another important case is where a fraud is intended to affect voting at an election. So, for example, section 106 of the Representation of the People Act 1983 creates a summary offence in circumstances where:

> (1) A person who, or any director of any body or association corporate which –
>
> (a) before or during an election,

the mere expression of unfounded 'opinion', which is commonly not subjected to criminal sanctions in liberal-democratic states.

[6] Although there may be some circumstances in which there is an excuse or justification: see the discussion in the Canadian case of *Zundel v R* [1992] 2 SCR 731.

[7] *Pfeifer v Austria* (2007) Appl No 12556/03.

[8] For example, defamation, as an action in private law, involves an element of victims' rights-based deterrent effect. Some examples of other less formal means by which the state expresses disapproval of false viewpoint statements are discussed in the conclusion. See generally, A Stone and F Schauer (eds), *The Oxford Handbook of Freedom of Speech* (Oxford, Oxford University Press, 2021).

[9] F Shauer and RH Pildes, 'Electoral Exceptionalism and the First Amendment' (1999) 77 *Texas Law Review* 1803, 1812, 1814.

[10] Compare, too, Art 32 of the Press Law 1881 (France), which defines criminal defamation as, 'any allegation or accusation of a fact that causes an attack on the honour or consideration of a person', and permits a maximum fine of €45,000 when the victim is a public official, as compared with €12,000 when the victim is a private individual. See Horder (n 4) ch 2.

(b) for the purpose of affecting the return of any candidate at the election, makes or publishes any false statement of fact in relation to the candidate's personal character or conduct shall be guilty of an illegal practice, unless he can show that he had reasonable grounds for believing, and did believe, that statement to be true.[11]

We should note two important points about the scope of this offence. First, it covers some instances in which a false statement of the relevant kind is unwittingly made, if the statement was made in the absence of reasonable grounds for believing it to be true. Such extensive coverage is controversial.[12] Secondly, the speech-focused wrongdoing at the heart of this offence is a limited kind of defamation, a false claim about the *personal* conduct or character of a candidate.[13] The abolition, more generally, of criminal defamation in England and Wales[14] is something else that makes this offence controversial, albeit less controversial than the more expansive versions employed in other jurisdictions (as we shall see). These more expansive versions of the offence extend liability to false statements about a candidate's *political* conduct and character.

Even so, the section 106 offence is controversial, fundamentally because it clearly detracts from the important free speech principle that false or misleading speech should (especially in political contexts) be met and countered with counter-speech, and not with state sanctions. As Justice Brandeis famously put it in *Whitney v California*.

> To courageous, self-reliant men [*sic*], with confidence in the power of free and fearless reasoning applied through the processes of popular government … [i]f there be time to expose through discussion the falsehood and fallacies, to avert the evil by the processes of education, the remedy to be applied is more speech, not enforced silence.[15]

In that regard, it is important to bear in mind that, even when concerned with falsely negative as opposed to falsely positive statements, the offence targets a somewhat different range of conduct from, say, crimes of hate or intimidation, although there will be overlaps. So, the justification for having crimes of hate or intimidation does not apply to this offence (and I will cast no doubt here on the justification for hate crimes or crimes of intimidation). For example, a false claim that a candidate has an unfortunate medical condition that will make them unfit for office may be a false statement falling within the scope of the prohibition; but it is not a statement aimed at intimidating or creating hate.

[11] Discussed in Horder (n 4) ch 3.

[12] It is controversial because it is strongly arguable that false statements of this nature should not be criminalised – if the criminal law is properly applied at all – unless the statements were fraudulent: made knowing that they were or might be false, as in the United States: see text at n 17 below.

[13] Although the offence extends to false positive claims made about a candidate to boost their vote return: *Morrison v Carmichael* [2016] SC 598. The significance of 'false positive' claims is discussed in J Horder, 'Criminal Law at the Limit: Countering False Claims in Elections and Referendums' (2021) 84 *MLR* 429.

[14] Coroners and Justice Act 2009, s 73.

[15] *Whitney v California (No 3)*, 74 US 357, 377 (1927) (Brandeis J).

In other jurisdictions, some versions of this offence are more restricted, and some less restricted, in different ways. An example that provides a convenient focus is to be found in Ohio's election law code. It is an offence to:

> Post, publish, circulate, distribute, or otherwise disseminate a false statement concerning a candidate, either knowing the same to be false or with reckless disregard of whether it was false or not, if the statement is designed to promote the election, nomination, or defeat of the candidate.[16]

In terms of its breadth, there are two important features of this example. First, in common with many similar provisions in US state codes, it is in one way narrower in scope than the equivalent UK provision: it requires what I term 'fraud', namely proof of intention or recklessness with regard to the falsity of the false statement made.[17] By way of contrast with the position under UK law, under Ohio law an honest belief (whether or not reasonable) in the truth of the false statement ensures that any such false statement. falls outside the scope of the offence. Secondly, though, the Ohio prohibition is significantly broader than UK law, in that there are no restrictions on the kind of false statement caught by it, so long as the false statement is intended to promote or defeat an election candidate. The equivalent provision in Minnesota is more explicit on this point, stating expressly that the false statement may concern, 'the personal *or political* character or acts of a candidate'.[18] I will come back to the latter point in section V.

II. Is Fraudulent Political Speech Constitutionally Protected?

We should first consider the strong view that frauds enjoy no special protection in virtue of being a form of speech. The strong view was expressed by Lord Hobhouse in the private law libel case of *Times Newspapers v Reynolds*:

> There is no human right to disseminate information that is not true. No public interest is served by publishing or communicating misinformation. The working of a democratic society depends on the members of that society being informed not misinformed. Misleading people and the purveying as facts statements which are not true is destructive of democratic society and should form no part of such a society. There is no duty to publish what is not true: there is no interest in being misinformed. These are general propositions going far beyond the mere protection of reputations.[19]

[16] Ohio Revised Code, § 3517.21(10).

[17] *Garrison v Louisiana*, 379 US 64, 75 (1964) (Brennan J): 'Although honest utterance, even if inaccurate, may further the fruitful exercise of the right of free speech, it does not follow that the lie, knowingly and deliberately published about a public official, should enjoy a like immunity.'

[18] Minnesota Statutes, § 211B.06.

[19] *Reynolds v Times Newspapers* [2001] 2 AC 127, 268.

In a US First Amendment context, similar sentiments have been expressed by the US Supreme Court, albeit with more care taken to confine the scope of constitutionally unprotected falsehoods to falsehoods intentionally or recklessly propagated,[20] something unfortunately left unclear in Lord Hobhouse's exposition of the matter, just cited. In *Garrison v Louisiana*, Brennan J said:

> That speech is used as a tool for political ends does not automatically bring it under the protective mantle of the Constitution. For the use of the known lie as a tool is at once at odds with the premises of democratic government and with the orderly manner in which economic, social, or political change is to be effected. … Hence the knowingly false statement and the false statement made with reckless disregard of the truth, do not enjoy constitutional protection.[21]

Do these statements imply that lying can, *as such*, justifiably be criminalised? They do not.

If it is to be justified, a criminal prohibition must be a necessary and proportionate step, in response to a wrong, even if the commission of the wrong does not enjoy constitutional protection. An illustration of this point from the United States is the striking down of criminal legislation in the case of *US v Alvarez*.[22] At his first meeting as a Board member of the Three Valley Water District Board, D falsely claimed to have received a Congressional Medal of Honour. The making of such a false claim was at that time expressly prohibited by the Stolen Valor Act of 2005, under which D was initially convicted.[23] The Supreme Court overturned D's conviction and struck the 2005 Act down as unconstitutional. In the Court's opinion:

> The Court has never endorsed the categorical rule the Government advances: that false statements receive no First Amendment protection. Our prior decisions have not confronted a measure, like the Stolen Valor Act, that targets falsity and nothing more.[24]

In the Supreme Court's view, that means that criminal – or indeed civil – measures to deter and punish lying must be targeted at, 'defamation, fraud, or some other legally cognizable harm associated with a false statement, such as an invasion of privacy'.[25] Most importantly, in the Supreme Court's view, the concern with intentional or reckless lying is a concern to *limit* the state's scope to prohibit or provide civil remedies for falsehoods in, say, the law of defamation. It is not a concern designed to justify the creation of new civil actions or offences.[26] In the wake of *US v Alvarez*, Congress passed the Stolen Valor Act 2013, which limits the

[20] See eg *Hustler Magazine Inc v Falwell*, 485 US 46 (1988).

[21] *Garrison v Louisiana*, 379 US 64, 76 (1964). See also *Herbert v Lando*, 441 US 153 (1979).

[22] *United States v Alvarez*, 132 S Ct 2537 (2012).

[23] 'Whoever falsely represents himself or herself, verbally or in writing, to have been awarded any decoration or medal authorized by Congress for the Armed Forces of the United States … shall be fined under this title, imprisoned not more than six months, or both.'

[24] *United States v Alvarez* 567 US 709, 711 (2012) (Kennedy J).

[25] ibid.

[26] ibid.

criminalisation of false claims to have received honours, or to have served in the military, to cases in which there was an intention thereby to obtain money, property or some other intangible benefit.[27]

A UK illustration comes from proposed reforms to the criminal law governing false communications. Hitherto, the offences in England and Wales concerned with malicious communication have been extraordinarily wide, breaching the general principle that such measures ought to be necessary and proportionate in their reach. This has been especially significant in their potential application to political debate and disagreement. For example, section 127(2) of the Communications Act 2003 says, in relation to improper use of a public electronic communications network:

> A person is guilty of an offence if, for the purpose of causing annoyance, inconvenience or needless anxiety to another, he –
>
> (a) sends by means of a public electronic communications network, a message that he knows to be false, [or]
>
> (b) causes such a message to be sent …[28]

Can it really be right, say, in the context of a heated political contest between two embittered rival candidates wooing votes from an already highly polarised and partisan electorate, that it is a criminal offence for a politically engaged voter to send a message they know to be false over the internet about the policies of one candidate, solely with a view to 'annoying' that candidate? In as much as it extends so far, section 127 cannot possibly be consistent with a genuine commitment to Article 10 rights, and to proportionate use of the criminal law. The Law Commission recommended in 2020 that the sending of false messages should be an offence only when 'they are intended to cause non-trivial emotional, psychological, or physical harm to a likely audience; and the defendant sent the communication without reasonable excuse'.[29] The Online Harms Bill 2022 will turn that recommendation into law.[30] The need for the prosecution to prove that D's false message was intended to cause non-trivial harm to a likely audience makes criminalisation somewhat more proportionate, although it remains unclear why the offence is not based on non-trivial harm intentionally caused, with cases in which such harm was only intended left to the law of criminal attempts.[31]

Against that background, we can consider the UK case of *R (Woolas) v Parliamentary Election Court*.[32] In *Woolas*, Mr Woolas had very narrowly won a

[27] See, further, S Lieffring, 'First Amendment and the Right to Lie: Regulating Knowingly False Campaign Speech after *United States v Alvarez*' (2013) 97 *Minnesota Law Review* 1047.

[28] The penalty upon summary conviction is a sentence of imprisonment for a term not exceeding six months or a fine not exceeding level 5 on the standard scale, or both.

[29] LCCP No 248, *Harmful Online Communications* (London, HMSO, 2020) para 6.32.

[30] https://www.gov.uk/government/news/online-safety-law-to-be-strengthened-to-stamp-out-illegal-content- (last accessed 8 February 2022).

[31] For further discussion, see Horder (n 4) ch 3.

[32] *R (Woolas) v Parliamentary Election Court* [2010] EWHC 3169.

seat in a general election, having made a series of false claims about his Liberal Democrat opponent during the course of the campaign. Woolas was not charged with an offence contrary to section 106; instead, the issue was whether Woolas's election should be annulled in virtue of his breaches of section 106. A key question, thus, was whether Woolas's lies about his Liberal Democrat election opponent, Robert Watkins, were a protected kind of speech, especially given the bitterly contested electoral context in which the lies were told. Woolas, a Labour Party candidate, made three false claims during the election process:

(a) That Robert Watkins had attempted to woo the vote of 'extremist' Muslims who advocated violence towards Mr Woolas.
(b) That Robert Watkins had refused to condemn extremists who advocated violence against Mr Woolas.
(c) That Robert Watkins had reneged on his promise to live in the constituency.

Rejecting the argument that claims of this kind enjoyed some kind of constitutional protection, notwithstanding their falsity, the High Court invoked Article 17 of the European Convention on Human Rights (ECHR) to deny Article 10 protection to false and dishonest statements, even when those statements were made in a political context. Article 17 makes it clear that the Convention is not to be interpreted in such a way as to grant a right to 'engage in any activity or perform any act aimed at the destruction on any of the [Convention] rights and freedoms'.[33] The *Woolas* Court took the view that Article 17 was engaged when false political claims caused harm to a candidate's electoral prospects, in that:

> Dishonest statements are aimed at the destruction of the rights of the public to free elections (Article 3 of the First Protocol) and the right of each candidate to his reputation (Article 8(1)).[34]

The significance of the ruling in *Woolas* is that, as indicated above, the making of such false political statements is a criminal offence contrary to section 106 of the Representation of the People Act 1983, and not just a ground for invalidating an election result (as occurred in this case), if the statements concern a candidate's 'personal conduct or character', an issue addressed in due course. Clearly, in so far as they amount to an offence, the false statements made in *Woolas* are not criminalised merely because they are false. They will only pass the *Alvarez* test if and in so far as the false statements lead to (to use the *Alvarez* terminology) a 'legally cognizable harm'. In the *Woolas* Court's view, such a harm takes the form of an invasion of the rights of the public to free elections and of a candidate's right to their reputation. However, even if one accepts this as a basis for the decision in *Woolas*, and as an interpretation the scope of UK election law, is such harm really enough to justify criminalisation?

[33] See further the discussion in J Rowbottom, 'Lies, Manipulation and Elections – Controlling False Campaign Statements' (2012) 32 *OJLS* 507, 519–20.
[34] *Woolas* (n 32) [105].

III. Fraud that Causes Harm: An Adequate Case for Criminalisation?

In interpreting the scope of and weight to be attached to rights under the ECHR, the *Woolas* Court invokes Article 17 to deny that there can be a 'right to defraud' where the fraud threatens rights under the First Protocol to Article 3 (free elections), and under Article 8 (right to protection of reputation). The broader question this ruling raises is whether, and when, it is appropriate to use the criminal law to deter and punish such frauds if harm is caused. Bear in mind that the right to free elections is already protected from fraud by the courts' public law power to annul an election tainted by fraud,[35] and that the right to one's reputation is protected under the private law of defamation and, increasingly, through the right to have defamatory information posted online taken down by the internet provider under the provider's community rules. This might suggest that the most important cases in which a fraud aimed at causing harm may proportionately be criminalised are those cases where, inter alia, the invasion of Convention rights involved lacks such alternative (non-criminal) means of protection.

Suppose that X, who was adopted, contacts the private adoption agency that handled the adoption, saying she wishes to find out about and follow her birth parents' religion. An agency worker deceives her into believing that her parents were Christians when in fact they were Jewish, leading X to undergo baptism. No offence is committed in English law on such facts, even though the fraud is intended to infringe X's right to freedom of religion. Moreover, it is unclear whether any civil wrong is done to X that could form the basis of a compensation claim. Nonetheless, perhaps the possibility of such an event's occurrence is too remote to justify state intervention.[36] A general offence of 'fraudulently breaching another's Convention right' would meet that point by covering a much wider range of rights-invading frauds. However, such a broad offence would surely suffer unduly from vagueness in scope, thus putting the law in tension with the demands of Article 7.[37] In practice, there is no alternative to identifying a particular type of harm brought about by fraud, and asking whether its nature and (likely) prevalence are such as to justify the application of criminal sanctions rather than leaving any injured person to a private law or similar remedy.

An obvious case for criminalisation is where a false statement intentionally or recklessly made leads to physical harm. Suppose that I tell you that a path through

[35] Representation of the People Act 1983, s 164.

[36] After all, largely for such reasons, the United Kingdom does not criminalise forced conversion to another religion, in cases involving threats falling outside the scope of existing offences where the making of the threat (eg a threat of death) itself is criminalised.

[37] Bob Sullivan has, of course, been at the forefront of efforts to ensure that the law of criminal fraud is not beset by uncertainty, in the quest to ensure extensive coverage and the avoidance of technicality in application: see eg GR Sullivan, 'Fraud – The Latest Law Commission Proposals' (2003) *Journal of Criminal Law* 139.

the woods is safe to walk down in the dark, when I know it leads directly to a concealed cliff edge. Having followed my advice, you then fall over the cliff and are killed. I may be convicted of murder or manslaughter (depending on what I intended or foresaw). In this example, the fraud is no more than a means or instrument for causing your death. However, it is not in every case of an offence against the person that there will be nothing more than this to say. An important example is fraud instrumental in persuading another (V) to engage in a sexual act. Such frauds may indeed be a mere means by which V is inexcusably persuaded to surrender their sexual autonomy and submit to D's will. However, some scholars have raised the important point that the fraud may come about through D's ex hypothesi legitimate concern for privacy in relation to certain information, notwithstanding its importance to V.[38] Suppose D was trafficked into sex slavery when young. Years later, she is dating V, who tells D he would never agree to have sexual intercourse with someone who had been a sex worker. Ashamed of her past, D says she has never worked in the sex industry. D and V subsequently enjoy sexual intercourse together. One reason for thinking that D should not be regarded as committing a sexual offence here is that D is entitled to conceal her past, as a matter of privacy, and thus lacks what ought to be a key element of fault:

> The right to privacy is of paramount importance to human dignity, personhood, and communal life. It is essential to the free development of an individual's personality and identity because it allows us to think freely, to leave our past behind us, and to avoid unjust discrimination.[39]

In this example, the undermining of V's sexual autonomy by D's deception is something that we may say that D has a (privacy-based) liberty to do in the circumstances. Such cases are thus distinct from cases in which the inapplicability of a criminal sanction in a fraud case has a more excusatory basis, such as many (albeit not all) cases in which D admits causing some harm through fraud, but denies that their conduct was dishonest.[40] Nevertheless, a different analysis may be required to account for the examples that are my principal focus, political viewpoint frauds that lead to the loss of an election or a wasted vote. That is because, in such cases, it may be admitted that there was neither excuse nor justification for the fraud. Instead, the claim is that – unjustifiable and inexcusable though it may have been, morally speaking – the fraud is one that ought to be tolerated. In that regard, it is helpful to draw on Bernard Williams's distinction between toleration

[38] See eg the discussion in N Scheidegger, 'Balancing Sexual Autonomy, Responsibility, and the Right to Privacy: Principles for Criminalizing Sex by Deception' (2021) 22 *German Law Journal* 769.

[39] ibid, text at n 110.

[40] For a helpful discussion, see J Gardner, 'Wrongs and Faults' in AP Simester (ed), *Appraising Strict Liability* (Oxford, Oxford University Press, 2005) 51, 67–70. A denial of dishonesty may involve a claim of right or liberty – 'It is permissible to keep small sums of money found in the street' – but may also concede that an appropriation was wrongful whilst offering an excuse: 'My employer permitted a fellow employee to take unsold bread rolls home from the bakery, so I just assumed that it would be alright for me to do so too.'

as a political doctrine and toleration as a moral doctrine.[41] Toleration as a moral doctrine is in play when, although we may have doubts about the ethical propriety of certain conduct – or, indeed, disapprove of the conduct – we nonetheless think that it is up to the conscience of the individual whether or not to engage in it. This, I suggest, is the approach many would take to the example of the former sex worker's deception just given, in so far as we disapprove of her lying. Her liberty to deceive stems in part from a sense that it is just 'up to her' whether or not she should tell the lie.

By contrast, when toleration is instantiated purely as a political doctrine, the toleration is focused narrowly on the (permissive) legal approach to the conduct. In such cases it is not appropriate that the power of the state be used to deter and punish those who engage in the conduct in question. However, it is perfectly consistent with the adoption of tolerance as a political doctrine that, as Williams puts it,

> we should do everything we decently can to persuade [someone] to change his ways and to discourage other people from living like him. We may … discourage as many people as we can from thinking well of him so long as he lives in this way.[42]

Such a response, which JS Mill was almost certainly thinking of when speaking of his distaste for 'moral coercion',[43] would not be appropriate (being too harsh and condemnatory) in the former sex worker example, where toleration as a moral doctrine is in play. By contrast, it is submitted that what Williams says here about the political doctrine of toleration is the appropriate attitude towards false political statements about election candidates, even when such statements may lead to a candidate's losing the election, and to votes being cast on a false factual basis. We are, morally, free to shun and openly to condemn those who knowingly employ political falsehoods (indeed, perhaps we positively ought to adopt such attitudes), but we ought not to seek to deter and punish them through criminal prohibition. There are, to be sure, complexities that make this distinction less clear-cut in its application to non-state agencies than it might appear. For example, obligations of 'net-neutrality' may oblige internet platforms to adopt toleration as a moral doctrine in their own approach to political viewpoint falsehoods, since it is in general for platform users, not for platforms themselves, to call out liars in politics.[44] However, I will concentrate on the simple application of Williams's distinction, according to which, whilst individuals – including individual politicians – are entitled to criticise and condemn lying and liars in politics, the criminal law should stay its hand.[45]

[41] B Williams, *In the Beginning Was the Deed* (Princeton, NJ, Princeton University Press, 2007) ch 10.

[42] ibid 131.

[43] JS Mill, *On Liberty* (London, JW Parker & Son, 1859) 13.

[44] See Horder (n 4) ch 2, where the limits and complexities of this claim are discussed in detail. I am not suggesting, for example, that someone who persistently abuses a platform's morally tolerant approach to lying is entitled to remain on the platform to continue lying.

[45] I shall not be concerned here with the appropriate limits of private law, and in particular the law of defamation.

IV. Freedom of (Uncivilised) Speech: Mill's Complacency about the Law

Finding a breach of individual rights contrary to the ECHR is not necessary if one is to justify the imposition of criminal liability for instances of lying or misleading that may cause such breaches. It is not necessary because, for example, a prohibition on lying or misleading may be justified by the need to protect an important public good rather than individual rights. Indeed, public-good-focused prohibitions on false or misleading statements are by far the most common form of such prohibitions. A long-standing example is perjury, but far more numerous are examples in which the prohibition is designed to deter and punish acts that are liable to frustrate the achievement of a regulatory goal. An example (albeit expressed negatively as a failure to tell the truth) is the offence of failing to give a true name and address when asked to do so by a constable in connection with a demand to see a firearm certificate, contrary to section 48(3) of the Firearms Act 1968.[46]

Granting that, however, as indicated in the last section, my concern is with instances in which (as I argue) a breach of individual rights, whether or not contravening the ECHR, is not a sufficient basis to justify a criminal prohibition of the fraud that brings about that breach, because the doctrine of toleration requires that the state should stay its hand. In that regard, it is important to appreciate the different ways in which the nature of pluralism poses challenges for moral and political toleration, with implications for the law. The case for toleration, both moral and political, hinges on the rise of value pluralism in a society. Value pluralism may manifest itself in a variety of ways that pose different challenges to doctrines of toleration. For example, one might distinguish a 'mutual respect' model of pluralism from a 'rivalrous' model, and also distinguish a rivalrous model from a 'enmity' model of pluralism. Under the mutual respect model, tolerance as a moral doctrine will be widespread, because different groups mind their own business and pursue their own agenda largely in a way calculated not to come into serious conflict or competition with other groups. This is, perhaps, characteristic of modern sects or churches in the United Kingdom coming under the banner of, say, the Protestant faith. With the mutual respect model, the legal doctrine of toleration has relatively little work to do, other than securing permission for the different groups to emerge and establish themselves in society.

By contrast, when pluralism is rivalrous, groups will – typically – seek to gain advantages at the expense of other groups (perceived as competitors) and may much more strongly denounce or criticise their rivals to undermine the latter's perceived legitimacy. There may be some degree of moral toleration, as between

[46] Discussed in LCCP No 195, *Criminal Liability in Regulatory Contexts* (London, HMSO, 2010) para 3.126.

rival groups, but – depending on the nature and intensity of the rivalry between the groups – its existence will be far more fragile than under the mutual respect model. This is, of course, the normal position in the case of rival political groupings and parties in a democracy. In such circumstances, there will be more work for a legal doctrine of toleration to do. For example, germane to this chapter will be the need to decide whether potentially harmful public denunciation, criticisms and accusations by one group respecting another are to be permitted (and if so to what extent), when such public statements contain false or misleading claims. Finally, there is the 'enmity' model of pluralism. Under this model, there is little or no scope for moral toleration. Rival groups do not recognise each other as having any right to exist; indeed, each regards the existence of the others as a threat to the public good.[47] Under the enmity model, groups go beyond public criticism and advancing their own agenda, at the expense of other groups. They seek, in addition, to use – or to persuade officials to use – the power of the state to restrict the scope for their rivals' activities (and the activities of their supporters) or to prohibit them altogether. Historically, the enmity model characterised the attitude of the Protestant and Catholic branches of Christianity towards each other at the time of the reformation.[48] The model is in some ways also characteristic of the contemporary attitude of the US Republican Party towards its US Democratic Party rival. For example, Republicans have moved beyond simple political rivalry with Democrats within the existing adversarial electoral framework, to making concerted efforts to inhibit – both in law and in practice – the ability of likely democratic voters to cast their votes.[49] In the field of free expression, stringent criminal laws prohibiting the publishing of 'fake news' about officials or election candidates are especially apt to be used in a partisan way, whether by authoritarian governments[50] or by rivals in conditions of enmity pluralism. For obvious reasons, the enmity model of pluralism, and in particular, groups' attempts to use the legal system to disadvantage or to delegitimise their rivals, is likely simply to clash irreconcilably with any doctrine of toleration.

I will be concerned mainly with the 'mutual respect' and 'rivalrous' models of pluralism. I will seek to show how an assumption that value pluralism by its nature involves mutual respect may leave the legal system ill-equipped to confront the challenges of giving full effect to legal toleration in conditions of rivalrous pluralism. Such an assumption may also lead to the downplaying or neglect of residual powers within a legal system that could be exploited, in conditions of enmity pluralism, by groups intent on restricting or punishing the activities – and in particular, the free expression – of their rivals: widely drawn defamation laws, or law outlawing blasphemy or heresy, being examples. In that regard, it is helpful

[47] For further discussion, in terms of the distinction between adversaries and enemies, see C Mouffe, *On the Political* (London, Routledge, 2005).

[48] See the discussion in Williams (n 41).

[49] See the discussion in Horder (n 4).

[50] See ibid ch 2.

to examine what JS Mill had to say about the rise of religious toleration. As we shall see, his account (wrongly) understands religious pluralism as a non-rivalrous, mutual-respect-based phenomenon, characterised by the moral doctrine of toleration. In fact, different religious sects in Victorian England were rivalrous, and the law's Church of England-inspired response to this was to implement merely a 'thin' political doctrine of toleration. This was a doctrine that permitted only civilised or 'reverent' critique, a doctrine that was also applied in the political sphere to criticism of government. Yet, a commitment to republican freedom in the democratic state requires an approach that is more robustly supportive of free expression in conditions of rivalrous pluralism. Such a commitment is not consistent with a policy in which officials, electoral candidates and other political agents are shielded by the criminal law[51] from uncivilised speech: from biased, partisan, false or misleading attacks, however regrettable such attacks might be. The Victorians' thin doctrine of toleration, which still overshadows the modern law, has no place in a politically vibrant democracy.

The background to Mill's articulation of the harm principle is his concern – later echoed in Ronald Dworkin's development of the notion of rights as 'trumps'[52] – with the protection of a minority from the 'tyranny of the majority'.[53] In terms of liberal-democratic political progress, for Mill, it is not enough to have ensured the accountability through the democratic process of those who hold political office. Beyond that, Mill says:

> There is a limit to the legitimate interference of collective opinion with individual independence: and to find that limit, and maintain it against encroachment, is as indispensable to a good condition of human affairs, as protection against political despotism.[54]

The idea, implicit here, that the protection of individual independence is a separate (albeit related) goal from the elimination of political despotism, comes from Mill's primary focus in *On Liberty* on the individual's *moral* independence: the individual's freedom to form and act on their own conception of what is good in their personal and social lives.[55] However, the protection of 'individual independence' and the suppression of despotism become part of the same goal once one expands the notion of individual independence to include the individual's *political* independence. This is the freedom to form and act on one's own ideas of governance, alone or in combination with others, and to comment critically on the ideas of others, in what Habermas later refers to as the 'public sphere'.[56] The republican significance of this point has, of course, been expounded with great

[51] I am not concerned here with the proper scope of the private law of defamation.

[52] Ronald Dworkin, *Taking Rights Seriously* (London, Duckworth, 1977) ch 11.

[53] Mill (n 43) 9.

[54] ibid.

[55] See, similarly, R Dworkin, 'Is There a Right to Pornography?' (1981) 1 *OJLS* 177.

[56] See eg J Habermas, *The Structural Transformation of the Public Sphere: An Inquiry into a Category of Bourgeois Society* (MIT Press, Cambridge, MA, 1989).

force and clarity in more recent times by Philip Pettit. In explaining what he calls the 'resilient property' of non-interference by the state,[57] Pettit says that, in a state that protects such non-interference,

> free persons can walk tall, and look each other in the eye. … [T]hey relate to one another in a shared, mutually reinforcing consciousness of enjoying this independence.[58]

I will come back to the significance of this claim at the beginning of section V. It is the foundation of any plausible defence of the citizen's liberty to lie in politics. First, though, we must turn to some of Mill's observations on moral independence, for they have a bearing on Pettit's claim.

For Mill, widely held suspicion about the benefits of government interventionism had hitherto ensured that the law was not as commonly used in England to suppress what he called 'individual independence' as it was in mainland Europe.[59] In England, Mill thought, the worst a moral or religious dissenter might ordinarily expect to face was social stigma and 'merely social intolerance',[60] a contentious view disputed below. Even so, Mill considered it to be a defect of the English approach that, other than in matters of religious belief, people were in general more concerned with what they (and others) ought to think and believe than with the principles that should guide law and public policy in circumstances where significant differences in thought and belief had emerged. For Mill, the 'harm principle' was to be the means by which this deficit would be remedied. It would act as a safeguard against the 'tyranny of the (democratic) majority'.[61] Nonetheless, in Mill's view, in the field of religious belief and practice one could *already* find that, 'the higher ground [respect for the right to moral independence] has been taken on principle and maintained with consistency'.[62] How did Mill think that the state's approach to religious belief had come to be characterised by such 'mutual respect' pluralism (as I have called it)?

In Mill's account, when the religious conflict of post-Reformation England ended, 'without giving a complete victory to any party':

> [E]ach church or sect was reduced to limit its hopes to retaining possession of the ground it already occupied; [and] minorities, seeing that they had no chance of becoming majorities, were under the necessity of pleading to those whom they could not convert, for permission to differ.[63]

[57] P Pettit, 'Negative Liberty, Liberal and Republican' (1993) 1 *European Journal of Philosophy* 15, 16.

[58] P Pettit, 'Criminalisation in Republican Theory' in RA Duff et al, *Criminalisation: The Political Morality of the Criminal Law* (Oxford, Oxford University Press, 2014) 138.

[59] Mill (n 43) 12.

[60] ibid 431.

[61] ibid 8.

[62] ibid 11. In that regard, so far as religious belief was concerned, he commended 'the great writers' on religious liberty, for articulating and making mainstream the view that 'freedom of conscience [is] an indefeasible right', and for 'den[ying] 'absolutely that a human being is accountable to others for his religious belief' (ibid 12).

[63] ibid 11–12. For further discussion of the example of religion, in the context of an analysis of toleration, see Williams (n 41).

Mill probably had in mind here the relatively recent expansion of the Toleration Act 1689 to include Unitarians in 1813 and Roman Catholics in 1832. However, Mill does not support his claims that mutual respect pluralism had at this time emerged in England (whatever the position may now be) with any empirical evidence concerning how major religions regarded their faith, or rival faiths, and the passage is misleading in a number of respects. For example, by 1851, far from resting content with their minority status, Nonconformists had expanded the number of their adherents to make up about half of those attending church on Sundays, the 1830s and 1840s having witnessed thousands of conversions.[64] Correspondingly, having failed in its attempt to maintain the denial of basic liberties to Nonconformists (such as the right to hold public office),[65] the Anglican church then embarked on an aggressive programme to attract believers, building over 600 new churches between 1818 and 1884 and nearly doubling the number of clergy.[66] There is precious little evidence here of Mill's notion that each church or sect was simply content to '[retain] possession of the ground it already occupied' (a classic feature of mutual respect pluralism). It is also incorrect to say that churches and their followers were primarily concerned with securing 'permission to differ' from their rivals, this being another typical feature of mutual respect pluralism. From the 1840s, high church Tractarians were causing outrage by introducing 'Catholic' elements to Anglican services, such as incense and vestments. Protestants reacted with lawsuits, legislation and in some instances violence, in a campaign to halt the 'ritualist plague'.[67] Such was the strength of feeling that, only a few years after the publication of *On Liberty*, Parliament passed the Public Worship Regulation Act 1874, in effect making it a criminal contempt of court for a Church of England cleric to refuse to abide by an order to avoid high-church rituals in conducting Church of England services.[68] Predictably, the move produced a number of 'martyrs' willing to undergo prosecution and imprisonment for their high-church practices.[69] What we see here, then, is clear evidence of rivalrous pluralism, and indeed enmity pluralism, in which state law is used to suppress the activities of rivals.[70]

This background is important because, in his defence of personal independence, in so far as it relates to religion, Mill's concern seems to be mainly with the

[64] DA Johnson, *The Changing Shape of English Nonconformity, 1825–1925* (Oxford, Oxford University Press, 1999) 77; S Mitchell, *Victorian Britain: An Encyclopedia* (London, Taylor & Francis, 2011) 23.

[65] GIT Machin, 'Resistance to Repeal of the Test and Corporation Acts, 1828' (1979) 22 *Historical Journal* 115.

[66] Mill may be referring to this when he speaks of the 'revival of religion': Mill (n 43) 31.

[67] N Yates, *Anglican Ritualism in Victorian Britain, 1830–1910* (Oxford, Oxford University Press, 1999) 82.

[68] http://etheses.dur.ac.uk/1581/1/1581.pdf. The Act was not abolished until 1965.

[69] See eg http://anglicanhistory.org/england/ecu/roberts/1884.html.

[70] Almost needless to say, even 'permission to differ' was at this time not tolerated in far as it might extend to anyone advocating atheism. See generally, NG Conrad, *The Marginalisation of Atheism in Victorian Britain: The Trials of Annie Besant and Charles Bradlaugh* (PhD thesis, Washington State University, 2009).

right to hold minority or controversial religious beliefs, to manifest or advocate one's faith (or the lack of it), and to pose challenges in argument to the foundations of rival faiths.[71] These are legal aspects of toleration associated largely with mutual respect pluralism. He says far less about what toleration demands under conditions of rivalrous religious pluralism, in which speakers are liable to go beyond 'civilised' limits by (say) traducing, denouncing or abusing other religions. So, how should the uncivilised speech associated with rivalrous pluralism be viewed, in the light of the harm principle? As Mill was well aware, the authoritarian and partisan common law gave no support to the freedom to engage in uncivilised speech, in so far as such speech might bring state religion into disrepute. In *Shore v Wilson*,[72] a case that concerned the right of Unitarians to receive trust funds reserved for 'Christians', Sir John Coleridge had said, 'there is nothing unlawful at common law in *reverently* doubting or denying doctrines part and parcel of Christianity, however fundamental'.[73] The precarious position in which vehement critics of state religion still at that time found themselves is only too well illustrated here by the need – spelled out by Sir John Coleridge – for sceptical criticism to be 'reverent' in character if it was to escape state censure. That position was underpinned at the time by the continuing legal significance of the offence of blasphemy (together with heresy[74]). As Mill himself points out in *On Liberty*,[75] in 1857 a well-digger named Thomas Pooley was convicted of blasphemy and sentenced to 21 months in prison for, amongst other things, shouting, 'if it had not been for the blackguard Jesus Christ, when he stole the donkey, police would not be wanted. … He was the forerunner of all theft and whoredom.'[76] Pooley was later found to be mentally disturbed, but luminaries such as Macaulay and Thomas Starkie more generally defended the view that, whilst casting doubt on Christian beliefs and practices was acceptable, contempt or ridicule, and in particular knowingly spreading (supposed) falsehoods, was not. Starkie wrote:

> [T]he law visits not the honest errors, but the malice of mankind. A wilful intention to pervert, insult, and mislead others, by means of licentious and contumelious abuse applied to sacred subjects, or by wilful misrepresentations or artful sophistry, calculated to mislead the ignorant or unwary, is the criterion and test of guilt.[77]

[71] See the discussion of religious liberty in Mill (n 43) 24–34.

[72] *Shore v Wilson* (1839, 1842) 9 Clark & Finnelly 359.

[73] ibid (emphasis added).

[74] At common law, Hawkins gave as an example of non-capital heresy, 'seditious words in derogation of the established religion [such] as these: "Your religion is a new religion and preaching is but prattling and prayer once day is more edifying"': W Hawkins, *A Treatise of the Pleas of the Crown*, vol 1, 2nd edn (London, Nutt and Gosling, 1724) ch 5, § 6.

[75] Mill (n 43) 29–30.

[76] GJ Holyoake, *The Case of Thomas Pooley, the Cornish Well Sinker* (London, Holyoake and Company, 1857) 12; cited by TJ Toohey, 'Blasphemy in Nineteenth Century England: The Pooley Case and its Background.' (1987) 30 *Victorian Studies* 315.

[77] T Starkie, *A Treatise on the Law of Slander and Libel*, 2nd edn (London, I and WT Clarke, 1830) vol II, 130.

Most importantly, in general, a similarly authoritarian approach guided the law's approach to seditious libel. Holdsworth cites Lord Ellenborough as authority for the view that, whilst 'it is competent for all the subjects of his Majesty [to discuss] every question connected with public policy', the law will step in when someone, 'makes this privilege a cloak to cover a malicious intention'.[78] In the famous trial for seditious libel of Thomas Paine, Sir Thomas Erskine (Paine's barrister) set out what he regarded as the limits of permissible political critique, as follows:

> That every man, *not intending to mislead* but seeking to enlighten others with what his own reason and conscience however erroneously, have dictated to him as truth, may address himself to the universal reason of a whole nation.[79]

At this time, of course, the law's understanding of what is 'intentionally misleading' or involves 'an intention to pervert' was suspiciously capacious. In 1817, there were more than twenty prosecutions of radical publishers for seditious libel, and many more publishers were imprisoned without trial.[80] In the 1820s, some 150 people were prosecuted for blasphemy for publishing and selling Paine's *The Age of Reason* (more prosecutions than for the whole of the eighteenth century),[81] in virtue of its claim that the Bible and Christianity themselves blasphemed God.[82] Mill's work was itself the subject of an inquiry made to the Law Officers whether a blasphemy prosecution could be brought against him.[83] But such vigorous assertions of legal authoritarianism, and Mill's knowledge of other infamous prosecutions for seditious libel,[84] did not lead him to change his view that, other than in exceptional circumstances, the law was not the main enemy of moral independence in England.[85] On his account, it is '*without* the unpleasant process of fining or imprisoning anybody', that the law, 'maintains all prevailing opinions outwardly undisturbed, while it does not absolutely interdict the exercise of reason by dissentients afflicted with the malady of thought'.[86] Accordingly, Mill misses the important republican point, rightly emphasised in recent times by Pettit, that to be subject to improper domination in the political sphere is wrongly

[78] Sir W Holdsworth, *A History of English Law* (London, 1903–72) vol X, 673 n i.

[79] *Rex v Paine* (1792) 22 How St Tr 357, 414 (emphasis added).

[80] Conrad (n 71) 22.

[81] Toohey (n 77) 318–19.

[82] LW Levy, *Blasphemy: Verbal Offence Against the Sacred from Moses to Salman Rushdie* (Chapel Hill, NC, University of North Carolina Press, 1993) 333.

[83] Toohey (n 77) 322.

[84] Such as the prosecution of the radical Edward Truelove for publishing William Edwin Adams's *Tyrannicide: Is it Justifiable?*: see https://newspapers.library.wales/view/3055061/3055063.

[85] About the Truelove prosecution (see n 84), Mill said: 'That ill-judged interference with the liberty of public discussion has not, however, induced me to alter a single word in the text, nor has it at all weakened my conviction that, moments of panic excepted, the era of pains and penalties for political discussion has, in our own country, passed away': Mill (n 43) 106. It would be right to point out that blasphemy prosecutions declined from the middle years of the nineteenth century (see Toohey, n 77), but Mill is not making an empirical point. His claim is about the disposition of the English more generally with regard to prosecution.

[86] Mill (n 43) 32 (emphasis added).

to find oneself subject to an arbitrary power, *whether or not* the person possessing that power is disposed or likely to exercise it.[87] That is why, for example, it was important that, in 2009, Parliament abolished the three notorious loci of arbitrary power in relation to controversial speech – the offences of seditious, obscene and defamatory libel – even though these offences had fallen into disuse.[88]

Mill's concern was, famously, with the possibility that erroneous but adequately thought-out opinion should be permitted to flourish, to aid the discovery and promotion of truth:

> Truth gains more even by the errors of one who, *with due study and preparation*, thinks for himself, than by the true opinions of those who only hold them because they do not suffer themselves to think.[89]

Further, he defended oppositional party politics, with one party advocating 'order or stability' and its opposite number advocating 'progress of reform' as 'necessary elements of a healthy state of political life', because 'it is in a great measure the opposition of the other that keeps each *within the limits of reason and sanity*'.[90] Mill does not address the question of whether or not the state has a role in promoting civilised disagreement of this kind, in relation to religious or political debate, by using coercion to deter and punish knowingly false or malevolent claims in either the religious or the political sphere (or both). Yet, this is a critical matter. The intensely rivalrous nature of both religious and political pluralism is liable to give rise to malicious criticism, conspiracy theories, (defamatory) caricatures of people and their views, and other damaging falsehoods liable to cause harm to – for example – religious and political careers and prospects.[91] Additionally, those persons effectively – or, indeed, legally – excluded from influence in the public domain, however much 'due study and preparation' (to use Mill's words[92]) is put into their advocacy of a political agenda, are liable to turn to so-called 'counter-public' speech.[93] This is dialogue with its own standards for truth and falsity, and for persuasive and unpersuasive lines of argument, that self-consciously rejects the dominant understanding of the acceptable limits to forms and styles of argument.[94] In that regard, emotionally charged religious or political

[87] See P Pettit, *The Common Mind: An Essay on Psychology, Society and Politics* (Oxford, Oxford University Press, 1996) 311.

[88] https://humanrightshouse.org/articles/uk-government-abolishes-seditious-libel-and-criminal-defamation/ (last accessed 16 March 2022).

[89] Mill (n 43) 33 (emphasis added).

[90] ibid 45 (emphasis added).

[91] An important example from a later period was the language used to associate strikers in industrial disputes in the inter-war period with 'Bolshevism': see L Beers, '"Is This Man an Anarchist?" Industrial Action and the Battle for Public Opinion in Interwar Britain' (2010) 82 *Journal of Modern History* 30.

[92] See text at n 90.

[93] For an early exploration of the subject, see M Warner, *Publics and Counterpublics* (New York, Zone Books, 2005).

[94] See, generally, J Marsh, *Word Crimes: Blasphemy, Culture, and Literature in Nineteenth-Century England* (Chicago, University of Chicago Press, 1998).

discourse is liable to gain significant traction in the battle for public opinion. For, as Lord Diplock memorably put it:

> In ordinary life it is rare indeed for people to form their beliefs by a process of logical deduction from facts ascertained by a rigorous search for all available evidence and a judicious assessment of its probative value. In greater or in less degree according to their temperaments, their training, their intelligence, they are swayed by prejudice, rely on intuition instead of reasoning, leap to conclusions on inadequate evidence and fail to recognize the cogency of material which might cast doubt on the validity of the conclusions they reach.[95]

There is, indeed, at least some evidence in *On Liberty* that Mill would not have objected to measures being taken to suppress the intentional dissemination of religious and political falsehood. As indicated above, for Mill, what is wrong about coercing people into silence is that the silenced opinion, 'may, and very commonly does, contain a portion of truth'.[96] He goes on to say:

> When there are persons to be found who form an exception to the apparent unanimity of the world on any subject, even if the world is in the right, it is always probable that dissentients have something worth hearing to say for themselves, and that truth would lose something by their silence.[97]

This point about the importance of having 'something worth hearing' can scarcely be said of those who disseminate known falsehoods, baseless conspiracy theories and the like. So, such uncivilised discourse seems vulnerable, on Mill's account, to suppression at the hands of the state. For, as the Attorney General put it in his address to the jury in the Truelove case, when speaking of the offence of seditious libel, 'the people of England, of whom you form a part, would never tolerate or endure the dissemination of doctrines which ought to be rejected and denounced with disapprobation and disgust by every patriot in every country, and by every honest man throughout the world'.[98] Seemingly preoccupied with the benefits of giving free rein to sceptical intellectualism, Mill fails to acknowledge what Sir James Stephen was later to claim, that the English law of blasphemy and seditious libel had created one (repressive) law for 'the vulgar' and another (politically tolerant) law for 'the sophisticated', and hence violated what Stephen called the 'manly simplicity which ought to be the characteristic of the law'.[99]

The idea of uninhibited civic and discursive freedom as naturally allied to masculinity was later taken up by Parliament, when the predecessor to section 106 of the 1983 Act was enacted in 1895.[100] The increasingly contested and rivalrous

[95] *Horrocks v Lowe* [1975] 1 AC 135, 150.
[96] Mill (n 43) 50.
[97] ibid 46.
[98] *R v Truelove*, 25 June 1858, https://newspapers.library.wales/view/3055061/3055063.
[99] JF Stephen, 'Blasphemy and Blasphemous Libel' (1884) 27 NS *Fortnightly Review* 289, 307; cited by Toohey (n 77) 321, n 21.
[100] See text at n 11.

nature of elections had (as in the case of intense rivalry between religions) led to the widespread use of falsehoods to discredit opponents and their policies.[101] To police such developments came a new distinction, related to the legal distinction between 'reverent' criticism (permissible) and the 'wilful intention to pervert, insult, and mislead others' (impermissible).[102] This was the distinction between falsehoods used to discredit election candidates *politically* (permissible) and falsehoods used to make *personal* attacks on candidates (impermissible). Speaking of the use of election lies about candidates, Sir Frederick Milner, Conservative MP for Bassetlaw, fulminated:

> What right had a candidate, or his agent, to go fishing about and try to take up some rumour about the gentleman who was opposing him? They ought to fight their battles like men, on *purely political* issues, and if they did try to fish up scandals, whether they believed them or not, they ought to receive just retribution.[103]

This new distinction – between personal and political attacks – remains foundational today as part of the election law in many jurisdictions, including the United Kingdom. Its unsatisfactory nature as a basis for criminalisation of false information or claims made about candidates will be explored in the next section. More broadly, though, Mill's failure clearly to address the limits of toleration under conditions of rivalrous (as opposed to mutual respect) pluralism in religion and politics, is a flaw that has continued to characterise English law.

V. The Criminalisation of Political Speech

It may readily be granted that there are rights to be free from intimidation, harassment and hate, and that such is the nature of the threat to freedom posed by wrongdoing of this kind that criminalisation is a necessary and proportionate response.[104] However, those are rights that have no special connection or link to engaging in politics or seeking political office. By way of contrast, as indicated earlier, whatever they may think of 'uncivilised' rabble rousing, the spreading of unfounded conspiracy theories, character assassination (and other forms of counter-public speech), officials and election candidates – whether periodically replaceable or not – have only very limited moral scope to employ state coercion to dictate the terms on which citizens assess their political merits. In declaring unconstitutional a prohibition on the malicious publication of a false statement of material fact about a candidate for public office, the Washington Supreme Court

[101] For a historical examination, see Horder (n 4) ch 3.
[102] See text at n 78.
[103] HC Deb 01 May 1895 vol 33, 227 (emphasis added). He went on to complain of 'unmanly and un-English tactics' (such as revealing a candidate's wealth) now being deployed to discredit rival candidates.
[104] See, further, Horder (n 4) ch 3.

said the statute was unconstitutional because it caused 'the government, rather than the people, [to] be the final arbiter of truth in political debate'.[105] As another US court put it, the state cannot 'substitute its judgment as to how best to speak for that of speakers and listeners; free and robust debate cannot thrive if directed by the government'.[106] That captures the spirit of republican theories such as that of Pettit, with his emphasis on the right of citizens of the republic to 'walk tall' in speech and deed.[107]

How do these republican ideals fit with the existence of offences specifically concerned with false claims about election candidates? In the United States, some seventeen states have such provisions, and they may be found in many other jurisdictions as well as in the United Kingdom.[108] The criminalisation of the making of such claims is not a minor matter. It has been estimated that in the 2016 US Presidential election, false stories relating to the two candidates were shared at least 38 million times on Facebook, with just over half of Americans who recalled seeing these statements believing them.[109] We saw that, in *Alvarez*, the US Supreme Court cast doubt on the constitutional propriety of criminalising lying, in the absence of a sufficiently substantial aggravating factor connected to the lying such as the occurrence of a legally recognised harm the lie was meant to bring about.[110] It is commonly assumed, in a number of jurisdictions including the United States and the United Kingdom, that where the aim of someone's false statement was the reduction of a candidate's vote share, having such an aim is an aggravating factor sufficient to justify criminalisation.[111] But how consistent is that assumption with a republican emphasis on the need for political toleration of robust, uninhibited and generally uncivilised election-related speech? The problem with regarding the possession of this aim as an aggravating factor in electoral viewpoint fraud is that, in political debate at election time, a very large proportion of election-related political speech – whether or not it involves falsehoods – will be aimed at increasing or reducing a candidate's vote share. Unless it might have that effect, for many people, it would hardly be worth engaging in the relevant speech

[105] *Rickert v Public Disclosure Commission*, 168 P 3d 826, 827 (2007).

[106] *Riley v National Federation of the Blind*, 487 US 781, 791 (1988).

[107] Text at n 60. This claim does not imply that there should be no private law remedy for defamation in appropriate cases, even in political and electoral contexts: see, for example, the Arlene Foster case: https://www.bbc.co.uk/news/uk-northern-ireland-57268308. Even so, there is a strong case for saying that where what officials or election candidates seek is a form or prior restraint (in the form of an injunction), as opposed to damages after the event, it should be necessary to prove that the person who engaged in the defamatory speech knew that it was false. For the requirement to prove knowledge or recklessness, when public figures are defamed, see *New York Times Co v Sullivan*, 376 US 254 (1964). For further discussion of private law rights in this context, see Rowbottom (n 33).

[108] See Lieffring (n 27); Horder (n 4), ch 3.

[109] See H Allcot and M Gentzkow, 'Social Media and Fake News in the 2016 Election' (2017) 31 *Journal of Economic Perspectives* 211.

[110] See text at n 22.

[111] See the helpful discussion in SP Green, 'Lying and the Law' in J Meibauer (ed), *The Oxford Handbook of Lying* (Oxford, Oxford University Press, 2018).

in the first place. So, the mere fact that false political speech has that aim does not really enhance the argument for prohibition, assuming one takes seriously the right provided in Article 10 to engage in (hate-)free political debate.

Moreover, the existence of such criminal prohibitions may cause as many problems as it solves. One problem is that, as is the case in defamation law, such prohibitions provide a way for the powerful and influential to silence or simply punish their (intemperate) critics.[112] Another problem is that these prohibitions have opened up a new means by which election candidates can be tarred by a false accusation that they – the candidates – have themselves lied, thus requiring the candidates to divert attention from their campaign to deal with that issue. As one US court put it:

> Complaints can be filed at a tactically calculated time so as to divert the attention of an entire campaign from the meritorious task at hand of supporting or defeating a ballot question, possibly diffusing public sentiment and requiring the speaker to defend a claim … thus inflicting political damage.[113]

This is not just a hypothetical possibility. In Ohio, where an Election Commission hears cases under its false statement statute, whilst between 2001 and 2010 the Commission upheld 90 complaints, no less than 420 were dismissed, with the biggest single proportion of the failed cases being ones in which no 'probable cause' was found.[114] Ironically, then, it seems likely that election fraud statutes themselves encourage the commission of a species of election fraud, namely the generation of fraudulent (politically motivated) complaints. So, even if it is true that there is a compelling state interest in the public good of honest and truthful debate in politics,[115] it is unclear that statutes criminalising viewpoint fraud do much to promote that interest or to protect the public good.

In the United Kingdom, as in some US states and in other jurisdictions,[116] viewpoint fraud statutes have been restricted to the criminalisation of, in effect, knowingly defamatory statements about candidates in the run-up to elections.[117] However, in the United States, defamation remains a general criminal offence in some fifteen states,[118] and such offences reinforce the chilling effect on speech of more specifically election-focused offences. For example, in 2002, a false claim that a mayor standing for re-election did not live – as required by law – in the county in which they held office was held to be a criminal libel under the Kansas

[112] An example is provided by the facts of *Rickert v Public Disclosure Commission (Rickert I)*, 168 P 3d 826 (Wash 2007), discussed in Horder (n 4) § 1(6)(i), and SA Rodell, 'False Statements v Free Debate: Is the First Amendment a License to Lie in Elections?' (2008) 60 *Florida Law Review* 947.

[113] *281 Care Comm v Arneson*, No 13-1229 (8th Cir Sep 2, 2014) para 25.

[114] ibid para 27.

[115] See eg *281 Care Comm v Arneson*, 638 F 3d 621, 633 (8th Cir 2011).

[116] See eg Canada Elections Act 2000, s 91.

[117] I have already pointed out that UK law (in common with the law in jurisdictions with similar provisions) extends more widely than this. See text following n 11.

[118] EP Robinson, 'Criminal Libel' (2009) www.mtsu.edu/first-amendment/article/941/criminal-libel.

law of criminal defamation.[119] In the United Kingdom, the continued existence of an 'election defamation' offence is more of an anomaly, given the abolition of the broader offence of criminal defamation.[120] Its continued existence must therefore be justified in virtue of the unique combination of defamatory content and the aggravating element[121] – the intent to influence voters – but, as I have already argued, that justification will not suffice in a free speech culture.[122] Moreover, an attempt to narrow the focus of electoral viewpoint fraud offences to frauds consisting of defamatory content involves the law in making arbitrary and politically controversial distinctions.

In the case of *Woolas* (discussed earlier),[123] for example, the Election Court had found that a false claim that a candidate had betrayed a promise to live in the constituency was a claim that related directly to the candidate's *personal* character: 'a person who breaks his promise is untrustworthy'.[124] The Election Court thus found that the false claim fell within the scope of section 106. The difficulty with that argument is that politicians commonly politicise matters of personal trustworthiness and moral integrity, in order to gain electoral advantage. As the US Supreme Court said of this link between the personal and the political, in *Monitor Patriot Co v Roy*:

> A candidate who, for example, seeks to further his cause through the prominent display of his wife and children can hardly argue that his qualities as a husband or father remain of 'purely private' concern.[125]

Similarly, the High Court overturned the part of the Election Court's decision in *Woolas* relating to the 'living in the constituency' claim, on the grounds that the claim related to the candidate's trustworthiness in relation to a *political* position, and thus it fell outside the scope of section 106. The High Court went on to observe that, were such a statement to be held to fall within section 106, that would have a significant inhibiting effect on ordinary political debate.[126] No doubt that is right, but the differing views of the judges in *Woolas* on the point are very understandable. For, as the Supreme Court put it, in *Garrison v Louisiana*:

> Few personal attributes are more germane to fitness for office than dishonesty, malfeasance, or improper motivation, even though these characteristics may also affect the official's private character.[127]

[119] https://ajrarchive.org/Article.asp?id=2606&id=2606.

[120] See text following n 11.

[121] This is the *Alvarez* point about the minimum content of fraud offences, namely that the fraud must have some aggravating element: see text at n 22.

[122] See text at n 112. See, further, Horder (n 4) ch 3.

[123] See text at n 11.

[124] *Watkins v Woolas* [2010] EWHC 2702 (QB), [109].

[125] *Monitor Patriot Co v Roy*, 401 US 265, 275 (1971) (Stuart J).

[126] *R (on the application of Woolas) v The Parliamentary Election Court* [2010] EWHC 3169 (Admin) [117].

[127] *Garrison v Louisiana* 379 US 64, 76–77 (1964).

This illustrates the difficulty of asking the courts to become involved in adjudicating such claims, as a matter of the application of the criminal law. As I have already indicated, an election outcome tainted by fraud can be overturned as a matter of public law.[128] Any candidate also has the right to seek a private law remedy for defamation, or to seek the removal of defamatory content from an internet platform.[129] In short, the case for the continued criminalisation of electoral viewpoint fraud is weak.

VI. Conclusion

It is worth starting a conclusion with the ringing endorsement in *Alvarez* of (republican) freedom to speak, an endorsement that echoes the 'more speech' solution to political falsehoods and half-truth advocated by Brandeis J in *Whitney v California*.[130] The *Alvarez* Court said:

> The remedy for speech that is false is speech that is true. This is the ordinary course in a free society. The response to the unreasoned is the rational; to the uniformed, the enlightened; to the straight-out lie, the simple truth. … Freedom of speech and thought flows not from the beneficence of the state but from the inalienable rights of the person. And suppression of speech by the government can make exposure of falsity more difficult, not less so. Society has the right and civic duty to engage in open, dynamic, rational discourse. These ends are not well served when the government seeks to orchestrate public discussion through content-based mandates.[131]

An important question these sentiments raise is whether, if a state decriminalises false political viewpoint claims made with a view to influencing voters, it is in some sense abdicating an important responsibility to discourage lying and misleading in politics. Some might argue that the state has no such responsibility, but that argument takes an unduly narrow view of the state's role in relation to the promotion of important public goods. To begin with, there may be special public contexts in which the obligation to be truthful and honest, in relation to viewpoint politics, takes precedence over freedom of speech. So, for example, someone commits a contempt of Parliament when

> deliberately attempting to mislead the House or a committee (by way of statement, evidence, or petition);
>
> - deliberately publishing a false or misleading report of the proceedings of a House or a committee.[132]

[128] See text at n 35.
[129] See generally Defamation Act 2013; Defamation (Operation of Websites) Regulations 2013.
[130] See text at n 15.
[131] *United States v Alvarez*, 132 S Ct 2537, 2550 (2012).
[132] https://publications.parliament.uk/pa/jt199899/jtselect/jtpriv/43/4310.htm.

Similarly, under the Ministerial Code:

> It is of paramount importance that Ministers give accurate and truthful information to Parliament, correcting any inadvertent error at the earliest opportunity. Ministers who knowingly mislead Parliament will be expected to offer their resignation to the Prime Minister.[133]

Continued membership of political organisations can also be made to depend on the observance of truthfulness.[134] More broadly, those who persistently lie about certain issues on social media platforms may find their access to those platforms restricted.[135] Further, beyond the use of (softly) coercive measures, agreements to voluntary codes of conduct for political campaigning, which include commitments to truthfulness and honesty, are something that the state, and social media platforms, are fully entitled to promote.[136]

No one – and certainly not any individual government – has privileged insight into political 'truths',[137] which is an important reason for state toleration of political (or religious) viewpoint untruths. However, that proposition is not inconsistent with defending the legitimacy of official campaigns to encourage people to engage critically with the evidential basis for political argument and judgement.[138] The non-coercive promotion of engagement by citizens with evidence, and with competing argument and perspectives,[139] is arguably one of the most important challenges facing liberal-democratic states in their attempts to create a flourishing and vibrant political environment.[140]

[133] Cabinet Office, *Ministerial Code* (2019) para 1.3(c); but see A Tomkins, 'A Right to Mislead Parliament?' (1996) 16 *LS* 63.

[134] For example, see Conservative Party, 'Code of Conduct for Conservative Party Representatives' (July 2021) www.conservatives.com/code-of-conduct, 6 ('Honesty: – Holders of public office should be truthful').

[135] www.facebook.com/formedia/blog/working-to-stop-misinformation-and-false-news (last accessed 17 March 2022).

[136] P Butcher and J Greubel, 'Towards a European Code of Conduct for Ethical Campaigning' (Brussels, European Policy Centre, 2021), http://aei.pitt.edu/103725/1/PRO-RES_PB.pdf.

[137] 'Any purely governmental response [along such lines] … is bound to be regarded as biased and propagandist': J-BJ Vilmer at al, *Information Manipulation: A Challenge for Our Democracies* (2018) www.diplomatie.gouv.fr/IMG/pdf/information_manipulation_rvb_cle838736.pdf.

[138] See, in the context of a discussion of the duties of internet platforms, Horder (n 4) ch 2.

[139] For example, by encouraging the practice of attaching warnings to unreliable online content, together with links to content involving alternative perspectives. See Horder, ibid.

[140] See, generally, Vilmer (n 138) 170.

6

Where Is the Harm in Theft?

JOHN STANTON-IFE

> They know they can tell a lie, as every day millions of people do, and the heavens will not fall; if the heavens were going to fall, they would have fallen already.[1]

I. Introduction

There is no doubt that theft can cause harm. *Bicycle Thieves* (1948),[2] a classic of Italian neorealist cinema, depicts the havoc a single act of theft can leave in its wake. The story is fictional but rings true. The central character, Antonio, has his bicycle stolen by a thief whose name, we later learn, is Alfredo. He exhausts himself searching the streets of Rome in a vain attempt to retrieve it, eventually resorting to stealing a bicycle himself. Poverty is rife in the aftermath of the Second World War, jobs are scarce and, without a means of traversing the city quickly, nigh on impossible to hold on to. The film is about two thefts: a first theft, by Alfredo, its effect on Antonio and his family, and the reactive attitudes of the Roman population to it, culminating eventually in the second theft – that by Antonio himself. In his fine study of the film, Robert Gordon observes that the bicycle is not only Antonio's means of supporting himself, his wife (Maria) and son (Bruno):

> Antonio's bike is a guarantee of autonomy, of the freedom to move around the city, to commute to a place of work, not to be thrust in the maelstrom of the bus queue or to be stuck out on the periphery.[3]

And Gordon continues:

> The economics are flagged up more than once simply in hard-cash calculations: Antonio has pawned the bike to pay for food before the film begins; and now Maria sacrifices their bedlinen (for 7500 lire: the clerk counts out the notes) to redeem the bike (for 6100

[1] B Williams, *Truth and Truthfulness* (Princeton, NJ, Princeton University Press, 2002) 85.
[2] V De Sica (dir), *Ladri di Biciclette* (*Bicycle Thieves*) (Produzioni De Sica SA, 1948).
[3] R Gordon, *Bicycle Thieves* (London, British Film Institute, 2008) 43.

lire, including one month's interest at 20 per cent) and let Antonio re-enter the world of labour.[4]

> The first arc of the film … moves through a 'comic', upward trajectory of romance and resolution, a narrative of Antonio's reintegration into the institutions of family and work. A problem is posed by a new situation (a job, but no bike) and is overcome at a cost (pawning the sheets) that draws husband and wife together, leading to happiness (Antonio and Maria together in the city, on their bike or laughing and playful), family unity (Bruno admiring the bike and his father) and integration (Antonio part of a happy army of municipal workers). The theft shatters the romance, and revealed that opening mini-narrative as illusory, ironic, casting the scale of the problem onto a new level.[5]

'Harm', as Joel Feinberg understands it,[6] is a 'setback to interests' and, as Joseph Raz understands it, a setback to autonomy[7] (or prospect-harm, as John Gardner glosses it[8]). On either view, Antonio and his family are harmed by the theft. His and their interests are set back by the theft, as is Antonio's autonomy, his ability (as Raz would have it) to choose between an adequate range of valuable options.

As well as representing the deleterious consequences of theft for the victim (ie the *harm*), *Bicycle Thieves* also focuses on the *wrongfulness* of the perpetrator's conduct, and more widely on the belief within the society that theft is wrong and the stigma in being thought a thief. Although there are formidable problems of proof and evidence on display in establishing that property was in fact stolen – and hence in involving the law – there is a universal belief among the Roman population encountered in the film that theft is morally wrong, something to be resented by all, not just the victim in a given instance. Yet Antonio, for so long the victim, turns perpetrator in the last part of the film. In Gordon's words:

> If we jump forward to the final sequence of the film, we find a narrative of the Fall, of transgression and exile: the collapse of the search, the collapse of Antonio's moral compass ('Thou shalt not steal') and dignity, in the face of his son, a mirror of his innocent self and hope. This fall is also [a] collapse of distinction. … He is now no different from Alfredo (both thieves: hence, we now learn, the plural *Thieves* of the title) any bicycle (the plural *biciclette* of the title, not rendered in the English) is now the object of his desperate grabbing, not *his* bicycle, his intimate property.[9]

The law does not take centre stage in the film, even if there are episodes involving the police. It does not develop into a courtroom or a prison cell drama. Neither culprit is arrested. Despite his discovery that it was Alfredo who stole his bicycle,

[4] ibid 45.
[5] ibid 47.
[6] J Feinberg, *Harm to Others* (New York, Oxford University Press, 1984).
[7] J Raz *The Morality of Freedom* (Oxford, Oxford University Press, 1986).
[8] J Gardner, *Offences and Defences* (Oxford, Oxford University Press, 2007).
[9] Gordon (n 3) 47–48.

Antonio can prove nothing. Since he chased (and lost) Alfredo in the immediate aftermath of the theft, he had garnered no witnesses. Alfredo's neighbours also use other means to fend Antonio off, for example the counter-accusation that Antonio is defaming Alfredo's name. And as for the immediate aftermath of theft number two, as Antonio furiously pedals away on the bike he has grabbed, the theft only culminates in his humiliating apprehension by a chasing group, including the owner of the bicycle. He avoids arrest, however, when the owner decides not to involve the police. Taking pity on Antonio, he is moved by the arrival of Antonio's crestfallen little son Bruno and settles for no more than the repossession of his bike. This was an act of mercy that did not meet with the approval of the passers-by who had helped Antonio's victim catch Antonio. Their resentment of Antonio was of a piece with Antonio's own resentment of Alfredo. As is true of numerous thefts the world over, the crimes perpetrated in *Bicycle Thieves* are not processed, let alone resolved, by the relevant criminal justice system, a point we will touch upon again.

One interesting facet of the reaction of ordinary Romans to thefts, as depicted in the film, is their sympathy for and ready willingness to aid strangers if perceived to be victims; and, by contrast, their antipathy and resentment towards presumptive thieves, even when not themselves the victims. It seems to me that this attitude, perhaps with some minor differences in degree, remains common in modern society. Antonio is brought down by the righteous indignation of the pursuing crowd who know nothing of his own status as a victim, of the harm he had suffered, or of the tortured journey he had just endured. Such considerations appear irrelevant to the question of his wrongdoing, as is the virtue or vice (as the case may be) of his own victim. Although his victim turns out to be a decent sort, given his kindness to Antonio and his little son, none of that would have been known to those who came to his aid or would even have mattered on the assumption that the property was *his*. Jeremy Waldron has coined the term 'normative resilience' to characterise an aspect of popular attitudes of ordinary people in modern societies to property.[10] At its most simple, the 'normative resilience' of property is constituted by its relative insensitivity to the ultimate justifiability of a society's system of property. Even if the system of property rights that holds sway is at bottom unjust, it is yet perceived to be *dishonest* to steal items of such property and *honest* to refrain from doing so. Judgements of the order, 'Y is a thief' or 'Object O belongs to X' are 'normatively resilient', Waldron explains, to the question whether 'private property is morally justified.' To elucidate the idea of normative resilience, Waldron contrasts other kinds of judgement that are *not* normatively resilient, such as 'Y is a heretic'. Imputations of heresy, says Waldron, will not be levelled by someone who has come to reject judgments of the order 'C is the true religion.' As such, imputations of the latter kind are not normatively resilient, since whether or not they are

[10] J Waldron, 'The Normative Resilience of Property' (1998) 9 *Otago Law Review* 195, 198.

asserted is far more sensitive to the question of ultimate justifiability.[11] Waldron explains his concern thus:

> I want to ask about the relation between existing patterns of property-holdings and the virtues and sentiments that property rights often involve: the sentiment of belonging, the condemnation of theft and trespass, the vice of dishonesty, as well as the general sense of mine and thine. These are undoubtedly moral sentiments, and they involve powerful thoughts about right and wrong; but it is intriguing that even when the overall morality of some existing set of property rights is called in question, these sentiments tend to associate themselves with the status quo rather than with the moral basis on which the status quo is being criticised.[12]

Thus far, I have made a few scattered remarks about theft based on its depiction in *Bicycle Thieves*, highlighting both the harm theft can do and its moral wrongfulness – as well as the strong perception of such wrongfulness among ordinary people. Such perception is part constituted, Waldron plausibly argues, by a measure of 'normative resilience.'

II. Why Is Theft Legitimately Criminalised?

My topic in what follows very much concerns the law, more specifically the *crime* of theft and its moral legitimacy. (Where the law of any jurisdiction is mentioned it will be England and Wales unless otherwise stated.) The question of the legitimacy of the law is here the question of what, if anything, can justify two aspects of a crime such as theft. First, what justifies the public blaming of a defendant by means of a criminal conviction given its meaning, stigma and other consequences? Secondly, what justifies the punishment of those convicted, including sometimes their imprisonment? These forms of hard treatment stand in need of justification. A criminal conviction brings a stigma, a criminal record, as well as sundry other potential consequences.[13] So far as imprisonment is concerned, there are 'material' and 'symbolic' dimensions of incarceration. The latter include the messages imprisonment communicates both to inmates themselves and to the public about those inmates.[14] The material dimensions include restrictions on freedom of movement; low levels of comfort and amenity; idleness (especially, a paucity of opportunities for labour); relative isolation from family members, friends and the larger community; as well as significant diminution of autonomy, especially insofar as prisons subject their inhabitants to a degree of bureaucratic control which

[11] ibid 201–02.

[12] ibid 196–97.

[13] Z Hoskins, *Beyond Punishment: A Normative Account of the Collateral Consequences of Conviction* (Oxford, Oxford University Press, 2019).

[14] R Lippke, 'No Easy Way Out: Dangerous Offenders and Preventive Detention' (2008) 27 *Law and Philosophy* 383, 408.

might be categorised as the 'subservience of youth'; and diminishment of privacy.[15] Beyond imprisonment, other criminal sanctions, fines and community penalties are also potentially highly burdensome.[16]

To say that the consequences of a theft conviction are often severe and that they require justification is not to say anything controversial. The justification, it might be said, is not far away. Often, it will be readily to hand in the two sorts of consideration stressed above: either the harm of theft or the wrong of theft. Do not states criminalise theft to prevent or respond to harm or wrongdoing? Indeed, they do, but my question is, *which is it*? Is theft legitimately criminalised because it is *harmful* or because it is *wrongful*? Now, even before this question gets off the ground, I imagine an immediate challenge may be made querying whether the question is well posed. Why *either* harm *or* wrong? Why not *both*? Why not say theft is criminalised both because it is harmful *and* wrongful? Indeed. I agree that on certain assumptions the answer is going to be, both. There is something to this challenge and I should thus explain the sense in which I am asking the either-or question.

What is at stake here is the debate between proponents of some version of 'the harm principle' and some of their opponents. Although there are a number of possible formulations of 'the harm principle' the best known remains John Stuart Mill's canonical formulation from *On Liberty*: 'the only purpose for which power can be rightfully exercised over any member of a civilized community, against his will, is to prevent harm to others'.[17] On this formulation, moral grounds (other than harm prevention itself) should be excluded as justifications for criminalisation. Alternatively, one might support the harm principle in a less strong form. One might allow that moral grounds other than harm itself may be valid grounds for criminalisation, but only if harm prevention is also involved. Either way, harm prevention is indispensable to the legitimacy of criminalisation. It is a sine qua non: no harm in the offing, no legitimate criminalisation. Let us call somebody who holds such a view a *harm-essentialist*. By contrast, harm-*non*-essentialists claim that there *can* be legitimate moral grounds, beyond those based on harm, for legitimate criminalisation; and deny that such grounds necessarily require support from harm-based considerations. Theft might be legitimately criminalised because, say, it is conduct manifesting the vice of dishonesty,[18] or because it wrongfully interferes with the 'sovereignty' of others.[19]

[15] ibid 408; cp Richard Lippke, *Rethinking Imprisonment* (Oxford, Oxford University Press, 2007).

[16] Sentencing Council, *Theft Act, Sentencing Guidelines* (2023) www.sentencingcouncil.org.uk/.

[17] JS Mill, *On Liberty* (London, Parker & Son, 1859); reprinted in JS Mill, *Utilitarianism, On Liberty and Considerations on Representative Government* (London, Dent, 1993).

[18] cp RA Duff, 'Virtue, Vice, and Criminal Liability: Do We Want an Aristotelian Criminal Law?' (2002) 6 *Buffalo Criminal Law Review* 147 on this argument and its limitations. See also R Hursthouse, *On Virtue Ethics* (Oxford, Oxford University Press, 1999). I am grateful to Andrew Simester for suggesting the 'harm essentialist' versus 'non-essentialist' terminology adopted in the text, in place of my original more clunky 'harm principlist' versus 'anti-harm principlist' distinction.

[19] A Ripstein, 'Beyond the Harm Principle' (2006) 34 *Philosophy and Public Affairs* 214, 231.

It is not that proponents of the harm principle need to, or are likely to, deny that there is *some* place for wrongdoing in legitimate criminalisation. They insist rather on the indispensability of harm. In the specific context of the criminal law, the most thoroughgoing defender of the harm principle, Joel Feinberg, argues that the focus should be 'on the subclass' of harmed conditions that 'are wrongs'. He identifies two notions of harm, a non-normative sense and a normative sense. In the first non-normative sense, harm is 'a setback to interests', as we noted earlier. If the windows in my front room are smashed, that sets back my interest. We can say I am harmed in this first sense without knowing anything about what caused the windows to be smashed. There could be a variety of causally contributory factors: my window smashed because somebody who wished me ill deliberately broke it; or because extreme weather conditions caused a tree to crash into it; and so on. Feinberg takes the second sense of harm, by contrast, to be normative, understanding it as pertaining specifically to wrongful human actions. In this second sense, I am harmed by the breaking of my window where it was the deliberate act of a person wishing me ill, but not when it was a natural event, since the natural event is not wrongful. In order to adjudge me harmed by the breaking of my window in this second sense we need to know therefore what caused the break. For harm-essentialists of this stripe, it is only harms that are also wrongs that are of concern here.

On the other hand, a harm-non-essentialist may be quite content to accept that conduct can be wrongful *because* harmful and thus harm may very well enter into their own story. To agree that wrongs *can* be wrongs because harmful is not to agree that wrongs *must* be harmful: they could be wrongful for some other reason. Again, the bone of contention between harm-essentialists and their opponents is essentially the *indispensability* or otherwise of harm. Rather than ask, curtly, 'is theft legitimately criminalized because it is wrongful or because it is harmful?', the fuller and more accurate question would be: 'is theft legitimately criminalized because it is wrongful – be that wrongful because harmful or for some other reason – *or* because it is harmful – from that subset of harms that are also wrongs?' In what follows I shall, however, use the shorter question as shorthand. I will mainly examine the harm-essentialist account offered by Andrew Simester and Bob Sullivan.[20] Theft, they argue, has a nature and rationale, and one essential part of the rationale is that it satisfies 'the demands of the Harm Principle'.[21] The crucial harm in play is 'harm to the proprietary regime as a whole'. A similar

[20] AP Simester and GR Sullivan, 'On the Nature and Rationale of Property Offences' in RA Duff and Stuart P Green (eds), *Defining Crimes: Essays on the Special Part of the Criminal Law* (Oxford, Oxford University Press, 2005) 168. Among numerous discussions, see AD Steel, 'The Harms and Wrongs of Stealing: The Harm Principle and Dishonesty in Theft' (2008) 31 *University of New South Wales Law Journal* 712; S Green, 'Theft and Conversion – Tangibly Different?' (2012) 128 *LQR* 564; SP Green, *Thirteen Ways to Steal a Bicycle: Theft Law in the Information Age* (Cambridge, MA, Harvard University Press, 2012).

[21] Simester and Sullivan (n 20) 169.

harm-essentialist argument has also been made by John Gardner,[22] which I shall touch upon below; but, since it is much less fully worked out than that of Simester and Sullivan, I shall concentrate on the case they build. I leave for now an altogether different harm-essentialist response: that of Joel Feinberg. Nowhere in his justly renowned four-volume defence of the harm principle in the context of the criminal law does Feinberg dedicate a specific section to the crime of theft. But there are numerous scattered remarks from which one can piece his view on theft together. That is for another occasion.[23]

III. Simester and Sullivan on the Harm in Theft

Posing any question about the legitimation of theft is complicated by the fact that there is no one definition of theft in force globally or accepted by lawyers or commentators. The law of England and Wales has it that:

> A person is guilty of theft if he dishonestly appropriates property belonging to another with the intention of permanently depriving the other of it.[24]

On the face of it, given the understanding of dishonesty as that which is dishonest by the standards of 'ordinary, decent people',[25] coupled with the fact that a conviction for theft requires no evidence of any harm caused, the rationale of the England and Wales theft offence looks on its face to be harm-non-essentialist – in terms of the manifestation in property-related conduct of the vice of dishonesty. However, one should not assume without argument that a factor such as harm needs explicitly to be a required element in an offence for it to operate as the rationale or an essential part of the rationale of the offence. In any case, Simester and Sullivan do not assume the specific law of England and Wales in presenting their harm-essentialist defence of the legitimacy of theft. Far from it. The authors consider that extant law is not in good shape. In the authors' view, theft true to 'its nature' is constituted by:

> A misappropriation of property belonging to another–as exclusively determined by the civil law – without claim of right on the part of the defendant, and with the intention, on the part of the defendant, of keeping or disposing of the property in question.[26]

This is not the law of England and Wales, the two most obvious differences being the absence of a dishonesty requirement and the substitution of 'misappropriation' for the neutral 'appropriation' in the England and Wales position. It is, however,

[22] Gardner (n 8).
[23] Feinberg (n 6); *Offense to Others* (1985); *Harm to Self* (1986); *Harmless Wrongdoing* (1990), all Oxford, Oxford University Press.
[24] Theft Act 1968, s 1.
[25] *Ivey v Genting Casinos* [2017] UKSC 67; *Barton* [2020] EWCA Crim 575.
[26] Simester and Sullivan (n 20).

the understanding of theft that the authors have in mind while presenting their harm-essentialist argument. The authors' defence of the harm principle in relation to theft has some complexity and requires explanation. Their answer to the question 'where is the harm in theft?' is, I suggest, best taken in three stages. At the first stage, the authors offer a definition of the harm of theft which, as we will see, is puzzling on initial reading since it does not appear to have any necessary link to harm at all. However, this is addressed at the second stage, in which they explain what they take the link between their definition and harm to be. Finally, at the third stage more is said about what they take the nature of the relevant harm to be, about its ultimately indirect rather than direct nature.

Begin, then, with step one. The authors early in their presentation and, at various points thereafter, appear to endorse either the Feinbergian understanding of harm as setback to interest or the Razian understanding as setback to autonomy that I mentioned in section I.[27] When these two understandings were touched on earlier I made no effort to adjudicate which was the more plausible understanding of harm. The authors likewise appear to assume both or either for their purposes without choosing between them. It comes initially as a surprise, then, that when they arrive at their specific definition of the harm of theft, it is not in terms of setbacks to interests or autonomy. It is rather, they say, the 'unauthorised appropriation' of property.[28] We will come to this in a moment. First, though, a word about the relation between harm and wrongfulness as understood by the authors.

Like Feinberg, what for the authors is required is a harm that is also a wrong. 'Within the framework of theft', they say, '*harm* (both to V and the proprietary regime) is constituted by the unauthorized appropriation of V's property',[29] also formulated as 'the misappropriation of a person's property';[30] while the *wrong* of theft 'is to take property without claim of right to it and intending to keep or dispose of it'.[31] Hence, they do not see the wrong of theft in terms of two of the possibilities a harm-non-essentialist might adopt. That is, they do not take the wrong of theft, first, in virtue-ethical terms – ie to be the manifestation in relation to property of the vice of dishonesty. Indeed, as noted, they believe dishonesty qua the standards of ordinary decent people should be dispensed with by the theft law of England and Wales. They also do not take the broadly Kantian line of seeing the wrong of theft as the wrongful interference with the sovereignty of victims, a denial of equal freedom.[32] They understand the wrong of theft to lie in the misappropriation of the property of others while intending to keep or discard it and in the absence of

[27] ibid, eg 169–72, 175.
[28] ibid 177.
[29] ibid.
[30] ibid, 179.
[31] ibid.
[32] Ripstein 'Beyond the Harm Principle' (n 19).

certain beliefs summarised by the term 'claim of right'. 'Claim of right' could be a belief on the part of the defendant that 'he has in law the right to deprive the other', or a belief that 'he would have the other's consent if the other knew of the appropriation and the circumstances of it', or a belief in certain circumstances that 'the person to whom the property belongs cannot be discovered by taking reasonable steps'.[33] The authors would allow an acquittal on a charge of theft based on claim of right, and on this point their preferred formulation of theft *is* in harmony with the position in England and Wales. None of these negations of liability, the authors point out, involves any challenge to 'the overarching societal distribution of property rights':

> All these negations fit snugly with the legal proprietary framework: the property was lost, or thought by D to be his own, or taken with V's assumed consent.[34]

'Those who steal', they conclude, 'attack the practices of creating and exchanging property rights.'[35] Hence, if it can be established that D has a 'claim of right', it cannot be said that D is attacking the practice of creating and exchanging property rights, even if he is in fact taking without authorisation what is not his, with intent to keep or dispose of it.

Their understanding of harm as unauthorised appropriation is initially puzzling; it is not on the face of it about harm at all, if harm is understood in either of the senses identified earlier, the Feinbergian setback to interests or the Razian setback to autonomy. Certainly, *many* such appropriations will cause harm (as in Antonio's case in *Bicycle Thieves*) but there will also surely be numerous cases where there is *no* such harm. Take a simple case of Ben Bradley's (from another context):

> *Bill Gates:*
> [S]uppose you steal $100 from Bill Gates's wallet while he isn't looking. He has so much money that he never notices. He is no worse off for not having that money, but you have still violated his rights.[36]

One might readily agree with Bradley that Bill Gates's rights have been violated; one might also take the view that the conduct is rightly criminalised as theft for that or some connected reason (it violates the sovereignty principle or it is dishonest by the standards of ordinary, decent people, etc). What seems on the face of it entirely absent, however, is any harm – there is no non-trivial setback to Bill Gates's interests or to his autonomy. However, on the Simester and Sullivan unauthorised appropriation definition, this *is* harmful to Bill Gates since the definition renders the conduct harmful by stipulation. 'Harm, including harm to V', would be *constituted* by the unauthorised appropriation of the $100 from him. Since harming *just*

[33] Theft Act 1968, s 2(1).
[34] Simester and Sullivan (n 20) 176.
[35] ibid 172.
[36] B Bradley, *Wellbeing* (Cambridge, Polity Press, 2015) 96.

is unauthorised appropriation, Bill Gates is harmed. Indeed, the authors explicitly accept that one can be harmed according to their proposal 'only formally'.[37]

So, an initial worry is that this formal move, insensitive as it is to any actual harm caused in the original sense, is an uninformative tautology that gets us nowhere. Yes, one might say, unauthorised appropriations will often do harm, as in Antonio's case, but especially in modern, highly unequal societies, they will also often be harmless or involve no more than de minimis harm on any understanding of harm in Feinbergian or Razian terms. The point generalises well beyond someone as enormously wealthy as Bill Gates. Roughly the wealthiest 10 percent of people in countries such as France, Germany, Britain and Italy own around 60 percent of national wealth, while half the population, the bottom half, owns less than 10 percent and generally less than 5 percent.[38] The figures are still more stark when one considers the share of a smaller subset at the top of the top 10 percent.[39] On the most recent available figures for the UK 'the best-off 0.1% were receiving 70 times the national average income each year; the best-off 1%, 16 times; and the best-off 10% of people, four times'. And these last figures do not fully take account of the effect on inequality of inherited wealth.[40] Of course, there are factors other than monetary value that are pertinent to the question of how significant personal property is to its owner, not least questions of sentimental value. However, it remains an obvious implication that the value to the owner of a sum of money or of an object readily replaceable at some price is going to vary enormously according to the wealth of its owner. It is not that one cannot set back the interests or autonomy of those in the very wealthiest financial brackets by stealing from them, but the amount stolen generally needs to be much more, relative to people in the poorest brackets. Even if one accepts that *any* unauthorised appropriation from *any* victim, rich or poor, is wrongful (and even that it should be criminal subject to emergency cases, the defence of necessity, etc), it is another matter altogether to suggest they are also uniformly harmful. We will refer to the problem that in modern societies some thefts are directly harmful, while some thefts are not as the 'subset problem'. As we will see, Simester and Sullivan directly address a version of this issue with a couple of imaginative examples that we will come to.[41]

For now, we should note that they are aware that their definition of the harm in theft might invite objections, of 'circularity', as they put it. As stated above, their argument comes in three stages and only one has been mentioned so far. So we must proceed to the other two before being in any position to assess the argument as a whole. It is with step two of the authors' account of harm that they make the

[37] Simester and Sullivan (n 20) 175.

[38] T Picketty, *Capital in the Twenty-First Century* (Cambridge MA, Harvard University Press, 2017) 321–22.

[39] D Dorling, *Inequality and the 1%*, 3rd edn (London, Verso, 2019).

[40] D Dorling, 'Are Things About to Get Better?' *Prospect Magazine* May 2023, 38.

[41] 'Forgotten Garment' and 'Immolator': section IV below.

crucial move. The key harm in play, they argue, is harm to the *regime* of property rights. Theft can be justifiably criminal in accordance with the harm principle where it prevents harm to a 'public good', the public good that is 'the proprietary regime' of property rights as defined by the civil law.[42] The harm to be prevented is harm to the property-rights system as a whole. As the authors see it, cases such as *Bill Gates* that lack direct harm to the victim nonetheless threaten harm to the regime of property rights, just as direct-harm cases such as Antonio's do.

This harm to the regime of property rights, as they see it, appears to be an 'imagined otherwise', to borrow George Eliot's term, albeit a dystopic one rather than Eliot's 'practical heaven'.[43] We are to imagine an otherwise in which 'the institution' is 'lost':

> [I]n the circumstances of the particular jurisdiction under discussion, the law of property facilitates the creation of forms of welfare and human flourishing that would become unattainable should that institution be lost. Where this is so, the Harm Principle is brought into play by the property regime itself. The regime itself serves our well-being; it provides a reliable means by which we can pursue a good life, through the voluntary acquisition, use, and exchange of resources. Having such a system may promote our well-being even if the particular form of the regime is imperfect, provided the community as a whole benefits by having a predictable, reliable, set of rules with which to organise their lives. Assuming minimum standards of just distribution of property, the proprietary regime is a public good.[44]

The law of theft is thus justified lest the system of property rights is 'lost' or becomes 'ineffective':

> By prohibiting crimes such as theft, the criminal law both protects individuals from any particular loss they may suffer and safeguards the regime of property law more generally. Those who steal attack the practices of creating and exchanging property rights.[45]

So, the crucial harm at stake is a counterfactual harm, an imagined otherwise, a state of affairs where the system of property rights is lost or, as the authors also put it, has become ineffective. The law of theft serves to prevent this.

The final and perhaps simplest step of the authors' argument ties the account back to the original (Feinbergian and Razian) senses of harm discussed above:

> Absent state intervention, however, the regime would be ineffective, and its ineffectiveness would result in lost opportunities for personal and social advancement through reliable coordinated economic activity, and for other forms of welfare and personal realisation that only the peaceful ownership and possession of property can deliver. Preventing that community-wide harm justifies state intervention to enforce the institution of property.[46]

[42] Simester and Sullivan (n 20) 171.
[43] G Eliot, *Middlemarch* [1871–72] (London, Collins Classics, 2021) ch 47.
[44] Simester and Sullivan (n 20) 171.
[45] ibid 172.
[46] ibid 171.

Broadly speaking, the considerations at play thus link the harm qua unauthorised appropriation with the Feinbergian and Razian notions of harm as setback to interests and setback to autonomy mentioned above. The authors also point to 'the community-wide' nature of the loss of opportunity and notions. This seems significant given that a large part of the point of the harm principle is to account for the legitimacy of convicting and punishing (including incarcerating) those found guilty of theft. Crucial here seems to be the spread of the potential harm, the systemic nature of it. This move, it might well be thought, puts the authors in a position to fend off one common line of attack against harm-principle accounts in general. Take John Gray, for example:

> It is true that, in forbidding restraint of liberty save when harm to others is at issue, Mill's Principle of Liberty rules out any number of illiberal limits on liberty such as are demanded by paternalist and moralist considerations. It rules these out because, unless and until harm to others is at issue, no other consideration – and, in particular, no utilitarian consideration – can even count as a good reason in favour of restraint of liberty. The problem is that, once the trip-wire set by the Principle of Liberty has been crossed, even trivial harms to others, could sanction substantial restraints of liberty. The protection afforded the priority of liberty by Mill's principle, though apparently stringent, is for this reason in reality slight.[47]

The allegation is that the harm principle is in the end a feeble constraint. Provided one can identify *some* harm to *some* small number of people, the 'trip-wire' is 'set' and the criminal law can limit the liberty of millions. Now one possible response among harm-essentialists to this kind of objection is to posit a proportionality constraint on the harm principle. The harm principle, 'perhaps', says John Gardner, 'adds that the law should not restrict or punish harmful activities in ways which are disproportionate to the harm'.[48] Whether or not, and if so in what form, harm-essentialists should adopt such a proportionality constraint is not something we need to settle for present purposes. But should arguments such as Gray's (above) be pressed against the authors, it would seem they have a reply by means of the expansive scope ('community wide') of the harm they have in mind.

There we have it. According to the authors, the harm in theft that ultimately justifies its criminalisation is regime harm, harm to the property rights regime as a whole; such harm, they claim, is at stake in *all* unauthorised appropriations short of emergency/necessity, not merely those that directly set back the interests or autonomy of victims. This gives an answer to the subset problem. Even if only a subset of thefts are *directly* harmful in the Razian or Feinbergian senses, all are harmful in the 'regime-harm' sense and, ultimately, that means that their criminalisation in an *indirect* sense is underwritten by harm in the Razian or Feinbergian sense.

[47] J Gray, *Mill on Liberty: A Defence*, 2nd edn (London, Routledge, 1996) 136–37.

[48] Gardner (n 8) 45; cp Raz, *Morality of Freedom* (n 7) and James Edwards, 'Harm Principles' (2015) 20 *Legal Theory* 253.

Hence, to get to this position they use 'harm' in two different ways, harm qua unauthorised appropriation and harm qua (community-wide) setback to interests or autonomy. The authors' understanding of the harm of theft qua unauthorised appropriation does not differentiate the harm to Antonio in *Bicycle Thieves* from the harm to Bill Gates. It is true that the authors do say that their argument 'accepts that violation of a property right may harm the victim directly',[49] as it plainly does in Antonio's case and does not in Bill Gates's case. However, this harm, they emphasise, is '*parasitic*'; it 'provides a justification for intervention only once it is accepted that the institution of property should be defended by the state'.[50] If the authors' main argument – their 'host' argument so to speak – does not go through, then neither will the parasitic one based on direct harms to victims such as Antonio. The parasite will die with the host. The authors' harm-essentialist argument does not, then, proceed by assembling the rock-solid cases of direct harming of a kind with Antonio's and then proceed to an account of harder cases. Antonio's case is relevant in the same way as Bill Gates's: both share the feature of unauthorised appropriation. The direct harms of cases such as Antonio's are not of independent force, merely a buttressing force 'parasitic' on the regime harm of the unauthorised appropriation.

IV. The Crime of Theft and Regime Harm

We need to know how the argument just sketched is to work. Unauthorised appropriations, whether or not directly harmful, are harmful in the regime-harm sense, hence the criminal law may intervene in the shape of the crime of theft to protect the property rights regime. Thus, the demands of the harm principle are satisfied. Such is the argument. The *Bill Gates* example we looked at above is not one considered by the authors. They do, however, devise a couple of imaginative cases designed to be hard cases for their own position. *Bill Gates* concerned an unauthorised appropriation that did not appear to do any harm. Their examples, which we will now look at, incorporate that feature, with the added twist that the defendant seriously needs the property for herself or for someone else. Their aim is to show that there is harm to V in these cases, despite initial impressions to the contrary, and thereby to show how the wider argument works. I will give the examples the labels, *Forgotten Garment* and *Immolator.*

> *Forgotten Garment:*[51]
> D misappropriates a garment from V. The garment is worthless, it is of no use to V; in fact, V normally throws out his old clothing and has forgotten its existence. 'Its misappropriation … affects [V] not at all.' On the other hand, D is

[49] Simester and Sullivan (n 20) 172.
[50] ibid (emphasis added).
[51] ibid 170.

destitute and in great need of clothing. D later discovers the loss and selfishly recovers the garment from V, thereby damaging D's welfare.

Immolator:[52]

V is a 'misanthropic billionaire'. His wealth is in the form of massive stores of cash, stored in boxes. He is 'determined that no-one shall have any use or pleasure from his wealth and has resolved that when his time is nigh, he will immolate himself and his cash'. From time to time D (who is V's selfless housekeeper), takes money from one or other of the boxes in order to help friends and acquaintances in dire economic straits. She takes no more than is necessary 'to stave off the worst consequences of the privations that afflict the people she helps'.

The harm-non-essentialists may say, as it is open to them to do, that these cases merely show that harm is *not* required for legitimate criminalisation. Subject to emergency or necessity, we have a wrong in this case, be that because D, in each case, manifests dishonesty in their dealings with V's property or D violates the sovereignty principle (or however the wrongfulness is to be spelt out). That D does not cause harm does not matter; it is not required. Of course, this is the main point in contention; how do the authors pursue their harm-essentialist argument?

One road not taken by the authors that would be open to harm-essentialists is to build an *exception* for cases sharing the relevant features of these examples, ie where both V is to dispose of, abandon or destroy the relevant property in short order *and* the person in the position of D genuinely needs the property (for D or another). Some means could be built into the law to allow for such exceptions, perhaps in the form of a defence to theft. *Forgotten Garment* and *Immolator* and like cases would be dealt with and would be no counterexample for at least some harm-essentialists. Whatever the strengths or weaknesses of such an argument, however, it is not the authors'. They, as we have seen, suggest there would be regime-harm in these cases, that criminalising the conduct is in accordance with the harm principle so that the regime of property rights is protected from harm. How would such harm come about? By 'undermining' the regime, the authors respond.[53] Undermining comes in two forms, 'immediate' and 'indirect'. Referring to *Forgotten Garment*, they say, the 'misappropriation' of V's old clothes is harmful because:

> [I]t … undermines the regime by which V's property right in the clothes is recognised. It does so even if the survival and functioning of that regime is ultimately, on this occasion, unaffected by D's wrong. The undermining is both immediate – through D's denying, or at least failing to recognise and respect, the demands of that regime – and indirect: absent some reason for treating D's case as special (eg, in circumstances of necessity or emergency) the widespread replication of such conduct by others would tend to damage the operation of the regime itself.[54]

[52] ibid 174.
[53] ibid 172.
[54] ibid.

Like our imagined harm-non-essentialists mentioned in the previous paragraph, the authors make their claim subject to emergency or necessity. But what does what they call 'immediate' undermining have to do with harm? For 'D's denying, or at least failing to recognise and respect, the demands of [the] regime' hardly seems to tell us anything about harm, even if it might say something about wrongdoing. The destitute man and the housekeeper in the above examples are thought by the authors not to recognise and respect the demands of the regime of civil property, or to deny it altogether. This is largely a question of attitude, specifically of the attitudes of the putative defendants which, without more, says nothing about any harm. Moreover, in the stories the authors tell, is it even clear that their destitute man and 'selfless' housekeeper *are* disrespecting the civil law regime of property by appropriating the relevant property? They may understand their actions as exceptional or necessary or both. Indeed, the idea of harm itself – or the lack of it – may loom large in their thinking; they could even be deliberating precisely in terms of harm and need. The attitude is not necessarily: 'I will take the property of others whenever it suits me.' It could be: 'I will not interfere with the property of others without permission, save for unusual cases where I am sure they have no use at all for the property in question and I have or someone else has a very strong need for it.' The authors themselves portray their kind housekeeper's appropriations on behalf of others as involving 'no profligacy'. 'She takes enough', they say, 'just enough, to stave off the worst consequences of the privations that afflict the people she helps.'[55] But why, disrespecter of property rights that she is alleged to be, does she not just fill her boots and take as much money as she can get away with? Her misanthropic employer is going to burn it all anyway! Might it be that she does in fact respect such rights, hence the scruples? If she and the destitute man take property to meet needs in circumstances in which the property will otherwise be destroyed or dumped in landfill, this does not yet tell us they would not scrupulously avoid taking property in normal circumstances out of respect for property rights where these conditions do not apply.

The 'indirect undermining' category, by contrast, does seem to be a consideration of the right sort, a consideration that one might believe may 'tend to damage the operation of the regime itself'.[56] However, given its context in cases such as *Forgotten Garment* and *Immolator*, how is the argument to work? For it is 'the widespread *replication* of such conduct', it is said, that would tend towards the relevant damage to the property regime. But how would it do that? Thus far no harm to the garment owner or the billionaire has been identified. And if the harm is zero in these cases, it does not matter how much you replicate *that* behaviour since zero multiplied by any number will amount to zero. Might one not further argue, on the contrary, that D in these examples is setting a *good* example, because

[55] ibid 174.
[56] ibid 172.

their conduct encourages the taking of the property of others only when there are strong enough moral reasons for it?[57] Perhaps the suggestion is that in some way these thefts that do not involve direct harm in *Forgotten Garment* and *Immolator* will somehow inspire or cause not replication as such, but conduct with different features which *are* harmful, which *do* lead to harm and override any good example set by such morally tailored conduct. But in that case, an account is needed of how such a mechanism would work. We will probe the mechanics of the argument for indirect undermining further in the next section.

V. When and How Does the System of Property Rights Break Down?

The strongest indication the authors give of *how* the system of property rights could potentially be undermined to the point of loss is, as we saw in the last section, the notion of 'replication'. Where one person engages in unauthorised appropriation, this leads others to do likewise. Each unauthorised appropriation sets a bad example. Replicated many times over to the *n*th degree we come to the point of collapse of the property system. We queried whether D in *Immolator* and *Forgotten Garment* may not be setting a *good* example, rather than bad, or at worst mixed, given their apparent sensitivity to justifying moral grounds and whether all that would be replicated would simply be more *harmless* conduct. That question, however, assumes that any imitator of their conduct would replicate faithfully and correctly the relevant features. But perhaps replicators would not be that discriminating and would be inclined to unauthorised appropriations of property without the special grounds present in *Immolator* and *Forgotten Garment*.

It is interesting to note a related issue in one of the classic arguments in jurisprudence. The argument in question is over whether there is a moral obligation to obey the law. It is consequentialist in nature and concludes that there is a moral obligation to obey the law because disobedience to even a bad law 'sets an example and inclines other people to disobey'. Joseph Raz in *The Authority of Law* takes the argument on, describing it as 'important' and he counsels against 'belittling its weight'.[58] He says, it should not be 'dismissed on the ground that the action of one private individual has too little impact to be worth considering'. After all, he adds, '[a] public atmosphere of respect for law rests on the cumulative effect of individual behaviour'[59] and 'we do affect other people's attitudes'.[60] But the argument

[57] cp J Raz, 'The Obligation to Obey the Law' in *The Authority of Law* (Oxford, Oxford University Press, 2009) 233, 238.

[58] ibid 237.

[59] ibid.

[60] ibid 238.

fails in Raz's view to establish the existence of a general duty to obey the law. For if it applies to many cases, it does not apply to many others:

> There are offences which when committed by certain people or in certain circumstances do revolt people and strengthen the law-abiding inclinations in the population. In other cases the example set is a good one because on the whole it encourages disobedience only when it is justified. ... There are ... countless offences the commission of which is never known. Countless traffic offences and many small tax offences, for example, are never detected at all. Moreover, in many cases it is practically certain in advance that the offence, if committed, will remain undetected. Such offences naturally do not set any example whatsoever. Hence the argument from setting a bad example fails to apply to many instances of possible offences.[61]

Of course, the question of whether there is a moral duty to obey the law is not the question of what legitimates the law of theft or, more specifically, the question of whether harm is indispensable to the latter. However, there does seem to be a parallel. Raz is asking about the effects on the general public of discrete acts of disobedience to the law and our question is about the effects on others of discrete instances of unauthorised appropriations. We've just repeated the possibility that some thefts akin to *Immolator* and *Forgotten Garment* may set a good example or a subtly mixed one. Some thefts may also have the effect of 'revolting' people and strengthening sentiments about the need for honesty in property dealings. Thanks to action by the suspicious relatives of elderly and vulnerable people with live-in or visiting carers in installing CCTV cameras into their homes, the general public in many different local regions has in recent years witnessed online clips of carers surreptitiously stealing from their elderly and vulnerable charges. A quick internet search immediately yields video clips of many such instances, often on the website of local newspapers. Quite possibly the sharing of reactions to such footage strengthens dispositions not to steal. Of course, many thefts are not detected at all, and in other cases it is practically certain in advance that the offence, if committed, will remain undetected. In short, it is not reasonable to believe that there is some simple mechanism at work such that any unauthorised appropriation will be copied and copied in such a way that it is shorn of any redeeming features.[62]

[61] ibid.

[62] In his valuable comments on a draft of this paper, Andrew Simester questioned Raz's assertions in the quotation above in relation to offences that are 'practically certain never to be detected'. Take the 'countless traffic offences' of which Raz speaks. 'Minor offences', says Simester, 'are seen by other drivers' to whom a bad example is set, not to mention the bad example the offender 'who gets away with it' sets to himself. Part of Simester's point, as I understand it, is that Raz, in the quoted words, appears to limit 'non-detection of offences' to non-detection *by legal authorities*, but relevant bad example setting can be to the population in general. That point is surely correct. However, it does not do away with the issue of actual and possible offences undetected by anyone (and I do not understand Simester to be saying it does). I think what this above all suggests is that the notions of 'widespread replication' of conduct and 'bad example setting' are complex and in need of detailed consideration. It is insufficient to take the meaning and implications of these terms to be self-evident. Replication by whom? Of what? To what extent? Bad example to whom? With what effect? And so on. We will have more to say on this below.

We have been examining the harm-essentialist argument that theft is legitimate in a way that gets over what we called the subset problem by asking how it is that the alleged harm of theft (unauthorised appropriations) can, if not blocked, lead eventually to the loss of the system of property rights or the loss of effectiveness of such a system or to some damage to the system.[63] Discussing lying and promise breaking, Bernard Williams writes:

> Despite the fact that there are norms which lay it down that assertions are supposed to be true, many assertions are not true, often because they are not sincere. Granted this, it is a good question, how the assertion system replicates itself. Moral philosophers have been fond of the fantasy that the rules against lying and promise-breaking are sustained by the consideration that any particular lie or breaking of a promise tends to damage the institutions of assertion and promising. It may perhaps be true, at the limit, that promises and assertions could become worthless if the respective institutions were overwhelmed with defaulting behaviour. But, quite apart from the question of how this consideration is supposed to affect any given agent, it is quite unclear where the point of breakdown is supposed to be reached, and without some idea of that, and of the kinds of causality involved, this idea does not do much to help understand how these linguistic practices survive the level of abuse which year in and year out they regularly receive.[64]

Williams's questions and observations can be applied mutatis mutandis to our purposes. Stealing is as old as the hills. We know that, in some form and to some extent, it will continue come what may. There are norms against stealing and there is a crime of theft as well as related civil wrongs, but plenty of stealing has always gone on regardless. So, it is a relevant question how the property system sustains itself. One might say the property system must be protected on the basis that any unauthorised appropriation tends to damage the institution of property rights. Perhaps it is true, at the limit, that the system of property rights could become worthless if the respective institutions were overwhelmed with defaulting behaviour. But when, we might ask Williams's question in relation to theft, is the point of breakdown supposed to be reached?

It seems that Simester and Sullivan do not always identify one and the same point of breakdown for the purposes of their argument. They speak, as noted above, of the 'loss' of the system of property rights, of the system as a whole becoming 'ineffective'. Here they appear to have in mind something like the 'overwhelming' of the system of property with 'defaulting behaviour' in Williams's terms–essentially the end ('loss') of the system of property rights as we know it. Elsewhere, as we will see below, the talk is not of the loss of the system of property rights, but of the need for theft to make up for the 'sometimes' 'inadequate' civil law protection of property rights. Let us look at each in turn.

[63] These formulations are not equivalent. Losing something is of course very different from damaging or weakening it. The strength of the Simester and Sullivan claim is addressed below.

[64] Williams (n 1) 86.

The very idea that one could 'lose' the system of property rights is mind boggling and multifaceted. Money, to take just one object of property rights with which the law of theft commonly deals, is only money ultimately because it is believed to be so by enough people. That these notes and coins in front of me are money is not a brute fact like the fact there is a mountain in Gwynedd. If (weirdly) we stopped believing there was a mountain there, that would not change the (brute) fact that there is. Bank notes and coins, by contrast, would cease to be money as we understand it if enough people stopped believing they were. Money (and property in general) are in other words made up of what John Searle calls 'institutional' as opposed to 'brute' facts:

> The secret of understanding the continued existence of institutional facts is simply that the individuals directly involved and a sufficient number of members of the relevant community must continue to recognize and accept the existence of such facts. Because the status is constituted by its collective acceptance, and because the function, in order to be performed, requires the status, it is essential to the functioning that there be continued acceptance of the status. The moment, for example, that all or most of the members of society refuse to acknowledge property rights, as in a revolution or other upheaval, property rights cease to exist in that society.[65]

If it is possible to avoid that stark result by deploying the criminal law of theft, then it is most plausible to argue that we should do so; and that it would be harmful not to. But is it plausible to suggest that such a doomsday result – the entire collapse of the country's system of property rights – could be at stake even were there no crime of theft at all? The controversy we are examining is not between theft abolitionists and non-abolitionists, as we might call them, and one might consider modifications to the law of theft short of abolition. But surely even full abolition would not threaten the end of property rights as we know it? Searle conjectures such an outcome would take a revolution or an upheaval.

For one thing, it has been evident for a long time that clear-up rates for theft have been consistently low in England and Wales. According to Andrew Ashworth, writing in 2013 but referring back to figures from 1999, 'such a low proportion of those who steal are actually reported, detected, prosecuted and convicted (about 3–4 per cent)'.[66] More recent figures tell essentially the same story: '4 per cent of thefts … end in the offender being charged and [the figure is] 1 per cent for car theft', according to Home Office figures.'[67] Yet we have seen nothing approaching a

[65] J Searle, *The Construction of Social Reality* (London, Penguin, 1996) 113, 117. See further the exchange between Smith and Searle: B Smith and J Searle, 'The Construction of Social Reality: An Exchange' (2003) 62 *American Journal of Economics and Sociology* 285.

[66] A Ashworth, 'What if Imprisonment Were Abolished for Property Offences?' (2013) *Howard League for Penal Reform* 9.

[67] M Brunt, '"Unacceptable and Unsustainable": Police Watchdog Condemns Low Burglary and Theft Clear-up Rates' *Sky News*, 11 August 2022 https://news.sky.com/story/unacceptable-and-unsustainable-police-watchdog-condemns-low-burglary-and-theft-clear-up-rates-12670020 (accessed 17 May 2023).

collapse in the system of property rights as a whole. For another thing, were we to have no law of theft, that would not imply having *no legal regulation* of stealing or no means of legal redress. Among other legal forms the civil law, in the guise of the torts of conversion and trespass to goods, would remain.[68]

The authors are of course aware of the point that the civil law also regulates stealing. Indeed, a major motivation for their opposition to the 'dishonesty' element in the England and Wales definition of theft is their belief that it undermines or subverts the civil law of property.[69] In the following passage they consider whether unauthorised appropriations could be left to the civil law, and it is here they seem to have in mind a 'point of breakdown' very well short of the 'loss' of the system of property rights:

> No doubt V can sue D in the civil courts for the unlawful taking of, say, his car. Sometimes, however, leaving V to his own devices in terms of self-help and civil redress would inadequately protect his property and, by extrapolation, the system of property rights as a whole. This is partly a pragmatic point: mobilising public resources to protect private property augments deterrence and means that V can report his loss to the police who, at least in theory, will assume the task of seeking out D and the stolen property while V gets on with his own affairs. But it is also symbolic: the proprietary regime is reinforced by public denunciation of proprietary usurpations.[70]

Three kinds of factor – deterrence, investigatory and symbolic – are identified in the passage as leading to the marginal harm avoidance brought to bear by the criminal law over and above the civil law. The symbolic or communicative features which can be supported by harm-non-essentialists and harm-essentialists alike, however, seem not to be essentially harm-based; or not essentially harm-based independently of any deterrent effect such factors might have. Both sides at least can and generally do support such features on the basis that they have valuable expressive and communicative value, regardless of whether they also have harm avoiding consequences. Deterrence itself does seem to be the most pertinent feature when assessing the marginal difference between legal regulation with and without the crime of theft. As for the investigative resources brought by the criminal law, seeking out the culprit who may not be known to V and so on, these in

[68] It would even not necessarily imply the absence of *criminal* regulation. Robbery and burglary could remain, with the elements of theft only part constituting the offences with their respective features of violence and invasion of the home. Moreover, the relevant civil sanctions could in principle be backed up by the criminal law. Theft, as Feinberg observes, is a 'primary crime', in the sense that it describes certain conduct, places it under interdiction and threatens punishment for engaging in it (*Harm to Others* (n 6) 19). But in its place, there could in principle operate a 'back-up sanction', a 'derivative' crime, held in reserve to enforce other techniques, such as tort law: 'if the court orders the defendant to pay the plaintiff's damages, and the defendant flatly refuses, then the court order will be backed up by legal force. The disobedient litigant will pay up whether he chooses to or not, and he may be punished to boot for contempt of court' (ibid 20).

[69] Simester and Sullivan (n 20) 179.

[70] ibid 172.

principle could also be undertaken under the auspices of the civil law, subsidised, say, by legal aid.[71]

But leaving that aside, we are asking Williams's question of where the point of breakdown is supposed to be. The register in the quotation above has changed from the 'loss' of the whole edifice of property rights, or the rendering of it 'ineffective'. *Sometimes*, it is said, civil redress would be inadequate. At other times, this implies, it *would* be adequate. The discourse is now in terms of some 'inadequacies' in the protection of property rights as a whole and the possibility of 'augmentation' of other protections by means of the criminal law and the 'reinforcement' of symbolism and 'at least in theory' investigative help from the police. Nothing so large as the system of property rights itself is at stake, but some measure of augmentation or reinforcement of the pillars supporting property rights is (the civil law, moral and prudential norms, etc). This suggests the point of breakdown comes well before the doomsday scenario of the loss of the property rights system as a whole. But if so, where? And how are the inadequacies, whatever their extent, and failures of augmentation and reinforcement, whatever theirs, to be weighed against the various kinds of serious cost we mentioned above, of imprisonment and other punishments, to D and to society, and of the stigma and so on of a criminal conviction? One might put Williams's concern as a dilemma. If we legitimate the criminalisation as theft of all unauthorised appropriations to prevent the *loss* of our system of property rights, which ex hypothesi would otherwise be overwhelmed with defaulting behaviour, we can plausibly argue we are preventing something gravely harmful enough for criminalisation. Even if the conduct of one person in misappropriating property, although remote in the extreme from the eventual collapse of property rights as a whole, has some miniscule contribution to make to that eventual collapse, the potential cumulative harm is so enormous that the individual acts can and should be castigated by the criminal law. But the cost of seeing the point of breakdown as cataclysmic in this way is the absence of any plausible empirical evidence in favour of such a counterfactual occurring. If on the other hand we legitimate the criminalisation as theft of all unauthorised appropriations (sometimes) to prevent inadequacies in the overall system of property rights protection, in order not to forsake potential augmentations of other techniques and reinforced symbolism, somewhere down the line we might reasonably hope for some sort of empirical support for the theft law's efficacy, but on the other hand it is unclear how strong these credits in harm prevention, so to speak, are to be offset against the known debits of harm caused to those to be criminalised and punished. In other words, it is very unclear whether the harm principle – an indispensable condition of course for harm-essentialists – is met or is met proportionally.

[71] cp F Wilmot-Smith, *Fair Legal Systems in an Unfair World* (Cambridge MA, Harvard University Press, 2019).

HLA Hart, in assessing Lord Devlin's claim that the enforcement of a state's positive morality is required to prevent the distintegration of that society, famously challenged Lord Devlin to reveal 'the empirical claim which the thesis makes' and to explain 'in what directions it is conceivable that a search for evidence to substantiate this claim would be rewarding'.[72] This, I think, is surely also required of those who take the line of the authors (and of John Gardner and others) that the harm legitimating criminalisation of a given offence will lie in loss or disintegration or some serious cumulative consequence. What is surely needed is a clearly spelt out account 'of the kinds of causality involved', to use Williams's terms. What in more detail is the 'imagined otherwise' and what will take us to that state unless effectively prevented from doing so?

This is a potentially very large question. Why do those who steal, steal? And why do those who do not steal refrain from doing so? How far is it the case that people who otherwise would steal will not do so due to the existence of a crime of theft in a certain form? Certainly, there are numerous criminological studies that could surely be most helpful if examined in depth. That is not something I can undertake here. But a somewhat random and superficial glance does not initially offer a lot of promise for the thesis.

One most interesting recent study is the Peterborough Adolescent and Young Adult Development Study, undertaken over many years by the Cambridge Institute of Criminology.[73] Seven hundred young adults in Peterborough were followed and the extent of their involvement in crime examined. The focus was both on the personal characteristics of the young adults concerned and their environments. It emerged, among much else, that one-third committed no crime at all and the vast majority of the remainder committed crimes only very occasionally. A very small group (4 percent) were responsible for nearly half the total crime and an overwhelming number of the most serious property offences.[74] The study found highly significant the notion of 'crime propensity', ie 'the tendency to see and, if so, to choose acts of crime … as a viable action alternative in response to a motivation (temptation or provocation)'.[75] A person's crime propensity depended crucially on their own value system.[76] The interaction between the crime propensity of people and the 'criminogenic features of the settings to which they are exposed' was also of considerable significance.[77] However, while a very large proportion of, say,

[72] HLA Hart, 'Social Solidarity and the Enforcement of Morality' in *Essays in Jurisprudence and Philosophy* (Oxford, Oxford University Press, 1983) 248, 249; first published in (1967) 35 *University of Chicago Law Review* 1.

[73] P-OH Wikström, D Oberwittler, K Treiber and B Hardie, *Breaking Rules: The Social And Situational Dynamics of Young People's Urban Crime* (Oxford, Oxford University Press, 2012).

[74] University of Cambridge Institute of Criminology, *Morality Prevents Crime* (2012) www.cam.ac.uk/research/news/morality-prevents-crime (accessed 22 May 2023).

[75] ibid 11.

[76] ibid 15–16.

[77] ibid 11.

shoplifting takes place in shopping centres away from the homes of the people concerned:

> The number of crimes young people commit in a criminogenic setting is not primarily affected by the amount of time all young people spend in that setting, but rather by the amount of time crime prone young people spend in that setting. Criminogenic settings are not criminogenic for all young people.
>
> The study suggests that a major reason why certain young people refrain from crime is not because they fear the consequences; it's that their morality simply prevents them from even seeing crime as a possible course of action in the first place.[78]

While the Peterborough Adolescent Study is just one study, one might say a drop in the ocean, it is interestingly in tune with Searle's observation that property rights are constitutively sustained by the deep beliefs of the population at large and with Waldron's notion of 'normative resilience.' Bernard Williams, in turn, stresses how ethical values are often embodied in 'deliberative silence', arguing that this is for the best and that we should avoid any over-moralistic assumption that we must be constantly engaged in moral deliberation on all important matters. As he puts the point:

> An effective way for actions to be ruled out is that they never come into thought at all, and this is often the best way. One does not feel easy with the man who in the course of a discussion of how to deal with political or business rivals says, 'Of course, we could have them killed, but we should lay that aside right from the beginning.' It should never have come into his hands to be laid aside. It is characteristic of morality that it tends to overlook the possibility that some concerns are best embodied in this way, in deliberative silence.[79]

Indeed, the Peterborough study suggests that for many young people, the option of stealing or shoplifting simply does not occur to them. It does not seem from this that the criminal law is playing a very significant role. It is not, as the study says, that these young people fear the consequences of shoplifting. It is just that their value systems, reasoning and habits mean that stealing is not thought of as an option in numerous contexts.

What of those young people studied who are at the other end of the spectrum, carrying out a highly disproportionate number of offences?

> Young people at the other end of the spectrum don't care very much about breaking the rules of the law and tend to be impulsive and short-sighted, leaving them more vulnerable to the temptations of crime – they are 'crime-prone'.[80]

Here the question is not what prevented the crimes, since the crimes were not prevented. But what is interesting is the finding that they are a relatively small proportion of the population studied.

[78] ibid 363.
[79] B Williams, *Ethics and the Limits of Philosophy* (London, Fontana, 1985) 185.
[80] *Morality Prevents Crime* (n 74).

For all of the above it is difficult to believe that the criminal law of theft and its sanctions have *no* marginal deterrent effect. Even if it is correct that most people refrain in deliberative silence due to their value systems and the group that does carry out a very large proportion of the offences is itself small, it is also plausible to think that the various value systems that make people refrain or desist are somewhere down the line inspired by the fact that theft is not only a wrong, but also a crime. Many value systems can presumably have evolved inter alia from moral, prudential and legal norms in an inextricable mixture. Moreover, it is commonly said in criminological circles that what deters is more the certainty or near certainty of being caught in the act, rather than the extent of the sentence or sanction.[81] 'Being caught' here can mean being caught by the police or legal officials or being 'caught' by fellow citizens, in the way that Antonio in *Bicycle Thieves* was apprehended by a chasing group of fellow citizens but not processed through the criminal justice system. Again, it is not easy to separate the two senses.

Ultimately, for all the reasons canvassed it does seem implausible to suggest that each unauthorised appropriation in its own miniscule way is potentially part contributor to the loss of the system of property rights, an outcome that can be held off by the criminal law of theft. What does seem correct is that the property system does depend on the cumulative effect of the belief systems and inclinations of the population as a whole.

VI. What Else Might Be Criminalised to Prevent Regime Harm?

Before concluding, a word on one other concern I have about the regime-harm argument for a harm-essentialist legitimation of theft. This concern is different from anything voiced before. To explain it, let us imagine none of the doubts above amount to anything. Unauthorised appropriations in general do, as the authors argue, threaten the regime of property rights, thereby giving the criminal law a harm-based reason to coerce the population in the shape of the crime of theft. Let us accept, for the sake of argument, that unauthorised appropriations do have such causal power and that, because it can be countered by the criminal law, it ought to be, or at least can legitimately be. But might this argument, on such assumptions, prove too much? For if unauthorised appropriations really have such power and constitute such a threat to the system of property rights, what else would seem to threaten the system by parity of reasoning? Let us look at three possible answers.

[81] R Apel and DS Nagin, 'General Deterrence' in M Tonry (ed), *The Oxford Handbook of Crime and Criminal Justice* (Oxford, Oxford University Press, 2011) 180.

The first issue does not go beyond unauthorised appropriations as such, but asks whether the authors' argument does not favour criminalising more of them than they say. Why restrict the intent element to *permanent* deprivation, as the authors do in their preferred definition of theft (here their recommended theft offence is in line with the law of England and Wales)? Why not include *temporary* deprivation as well? Temporary appropriations can be just as much unauthorised as permanent appropriations. Secondly, beyond theft itself, what of trespass to land? The criminalisation of trespass in many jurisdictions, such as in England and Wales, remains the exception not the rule. *Some* forms of trespass might be criminalised, for example those perpetrated by D with intent to obstruct or disrupt V's lawful activity on the land in question, or to intimidate V so as to deter V from lawful activity on that land.[82] And while trespass is a constitutive element of burglary, trespass per se is not criminal. Yet is not the same harm to the property rights regime at stake? Why are these unauthorised violations of property rights not harmful in the way the authors claim unauthorised appropriations are? There is, after all, no burden by parity of reasoning with their theft argument to show *direct* harm in these cases. Finally, if the necessary harm is property-regime harm and a crime of theft can potentially work to block such harm, why should breach of contract not also be a crime? Why should it remain a mere civil wrong? Contract is also one of the pillars holding up the system of property rights, as the authors themselves assert. If existing civil remedies for unauthorised appropriations – conversion, trespass to goods – are insufficient (necessitating the criminal offence of theft), why is the civil law not also insufficient in the case of breach of contract? Why is there no criminal breach of contract?

I do not know. It is at least possible that the authors might be willing to accept the first two extensions of the criminal law as implications of their argument, or at least travel some of the distance. But, whether that is right or wrong, I would be surprised if they would accept the third. The authors, it will be remembered, characterise the value of the property system in terms of 'the voluntary acquisition, use, and exchange of resources'.[83] As for the first extension, allowing temporary misappropriation to count as theft, embracing it would put them in distinguished company. It is already the legal position in Canada: the necessary intent for theft, according to the Canadian Criminal Code, is to deprive '*temporarily or* absolutely'.[84] The proposal would also have the distinguished support of Glanville Williams, who concludes that temporary appropriation should be theft and en route to that conclusion stresses a feature of property rights also identified as important by the authors, namely *using* property even where there is no

[82] Criminal Justice and Public Order Act 1994, s 68.
[83] Simester and Sullivan (n 20) 171.
[84] Criminal Code, RSC 1985, c C-46, s 322.

substantial risk of permanent loss.[85] If they were to accept the extension of theft to temporary unauthorised appropriation, they would of course need to modify the italicised words in their statement of the wrong of theft – namely 'to take property without claim of right to it and *intending to keep or dispose* of it'.[86] However, they give no indication that they *would* in fact take that line and, if not, some account of why these unauthorised appropriations are distinct is needed.

As for the second case, bare trespass, again it is possible that they would be willing to accept at least some wider criminalisation of trespass by parity of reasoning with their position on theft. The numerous options canvassed for law reform in the treatise that carries their names is just one of its great strengths. One such proposal is the adoption of a general offence of trespass into people's homes, already an offence in France, Germany and Italy.[87] The argument given in favour of such offence is the importance of protecting people from 'extremely serious … violations of personal space'.[88] However, why the restriction to people's homes? Why not *any* trespass on people's property? Would not any trespass tend to undermine the property rights regime as a whole and would it not have the same causal power as is ascribed to unauthorised appropriations?

Breach of contract *as a crime*, by contrast, sounds entirely novel. But should we not draw the same conclusion about criminalising it as about unauthorised appropriations in theft? Some breaches of contract will be directly harmful, some will not, as was the case with unauthorised appropriations; but all, as the argument goes, will implicate damage to the practice of contracting and thus the property system itself, as contract is one of the pillars of the property system. Interestingly, Joseph Raz offers a rationale for understanding breach of contract in terms of the harm principle with an affinity to the Simester and Sullivan rationale for theft. According to Raz:

> The law must choose which harms to protect against and which not. The distinctive mark of contract law is that harms it protects against are harms to the practice of undertaking voluntary obligations and harms resulting from its abuse.[89]

We noted earlier Raz's scepticism about the 'setting a bad example' argument in relation to a putative moral duty to obey the law. In the light of that, one might have expected a bit more interrogation of what it means to harm 'the practice of undertaking voluntary obligations' in his argument about contract and of how discrete individual breaches of contract will do that. But Raz is nowhere arguing for the criminalisation of breach of contract. It is the civil law of contract he is seeking to legitimise by means of the argument. His argument, then, does not

[85] G Williams, 'Temporary Appropriation Should be Theft' [1981] *Crim LR* 129.

[86] Simester and Sullivan (n 20) 179.

[87] JJ Child, AP Simester, JR Spencer, F Stark and GJ Virgo, *Simester and Sullivan's Criminal Law: Theory and Doctrine*, 8th edn (Oxford, Hart Publishing, 2022) 689.

[88] ibid.

[89] J Raz, 'Promises in Morality and Law' (1982) 95 *Harvard Law Review* 938.

parallel the authors' theft argument, where the harm to the property system does double duty in legitimising the civil and criminal law of theft. He is not getting two for the price of one. John Gardner, on the other hand, appears entirely open to the idea of *criminalising* breach of contract:

> The law may proscribe breach of contract (whether by making it actionable in the civil courts or punishable in the criminal courts) and when it does so it complies with the harm principle. Breaches of contract tend to do harm even when they do not specifically harm the plaintiff by losing her the advantage (if any) of the contract, because even under these circumstances they tend to erode the practice of maintaining reliable voluntary obligations, thereby harming everyone who has reason, or might come to have reason, to enter into such obligations.[90]

Gardner's argument here is essentially the same as the authors', albeit the authors do not discuss breach of contract, let alone speak of criminalising it. Gardner does not develop the point. However, his willingness to contemplate a crime of breach of contract and his confidence that it would be underwritten by the harm principle points in a direction the authors might want to go. But, as I have said, I doubt they would, although that doubt may reflect nothing more than my own sense that, if the authors' argument implies the criminalisation of breach of contract, that is a reductio of the argument. Of course, the harm principle is always proposed, by the authors no less than all its proponents, as a *necessary* condition for legitimate coercion, not as a sufficient condition. Hence, they might accept that the harm principle does underwrite criminalising temporary unauthorised appropriations, criminalising bare trespass and breach of contract, but then argue that, all things considered, one, two or all of them should not be criminalised because defeated on other grounds. We would then need to know what are the defeating considerations, why they have the strength to defeat the regime-harm cases where they do, and why they do not have that strength in the case of theft.[91] As I have said in some detail, I am in any case sceptical of the 'damage to the practice' version of the harm principle as regards theft. But, even if I am wrong about that, it seems to me that the gravitational pull towards further criminalisation is a disadvantage of that view.[92]

[90] Gardner (n 8) 5.

[91] D Husak, *Overcriminalization* (Oxford, Oxford University Press, 2008) 136 argues that the choice between civil and criminal regulation should turn on when 'individuals who are wronged should retain the sole power to decide whether to initiate proceedings against tortfeasors and those who breach their agreements'. In some cases – the civil cases – he argues, the 'prerogative to forgive and forget' should be 'retained by the victim'. In other cases, the criminal ones, it is for the state or community to have the (final) say. As he acknowledges the argument depends on an independent account of just when the power of ultimate decision should rest with the victim. Effectively at the end of *Bicycle Thieves*, the victim of Antonio's theft did exercise 'the prerogative to forgive and forget'. I cannot pursue this interesting issue further here. For comment on Husak's argument, see V Tadros 'The Architecture of Criminalization' (2009) 28 *Criminal Justice Ethics* 74.

[92] It is open to the authors to go the opposite way. Rather than accept temporary unauthorised appropriations, bare trespasses and breaches of contract should be crimes if theft should (or that there is a pro tanto reason for that), they could argue none should be crimes, *including* theft. There is no indication in

VII. Conclusion

My question above, is theft legitimately criminalised because it is harmful or because it is wrongful, immediately received the answer 'both'. So, the question was modified. 'Both' in what combination? Harm-non-essentialists may well agree that conduct can be wrong (among other reasons) because it is harmful, but it is ultimately the wrongness that matters. Harm is dispensable. Harm-essentialists, by contrast, generally agree that crimes need not only be harmful in order legitimately to be crimes; they need to be wrongful too. But harm is indispensable. I have focused on Andrew Simester and Bob Sullivan's defence of the harm principle as the legitimating rationale of theft. To their credit, they have not simply relied on a defence of the harm principle as a legitimating ground for crime in general and just 'read off' the legitimacy of theft from that. Such approaches often take the lion's share of the examples of harm from other contexts, homicide, serious violence and sexual offences. Eschewing such an approach, the authors see that theft raises distinct issues and have given it special attention. They have argued that the relevant harm is regime harm, harm to the regime of property rights. That gets them round what I called the 'subset' problem: only a (significant) subset of thefts, especially in the circumstances of startling inequality reported by Stiglitz, Picketty, Dorling and others, cause direct harm. But they argue that all unauthorised appropriations conduce to regime harm and that is truly where the action is. The direct harms are relevant only 'parasitically'.

I began, I hope not too self-indulgently, with an examination of one of my favourite films, *Bicycle Thieves*. Watching the portrayal of the aftermath of theft so graphically relayed should convince anyone that theft can be very harmful. It is fitting, I think, that Amy Burrell and Matt Tonkin preface their volume on property crime with a dedication to 'victims of property crime who are often forgotten'.[93] While it may be an odd line to take against champions of the harm principle, I believe the authors at the very least need to drop their claim that direct harms are 'parasitic' on their other category of regime harms because – and this is the odd bit – that does not give harm its due.[94] Where is the harm of theft? It is there in the direct harms of the sort depicted in *Bicycle Thieves*. Above I have tried to explain why I am not quite convinced by the authors' and John Gardner's notion of regime harm, or of harm as damage to the practice, for all its highly interesting features. As I have tried to explain, largely by adapting Bernard

their writing, however, that they might be tempted down that path. In this connection it is interesting to note that Ashworth (n 66), though no theft abolitionist, argues for the removal of imprisonment as a sanction for theft.

[93] A Burrell and M Tonkin, *Property Crime: Criminological and Psychological Perspectives* (London, Routledge, 2020).

[94] The phrase, 'giving harm its due', is Antony Duff's: see *Answering for Crime* (Oxford, Hart Publishing, 2007) 138–40.

Williams's questions directed at a similar argument to do with lying, we need an unambiguous statement of 'where the point of breakdown' in such regime harm 'is supposed to be reached', and a fuller account of the 'kinds of causality involved'. Perhaps those challenges can be met. My hunch is that the harm-non-essentialist route – although I've not tried to suggest here what form it should take – is likely to be more promising. As for harm to the regime of property rights, I suspect that if the heavens were going to fall, they would have fallen already.[95]

[95] I am most grateful to Grant Lamond and Andrew Simester for their comments on a draft. It is a pleasure to be contributing to this volume in honour of Bob Sullivan. I was tempted initially to revisit the controversial case of *R v Turner (No 2)* [1971] 1 WLR 901 (CA) for this purpose but could not in the end get the idea I had to work. In that well known case, the defendant was convicted of theft after driving his own car away from an east London garage apparently to avoid paying for repairs the garage had made to the car. The car parked on the road outside the garage was close to the old West Ham United football ground at Upton Park, which reminds me of the West Ham games I attended with Bob at the now demolished Boleyn Ground. While watching these matches we discussed all sorts of things, such as why the West Ham left back was getting caught out of position so frequently (other spectators were also very audibly discussing that kind of thing). We also spent a fair bit of time ruminating out loud on knotty problems in the criminal law (no other spectators seemed inclined to join in). I have benefitted immeasurably both from reading Bob Sullivan's extensive writings and from talking about criminal law with him and not only in football grounds. Usually, I simply learn and inwardly digest, but somehow, we have never seemed to agree entirely on property offences. Indeed, I note I appear on the Simester and Sullivan list of rogues, those miscreants that have a good word to say about the case of *R v Hinks* [2001] 2 AC 241, named and shamed in footnote 30 of their paper, 'The Nature and Rationale of Property Offences' that I have been discussing above. I don't for a moment think Bob is going to agree with what I say here but I hope that carrying on the argument is a fitting way of honouring him, this time on the place of the harm principle in theft. In the end I do not know who is closer to the truth on this, but what I am sure of is that the subject, like so many others, is much enhanced for Bob's scholarship.

PART III

Defences

7

Not Guilty by Reasons Other than Insanity

CLAIRE HOGG AND JJ CHILD*

Debates about reforming the *M'Naghten* rules of legal insanity are as old as the rules themselves – which is to say, very old indeed.[1] In practice, however, these debates have had a limited impact, with *M'Naghten* becoming ever more entrenched across the common law world.[2] In England and Wales, commitment to the *M'Naghten* orthodoxy has left us with an approach to insanity that is, in several of its aspects, conspicuously inappropriate for a liberal criminal justice system.[3] While there are many possible explanations for stagnation here, one contributing factor has been the tendency for reform debates to drift towards absolutist normative positions – arguing for extremes of the expansion or abolition of the defence – that have failed to provide the consensus required for real change.[4] If reform is to be a realistic possibility, we must look beyond the established terms of the broader ideological debate and towards the precise structure, function and impact of insanity in operation.

* We would like to thank those who have provided comments on an earlier draft of this chapter – Prof Andrew Simester, Prof Antony Duff and Dr Matt Gibson – as well as discussion groups at King's College London and the Socio-Legal Studies Association. Dr Hogg would like especially to thank the European Research Council and Horizon Europe for funding her research as a post-doctoral fellow with the project *Roots of Responsibility* (ID: 789270) at UCL, during which time her work on this chapter was completed.

[1] Emanating from debate in the House of Lords following the case of *M'Naghten* (1843) 10 Cl & Fin 200.

[2] A version of the *M'Naghten* rules, or a codified insanity defence influenced by *M'Naghten*, applies in many common law jurisdictions. These include (but are not limited to): England and Wales (*M'Naghten* (n1)), Scotland (Criminal Procedure (Scotland) Act 1995, s 51A), Northern Ireland (Criminal Justice Act (Northern Ireland) 1966 (c 20), s1), Ireland (Criminal Law (Insanity) Act 2006, s5(1)), the USA (under Federal law (18 US Code §17) and at State level), Australia (under Federal law (Commonwealth Criminal Code, s7.3(1)) and at State level), Canada (Criminal Code (RSC 1985 c. C-46), 16(1)), New Zealand (Crimes Act 1961, s23), India (Indian Penal Code, s84), and Singapore (Penal Code 1871, s84).

[3] See Law Commission, *Insanity and Automatism* (Discussion Paper, 2013) ch 1. These aspects will be outlined and discussed in depth later on in this chapter.

[4] See, for example, the stalling of the most recent Law Commission project since 2013 (n3).

It is in this respect that Sullivan's insanity scholarship distinguishes itself. Though typically demonstrating a preference for expanding the defence's application,[5] his work challenges the terms of the debate by scrutinising the structure of the insanity rules as they apply in England and Wales. In particular, he identifies two distinct roles played by insanity: (1) the insanity defence *qua* defence, whose function is exculpatory, and (2) insanity as a diversionary (or inculpatory[6]) mechanism, applied to redirect certain defendants towards a qualified version of acquittal. This second role applies where a defendant who has not been proven to have committed the offence charged (either because he lacked mens rea or acted involuntarily), or who satisfies an alternative defence, is nonetheless found to fall within the scope of the insanity rules. In these cases, the court will substitute an unqualified acquittal for a 'special verdict' ('Not Guilty by Reason of Insanity'), opening up a range of disposal options that would not be available had the defendant been acquitted outright.[7]

Distinguishing the two roles of insanity provides an important step towards a more precise and actionable understanding of the operation of insanity in England and Wales. It is also a crucial issue absent from current reform debates, representing a point of internal conflict and potential contradiction. For those aiming to progress the debate around insanity reform in a useful and productive way, then, the next step must be to reach a comprehensive understanding of insanity's little-discussed secondary role: the diversionary function by which a defendant may be effectively redirected from acquittal to the special verdict. The first aim of this chapter, and the focus of Section I, is to do just this. By clarifying the nature and operation of the exculpatory/diversionary divide, we will provide a comprehensive accounting of the diversionary (or inculpatory) function of insanity. In so doing, we illuminate the internal contradictions in purpose and rationale that will inevitably continue to plague any reform proposal which fails to grapple with insanity's dual roles.

The second of this chapter's aims, and the focus of Section II, is to translate this analysis into feasible directions for reform. Earlier work by Sullivan and Child has remained within the confines of common law progression, with the more modest aim of ensuring basic fairness with respect to the application of insanity rules at common law.[8] By contrast, our objective is to endorse a fundamental change to

[5] Across several co-authored articles with JJ Child, the co-author of the current chapter, as well as editions of *Simester and Sullivan's Criminal Law* (Oxford, Hart Publishing).

[6] Sullivan and Child describe the application of insanity rules here as *inculpatory* in effect: they require a defendant to rely upon – and, due to the reversed burden of proof arising from a legal presumption of sanity, to prove – a defence of insanity, when otherwise an outright acquittal – and *not* a conviction – would be warranted.

[7] These include orders for hopsitalisation, treatment, and supervision within the community. See: Criminal Procedure (Insanity) Act 1964, s 5, as amended by the Domestic Violence, Crime and Victims Act 2004.

[8] See eg JJ Child and GR Sullivan, 'When Does the Insanity Defence Apply? Some Recent Cases' [2014] *Crim LR* 787; JJ Child, HS Crombag and GR Sullivan, 'Defending the Delusional, the Irrational, and the Dangerous' [2020] *Crim LR* 306; 'Drunk, Dangerous and Delusional' [2020] *Addiction* 2200 and 'Debating Intoxication' [2020] *Addiction* 2210.

the underlying operation of insanity, effected at statutory level. The position we take is one of partial abolition; abolition, that is, of insanity in its diversionary function only. Our contention is that, while insanity in its exculpatory function – insanity as a defence *qua* defence – plays an important role in the law, the use of insanity rules as a means of forestalling otherwise warranted acquittals must, for reasons of both fairness and coherency, be prohibited via statute. In this way, we chart a third way through the the more general and dominating expansion/abolition debate. By committing to a project of partial abolition, we contend, insanity doctrine in England and Wales can rid itself of the injustices that currently characterise its operation in practice, whilst providing the conceptual space and clarity of rationale required for the necessary reform of insanity as a genuine excusing defence.

I. The Dual Roles of Insanity

To understand our call for partial abolition, one must understand the two roles currently played by the insanity rules. Our first objective, then, is to clearly differentiate *insanity as exculpatory defence* from *insanity as inculpatory diversionary mechanism*. Our main focus here will be to bring out and distinguish the latter role. Once the inculpatory role is explained, we can begin to make clear the case for its abolition.

What Is the Exculpatory Insanity Defence?

The exculpatory insanity defence is the label we have used to describe insanity when it is playing the role of a defence *qua* defence (ie, D has committed all the elements of an offence, does not have an alternative defence and appeals to insanity as her route to acquittal via the special verdict). The effect of insanity in this role is that a defendant who acted voluntarily and with mens rea may be able to avoid a conviction if she can demonstrate that, due to a condition meeting the *M'Naghten* status test,[9] *either* she did not know what she was doing,[10] *or* she did not know that her actions were illegal.[11]

Even in this most obvious role, it should be acknowledged that questions remain as to the kind of defence *M'Naghten* insanity is intended to be. Specifically, we might ask whether it is better understood as a test for certain specific excusing

[9] 'A defect of reason caused by a disease of the mind'; note that this is not restricted to psychological illness (*Kemp* [1957] 1 QB 399).

[10] The courts' narrow interpretation of this limb may lead us to ask whether it is possible for a defendant to meet the first limb of *M'Naghten* and have mens rea. This is an important question, but not one we will attempt to address here.

[11] See *Windle* [1952] 2 QB 826 and *Johnson* [2007] EWCA Crim 1978.

factors that a mental condition can introduce, or as a test for a kind of mental incapacity, operant at the time of act,[12] that excludes a defendant from the class of persons who can be held culpable.[13] We return to this discussion in section II, not to seek a final resolution, but to demonstrate how the central contention of this chapter (ie, for partial abolition of insanity) can unlock both conceptual and reform debates about insanity in its exculpatory role.

What Is the Inculpatory Insanity 'Defence'?

In addition to providing a layer of protection to mentally ill defendants who are found to satisfy the elements of a crime, insanity can also be introduced as a means of qualifying the acquittal of defendants whose failure to satisfy those elements is attributable to the operation of a mental condition. Perhaps the clearest example of this inculpatory, or diversionary, function of insanity arises from the legal treatment of involuntary action; specifically, the legal distinction between 'sane' and 'insane' automatism. It is a well-accepted principle that criminality can be attributed only to a conscious, freely acting agent. To paraphrase Hart, it is morally incoherent for the law to hold a person to account for actions over which they lacked either the ability or the opportunity to exercise control.[14] Putting it another way: if we are to censure a person for their actions, we must be able to give some account of what we would have had them do instead; the individual who acts without choice or control cannot rightly or reasonably be asked to do otherwise. As a general rule, then, an act performed involuntarily and without prior fault cannot constitute a crime.[15]

In principle, this rule ought to hold equally in cases where the involuntary act was caused by a mental condition. D1, who acted unconsciously during a dissociative episode or fugue state, would seem just as entitled to an acquittal as D2, whose body was moved by an external physical force; in neither case is the prosecution able to prove a necessary element of the crime (voluntary action). In practice, however, the fate of the D1 is an open question, turning on whether the cause of his unconscious state can be classified as a 'disease of the mind' under the insanity defence. In the 1957 case of *Kemp*,[16] D's advanced arteriosclerosis had led to a loss of blood to the brain, causing a blackout during which he attacked his wife with a hammer. With D's act acknowledged by all parties as faultlessly

[12] Although not at the time of the criminal trial process, distinguishing it from fitness to plead.

[13] See B Livings et al (eds), *Mental Condition Defences and the Criminal Justice System* (Newcastle upon Tyne, Cambridge Scholars Publishing, 2015).

[14] HLA Hart, *Punishment and Responsibility: Essays in the Philosophy of Law* (Oxford, Oxford University Press, 2008) 181: '[U]nless a man has the capacity and fair opportunity to adjust his behaviour to the law its penalties ought not to be applied to him.'

[15] Prior-fault rules apply exceptionally to allow the court to take account of D's fault in becoming involuntary, most prominently through the use of drugs or alcohol. See eg *Lipman* [1970] 1 QB 152.

[16] *Kemp* [1957] 1 QB 399.

involuntary and conviction off the table, the court's deliberation turned to the kind of acquittal to which this manner of illness-induced involuntariness should give rise. The decision of the court was that cognitive impairments with physiological rather than psychological causes could be categorised as 'diseases of the mind' under the *M'Naghten* rules, despite falling outside lay conceptions of 'insanity'. As a consequence, D's unconscious condition at the relevant time was classed as *insane* automatism, and a verdict of not guilty by reason of insanity followed.

The language used to discuss automatism may easily obscure the reality here. When courts and commentators refer (as they quite often do) to the 'defence' of automatism, the natural implication is that the sane/insane automatism distinction amounts to a choice between one of two defences (automatism or insanity). In truth, however, automatism – a state of unwilled, involuntary action – is not a defence at all. It is an admission that definitional elements of a crime are absent.[17] Once this is understood, the operation of *M'Naghten* in *Kemp* (and similar cases) is clarified. The movements of the defendant in *Kemp*, having occurred without any input from a conscious will, did not amount to the commission of a crime and were in need of neither excuse nor justification. When insanity was introduced it was not, therefore, as a defence – none was necessary. Rather it was a means of qualifying Mr. Kemp's acquittal, diverting him away from a guaranteed absolute discharge and towards the special verdict.

The justification for this inculpatory, diversionary, operation of insanity is quite explicitly one of public protection. D who receives a special verdict remains under court powers and, should he be believed to pose an ongoing threat to others, can be made subject to a range of available disposal options – options that are unavailable in respect of a defendant acquitted outside of the special verdict. This rationale is set out very clearly in *Bratty*, where, speaking on voluntariness, Lord Denning expressed the view that while '[t]he requirement that it should be a voluntary act is essential … in every criminal case',[18] it did not follow from this that 'every involuntary act … leads to an acquittal'.[19] For reasons of public protection, this could not be the case where the involuntary act stemmed from an ongoing condition:

> Suppose a crime is committed by a man in a state of automatism or clouded consciousness due to a recurrent disease of the mind. Such an act is no doubt involuntary, but it does not give rise to an unqualified acquittal, for that would mean that he would be let at large to do it again. The only proper verdict is one which ensures that the person who suffers from the disease is kept secure in a hospital so as not to be a danger to himself or others. That is, a verdict of guilty but insane.[20]

[17] JJ Child and A Reed, 'Automatism Is Never a Defence' (2014) 65 *Northern Ireland Legal Quarterly* 167.

[18] *Bratty v Attorney-General for Northern Ireland* [1963] AC 386, 409.

[19] ibid 410.

[20] ibid.

In furtherance of this point, Lord Denning stressed that the prosecution must regard itself as having not only the ability, but also the obligation to raise insanity in order to prevent an outright acquittal in cases where the status test may be met.[21] It is an approach that has been confirmed in the now leading case of *Sullivan*.[22]

Although Denning's comments in *Bratty* were specifically directed towards insane automatism cases, his rationale has more extensive implications. If the sane/insane automatism distinction is justified by a public protection mandate, this would seem to apply equally well in cases where, due to a condition meeting the *M'Naghten* status test, a defendant acted voluntarily but without mens rea. Following the reasoning of Lord Denning and Lord Diplock (in *Bratty* and *Sullivan*, respectively) it would seem that the prosecution should be regarded as being under the same duty to raise insanity in these cases, in the interests of protecting the public from recurring dangerous behaviour. Certainly, in *Sullivan*, while the debate focused on automatism, there was no question as to whether the defendant possessed the mens rea of the violent offence charged, given that he was accepted as having been unconscious at the time. Nonetheless, rather than acquitting outright, the jury returned a special verdict of insanity, which was upheld both in the Court of Appeal and the House of Lords.

The same rationale appears to hold where D completes the elements of a crime and seeks to appeal to a defence other than insanity on the basis of a delusional mistaken belief. Where, for example, D makes an honest but delusional mistake as to the need for defensive force, the question arises as to whether he should be able to rely on self-defence, or whether that route should be excluded by mental disorder or insanity rules. The current approach at common law remains somewhat confused and inconsistent, but has broadly followed the same diversionary route discussed above, with diversion to insanity and the special verdict preferred.[23]

The relationship between delusional beliefs and self-defence is complicated by the two-prong objective–subjective test for self-defence, wherein a defendant is required to have responded with reasonable force to a threat that was honestly perceived.[24] In certain cases, the courts' approach has been to permit a defendant's mental condition to be relevant to the subjective honest belief test. In other words,

[21] ibid 411.

[22] *Sullivan* [1984] AC 156: 'The purpose of the legislation relating to the defence of insanity, ever since its origin in 1800, has been to protect society against recurrence of the dangerous conduct' per Lord Diplock at 182.

[23] See Child and Sullivan (n 8) 799: 'The rationale for the insanity defence is easily stated. Where D acts in a harmful manner, but lacks blameworthiness due to some internal condition that caused him to lack understanding of his acts and/or their wrongfulness, whilst his acts should be excused, the court should consider a disposal order that will protect the public from such harms in the future. … Whenever D satisfies the insanity defence, whether he commits every element of the full offence or not, and whether he may be able to rely on an alternative defence or not, the insanity defence must be applied in preference: the court must be enabled to consider how D can be helped, and others protected.'

[24] *Gladstone Williams* [1984] 78 Cr App R 276; Criminal Justice and Immigration Act (CJIA) 2008, s 76(3)–(4).

where the defendant acts with force in response to a delusional misperception of threat, the courts have asked whether that force was excessive or disproportionate in the circumstances as the defendant delusionally perceived them to be.[25] In theory, then, the courts have left open the possibility that a defendant could successfully argue self-defence on the basis of a delusional perception of threat, so long as the force they used in response to that threat was reasonable in the (perceived) circumstances.

However, subsequent case law demonstrates that courts are reluctant to permit this possibility in actuality, preferring an approach whereby a defendant who responds to a delusional misperception of threat will be diverted to insanity (albeit, interestingly, the courts seem hesitant to state this outright). This is well illustrated in the 2013 case of *Oye*, in which the Court of Appeal briefly considered the potential for self-defence in circumstances involving a psychotic defendant who caused injury to another person while believing himself to be under attack by demons.[26] While acknowledging that D was entitled to have his delusional perceptions adopted for the subjective 'honest belief' test, the court refused to allow self-defence to be successful on the grounds that the jury were entitled to find the force used by D (which amounted to a punch sufficient to fracture the victim's jaw, and the throwing of some crockery) was nonetheless unreasonable in the circumstances as the defendant perceived them to be. A starker illustration still is provided by the 2018 case of *Taj*,[27] a case involving a defendant who mistakenly believed he was acting to prevent a terror attack. Much of the appeal in *Taj* focused on intoxication as the likely cause for his mistaken delusion, which would straightforwardly have undermined his appeals to self-defence.[28] However, crucially for present purposes, at the time of Taj's appeal hearing a distinct mental condition (bipolar disorder) was recognised as an *alternative* cause.[29] Since this alternative cause was not caught by prior-fault rules (was not attributable to intoxication) and was not held to come within the insanity rules, the possibility of self-defence would appear to have been left open. As in *Oye*, however, the court dismissed this option on the facts. In doing so, it quite bizarrely suggested that while the belief test remains subjective, the test for reasonable force applies to the circumstances as they were in objective reality and *not* to D's subjective perception of them[30] – an interpretation that, if accepted, would thoroughly undercut the purpose of the subjective test, and seems to have been applied with the intention of preventing a delusional perception of threat from forming the basis of self-defence.

[25] See *Martin* [2001] EWCA Crim 2245.
[26] *Oye* [2013] EWCA Crim 1725. Discussed in Child and Sullivan (n 8).
[27] *Taj* [2018] EWCA Crim 1743. Discussed in JJ Child, HS Crombag and GR Sullivan, 'Defending the Delusional, the Irrational, and the Dangerous' [2020] *Crim LR* 306.
[28] See *O'Grady* (1987) 85 Cr App R 315 and *Hatton* (2006) 1 Cr App R 16. Even here *Taj* was not a typical case, as the court were tracing D's delusional state back to a *previous* state of intoxication. But that issue is outside the focus of the current chapter.
[29] *Taj* [2018] EWCA Crim 1743, [61]–[65].
[30] ibid [63]–[64].

Dual Roles and Dual Rationales

What the above discussion illustrates is that the insanity defence currently plays dual roles, supported by two distinct rationales. On one hand, it operates as an exculpatory defence, justified by the potential for mental disorder to negate culpability under certain conditions. On the other, it functions as an inculpatory measure justified by public protection concerns, bringing mentally disordered defendants within the scope of the criminal law and thereby enabling the court to retain powers of detention over them. This distinction is not always easy to discern, being obfuscated by the mislabelling of defences (automatism) or hidden within the complex construction and application of alternative rules (self-defence), but its presence and impact on liability is undeniable.

II. The Case for Partial Abolition

One response to the foregoing discussion would be to accept the dual roles played by the insanity defence, and to focus on tackling the unclarity and inconsistency of its application at common law. This is the approach taken in papers by Sullivan and Child, and we endorse it as an important exercise that will significantly improve the status quo. However, if we return to first principles, and if we allow ourselves to consider the potential for legislative reform, we must ask whether the dual-role structure of the insanity defence is something we ought to accept. Our position is that it is not, and that any statutory restatement of the law should abolish insanity's inculpatory role. In the discussions that follow, we set out three major problems with the current law that may be mitigated and/or resolved by partial abolition. We then discuss the benefits of partial abolition for the remaining exculpatory role of insanity as a defence, and address an important question of practical application.

Inculpatory Insanity and Inappropriate Liability

A perfectly functioning insanity defence, even in its inculpatory role, would leave no room for inappropriate convictions. All those caught within the insanity rules would be diverted to the special verdict and, while potentially subject to disposal orders, would be cleared of any criminal guilt. Unfortunately, the operation of the current law is far from perfect. Under the current application of the insanity rules, it is quite possible for D to submit to a conviction for an offence the elements of which she is accepted not to satisfy purely in order to avoid an insanity verdict. This is brought out in a particularly troubling way by *Sullivan*,[31] where D was

[31] *Sullivan* [1984] AC 156.

accepted by all parties as having acted unconsciously and, therefore, both involuntarily and without mens rea. At the close of evidence, the judge ruled that (if the jury accepted the evidence) it would not be open to them to return a verdict of not guilty to the grievous bodily harm offence charged, but rather it must be the special verdict of not guilty by reason of insanity. To avoid the potential consequences of this, D pleaded guilty to the lesser charge of inflicting actual bodily harm, a charge requiring proof of an assault committed either intentionally or recklessly – neither of which, it goes without saying, could have been established in respect of an unconscious defendant. In effect, then, what we have in *Sullivan* is a defendant accepting a conviction for a crime for which he did not have the mens rea in order to avoid an insanity verdict for a more serious crime for which he *also* did not have the mens rea.[32]

Cases of this kind are particularly concerning due to the reversal in the burden of proof that is attached to the insanity rules. The presumption of sanity established in *M'Naghten* lays the burden of proof for establishing *in*sanity on the defence.[33] This presumption, while arguably appropriate in the exculpatory context, means that any defendant caught by the inculpatory operation of *M'Naghten* suddenly finds himself subject to the requirement to prove a defence – a burden he would not be under had the rules of voluntariness and/or mens rea been permitted to apply to him in the usual way.[34] Troubling enough by itself, the worry is compounded when one recalls that a defence of insanity introduced via the inculpatory mechanism might still be rejected by a jury. Where such cases arise, there does not appear to be a clear process by which the court may ensure that all burdens of proof applicable prior to the diversion have been adequately discharged. This was the main ground of appeal in *Bratty*:[35] the defendant had initially raised automatism, but had been redirected by the trial judge to insanity, a defence the jury rejected. The defendant appealed his conviction on the grounds that the introduction and subsequent rejection of inculpatory insanity meant that the question of sane automatism had not been adequately resolved, a suggestion dismissed by the court on the grounds that the jury had, in rejecting insanity, implicitly rejected any claim that the defendant's actions were performed involuntarily.[36] On the particular facts of *Bratty*, this

[32] The circumstances leading to D's decision to plead guilty in *Sullivan* have changed with the reform of the special verdict, providing disposal options beyond indefinite detention. However, this has led to only a minor increase in the use of the insanity defence, despite a disproportionately high prevalence of mental disorders within the prison population. R Mackay, 'Ten More Years of the Insanity Defence' [2012] *Crim LR* 946.

[33] Discussed in *Bratty v Attorney-General for Northern Ireland* [1963] AC 386.

[34] T Jones, 'Insanity, Automatism, and the Burden of Proof on the Accused' (1995) *LQR* 475.

[35] *Bratty* [1963] AC 386.

[36] ibid 4: 'Where the possibility of an unconscious act depends on, and only on, the existence of a defect of reason from disease of the mind within the M'Naghten Rules, a rejection by the jury of this defence of insanity necessarily implies that they reject the possibility.' As an isolated statement this is worrying, and inaccurate – a jury may reject a defence of insanity on the basis that neither of the two limbs are met without denying the existence of any alleged condition meeting the status test. One could make the case that, since neither the 'nature and quality' nor the 'wrongness' limb of *M'Naghten* can

may have been a reasonable inference for the court to make; nonetheless, the case introduces a concern that it does not adequately resolve. Clearly, where a defendant is redirected to a defence of insanity that is subsequently rejected, the court cannot in principle convict without having determined whether an acquittal may yet be warranted on the basis of (non-insane) automatism, lack of mens rea, or any alternative line of defence from which the insanity rules intervened to divert D. In practice, however, the lack of a clear mechanism for such cases creates a real danger that the rejection of insanity will be treated as the end of the matter, with unresolved questions of voluntariness, mens rea, and alternative defences falling by the wayside.[37] Oversight of this kind risks the unjust and inappropriate conviction of non-culpable defendants in respect of whom the prosecution's burden of proof has not been fully discharged.

Exacerbating the problem of inappropriate outcomes is the uncertain application of threshold judgements for insanity, marking the point when the insanity rules will be engaged. This, of course, includes the notorious internal/external cause distinction – a much-criticised aspect of the current insanity defence,[38] and one that would largely be made irrelevant with the abolition of inculpatory insanity.[39] Another problematic threshold, already introduced, arises when D wishes to rely on an alternative defence, marking the point where D's mental condition or delusion will divert D from other potential defences to the application of insanity. In the most troubling examples, this threshold will be met more easily than the terms of the insanity defence itself, diverting D to a non-applicable insanity defence and therefore liability. In the case of *Taj*, discussed above, the Court of Appeal excluded D from the application of self-defence (making clear that defendants cannot rely on mistaken deluded beliefs), but subsequently did not find sufficient basis for an insanity verdict. The outcome was a significant term of imprisonment for a defendant who, had he been permitted to rely on his honest beliefs to establish self-defence, might well have been acquitted.

fail to apply to an unconscious defendant, any rejection of insanity contains an implicit rejection of automatism. Even this is inadequate, however, as it disregards potential cases where D lacks conscious control over his actions, but retains awareness of his surroundings. Given that both limbs have been narrowly interpreted in terms of D's specific knowledge at the time of the act, while explicitly ruling out the relevance of broader failings of agency and decision-making capacity, it is conceivable such a defendant might be not be regarded by a jury as having met either limb of *M'Naghten* despite having acted involuntarily (for recent confirmation of the wrongness limb as a knowledge-based test, see *R v Keal* [2022] EWCA Crim 341). As such, while a denial of automatism may have been implicit in the jury's rejection of insanity on the facts of *Bratty*, it is both incorrect and potentially dangerous to suggest that *any* rejection of insanity 'necessarily implies' a rejection of automatism so long as each claim relies on the presence of the same condition.

[37] See eg *Bratty v Attorney General for Northern Ireland* [1963] AC 386, and *Taj* [2018] EWCA Crim 1743, both discussed in section I.

[38] See eg J Rumbold, 'Diabetes and Criminal Responsibility' (2010) 174 *Criminal Law and Justice Weekly* 21.

[39] We discuss this further below, in the context of the retained exculpatory role of insanity.

Inculpatory Insanity, Answering for Crime, and Inappropriate Labelling

A further problem with inculpatory insanity concerns the duty incumbent upon any criminal justice system to enable defendants to answer for *pro tanto* wrongs.[40] It may be easy to assume that the route to an acquittal is of little importance, so long as the defendant is in fact acquitted (and, ideally, discharged). From a defendant's perspective, however, the path to the outcome can matter almost as much as the outcome itself. In 'The Mark of Responsibility', John Gardner discusses the preference among defendants for arguing provocation over diminished responsibility, despite the fact that each defence provides the same degree of partial exculpation and carries the same implications for sentencing.[41] Gardner posits that the crucial difference lies in the ability of each defence to provide a means by which defendants may account for their actions in rational terms. While provocation is a defence of excuse, diminished responsibility is neither excusing nor justifying; rather, it amounts to a concession that one is unable to give an account of oneself on that occasion as a rational, responsible agent.[42] *Ceteris paribus*, we prefer provocation over diminished responsibility because as rational beings it is natural for us to want to explain ourselves in rational terms; to have and to offer an intelligible account of our actions and behaviour.[43] As Gardner states:

> [I]t is part of the nature of self-respect that a self-respecting person wants to be able to give an intelligible rational account of herself, to be able to show that her actions were

[40] On the role and importance of 'answering', see RA Duff, *Answering for Crime* (Oxford, Hart Publishing, 2007).

[41] J Gardner, 'The Mark of Responsibility' in J Gardner (ed) *Offences and Defences: Selected Essays in the Philosophy of Criminal Law* (Oxford, Oxford University Press, 2007). Specifically, he references the debate that arose around these two partial defences regarding victims of domestic abuse who go on to kill their abusers. The debate concerned the requirement of the provocation defence that the relevant loss of control be 'sudden and temporary' – a specification which excluded from the defence many victims of long-term domestic abuse. Although these defendants were typically able to rely on an alternative defence of diminished responsibility, their exclusion from a specific defence of provocation was regarded as an injustice; it required these defendants to commit to a narrative of impaired capacity, rather than to one in which the killing was carried out as a (partially) excusable response to extreme and ongoing provocation. Successful campaigning spearheaded by organisations such as Justice for Women and the Southall Black Sisters ultimately led to legislation replacing provocation with a new partial defence of loss of control, formulated without the 'sudden and temporary' requirement. (Coroners and Justice Act 2009, s54).

[42] To understand this distinction one must understand that, for Gardner, to give either a justification or an excuse for one's action is to explain that action in terms of reasons; to justify an action is to claim that it was performed 'for adequate reasons' while to excuse an action is to claim that, while the reasons for acting may not have been adequate, the beliefs and desires motivating that action were supported by reasons that were (ibid 178–79). To be able to justify or excuse one's action is, therefore, to be able 'to explain oneself, to give an intelligible account of oneself, to answer for oneself, as a rational being' (ibid 182). It is in this ability, for Gardner, that basic responsibility consists.

[43] ibid 178: 'So as rational beings – beings who are able to follow reasons – we cannot but want to follow reasons – to excel in rationality.' Gardner is heavily influenced here by Aristotle's view that 'rationality is a capacity that makes the case for its own realization'. See fn 2, referencing Aristotle's *Nicomachean Ethics* 1097b24–1098a17, 1103a23–25, 1168a5–9.

> the actions of someone who aspired to live up to the proper standards for success in her life and fitness to lead it. She wants it to be the case that her actions were not truly wrongful, or if they were wrongful, that they were at any rate justified, or if they were not justified, that they were at any rate excused.[44]

It is easy to see the potential relevance of this analysis to the present discussion.[45] If we accept Gardner's position that people have an interest in accounting for themselves in terms of reasons for action, then exculpation on grounds of standard principles of mens rea, actus reus, excuse and mistaken justification will be preferable prima facie to exculpation on grounds of exclusion from the class of rational, and thus responsible, persons. If we accept, further, that this interest is rooted in respect for oneself as a person, it would seem to follow that there is an imperative upon makers and influencers of the law to enable such accounts to be given where possible, in recognition of that basic personhood. Applying the insanity defence to supervene over both a lack of mens rea and other potential defences qualifies a defendant's right to explain his actions as a self-respecting person. Regardless of his delusional mistake, it still makes sense for D to explain that he was not trying to commit a criminal wrong, and/or that he was acting on beliefs which, if true, would have afforded him a complete defence.

Within the current law, once the insanity defence is engaged D is not only restricted in his explanation to the terms of that narrow defence, but he also bears the legal burden of proving its elements on the balance of probabilities.[46] If he is successful, D is labelled 'not guilty *by reason of insanity*',[47] a label that discards (and implicitly discredits) D's denial of the offence itself, along with any claim to an alternative defence. In the context of any future comprehensive review of the law, this provides another principled reason for restricting the insanity defence to cases where D lacks alternative justifications or excuses for his conduct, maximising our engagement with D as a potentially rational actor.[48]

[44] J Gardner, *Offences and Defences* (Oxford, Oxford University Press, 2007) 133.

[45] Although Gardner himself would likely disagree with our conclusions, regarding mental condition-based exculpation as properly and appropriately understood in terms of the absence of reasons for action. For a critical analysis of this position from a therapeutic perspective, see A Acorn, 'Responsibility, Self-respect and the Ethics of Self-pathologization' in F Tanguay-Renaud and J Stribopoulos (eds) *Rethinking Criminal Law Theory: New Canadian Perspectives in the Philosophy of Domestic, Transnational, and International Criminal Law* (Oxford, Hart Publishing, 2002).

[46] In its practical effect, rather than the prosecution's proving D's mens rea and voluntariness to the criminal standard, the diversion forces D to prove his innocence by demonstrating that his condition caused him not to understand the nature or quality of his action. See T Jones, 'Insanity, Automatism, and the Burden of Proof on the Accused' (1995) *LQR* 475, 484–88.

[47] ie, the special verdict (emphasis added).

[48] One response is that if D qualifies for the insanity rules, then he is not a rational actor, and that an exclusion from criminal responsibility also excludes consideration of mens rea and alternative defences. We see something of this in Law Commission, *Insanity and Automatism* (Discussion Paper, 2013) ch 2. We find this argument unconvincing – whilst we agree that insanity is best understood as a denial of responsibility, it is still necessary to explain *what* D is not responsible *for*. Where this is anything other than an unjustified or unexcused criminal offence, there is a burden to explain why the same rule is not applied to the population at large, and why civil rules are not more appropriate (discussed further below).

Inculpatory Insanity and Public Protection

The third reason for favouring abolition is simply that the inculpatory insanity defence is not well suited to its (purported) aim. If we accept the narrative, exemplified by the judgment of Lord Denning in *Bratty*,[49] that the inculpatory role of insanity is necessary as a forward-looking measure for preventive detention and societal protection, we should also recognise that it performs this role extremely poorly.

This can be illustrated by a number of basic doctrinal impediments. There is a curiosity to the public protection argument, for example, in that it pretends the insanity rules are an essential mechanism for 'clutching' dangerous individuals whilst interpreting the elements of insanity so narrowly that it applies to only a handful of defendants each year.[50] Equally, the criteria employed do not provide a reliable measure for future dangerousness; just as internal causes (potentially caught by insanity) may be temporary or non-dangerous,[51] so external causes (excluded from insanity) may entail significant risks of reoccurrence[52] and, more generally, these criteria can be uncertain and unintuitive in application.[53] Finally, highlighted by Sullivan and Child,[54] it should be noted that the insanity defence is not applied to the public at large, but only to those who have completed a certain act – an act that must satisfy certain actus reus elements of a crime. But, as we have discussed, this act needs to be neither voluntary nor accompanied by mens rea. In this manner, the base threshold for application of the insanity defence (the initial filter for defendants) is constructed with a set of actus reus elements (varying across different offences) that were certainly not designed with this task in mind, with no attempt at risk-based justification. Civil detention rules are not predicated on criminal actus reus elements (ie they are not, independently, reliable markers of dangerousness),[55] and criminal offences are not established on the basis of a few actus reus elements either (ie they are not, independently, reliable markers of a criminal wrong[56]). What useful role are they playing within the insanity rules?

[49] *Bratty v Attorney General for Northern Ireland* [1963] AC 386.

[50] On the low rate of use, see R Mackay, B Mitchell, and L Howe, 'Yet More Facts About the Insanity Defence' [2006] *Crim LR* 399. For more on the relationship between criminal law and dangerousness, and preventive detention in particular, see eg AE Bottoms and R Brownsword, 'Dangerousness and Rights' in J Hinton (ed) *Dangerousness: Problems of Assessment and Prediction* (Crows Nest (Australia), Allen & Unwin, 1983); N Walker, 'Dangerous Mistakes' (1991) 158 *British Journal of Psychiatry* 752; N Walker, *Dangerous People* (London, Blackstone Press, 1996); J Floud, 'Dangerousness and Criminal Justice' (1982) 22 *British Journal of Criminology* 213; AE Bottoms and R Brownsword, 'The Dangerousness Debate After the Floud Report' (1982) 22 *British Journal of Criminology* 229.

[51] eg an operable congestion of blood on the brain (*Kemp* [1957] 1 QB 399).

[52] eg external events leading to post-traumatic stress disorder.

[53] See Law Commission, *Insanity and Automatism* (Discussion Paper, 2013) [1.37]–[1.47].

[54] Child and Sullivan (n 8) 799.

[55] Mental Health Act 1983, Part 2. We discuss civil detention further below.

[56] This includes so-called strict liability offences, which at least also require D's conduct to be voluntary.

There are further arguments of principle at issue here as well. The use of the insanity defence as a tool to safeguard powers of disposal over 'dangerous' mentally ill defendants raises concerns about the fair and equal application of the law. In all likelihood, there regularly come before the lower courts individuals with no relevant mental condition who may nonetheless be perceived, rightly or wrongly, to pose an ongoing risk to public safety. If, however, D's guilt cannot be adequately established in respect of the offence with which he is charged, then he is entitled to an acquittal irrespective of any threat he may be felt to pose. There is, in such cases, no suggestion that the principles of culpability ought to be amended or altered in order to ensure an outcome preferable to the court, on grounds of public protection or any other grounds. To permit this to happen in cases where insanity is raised as a diversionary measure would, therefore, require additional justification beyond a simple appeal to public safety.

To put it another way: given that we do not *generally* countenance the manipulation of culpability principles to forestall an acquittal on public protection grounds where such an outcome would otherwise be supported, it is difficult to see a non-discriminatory justification for the use of such an approach *exclusively* in cases where the apparent risk proceeds from mental difference on the part of the defendant.[57] Indeed, by diverting defendants away from unqualified acquittals and towards the special verdict on the basis of a mental condition, we may be in breach of obligations under the UN Convention on the Rights of Persons with Disabilities (CRPD).[58] While this is not a question with which this chapter will engage, it is important to be aware that the use of mental condition defences is regarded in some quarters as a contravention of human rights law, with the official position of the Committee of the Convention being that the abolition of such defences and the introduction of a 'disability neutral'[59] approach is required for compliance.[60]

But even beyond this, it is surely wrong to present the criminal law as the sole (or even the primary) mechanism for detaining dangerous individuals who

[57] The existence of a presumption of sanity and the requirement that actus reus is established before a special verdict is returned complicate the comparison drawn here. Nonetheless there is still a clear disparity, in that a non-mentally ill defendant who acted without mens rea (assuming the offence is not one of strict liability), or who acted involuntarily, will be entitled to an acquittal. This is not currently the case where the lack of either voluntariness or mens rea is due to a condition meeting the *M'Naghten* status test.

[58] In particular Art 12, which ensures for persons with disabilities the right 'to enjoy legal capacity on an equal basis with others in all aspects of life' (CRPD Art 12(2)), and Art 14, which prohibits the use of a disability as justification for a deprivation of liberty (CRPD Art 14(1)(b)) and ensures for persons with disabilities equal protection from deprivations of liberty under the law (CRPD Art 14(1-2)). The implications of these clauses for mental condition-specific defences are discussed in T Minkowitz, 'Rethinking Criminal Responsibility from a Critical Disability Perspective' (2014) 23 *Griffith Law Review* 434.

[59] For discussion of disability neutrality in a UK context, see J Peay, 'Mental Incapacity and Criminal Liability: Redrawing the Fault Lines?' (2015) *International Journal of Law and Psychiatry* 25.

[60] Committee on the Rights of Persons with Disabilities, *Guidelines on Article 14 of the Convention on the Rights of Persons with Disabilities* (14th session of the Committee, 2015). See especially s 14

have not committed a crime. The obvious alternative is the use of civil detention where D poses a threat to himself or others.[61] The Law Commission criticises civil detention rules as 'inadequate' for protecting the public,[62] citing two reasons: concern over a potential gap in time between criminal acquittal and civil detention, and a lack of oversight from the Secretary of State for individuals detained through the civil procedure. But these reasons are far from definitive. Regarding the first, powers could be given to the criminal courts to prevent such a gap (as the Commission appears to acknowledge).[63] Regarding the second, beyond a principled objection to added barriers for those detained without having committed an offence under the insanity rules,[64] an independent review chaired by Professor Sir Simon Wessely has cast considerable doubt on the policy and practical benefits of the Secretary of State's role.[65]

Exculpatory Insanity and the Benefits of Partial Abolition

The exculpatory insanity defence is the label we have used to describe insanity when it is playing the role of a defence properly so-called (ie D has committed all the elements of an offence, does not have an alternative defence and appeals to insanity as her route to acquittal via the special verdict). Abolishing insanity in its inculpatory role and restricting it to its function as a true defence would, we believe, have a clarifying effect on an area of law that has become untenably muddled and intractable. Detaching forward-looking, risk-based inculpatory insanity from backward-looking, culpability-assessing exculpatory insanity would: (i) eliminate

('Persons with disabilities are frequently denied equal protection under [criminal] laws by being diverted to a separate track of law, including through mental health laws') and s 16 ('declarations of unfitness to stand trial or incapacity to be found criminally responsible in criminal justice systems and the detention of persons based on those declarations, are contrary to Article 14 of the Convention since it deprives the person of his or her right to due process and safeguards that are applicable to every defendant').

[61] Mental Health Act 1983, Part 2.

[62] Law Commission, *Insanity and Automatism* (Discussion Paper, 2013) [2.23]–[2.29].

[63] There are various options to model this on, including the emergency admissions procedure (Mental Health Act 1983, s 4), or the process of diversion without conviction currently only open to magistrates (Mental Health Act 1983, s 37(3), and so on. See R Mackay, *Mental Condition Defences in the Criminal Law* (Oxford, Oxford University Press, 1995) 70–71 and 139. See also, for example, recent changes in the Netherlands where, since 2020, previous criminal law routes to ordering compulsory treatment for those not satisfying the elements of an offence have been abolished and replaced with entirely civil orders. Notably, these civil orders can be imposed directly by a criminal court (Forensic Care Act 2020, Art 2.3) eliminating the potential gap between criminal acquittal and civil detention.

[64] We are talking here about those caught by the insanity rules despite lacking mens rea or satisfying the terms of an alternative defence. Discussed in RA Duff, 'Incapacity and Insanity: Do We Need the Insanity Defence?' in Livings et al (n 13) 168–69.

[65] *Modernising the Mental Health Act: Final Report of the Independent Review of the Mental Health Act 1983* (HCWS1149, 2018). The report recommends the removal of the Secretary of State's role (201), and criticises the current system for creating delays (disruptive to patient recovery) without effective or worthwhile oversight (197–201).

most of the concern that currently exists surrounding burden of proof, since insanity would only be introduced as a proper defence in cases where both mens rea and voluntariness can be proven; (ii) ameliorate some of the concerns regarding fair labelling and equal access to justice (at least addressing the most egregiously inequitable aspects, where defendants with mental disability have acquittals withheld despite the accepted absence of mens rea); (iii) allow us to eliminate some of the more absurd aspects of the current insanity defence such as the internal/external causes distinction, which came about as the result of the courts trying to get *M'Naghten* to operate simultaneously as a backwards-looking test for culpability and a forwards-looking test for dangerousness, resulting in a nonsense that effectively serves neither purpose; and (iv) enable us to develop and even expand *M'Naghten* as a defence, without the limitations currently imposed by its function as a protective measure. The first three of these are essentially extrapolations from the problems discussed in previous sections, but the last requires some explanation.

If we aim to develop effective proposals for insanity defence reform, we must begin with a clear understanding of the purpose and function of insanity as a legal concept. Herein lies a problem. The current approach to legal insanity is driven by two quite distinct sets of normative questions generating different, potentially contradictory, answers. On the one hand, insanity in its exculpatory role purports to address questions of culpability, offering a means of determining the conditions under which evidence of a mental disorder should negate D's liability for an offence.[66] In its inculpatory role, meanwhile, the defence is driven not by questions of culpability but by those of risk assessment and harm prevention. These forward-looking questions are both legitimate and important, appropriately informing disposal options within the special verdict and non-criminal detention within the civil law.[67] They are, however, quite distinct from – and unlikely to generate the same answers as – those backwards-looking culpability questions with which, in principle, the defence concurrently attempts to engage. The effect of this in practice is a doctrine of insanity that is in some respects at odds with itself, pulled simultaneously in two different directions.

[66] Commentators may disagree whether mental incapacity *excuses* D's offending or *excludes* liability for lack of a responsible agent, but in either case, the focus is on defining the basis and extent of exculpation. This core normative question, as we identify it, still presents considerable and enduring challenges for the law (and for the scientific community informing the law). How and to what extent particular mental disorders qualify an offender's culpability remains contested as an abstraction, and this only becomes more difficult when we consider how a disorder is experienced by a specific individual (with diverse values, experiences and emotions) at a precise and previous moment in time. However, again, despite these difficulties, it is surely the correct question to ask when defining complete and/or partial mental incapacity defences.

[67] Disposal following the special verdict is governed by the Criminal Procedure (Insanity) Act 1964, s 5. Civil detention for the health or safety of the patient or for the protection of other persons is governed by the Mental Health Act 1983, Part 2 (as amended).

Left unaddressed, this tension between rationales is likely to create problems for any attempt to modify the scope of the defence.[68] The Law Commission's reform proposals in 2013 provide a useful example.[69] In its Discussion Paper, the Commission raised many valid criticisms of the current approach – that the sane/insane automatism distinction is unfair and incoherent, that the *M'Naghten* rules are interpreted excessively restrictively, etc; and it argued (as we do) that the rules around insanity need a significant legislative overhaul.[70] However, a significant part of the Commission's proposed reform was the fusing of sane and insane automatism (conceived by the Commission – in our opinion wrongly – as two alternative defences) into a single defence leading to a verdict of 'not criminally responsible by reason of recognised medical condition'.[71] The Commission's aims were commendable: to expand the scope of the existing defence, while distancing it from stigmatising terminology and removing the 'internal/external cause' distinction that has led to incoherent and counterintuitive outcomes. Unfortunately, its approach was compromised by a failure to acknowledge and address the diversionary operation of the current insanity rules, a failure that led it inadvertently to construct an approach the primary consequence of which would be the inculpation of more people whose actions would not otherwise amount to a crime. Had the inculpatory corollary been adequately grasped, it would have been clear to the Commission that the result of combining 'sane' and 'insane' automatism into a singular defence would be the diversion of greater numbers of defendants away from an absolute acquittal and discharge on grounds of involuntariness, and towards a (reconceived) special verdict.

The Commission's failure here was in some respects inevitable. So long as the inculpatory dimension of the insanity jurisprudence exists, any attempt to broaden the application of *M'Naghten* as a defence (whether through expansion of the scope of the status test, or reinterpretation of the two limbs) will come at the cost of a wider inculpatory net – and while an expanded reading of the current insanity rules may be necessary to protect (exculpate) those who fulfil the elements of an offence but are nonetheless undeserving of blame, whether we should expand the rules to capture more defendants who fail to fulfil those elements (on grounds of harm prevention/risk management) is a very different question. What the Law Commission's example illustrates is that, by fusing these questions within the current law, we run the risk of answering neither effectively. Abolishing the inculpatory aspect of insanity would ameliorate this problem, allowing the terms and scope of the defence to be designed in view of the culpability question alone.

[68] We see this alluded to in other writings, which criticise the inconsistent application of the current insanity rules and the unfairness of reversing the burden of proof. See discussion in W Wilson et al, 'Violence, Sleepwalking and the Criminal Law. Part 2: The Legal Aspects' (2005) *Crim LR* 614, 622–23; T Jones, 'Insanity, Automatism, and the Burden of Proof on the Accused' (1995) *LQR* 475, 512–16.

[69] Law Commission, *Insanity and Automatism* (Discussion Paper, 2013).

[70] ibid ch 1.

[71] ibid chs 3–4.

In concluding this point, let us consider the recent case of *Keal*.[72] D was found guilty of attempting to murder three members of his family, whom he attacked under the delusional belief that he was possessed and controlled by the devil. D repeatedly apologised to his victims during the attack, recognising the wrongness of his actions but believing that he had no choice in performing them. D appealed his convictions, arguing inter alia that a correct interpretation of *M'Naghten* should allow the insanity defence to apply where a mental disorder creates the perception of external control and manipulation. D's appeal was dismissed, with the clear statement from Lord Burnett that the 'defence of insanity is not available to a defendant who, although he knew what he was doing was wrong, he believed that he had no choice but to commit the act in question'.[73] We anticipate a negative academic response to this decision; the public interest in D's conviction for three counts of attempted murder is certainly questionable. But as this new debate unfolds, we encourage commentators to consider the full implications associated with expanding the insanity rules to include the events in *Keal*. As a basis for exculpation, we are broadly in favour of expansion: D should not be held liable for an offence if we believe that he experienced no choice in its commission. But the inculpatory corollary of the current law must not be forgotten. Any expansion of insanity to include the situation in *Keal* would necessitate (under the current law) an expansion of insanity to include all defendants who experience compulsion in completing the actus reus elements of a crime, even in the absence of mens rea; a numerically unpredictable, and essentially unjustified, expansion of inculpatory insanity.

Addressing Some Final Concerns

Were inculpatory insanity abolished, conduct previously caught within its terms would no longer be diverted to the insanity rules. We have set out the potential benefits of this. Nevertheless, the introduction of an abolitionist position – however careful its scope – may naturally give rise to concerns as to the practicality and/or appropriateness of applying standard criminal rules to delusional or irrational defendants. On this question, serious reservations have been raised, both by the Commission,[74] and by commentators such as Duff:

> [R]ational incapacities negate what the normal requirements of mens rea presuppose, an agent with ordinary rational capacities: absent such capacities, it is pointless, or perhaps even normatively senseless, to ask whether the defendant satisfied those requirements.[75]

[72] *Keal* [2022] EWCA Crim 341.
[73] ibid [48].
[74] Law Commission, *Insanity and Automatism* (Discussion Paper, 2013) [2.18]–[2.22].
[75] Duff (n 64) 167–68.

While there is some force to this objection, it is easily overstated. Although 'normal requirements' within the law might apply best to composed and thoughtful rational actors, the criminal legal system must (and does) engage with defendants of very different levels of capacity, including those who have made unreasonable mistakes as to factual circumstances. Indeed, the system is currently operating with an extremely narrow insanity defence that diverts very few defendants from this standard application, and other legal systems operate without a diverting mechanism at all.[76]

It is possible to imagine extreme examples where discussion of mens rea might seem inappropriate: for example, asking if D intended to cause death or serious harm where D kills V believing he is fighting a snake at the centre of the earth.[77] But the inappropriate feel of such discussion often masks the simple truth, that in examples of this kind mens rea may simply be absent: D did not know that V was a person.[78] Other examples may be more challenging, such as Duff's example in which D kills someone while believing them to have been 'taken over' by an alien.[79] Here, there may be legitimate doubt whether D believed V was still a person or not, relevant to potential liability for murder. It is important, however, to remember the role of the criminal burden of proof in such cases: the question is whether the prosecution can prove *beyond reasonable doubt* that D satisfied all elements of the offence. In cases of uncertainty, or where questions of mens rea do not make sense, the offence burden will not be met. Such individuals may warrant detention through civil means, but in the absence of a proven criminal offence there should be no need for a criminal defence.[80]

A variation on this concern, that we also reject, has attempted to equate delusions stemming from mental disorders with voluntary intoxication. For Storey and others, for example, if D 'cannot invoke his self-induced intoxication to support a plea of self-defence … then it *logically follows* that he cannot invoke his own insane delusions to do so either'.[81] But this is a false, and troublesome, equivalence.

[76] The German system, for example, allows self-defence and other defences to be raised even in the context of extreme delusional states.

[77] *Lipman* [1970] 1 QB 152.

[78] In the case of *Lipman* (ibid), liability was found using the prior-fault intoxication rules, substituting for D's missing *mens rea* to construct the basic intent offence of manslaughter.

[79] Duff (n 64) 168.

[80] D may alternatively satisfy the terms of an offence, such as gross negligence manslaughter, that does not require subjective mens rea. In such cases, the practical difficulty of demonstrating mens rea is removed. D will still be protected, under our approach, but a defence of insanity (in its exculpatory form).

[81] T Storey, 'Self-defence: Insane Delusions and Reasonable Force' (2014) *Journal of Criminal Law* 12, 15 (emphasis added). See also *Taj* [2018] EWCA Crim 1743, where the *Oye* precedent is presented as 'equally apposite' despite no finding of insanity; and support for this outcome in T Storey, 'The Meaning of 'Attributable to Intoxication': Self-defence and Mistaken Belief' (2018) *Journal of Criminal Law* 362, 365, and M Dsouza, 'Intoxication, Psychosis, and Self-defence: Evaluating *Taj*' (2018) 9 *Archbold Review* 6, 9. Dsouza's conclusion here also seem in tension with his broader views on the use of reasonableness in self-defence, set out in M Dsouza, *Rationale Based Defences in Criminal Law* (Oxford, Hart Publishing, 2017) 41–43. The criticism extends to those who would block complete defences, but substitute a partial defence: see Livings et al (n 13) ch 3 and ch 11 by C De Than and J Elvin.

D's intoxicated mistakes are held to undermine self-defence on the basis of prior fault; we blame D for voluntarily consuming a dangerous drug that he should have known risked uncontrolled and/or risky behaviour. Mistakes induced by mental disorders, absent prior fault, involve none of these grounds for blaming D. Thus, if we want to remove D's defence in the latter category, we need a different reason for doing so.

A final potential worry relates to broader concerns associated with abolitionist projects, and the degree to which these are engaged by our proposal. Although the diversionary function of insanity has been criticised within the existing literature, this has typically been in service of an argument for the abolition of insanity as a whole. While Christopher Slobogin and Tina Minkowitz have each argued that acquittals for mentally disordered defendants should, where possible, come through actus reus/mens rea and standard defences rather than through mental condition defences,[82] both regard such integration and abolition of insanity as closely connected projects, with the former largely motivated by the desirability of the latter. This has led to criticism and concern regarding the potential impact of their respective proposals upon defendants for whom the only plausible route to acquittal is a mental condition defence. In particular, Michael Perlin has raised the worry that removing the option of the special verdict would lead to higher numbers of severely mentally ill people becoming incarcerated in general prisons with limited access to support and treatment, where they would find themselves subject to disproportionate levels of violence and abuse.[83] In Perlin's opinion, well-intentioned calls to replace mental condition defences in favour of disability-neutral approaches would in reality inflict significant harm upon an already vulnerable population, and exacerbate existing problems of the rates and severity of mental illness among incarcerated people. In his words:

> The abolitionist position is short-sighted and, if adopted, would inevitably lead to a worsening of the lives of a segment of the population of persons with disabilities that has never been consulted in this conversation. … [Abolishing mental condition defences] would violate due process, dignity, and fair-trial mandates, and would inevitably lead to the torture of persons with mental disabilities who are charged with and convicted of crimes.[84]

These are very reasonable concerns, particularly when one considers the enduring unpopularity of the insanity defence combined with its highly restrictive judicial interpretation. Given that the realistic window for mental-condition-based

[82] Slobogin, in particular, set out a comprehensive proposal for the integration of mental condition sensitivity into existing culpability principles. See C Slobogin, 'An End to Insanity' (2000) 86 *Virginia Law Review* 1199. See also T Minkowitz, 'Rethinking Criminal Responsibility from a Critical Disability Perspective' (2014) 23 *Griffith Law Review* 434.

[83] M Perlin, 'God Said to Abraham/Kill Me a Son: Why the Insanity Defense and the Incompetency Status are Compatible with and Required by the Convention on the Rights of Persons with Disabilities and Basic Principles of Therapeutic Jurisprudence' (2017) 54 *American Criminal Law Review* 477.

[84] ibid 483.

exculpation is low, while the rates of mental illness among incarcerated people are high,[85] it is difficult not to sympathise with Perlin's hostility towards any proposal – however well-intentioned – that could narrow that window further. However, this is where our preferred approach has an advantage over the proposals of Slobogin and Minkowitz, since our aim is not to endorse the abolition of the insanity defence altogether,[86] but only to eliminate its inculpatory aspect. As we have argued, significant expansion of the exculpatory scope of the defence actually becomes easier to support once this aspect is removed, as it no longer has the consequence of inadvertently widening the inculpatory net.

III. Conclusion

Few would defend the insanity rules as they currently operate. Across this chapter, we have highlighted and explored the broad structural problems with the law, and the effect of these problems in contributing to unjust case outcomes. Sullivan and others have taken crucial steps towards ameliorating the current problems through recommendations to the courts. Our contention, however, is that there is a need to definitively shut down, by way of legislative intervention, the use of insanity rules as a means of qualifying the acquittals of defendants with mental disorder or difference.

Mentally disordered individuals are some of the most vulnerable in society. In the comparatively rare cases in which their conduct leads to harm, and subsequently to the intervention of the criminal justice system, that vulnerability ought not to be forgotten, and nor should their right to fair and equal access to justice be deprioritised. Our approach across this chapter has been to encourage greater respect and protection for such individuals by modelling an approach that recognises and engages with their reasons for acting, and provides principled restrictions for the boundaries of criminal rules. In proposing the partial abolition of insanity, we offer a new and compelling basis for statutory reform, of relevance not only to the law of England and Wales but across multiple common law jurisdictions where *M'Naghten* represents the current law. The potential statutory reform of the insanity rules continues to engage reform bodies internationally, but where these projects attempt to expand or contract the insanity rules as a whole (inculpatory *and* exculpatory), tensions and contradictions within such reform are inevitable, leading projects to stall and fail. Our approach offers a new way forward, with the best chance for conceptual clarity, and of achieving fairness in application.

[85] See House of Commons Committee of Public Accounts, *Mental Health in Prisons* (8th Report 2017–19, 2017).

[86] At least, not necessarily. We (in varying degrees) are open to the possibility that a thoroughgoing project of integration could render mental condition defences largely unnecessary, such that their abolition essentially becomes a formality. We do concede, however, that to abolish insanity without having first done the considerable work of integrating mental condition-sensitivity into existing culpability tests would be a mistake, for all the reasons Perlin gives.

8

Withdrawal from Attempts?

BEATRICE KREBS*

I. Introduction

I was very honoured to be asked to contribute to a *Festschrift* for a criminal law scholar and teacher whose work I have known and valued from my earliest student days. Then as now I admired Bob Sullivan's publications as much for their elegant prose as for the clarity and rigour of their argument. I came to know him as a person when he examined my DPhil on complicity – I was very grateful for his gentle, reassuring manner and his kindness. Since then, our paths have crossed in various places, and I am thankful for his continued support and the helpful advice he has given me on many occasions. Bob is, of course, a prolific writer who has published in almost every area relevant to the criminal law syllabus (and beyond). One topic that does not seem to have attracted his attention quite so much, however, is the 'defence' of withdrawal. I hope that Bob will find the below musings on this topic of interest.

Imagine the following situation: (1) D is jealous of V, his ex-wife's new partner. He decides to kill V by beating him to a pulp. He knows that V goes for a run in the evening, so one day D lies in wait for V with a baseball bat. As V jogs past him, D jumps out of the bushes and swings the baseball bat at him with force, but misses. D takes aim again, but seeing the fear in V's eyes, he experiences a sudden change of heart. He drops the baseball bat and walks away. Under the law as it stands, D will be criminally liable for assault by causing V to fear immediate harm. It is very likely that, in light of D's intention to kill V, D's swing of the bat makes for an act sufficiently proximate to the killing of V as to amount to attempted murder. Yet at that point in time, D's better self leads him to abandon his deadly project. Withdrawal is no defence to attempted crimes at common law. This is so even though D abandoned his crime voluntarily, before any physical harm occurred to V, and whilst it was still possible for the crime to come to fruition.

* I am profoundly grateful to Andrew Simester for helping me sharpen and focus the argument put forward in this chapter. Thanks are also due to Kesley Rati for her helpful research assistance.

Compare this instance with the following: (2) P tells S of his plans to cause V, his rival-in-love, grievous bodily harm by severely beating him. S considers this treatment too lenient and suggests that P kill V by shooting him in the head. He offers to get P a gun, which he does. The next day, S has a change of heart. Driving towards P's house, S calls P on his mobile, pleading with him not to go ahead with the shooting. By the time he arrives, and despite S's best efforts to persuade P to abandon his murderous plan, P has already gone ahead and shot V. In this case, S might well have done enough to withdraw from the criminal venture and thereby to extricate himself from liability. This is so even though the full crime has been committed; V was killed, and, what is more, because of S's prior involvement: without S's advice and assistance, P would not have thought of killing V, let alone have had the means to do so.

The difference in outcome for D and S arises because English law recognises withdrawal as a 'defence' only in the context of secondary participation (as in example 2); it does not avail principals who abandon their criminal purpose after having crossed the crucial threshold from mere preparatory acts to an attempt but before their crime has come to fruition (as in example 1).

The oddity of this distinction is graphically illustrated by considering the statutory offence of doing an act capable of assisting or encouraging a crime.[1] Liability for the statutory offence is incurred the moment that the act capable of assisting or encouraging P's crime has been done:[2] this liability is sustained whether or not the principal offence is committed. At common law, if S withdraws her assistance/encouragement prior to the commission of the principal offence in a manner that fulfils the conditions of the withdrawal 'defence', S will not be a party to P's offence. By contrast, her liability for the statutory offence of intentionally encouraging or assisting an offence by doing an act capable of encouraging or assisting P's crime *will*, in terms of the letter of the law, remain intact.[3] In other words, *on exactly the same set of facts*, recharacterising liability as inchoate leads to a different liability outcome: surely an undesirable state of affairs. As will be seen below, there are good reasons for allowing a withdrawal 'defence' in complicity. Those reasons extend to the statutory offence too. Indeed, they are part of the reason why the statutory offence is so problematic.

With all that said, withdrawal is rarely relied on even within the context of complicity. Concomitantly, what amounts to withdrawal and what legal consequences, if any, should follow a finding of withdrawal has attracted little interest from scholars in this jurisdiction,[4] even though other aspects of complicity have

[1] Serious Crime Act 2007, s 44.

[2] ibid s 49.

[3] S 50 of the Serious Crime Act 2007 does provide a defence of acting reasonably, but that provision only applies at the time of the actus reus of the statutory offence.

[4] Outside of what ME Badar and A Reed ('The Fault Element and Withdrawal Principles in Joint Criminal Enterprise: The Need for a Restatement' (2014) 1 *Journal of International and Comparative Law* 253, 274) refer to as 'a small circle of cognoscenti' writing mainly between 1981 and 2001: D Lanham, 'Accomplices and Withdrawals' (1981) 97 *LQR* 575; KJM Smith, 'Withdrawal from

proved a fertile (battle)ground for academic discourse. This lack of interest may be due not only to the still uncertain state of the law and its theoretical underpinnings, but also to some ignorance of the defence on the part of criminal law practitioners.[5] It may also be the case that the withdrawal 'defence' is more appealing in theory than in practice.[6] As Gideon Yaffe put it:

> Change of mind, as common as it is, is puzzling from a moral point of view. It is hard to know how to react to the person who acts in a way of which we disapprove, but changes his mind later. As the agent of a bad act, he seems worthy of censure; as the agent who prevented the bad act's occurrence, he seems worthy of praise. The puzzle arises from the fact that he is, indeed, both of these agents.[7]

This chapter will argue that withdrawal could be more readily available as a defence than it currently is. Allowing a voluntary withdrawal to let the defendant off the hook in example 2 but not in example 1 requires explanation. In what follows, I argue that a case can be made to treat both defendants alike, which is the position in German law. At least where the defendant's actions and the completion of the offence are distanced in time and/or space, extending the defence to principals is within the interpretative reach of English law and, indeed, warranted.

The chapter proceeds as follows: section II reviews the current state of English law, including the nature, scope and supporting rationales of withdrawal. What purpose is withdrawal meant to serve? What are its constituent elements? Is it a substantive *defence* or something else? And is it best justified as providing an incentive to offenders to rethink their crime and desist or because withdrawal demonstrates reduced dangerousness on their part? Building on the insights gained in section II, section III considers whether withdrawal should be more widely available, as a form of *actus contrarius* to criminal attempts by principal actors. The discussion here will reflect briefly on why the law criminalises attempts in the first place (ie what is the nature of the wrong involved in attempts?) and then consider whether attempt can justifiably be distinguished from complicity with reference to the recognition or otherwise of a withdrawal defence.

In gist, I argue that concerns which motivate the criminalisation of accessories also underpin the criminalising of attempts (whether the would-be perpetrator

Criminal Liability for Complicity and Inchoate Offenses' (1983) 12 *Anglo-American Law Review* 200; KJM Smith, 'Withdrawal in Complicity: A Restatement of Principles' [2001] *Crim LR* 769. More recent publications include A Reed, 'Repentance and Forgiveness: Withdrawal from Participation Liability and the Proportionality Test' in A Reed and M Bohlander (eds), *Participation in Crime: Domestic and Comparative Perspectives* (Farnham, Ashgate, 2013) and C Sjölin 'A Step Away from Liability – Withdrawal and Fundamental Difference *Post*-Jogee' in B Krebs (ed), *Accessorial Liability after Jogee* (Oxford, Hart Publishing, 2019) 69. This can be contrasted with a vast literature on the topic produced in Germany.

[5] This thought is supported by anecdotal evidence in the form of conversations I had with practitioners at a criminal bar conference who confessed to not knowing much about withdrawal or rarely considering it as a defence.

[6] GP Fletcher, *Rethinking Criminal Law* (Boston, MA, Little, Brown, 1978) 197.

[7] G Yaffe, *Attempts* (Oxford, Oxford University Press, 2012) 309.

acts alone or complicitly), and that there are good reasons to treat the situations alike when it comes to defendants who, having gone beyond mere preparation, voluntarily desist from completion of a crime (even if not necessarily for laudable motives). At the least, it should be possible to treat those instances of attempted perpetration similarly to withdrawal in complicity where there is a gap in time between necessary preparation to enable commission of the principal offence and the time chosen for its commission. Examples are cases in which the perpetrator puts poison in one of many bottles or prepares an explosive trap, the poison to be consumed or the trap to be tripped later by an unwitting victim. In these examples, crimes relating to the possession of poisons and explosives may well have been committed. Those crimes are not our concern. Our concern is when the poison is on the point of being taken or the trap is about to be trodden on. In both these cases there is strong evidence of attempted murder. Suppose at the point when V was about to swallow poison, D grabbed the bottle and no harm was done. Similarly, when V was mere yards from the trap, perhaps D disabled the device and again no harm was done. Each of these harm-preventing interventions was voluntary. The argument will be made that in both cases there should be no conviction for attempted murder. In developing this argument, for comparison, I will draw in section IV upon aspects of German law, where withdrawal is recognised as a ground for excluding criminal liability both for sole offenders and people *committing* crimes *en groupe*. Section V summarises my proposal, and section VI concludes.

II. The Law of Withdrawal: Doctrine and Rationales

At common law, withdrawal leads to outright acquittal of the accomplice as opposed to conviction of a lesser offence or a sentence reduction. The leading case, *Becerra and Cooper*,[8] involved the burglary of a house. The tenant of a first-floor flat surprised the two defendants inside the property. Becerra, who earlier on had handed Cooper a knife, exclaimed 'Let's go!', climbed out of a window and ran away. Cooper, however, responded by fatally stabbing the tenant. Both burglars were charged with murder. Becerra tried to defend himself by arguing that he had withdrawn from the joint enterprise before the fatal stabbing. His defence was rejected by the Court of Appeal which emphasised that withdrawal first and foremost required unequivocal notice to the other party of the intention to withdraw. What else might be required remains unclear because of the lack of guidance from any subsequent cases, including the review of complicity law by the Supreme Court in *Jogee*.[9] It is therefore generally assumed that the pre-*Jogee* case

[8] *Becerra and Cooper* (1976) 62 Cr App R 212 (CA).
[9] *Jogee* [2016] UKSC 8.

law on withdrawal remains applicable, even though its requirements are likely to have been distorted by the then existence of the doctrine of parasitic accessory liability.[10]

Requirements

If one were briefly to distil from the case law what makes for a successful case of withdrawal, it would look something like the following.[11] In order successfully to withdraw, an accessory needs to make:

(a) a voluntary[12] decision to withdraw[13] (not necessarily based on a penitent motive);
(b) the withdrawal must be made before commission of the (attempted or substantive) crime by the principal offender is complete,[14] which is when the accessory's criminal liability crystallises and becomes fixed. Repentance after the fact does not suffice;
(c) the voluntary decision to withdraw is communicated[15] to the principal offender in good time[16] (or, failing that, to the law enforcement agencies or the potential victim), in the form of an 'unequivocal' notice of withdrawal;
(d) which breaks the chain of responsibility[17] that otherwise would link the accessory's assistance or encouragement with the principal offence.

What (conduct) precisely is required appears to be governed by a proportionality requirement: the greater S's involvement up to the point at which he seeks to withdraw, the more substantial the effort he will need to make to succeed with the defence. The spectrum extends from S's simply attempting to communicate

[10] Sjölin (n 4) 70, 74.

[11] The requirements of withdrawal are shaped by the rationale that underpins the defence. Since the rationale remains unclear (as explained below), the requirements, too, remain uncertain and unsettled, and this, as well as interpretative difficulties with concepts such as 'unequivocal notice', hampers any attempt at restating them.

[12] *Otway* [2011] EWCA Crim 3.

[13] The case law and literature oscillate between change of mind and change of heart, see eg Smith, 'Withdrawal from Criminal Liability' (n 4) 211 ('D experiences a change of heart').

[14] It remains unclear whether withdrawal is possible once the threshold to an attempt has been passed but the crime remains incomplete. In *Perman* [1996] 1 Cr App R 24 (CA) 34, the Court observed: 'We would simply raise the question whether once the criminal activity contemplated in a joint enterprise has commenced, it is possible for a party to the joint enterprise to withdraw, and whether it is ever open to a party to a joint enterprise to say that he is not criminally responsible for all that is done in that criminal activity which is within the scope of the joint enterprise. … Certainly most of the instances given in Smith & Hogan, 7th ed at p 153, of withdrawal, are cases of withdrawal from a joint enterprise before the start of the contemplated criminal activity.'

[15] *Mitchell and King* [1990] Crim LR 496 (QBD) and *O'Flaherty* [2004] EWCA Crim 526, [2004] 2 Cr App R 20 (CA) found communication to be unnecessary in cases of spontaneous group violence.

[16] *Perman* [1996] 1 Cr App R 24 (CA).

[17] Older cases, eg *Whitehouse* [1941] 1 WWR 112 (CA BC), also speak of breaking the chain of causation, but modern case law does not presuppose a causal link in complicity.

to P his decision to withdraw to S's having to take active steps seeking to thwart P's commission of the offence (such as warning the intended victim, alerting the authorities or even physically preventing P from carrying out the previously joint plan).

An important factor in determining where on this spectrum S's case falls and what conduct is demanded of him to withdraw effectively seems to be the form of his complicity.[18] Cases such as *Mitchell and King*[19] suggest that the law distinguishes between preplanned and spontaneous criminal ventures, and that, in contrast to planned offending, it may be possible successfully to withdraw from spontaneous crimes without the need to communicate this to the other participants. While *Robinson*[20] casts doubt on the generality of this proposition, suggesting that communication of withdrawal is necessary even in situations of spontaneous violence unless it is not practicable or reasonable so to communicate, *O'Flaherty*[21] and *Rajakumar*[22] have since confirmed that 'what may suffice to constitute withdrawal in spontaneous and unplanned group violence may not necessarily so suffice in preplanned group violence.'[23] Both cases predate *Jogee*, however, and it may be that, with parasitic accessory liability gone, there no longer is any need to treat spontaneous violence differently from preplanned crimes. As Sjölin has argued, 'the generosity of approach in *Mitchell and King* and *O'Flaherty* is not necessary now that the prosecution must prove that S acted to assist/encourage P *in that offence* with the intention of so doing'.[24]

Nature and Scope

The recognition of withdrawal as a 'defence' unique to complicity is usually supported by reference to complicity's distinctive features. As such, it has been said that complicity's derivative nature and the possibility of some pre-inculpatory interlude offer 'an accessory special exculpatory possibilities not found in relation to principal liability'.[25] Correspondingly, the Law Commission has found that '[t]here is no authority to suggest that withdrawal from an attempt to commit an offence may at present be raised as a defence'.[26] Such literature as there is agrees: where the issue is discussed at all, commentators largely reject a wider application

[18] See Smith, 'Withdrawal from Criminal Liability' (n 4) 209.
[19] *Mitchell and King* [1999] Crim LR 496 (QBD).
[20] *Robinson* [2000] EWCA Crim 8.
[21] *O'Flaherty* [2004] EWCA Crim 526, [2004] 2 Cr App R 20 (CA).
[22] *Rajakumar* [2013] EWCA Crim 1512.
[23] ibid [42] (Davis LJ).
[24] Sjölin (n 4) 90.
[25] See Smith, 'Withdrawal in Complicity' (n 4) 769.
[26] Law Commission No 102, *Attempt, and Impossibility in Relation to Attempt, Conspiracy and Incitement* (London, HMSO, 1980) para 2.132. See, similarly, Smith, 'Withdrawal from Criminal Liability' (n 4) 205.

of the withdrawal 'defence', on the basis that 'the obvious practical difficulties and dangers entailed in catering for a few remote examples rules [*sic*] out a withdrawal defence for perpetrators'.[27] It would thus seem that withdrawal is no 'defence' to liability outside the context of secondary parties.

We shall return below to the question whether the position of an accessory is all that different from that of a principal offender who abandons further commission of his crime (or attempts to undo what he has previously done). Another matter of some debate is whether withdrawal really is a *defence*. Confusion over the latter question is sometimes caused by the different meanings a claim of withdrawal can carry. Indeed, the language of defences is at times employed when all the actor is trying to say is that some part of the actus reus or mens rea of the offence has not been made out (wherefore there is no prima facie case against which the accused needs to raise a defence – he never incurs any prima facie liability).[28] These situations must be distinguished from instances where, having satisfied both the actus reus and mens rea, the actor seeks to extricate himself from criminal liability, by taking steps that comply with the requirements of withdrawal as an affirmative defence or as a bar to accountability. Typically, in the context of complicity liability, this occurs where S has, with appropriate mens rea, done what will amount to complicity should P commit the principal offence, where P has not yet completed the offence.

Advocates of withdrawal as an affirmative defence (for accessories) are divided over whether this provides a justificatory defence (on the basis that it recognises the appropriateness of the accessory's actions) or an excusatory defence (as a concession to the accessory's particular circumstances). A compromise might be to treat withdrawal as excluding *punishment* that sits outside the dichotomy of justificatory and excusatory defences.[29] That way, any verdict of culpable wrongdoing remains untouched (which might make the 'defence' more palatable to victims and society at large); all the exclusion would do is recognise that the party who has withdrawn does not now need to be punished, even though he had crossed the threshold towards wrongdoing and done so culpably. His subsequent repentance, however, has done away with the need for society to step in and punish him for the wrong he has culpably committed. In other words, recasting the 'defence' as an exclusion ground for punishment would allow us still to point the finger and blame the accused for ever having gone as far as he did before withdrawing. In that way, this conception would allow us to uphold some of the reasons for criminalising the accused's actions in the first place whilst still providing an incentive for would-be offenders to reconsider and undo, as much as possible in the circumstances of their case, their involvement in crime (for they can now expect to escape

[27] KJM Smith, *A Modern Treatise on the Law of Criminal Complicity* (Oxford, Clarendon Press, 1991) 255.

[28] cp Smith, 'Withdrawal from Criminal Liability' (n 4) 207: 'A claim of withdrawal from a prior act of "complicity" can amount to an assertion that the [actus reus] of complicity does not exist.'

[29] See Badar and Reed (n 4) 275.

punishment, even though they may not necessarily be blameless). This reasoning, it is worth observing, applies to principals and attempts liability as much as it does to secondary parties.

Rationales

Which brings us to the question why withdrawal should lead to freedom from punishment. Commentators are divided on the matter. They disagree over whether withdrawal operates to incentivise a secondary party to disengage from a criminal enterprise or, alternatively, to reflect his reduced level of social dangerousness and/or blameworthiness.[30] While these are the two main rationales discussed in the English literature, further theories have been put forward in other jurisdictions. None of them is by itself entirely satisfactory, and it is probably a combination, rather than any one theory alone, that informs and explains the current law. There is room only to sketch the main lines of argument here.

The Law Commission has in the past suggested an incentivising rationale:

> [S]ince the object of the criminal law is to prevent crime it is equally important to give reasonable encouragement to … [an] attempter … to withdraw. … The absence of such a defence may operate to dissuade an individual who might otherwise decide to cease participating in the planning of a crime from taking that decision since having become a party to the inchoate offence there is no inducement for him to cease his activities before commission of the substantive offence takes place.[31]

It has been objected that the credibility of this rationale depends largely on whether offenders are aware of the existence of a withdrawal defence.[32] In light of the uncertainties surrounding the requirements of withdrawal in complicity, it seems unlikely that people generally are aware of it (to the extent necessary to make the inducement theory work). As Badar and Reed have observed: 'The suggestion that D2 modify their criminal behaviour in relation to offence-definitional criteria of which they are highly unlikely to be aware is counterfactual, and the apotheosis of recalcitrant conduct.'[33] Even so, this is not an in-principle objection. Ignorance of the 'defence' might well be a matter of fact: this, however, generates not so much an argument against the cogency of the incentive rationale as an objection that the law is not doing enough to fulfil its guiding function by communicating the availability of a withdrawal provision and its requirements.

The other main justification for giving legal recognition to withdrawal is in order to recognise the diminished dangerousness of act or actor.[34] Whilst the

[30] See Smith, 'Withdrawal in Complicity' (n 4).

[31] Law Commission Working Paper No 50, *Inchoate Offences: Conspiracy, Attempt and Incitement* (London, HMSO, 1973) 150.

[32] Smith, 'Withdrawal from Criminal Liability' (n 4) 204.

[33] Badar and Reed (n 4) 275.

[34] Smith, 'Withdrawal from Criminal Liability' (n 4) 214.

Law Commission has suggested that 'the social danger already manifested by the defendant's conduct made it appropriate that any effort he might make to nullify its effects should instead be reflected by mitigation of penalty',[35] Badar and Reed argue that '[t]he redemptive actor who has voluntarily renounced his complicitous behaviour has revealed himself as possessing more limited society danger characterisations, and should be inculcated a quasi-excuse'.[36] Fletcher considers this to make 'intuitive sense', although he also raises the question 'whether the criminal law should be grounded in case-by-case assessments of dangerousness'.[37] In his view, a more promising approach would be one that reflects 'that the intent required for an attempt is not merely a firm resolve up to the time the attempt is complete as a punishable act. The intent required is one to carry through'.[38] Horder puts it this way: 'voluntary renunciation shows that the original criminal purpose was not sufficiently firm',[39] which seems to locate the rationale for the withdrawal 'defence' in the actor's reduced culpability.

Both of these major lines of argument find some resonance in the United States, where the criminal law frequently classifies offences by hierarchy (as in 'first degree murder', 'second degree murder', and so on). Amongst US academics, there is a school of thought that posits the idea that a similar structure should be imposed on the defences side. Thus, Moriarty has commented as follows:

> [W]hile people should be encouraged to commit no harm rather than some harm, those that commit some harm should be encouraged to commit less rather than more. Just as the degree structure of criminal law threatens greater punishment for more aggravated forms of a given crime, thereby providing greater deterrence for the higher degrees of crime, so too can the reward of remission of punishment motivate persons who have not yet caused the more aggravated species of harm to abandon their enterprise and refrain from causing more damage than they have already.[40]

While English law has, at least for now, eschewed a similar hierarchical structure, it is certainly correct to say that outcomes matter – the greater the harm, the greater the punishment. If we are serious in our commitment to preventing harm, there is something to be said for an approach that aims to reward those who desist from causing (greater) harm, even if at the last possible moment.

It has been possible only to outline the foregoing rationales here in order to give a sense of their flavour. They tend to be presented as alternatives; however, it is more fruitful to think of them as complementary. Abandonment of a criminal purpose as an indication of lack of firm antisocial intent (and hence the absence of any real public danger) is not irreconcilable with an understanding that considers

[35] Law Commission No 102 (n 26) para 2.132.
[36] Badar and Reed (n 4) 275.
[37] Fletcher, *Rethinking Criminal Law* (n 6) 186–87.
[38] ibid 188.
[39] J Horder, *Ashworth's Principles of Criminal Law*, 9th edn (Oxford, Oxford University Press, 2019) 524.
[40] DG Moriarty, 'Extending the Defense of Renunciation' (1989) 62 *Temple Law Review* 1, 5.

the 'defence' first and foremost as a means to encourage people to abandon courses of criminal activity that they have already embarked upon. In fact, 'as a criminal plan nears fruition, the former notion diminishes in persuasive power, while the latter gains'.[41] For present purposes, the key point to add is that these defensive rationales for recognising withdrawal in law apply just as much to actions by the principal as they do to the accessory. They apply, that is to say, to attempts as well as complicity.

III. Withdrawal as a General *Actus Contrarius* to Criminal Attempts?[42]

Suppose that I am right about this. Suppose that many of the rationales for allowing withdrawal to *exculpate* in complicity carry over to attempts. That is not an end to the matter. We must also consider the grounds of *inculpation*. Before any argument can be made for extending the withdrawal 'defence' from complicity to criminal attempts, it is necessary to examine the grounds for criminalising attempts in the first place. As KJM Smith has observed, 'the acceptability of any excusatory defence turns on the underlying rationale for *imposition* of the specific form of liability concerned: would exculpation be consistent with the justifying aims of the particular form of liability at issue – would it undermine the basis for imposition?'[43] In other words, we need to consider whether there is something distinctive about the liability of principals, and in particular about attempts liability, that deprives the arguments for a withdrawal defence of their normative grip.

The Wrong in Attempted Crimes

Let us thus, briefly, investigate the grounds for imposing criminal liability for attempted crimes. Why do we criminalise attempts? Edwards and Simester suggest that 'those who try and those who succeed commit different wrongs'.[44] The question, therefore, becomes: what is the (distinctive) *wrong* in attempts? As is often the case with matters of criminal law theory or doctrine, there is no single, or even unequivocal, answer. Three principal explanations for imposing criminal liability for attempts can be distilled from the case law and academic literature. While their

[41] P Buscemi, 'Conspiracy: Statutory Reform since the Model Penal Code' (1975) 75 *Columbia Law Review* 1122, 1168.

[42] *Actus contrarius* approaches are premised on the idea that 'just as much as an attempt may show that D defies the law, the withdrawal can be evidence that he embraces the societal order again': M Bohlander, *Principles of German Criminal Law* (Oxford, Hart Publishing, 2009) 146.

[43] Smith, 'Withdrawal from Criminal Liability' (n 4) 202–03.

[44] J Edwards and AP Simester, 'Crime, Blameworthiness, and Outcomes' (2019) 39 *OJLS* 50, 54.

justifying features differ, they are unified in their perception of attempt as a wrong in itself, not just an attempted wrong.

One classic explanation of the distinctiveness of attempts is objective. A core function of criminal law is the prevention of harm. While attempts may not result in actual harm, they tend to endanger: it is often a matter of sheer luck whether the attempt succeeds and results in harm. Concomitantly, one school of thought locates the reason for the criminalisation of attempts in the objective endangerment of a legally protected right or interest. However, such an objective theory is difficult to square with section 1(2) of the Criminal Attempts Act 1981, according to which a conviction may lie even when attempting offences that are impossible to commit. For example, one cannot be in possession of a controlled drug if the white powder possessed is not a drug, but conviction for attempted possession can be returned if D believes he has purchased cocaine.[45] It is the hallmark of impossible attempts that there is no actual endangerment of the protected right or interest in such instances.

That objection lends weight to an alternative school of thought, one that locates the ground of liability *subjectively*, in the defendant's willingness to commit crime, as evidenced by the attempt. Advocates of subjective theories stress that even objectively harmless conduct, inasmuch as it demonstrates an attitude that is hostile to our legal order, is capable of disturbing society and causing alarm and distress to the general public. Attempters, one might say, are culpable, and deserve punishment, even when they are not actually dangerous. It might be objected, however, that section 1(1) of the Criminal Attempts Act 1981 is clear that, whilst the defendant's intention is of particular importance, he must also have performed an act that was more than merely preparatory to the commission of the offence; a hostile intent alone thus cannot support the imposition of criminal liability. Alternatively, one might point to considerations of social security: notably, to the *impression* that attempts *in general* tend to create in the mind of the general public, and in turn to 'the advantage [punishment] brings to the social order'.[46] Ultimately, this more integrative proposal takes the reason for criminalising attempts to be the proclivity of manifested criminal intents to interfere with our sense of security and to shake the public's trust in law and order.

Whatever one's preferred account of the wrongness of attempts and the justification of their criminalisation, one must ask the question: is it possible to square that account with a 'defence' of withdrawal? Or would allowing such a 'defence' undermine the basis for the imposition of criminal liability on attempts? If the reason for criminalising attempts lies in the endangerment of legally protected interests (as proponents of objective theories suggest), and withdrawal – as seen earlier – reflects a reduction in said danger, then the two are not incompatible.

[45] Contrast a situation where the objective is feasible but the means inadequate as when the ladder brought to gain access to the eighth-floor flat is not long enough. No need to apply the impossibility rule to convict of attempted burglary.

[46] J Burchell, *Principles of Criminal Law*, 3rd edn (Cape Town, Juta, 2005) 73.

Likewise, if attempts-liability is ultimately about the actor's commitment to crime (as the subjective theory posits), then a 'defence' that seeks to incentivise or reward D's change of mind would not undermine this rationale either. Explanations in terms of public perceptions of social order and security may seem more difficult to square. As KJM Smith has argued, albeit without giving concrete evidence or examples, 'the usually more overt and immediate nature of the act of attempt may cause types of social alarm which cannot be satisfactorily assuaged by withdrawal'.[47] It is not obvious, however, why those who assist or encourage others (who may not have committed any crime but for said assistance or encouragement) should benefit from a withdrawal defence, but principals should not. After all, one of the reasons often given for imposing liability on accessories is the perception that crimes committed *en groupe* are more dangerous or likely to succeed/go ahead due to peer pressure and other group dynamics. Such pressure applies irrespective of what role an individual is playing. In any event, while it may be true that society's sense of security cannot always be fully vindicated where an offender abandons his offence only once the threshold from merely preparatory act towards an attempt has been crossed, it might cost society (and its sense of security) more dearly in the longer run not to leave open the door to legality for those who abandon their attempt, if at the last possible moment. It is submitted that withdrawal is not inherently incompatible with the rationales (surveyed above) underpinning the imposition of liability for criminal attempts.

Withdrawal from Attempted Crimes

Assuming, then, that extending the defence to cover criminal attempts could in theory be justified, could we make it work in practice?

Consider, first, the possibility of failed attempts. It may be objected that some attempts are abandoned not because the offender experienced a (genuine) change of heart but because the attempt went awry. If withdrawal were a defence to attempts, should we be concerned that it might benefit people who do not deserve freedom from punishment? To some extent, the requirement of voluntariness, noted above in section II, can take account of these concerns. Where the evidence suggests that D abandoned his crime because he believed he could no longer succeed (or that apprehension was imminent and D did not fancy being 'caught in the act'), we may conclude that the withdrawal was not voluntary (a conclusion that would, of course, require some clarification of doctrine). Perhaps more interesting is the question whether D can withdraw where the offence has become objectively impossible, but D has not realised this and believes it can still occur. If

[47] Smith, 'Withdrawal from Criminal Liability' (n 4) 206.

he now has a change of heart, should he be able to benefit from a withdrawal provision? I would suggest that the law should follow the lead of the Criminal Attempts Act 1971: if an offender can be punished for an impossible attempt, he should also be able to withdraw from an impossible attempt. This possibility would, of course, be subject to the proviso that he subjectively believed he could still have succeeded – it does not seem appropriate for him to benefit from a withdrawal 'defence' where desistance is owed to external circumstances rather than to a free and autonomous decision by the actor.

Concerns around failed attempts led KJM Smith to suggest that the 'delineation of a point of no return could possibly be approached through a concept of "complete" and "incomplete" attempt, withdrawal being permitted only in the latter'.[48] He described 'incomplete' attempts as involving situations where 'the actor has still to perform a final act, such as pulling the trigger of a gun'.[49] In such a case, because the actor has not done all he needed to do for the attempt to be truly underway, and in that sense, the actor still has a choice whether or not to go ahead, there remains scope for a change of heart and hence withdrawal. By contrast, where the attempt is complete, because the actor has done all he needed to do, so that it is now out of his hands whether the attempt will succeed, it will be too late to withdraw. As a conceptual distinction, this is both coherent and compatible with the rationales for criminalising attempts that we canvassed earlier.

Of course, identifying the relevant last act can be difficult and even contrived. (Indeed, even a sufficient 'last act' might be susceptible of counteraction by the actor.) Smith himself conceded that 'identifying the last or final act is unlikely to prove much more satisfactory than it did when used to determine proximity for the imposition of liability for attempt'.[50] He thought that '[e]ven if the formula is modified so as not to exclude last acts until failure becomes apparent there remains the problem of identifying the relevant last act'.[51]

Smith's 'last act' proposal is evocative of a similar distinction drawn by German criminal law, albeit that German law allows for withdrawal in both complete and incomplete attempt situations. Complete attempts[52] are governed by stricter requirements, however. A closer look at this rival conception appears warranted, if only to see whether any lessons can be learned when considering whether Smith's proposal might be adopted for English law.

[48] ibid.
[49] ibid 206.
[50] ibid.
[51] ibid.
[52] Bohlander (n 42) 146–51, 177, refers to these as 'finished attempts' which arguably better reflects that the defendant has done all he needed to do, albeit that this did not lead to 'complete' success. However, in keeping with the terminology used by KJM Smith whose discussion of 'completed' and 'incompleted' attempts inspired this chapter, I shall stick with the language of 'complete' and 'incomplete' attempts.

IV. A Rival Conception: German Law[53]

While German criminal law rests on different foundations and has a different structure from the common law, the factual situations with which it – like any criminal legal system – must grapple are more or less the same. Looking at its approach can therefore be helpful in *illustrating* alternative ways of responding to the normative challenges that arise from those factual situations. The German penal code[54] contains two general provisions that deal with liability-extinguishing withdrawal:[55] § 31 StGB (governing withdrawal from attempted participation and conspiracy) and § 24 StGB (governing withdrawal from criminal attempts).

§ 31 StGB allows for withdrawal in situations where the accused conspired or attempted to participate in a serious crime.[56] The provision applies to situations that have not yet reached the attempts stage and thus covers preparatory acts/inchoate offending. It states:

> (1) Whoever voluntarily
>
> 1. abandons the attempt to induce another to commit a serious criminal offence and averts any existing danger that the other may commit the offence,
> 2. abandons his plans having declared his willingness to commit a serious criminal offence or
> 3. prevents the commission of an offence having agreed to commit a serious criminal offence or having accepted the offer of another to commit a serious criminal offence
>
> does not incur the penalty under § 30 [conspiracy].
>
> (2) If the offence is not completed without any action on the offender's part or if it is committed independently of his previous conduct, the offender's voluntary and earnest effort to prevent the completion of the offence suffices for exemption from punishment.

The scope of § 31 StGB extends to the conduct specifically mentioned in § 30 StGB, being attempts to induce or incite another person to commit a serious criminal offence as well as declarations of willingness or acceptance of the offer of another or agreements with another to commit or incite the commission of a serious offence. The two provisions together operate as the functional equivalent of what English law would term conspiracy, albeit that the German law is 'closely modelled on the general concept of attempts'.[57]

[53] There are also common law jurisdictions that allow for a withdrawal defence in the context of attempts, eg those US states that follow the Model Penal Code. The German law is of interest here because of the similarity to KJM Smith's proposal.

[54] *Strafgesetzbuch* (abbreviated StGB).

[55] There are also several withdrawal provisions that apply to specific offences (such as treason and subsidy fraud): see Bohlander (n 42) 138.

[56] Defined as the opposite of a misdemeanour.

[57] Bohlander (n 42) 175.

Once the offender has crossed the threshold from mere preparatory acts to a criminal attempt, § 31 StGB ceases to be applicable and § 24 StGB takes over. The latter allows for withdrawal from criminal attempts[58] if the offender either voluntarily desisted from committing the offence or prevented its completion. Specifically, § 24 StGB provides:

> (1) A person who of his own volition gives up the further execution of the offence or prevents its completion shall not be liable for the attempt. If the offence is not completed regardless of his actions, that person shall not be liable if he has made a voluntary and earnest effort to prevent the completion of the offence.
>
> (2) If more than one person participates in the offence, the person who voluntarily prevents its completion shall not be liable for the attempt. His voluntary and earnest effort to prevent the completion of the offence shall suffice for exemption from liability if the offence is not completed regardless of his actions or is committed independently of his earlier contribution to the offence.

Withdrawal as a Personal Exemption from Punishment

Under German legal doctrine, withdrawal does not negate an offence element; neither is it seen as a justificatory or excusatory defence. Rather, it is predominantly recognised as a *personal exemption from punishment* (*persönlicher Strafaufhebungsgrund*).[59] This categorisation acknowledges that the actus reus and mens rea of a criminal attempt were present, that this constituted a wrong committed with (some level of) culpability: but, provided the offender voluntarily abandoned his criminal venture, D becomes exempt from the punishment that would otherwise have followed. In practice, the accused is acquitted from the charge of having attempted a particular substantive offence.[60]

As can be seen above, § 24 StGB makes separate provision for sole offenders and those participating in a joint criminal enterprise. While different requirements apply depending on the type of involvement, both § 24(1) StGB (sole offenders) and § 24(2) StGB (joint criminal enterprises) presuppose that the relevant crime has not been fully executed. Neither must the attempt have 'failed', in that the

[58] Defined in § 22 StGB as requiring steps that will imminently lead to the completion of the offence as envisaged by the actor. § 23(1) StGB clarifies that attempts to commit a serious offence will generally incur criminal liability, whilst attempts of misdemeanours will only lead to liability where the penal code explicitly says so. Whether the attempts stage has been reached depends largely on the actor's subjective perspective, which according to the jurisprudence of the Bundesgerichtshof is determined with reference to the surprisingly casual (for a legal test) formula of *Jetzt geht's los!* ('Here we go!'): see eg BGHSt 26, 201ff; BGHST 28, 162–63.

[59] B von Heintschel-Heinegg (ed), *Beck'scher Online Kommentar*, 53rd edn (Munich, CH Beck, 1 May 2022) K Cornelius § 24 StGB [3] (hereafter BeckOK StGB/Cornelius); BGHSt 7, 296, 299.

[60] Bohlander (n 42) 151.

defendant comes to believe, rightly or wrongly, that he can no longer achieve success.[61] By contrast, where commission of the full offence has become objectively impossible, but the actor did not realise this, he can still successfully withdraw – provided the applicable requirements of § 24 StGB are met. To these we now turn.[62]

Complete Attempts

§ 24(1) StGB distinguishes between two situations which have come to be known as 'incomplete' (*unbeendeter Versuch*) and 'complete' attempts (*beendeter Versuch*), respectively (even though § 24 StGB itself eschews this terminology).[63] Starting with the latter, an attempt is 'complete' if the offender *believes* that he has done everything necessary for the prohibited consequence to come about.[64] For example, if D intended to kill V with a box of poisoned chocolates, and he sent these to V by post, he did everything *he* needed to do to poison V (that V still must eat the chocolates for death to occur is immaterial, for it is the steps that D himself needs to take that count). To withdraw in a complete attempt scenario, the offender must actively prevent completion of the crime.[65] While he does not need to select the most promising means available, his efforts must be causal for the crime's non-occurrence.[66] In the poisoned chocolates example, D would have to warn V not to eat the chocolates or visit him and take away the box. Another example would be the planting of a time-bomb in a building. Where D has activated the bomb so that it will explode at a preset time, he has done everything he needs to do to set the offence (depending on the circumstances, it will be criminal damage or a fatal or non-fatal offence against the person) in motion. To withdraw, he will need to disarm the bomb or warn the authorities so that they can prevent the explosion in a timely manner. If the offence did not occur for reasons

[61] BeckOK StGB/Cornelius § 24 StGB [12]–[13].

[62] In what follows, I focus on § 24(1) StGB, which governs withdrawal by sole perpetrators. The requirements for withdrawal become significantly more demanding where several offenders were involved in the attempt: they are governed by § 24(2) StGB (Withdrawal from Joint Criminal Enterprises).

[63] According to the wording of § 24(1) StGB, the law requires no more than that the actor voluntarily desisted from committing the crime or prevented its completion. The statutory provisions do not mention the concepts of *Fehlschlag* (failed attempt) or *beendeter* (complete) and *unbeendeter Versuch* (incomplete attempt). Nevertheless, the judiciary tends to commence analyses of withdrawal by asking whether the attempt had gone awry and then distinguishes between complete and incomplete attempts (see eg BGHSt 34, 53ff; BGHSt 39, 221, 228; BGH NStZ 2013, 156, 157). It does so because the statutory requirements (in terms of what action needs to be taken) imposed on the perpetrator who wishes to withdraw depend logically on whether he had already done everything he subjectively considered necessary to bring about the crime or not.

[64] BeckOK StGB/Cornelius § 24 StGB [22].

[65] ibid § 24 StGB [21].

[66] Bohlander (n 42) 149.

unconnected to his efforts, D can still withdraw, provided he did everything that, from his perspective, would have been necessary and appropriate to prevent the full offence.[67]

Incomplete Attempts

An attempt remains incomplete if D believes he has not yet done everything he needs to do to bring about the crime.[68] In such a scenario, to withdraw from his attempt it will be enough for him to abandon his criminal endeavour.[69] For example, if D intended to kill V and had already pointed the gun at him, but then experienced a change of heart, he can successfully withdraw by lowering the gun and abandoning his plan to shoot V. The attempt remained unfinished, for D still had to pull the trigger to complete his attempt of killing V by gunshot wound.

Failed Attempts

Withdrawal will be unavailable, however, where the attempt was abandoned because the defendant believed (rightly or wrongly) that he could no longer achieve success. This is known as *subjektiver Fehlschlag* (subjectively failed attempts).[70] Conversely, where commission of the full offence is objectively impossible, but D does not realise this, he can still successfully withdraw.[71] This follows from the last sentence in § 24(1) StGB, according to which an actor can withdraw even if it is impossible for his actions to result in completion of the crime, provided he engaged in a voluntary and earnest effort to prevent the completion of the offence. The following are (textbook) examples of withdrawal-preventing failed attempts:[72]

1. D breaks into V's house in order to steal money and other valuables. The house is empty, however, V having recently moved.
2. D goes for a walk by the river and sees his enemy V on the other bank. He discharges a pistol aimed at V, but misses. V flees and thus escapes being hit by D's further shots.
3. D burgles V's house in order to steal a valuable painting, only to discover that it is in fact a cheap copy.

[67] ibid 149. Alerting the authorities must, of course, be grounded in a genuine wish to resile from the planned offence. Thus, a terrorist causing disruption by planting live bombs and then telling the police about them would not be taken to have withdrawn.

[68] BeckOK StGB/Cornelius § 24 StGB [22]; BGHSt 4, 180; BGHSt 31, 170.

[69] ibid [21].

[70] ibid [12].

[71] See BGHSt 9, 52; BGH NStZ 2011, 629; BGH NStZ-RR 2015, 105.

[72] V Krey and R Esser, *Deutsches Strafrecht Allgemeiner Teil*, 6th rev edn (Stuttgart, Kohlhammer Verlag, 2016) 557.

4. D wants to rob V and hits him over the head. V pretends not to have any valuables on his person, claiming that his wallet and watch have just been stolen. D believes V and flees.

Unsurprisingly, determining whether an attempt has failed may be easier in abstract than in application. Imagine D had planned to shoot V dead, but missed. He only had one shot. Yet D could still bring about V's death by strangling him. There is a debate in German law as to how this situation is to be resolved.[73] This is because trying faithfully to apply the principles in § 24(1) StGB might lead us to two different, diametrically opposed, propositions. On the one hand, it could be argued that the attempt (to shoot V dead) has *failed*, as it is now impossible to execute D's original plan and D is aware of this: he intended to shoot V dead and he knew he only had the one shot which missed its target. On the other hand, if D is aware that there are other immediate means by which he could bring about V's death, one might conclude that the attempt situation remains, in law, *incomplete*, in which case withdrawal would still be possible according to the second sentence in § 24(1) StGB.

The issue tends to arise in what German legal scholars call '*mehraktige Geschehensabläufe*':[74] that is, in instances where a series of criminal events form, in effect, one continuous sequence. In the past, the German judiciary treated such instances as involving a failed attempt whenever the accused had not considered and endorsed alternative means (to implement his criminal endeavour) prior to embarking on his first attempt.[75] The decisive element under this approach was the accused's 'planning horizon' (*Planungshorizont*). An attempt was deemed complete whenever the accused had done everything he had *planned* to do to bring about the offence. If this did not lead to the commission of the full offence, then the attempt would count as failed, even if other means by which the crime could still be executed (in temporal and spatial proximity to the acts already performed[76]) had become available. If, by contrast, the accused, when planning his crime, had contemplated and endorsed different ways in which he might proceed, then an attempt was not considered to have failed when one method could no longer succeed, and it remained possible for him to withdraw by desisting from further action. The problem with this approach was that it benefited actors whose planning had considered alternative ways by which to achieve their criminal goal. Arguably, perpetrators who go to such lengths are more dangerous and exhibit greater criminal energy than those whose plans do not include 'fall-back' options. It is difficult to see why the former should be given more opportunity to withdraw than the latter.

More recent judgments have therefore been treating the so-called *Rücktrittshorizont* (ie the offender's 'withdrawal horizon') as decisive; or have

[73] BeckOK StGB/Cornelius § 24 StGB [16].
[74] ibid.
[75] BeckOK StGB/Cornelius § 24 StGB [17]; BGHSt 14, 74; BGHSt 21, 319, 322.
[76] Bohlander (n 42) 148.

adopted a holistic approach, favoured by the majority of academic commentators, which looks to how the actor imagined his crime would evolve *after* the last act he took towards its completion.[77] Under such an approach, an attempt remains incomplete if the actor, whilst considering his actions up to that point as failed, appreciates that he still has other means by which he could bring about the crime in a timely manner. If in such circumstances he desists from acting further, this amounts to a voluntary withdrawal from an incomplete attempt.[78] By contrast, if the accused considered it impossible to still achieve the crime after the last step he took towards its completion, his attempt would have failed. This (admittedly more generous) approach is grounded in the thought, echoing some of the Anglo-American theory canvassed earlier, that there is no need for punishment if an accused refrains from taking steps that, although different to his original plan, would be no less promising to bring about the relevant crime. An accused who desists in such circumstances is said to have returned to the path of legality.[79] Were the situation resolved any differently, so that the accused were treated as having committed a criminal attempt, there would be no incentive for him to withdraw at that point. Rewarding an accused who refrains from acting again after his initial attempt has failed also vindicates the victim's interests (in not being harmed any further).

Going back to the example of D, who had one shot with which to kill V, but who appreciates that he can still achieve his goal by strangulation, under the current judicial approach this is likely to be held an incomplete attempt from which D can withdraw by refraining from further action, provided he desists 'of his own volition'.

Voluntariness

Withdrawal, in German law too, presupposes voluntariness. What voluntariness requires, however, is contentious – unsurprisingly; no legal system can side-step the underlying normative issues by definitional fiat. German academic literature tends to interpret this requirement as demanding that the accused desisted because of *autonomous motives* (at the time the decision to withdraw is taken). A decision to desist will count as autonomous if it was free and self-determined. It does not require a virtuous motive.[80] On such a view, withdrawal is precluded whenever the accused desisted because of heteronomous motives, ie reasons that are independent of the will of the actor. The judiciary takes a similar approach, enquiring whether the actor was 'master of his decisions' (*Herr seiner Entschlüsse*),[81] or whether these

[77] BeckOK StGB/Cornelius § 24 StGB [18].
[78] BGH NStZ-RR 2017, 335.
[79] H Otto, 'Fehlgeschlagener Versuch und Rücktritt' (1992) *Juristische Ausbildung* 423, 428.
[80] Bohlander (n 42) 150.
[81] BeckOK StGB/Cornelius § 24 StGB [38]; BGHSt 35, 186; BGH NStZ-RR 2014, 241.

were rather the result of external pressures (*äußere Zwangslage*)[82] or psychological inhibitions/mental pressure (*psychische Hemmungen/seelischer Druck*).[83] The so-called 'Frank Formula' (named after Professor Reinhard Frank who came up with the relevant test) can help decide whether withdrawal was voluntary or not. Under this approach, a withdrawal will be considered voluntary if D thought 'I do not want to continue even if I could' and involuntary if D thought 'I cannot continue even if I wanted to'.[84]

Some Comparative Observations

The German model is not bereft of hard cases, as we have noted: that is an inevitable feature of any sophisticated legal system. Yet it illustrates the possibility of a feasible alternative approach. It allows for withdrawal not just in the context of complicity but also makes provision for certain principals who wish to disengage from criminal attempts. English common law, by contrast, disallows withdrawal for attempts by would-be perpetrators. The latter, once they have engaged in a more than merely preparatory act, can no longer extinguish their liability by withdrawing, whereas under the German model withdrawal remains a possibility unless the attempt has failed and the offender lacked the (subjective) belief that he could still succeed in his crime.

We have seen that the German withdrawal provision for sole offenders differentiates between complete and incomplete attempts. A similar distinction has been proposed by KJM Smith for English law. He envisages extending withdrawal to *incomplete* attempts. His definition of 'incomplete' attempts, like the German conception, would look to whether there are one or more further acts that D needs to take to achieve his goal. Similar to the approach adopted by the German courts, Smith seems to envisage a *subjective* perspective when assessing whether an attempt ought to be considered completed or incomplete. Mindful that English law already takes a subjective approach to the issue of impossible attempts (considering the facts as the defendant believed them to be),[85] this seems in principle possible.

V. A Proposal

Indeed, one might go further. Under certain circumstances, the German model allows withdrawal also in instances of *completed* attempts, specifically where D has further means by which he, imminently, could have another go at committing/

[82] See BGH NStZ-RR 2014, 171.
[83] See BGH NStZ 2014, 450.
[84] See Bohlander (n 42) 150.
[85] See s 1(3)(b) of the Criminal Attempts Act 1981.

attempting the offence. It is likely that such a move, in England, would require legislative reform. Be that as it may, it is also worth noting one category of complete attempts – understood as attempts where D has done all he needed to do to set the offence in motion – which one might want to include were one to extend the scope of the withdrawal 'defence' to would-be perpetrators. These might be termed 'non-proximate attempts'.

Non-proximate Attempts

One of the reasons given for treating secondary parties and sole offenders differently under English law when it comes to withdrawal is the argument that secondary liability is *structurally different*: whereas with inchoate offences, once the elements of attempt are satisfied, the offence is complete and cannot be 'uncommitted', secondary participation can be undone before the commission of an offence. In particular, it is argued that the perpetrator has a choice whether or not to go through with the crime, whereas a secondary party has no such choice (or chance to think again), once the assistance or encouragement is rendered. This can be seen most clearly in cases of conditional intent, ie where, at time T1,[86] P may intend to commit robbery and if met with resistance also murder. P's intent can change if and when (at T2) he finds himself in the actual situation of being met with resistance. S's intent, however, is fixed (for both robbery and murder) at point T1. So once assistance is given at T1, S is implicated and will now need withdrawal if, between T1 and T2, he has a change of mind, in order to escape liability for murder should P go on to commit it. Absent the possibility of withdrawal, S's liability is no longer in his hands. By contrast, P only needs to refrain from acting upon his original intent to escape liability. Refraining from doing more is not an option for S, who is committed (for both crimes) at T1.

Yet a similar logic applies to crimes where there is a delay (between T1 and T2) for the perpetrator during which he can experience a change of heart: as, for example, where he has planted a bomb with a timer or laid a trap that will be triggered at some future point by the victim. In such cases, even though, technically, a completed criminal attempt has occurred, there is a case for allowing the offender to repent and to benefit from withdrawal.

A General Test

Suppose that we accept the broad argument that I have made in this chapter. What should be asked of a perpetrator who wishes to withdraw from his

[86] I am adopting the terminology for 'future-conduct offence constructions' from JJ Child and A Hunt, 'Beyond the Present-fault Paradigm: Expanding Mens Rea Definition in the General Part' (2022) 42 *OJLS* 438.

attempt (whether incomplete or complete but non-proximate)? In parallel to what English law already requires from secondary parties who wish to withdraw, and drawing on the above distinctions between failed, incomplete and complete attempts, I would propose that withdrawal from a criminal attempt should be possible where:

(a) the criminal purpose has been abandoned voluntarily (ie for autonomous, though not necessarily penitent or virtuous, motives);
(b) whilst completion of the offence was still objectively possible or subjectively believed possible by the actor (in other words, the attempt must not have failed); and
(c) fair effort has been made by the actor to prevent completion of the relevant substantive offence (in incomplete attempt situations) and to countermand any endangerment for the protected legal interest (where the attempt was complete at the stage of withdrawal).

What amounts to 'fair effort' would be a question of fact and degree for the jury. As with accessories who wish to withdraw, this can be guided by a proportionality principle. Over time, case law might help to get a clearer picture of what is required in typical situations.

VI. Concluding Remarks

Jogee did not consider withdrawal in its restatement of the principles of accessorial liability. One problem with reforming, and possibly extending, the law of withdrawal is that its scope is shaped by the grounds for accepting the 'defence' in the first place, and these remain uncertain:

> The more credence given to the efficacy of the defence as an inducement to renounce, the less stringent are likely to be the qualifying demands. Alternatively, if the defence is viewed more as an instrument for demonstrating absence of entrenched criminal purpose then only rather more strenuous efforts are likely to be sufficiently convincing.[87]

The uncertainties around the scope and application of withdrawal might be considered a reason not to extend the 'defence' to cover perpetrators and their criminal attempts. However, as this chapter has sought to demonstrate, German law is not fully clear or explicit on the underlying theory either, yet has been able to make some provision to allow sole offenders to withdraw from criminal attempts. This is not to overlook that many aspects of the relevant law are contentious and subject to debate. However, even conceding the (practical) problems involved in fashioning a withdrawal 'defence' for criminal attempts, there are good reasons for extending it to at least some would-be perpetrators: although complicity is

[87] Smith, 'Withdrawal from Criminal Liability' (n 4) 204.

formally distinguishable from attempts (in that for the former the renunciatory conduct must precede rather than follow crystallisation of liability), the possible justifications for a defence of withdrawal are comparable.[88] As such, it should be possible – and warranted, if like cases are to be treated alike – to extend the scope of withdrawal to incomplete attempts, and even to those instances of complete attempts that are structurally akin to complicity, in that there is a gap between the time when the ingredients necessary to commit the crime are put in place and when it is finalised. In such cases, there remains a window of opportunity between commencement and completion of the crime, during which a perpetrator can experience and act upon a change of heart such that he should not, ultimately, be punished. Allowing withdrawal in cases of what might be termed non-proximate attempts would not undermine the rationales underpinning attempts liability. As with accessorial liability, there are good reasons to allow a route back into legality for those who, albeit at the last possible moment, wish to change tack and abandon their criminal endeavour.

[88] ibid 215.

9

Emergencies, Necessity and the Prevention of Crime

HENRY MARES*

Consider the following scenario:[1]

> *Emergency*: P is instructed by A to kill V. If P does not kill V, A credibly threatens to kill immediately thirty schoolchildren for whom P is responsible.

In this scenario, if P does choose to kill V, P will become guilty of murder unless she has a defence. The purpose of this chapter is to explore whether P may indeed have a defence: first, by briefly considering the common law, and, secondly, by considering in more detail the statutory defence under section 3 of the Criminal Law Act 1967. I will offer an argument that the current law has the resources to allow a defence to P in situations such as *Emergency* – that a case can be made for putting the matter to a jury both at common law and under the 1967 Act.

In what follows, I begin by considering common law defences, especially the defence of necessity. I suggest that there is some traditional authority that lethal force can be used in emergencies of the kind envisaged. I then make a similar argument for the scope of the section 3 defence, in light both of its genesis and

* For help with the provision of primary materials for this paper during the pandemic, thanks are due to the Library of the Institute of Advanced Legal Studies, London; the Maughan Library at King's College, London; the British Library, and especially to Dr L Garcia-Moreno; the Library of the London School of Economics; the Library of Trinity College, Cambridge; the House of Commons Enquiries service; and the Parliamentary Archives. Thanks are due as well to Mr J Bernhardt, Dr B Spagnolo, Dr J Stanton-Ife, and especially Professor A Simester and Professor F Stark whose comments have greatly improved this paper. All errors remain those of the author.

[1] Variations on this hypothetical are clearly possible, eg with fewer schoolchildren, more or less certainty over the extent of the threat, or with more or less immediacy in its execution: compare the discussion in L Alexander, 'Deontology at the Threshold' (2000) 37 *San Diego Law Review* 893. Note that this situation contemplates a private actor; for discussion of state actors in situations of self-defence or necessity, see GR Sullivan, 'The Hard Treatment of Innocent Persons in State Responses to the Threat of Large Scale and Imminent and Terrorist Violence: Examining the Legal Constraints' in GR Sullivan and I Dennis (eds), *Seeking Security: Pre-empting the Commission of Criminal Harms* (London, Hart Publishing, 2012) 293.

of subsequent case law. After considering various possible objections to the arguments developed in the chapter, I conclude that there is reason to think that both necessity and the section 3 defence are available in *Emergency*.

I. The Common Law

One might have thought that duress would be the most obvious possible defence in this scenario, as it deals with what would otherwise be crimes committed under pressure. The duress defence is entirely a creature of the common law; the current test was set out in *Graham*:

> The Crown having conceded that the issue of duress was open to the appellant and was raised on the evidence, the correct approach on the facts of this case would have been as follows:
>
> (1) Was the defendant, or may he have been, impelled to act as he did because, as a result of what he reasonably believed King had said or done, he had good cause to fear that if he did not so act King would kill him or (if this is to be added) cause him serious physical injury?
>
> (2) If so, have the prosecution made the jury sure that a sober person of reasonable firmness, sharing the characteristics of the defendant, would not have responded to whatever he reasonably believed King said or did by taking part in the killing?[2]

Although the dominant rationale of the defence has been that the will of the defendant was overborne by the pressure, there is also a thread of authority suggesting that the rationale of a lesser evil was being chosen.[3] Either rationale would in principle apply to *Emergency*, and the case seems capable of meeting the criteria set out in *Graham*. Notoriously, however, there is a snag: following the House of Lords decision in *Howe*, the defence is not available to murder.[4] The rationale for that restriction is contestable,[5] a matter to which we return later. In principle, there seems no reason why the reasonable firmness constraint in *Graham* requires ad hoc supplementation of the *Howe* kind; especially where, as in *Emergency*, the threat is not to the protagonist herself, but to others for whom the protagonist is responsible – a scenario not contemplated in *Howe*. In the absence of legislative reform, however, the rule is clear: our protagonist in *Emergency* has no defence of duress.

[2] *R v Graham* (1982) 74 Cr App R 235, 241.

[3] Compare *R v Howe* [1987] 1 AC 417, 435 (Lord Hailsham) with *R v Graham* (1982) 74 Cr App R 235, 241.

[4] Duress may have been a defence to what would otherwise be homicide in the past: see JH Baker, *Oxford History of the Laws of England*, vol VI (Oxford, Oxford University Press, 2003) 562 and sources therein.

[5] See eg F Stark, '*R* v *Howe* (1987)' in P Handler, H Mares and I Williams (eds), *Landmark Cases in Criminal Law* (Oxford, Hart Publishing, 2017) 309.

As things stand, the most plausible common law defence is that of (lesser-evils) necessity.[6] Necessity, to the extent it exists as a defence in criminal law,[7] has not always been thought to be available as a defence to what would otherwise be murder; as is well known, it was excluded in the 1884 case of *Dudley and Stephens*.[8] Glanville Williams argued for the existence of such a defence 'where the killing results in a net saving of life',[9] as in *Emergency*, and, more recently, such a defence was recognised by Brooke LJ on the facts arising in *Re A*:

> According to Sir James Stephen there are three necessary requirements for the application of the doctrine of necessity:
>
> i. the act is needed to avoid inevitable and irreparable evil;
> ii. no more should be done than is reasonably necessary for the purpose to be achieved;
> iii. the evil inflicted must not be disproportionate to the evil avoided.[10]

These criteria would indeed be met in *Emergency*, but there has not been much enthusiasm for extending the defence beyond conjoined twins cases; an extension of the defence of necessity to assisted suicide was, for example, avoided in *Nicklinson*.[11] In *Re A*, Brooke LJ noted that neither of the leading judgments in *Howe* 'displays any evidence that they had in mind a situation in which a court was invited to sanction a defence … on facts comparable to those with which we are confronted in the present case'.[12] The same might be thought to be true in applying that test from *Re A* to *Emergency*. Yet an argument for doing so can be made.

The first point to notice here is that *Emergency* is clearly distinguishable from the facts of *Dudley and Stephens*. In the latter case, no crime was threatened against any victim, there was not even a moral wrong, *apart* from the very wrong perpetrated by the defendants. The defendants killed and ate the cabin boy purely to serve their own ends. By contrast, in *Emergency*, P acts to avert a profound wrong, an abhorrent crime. It would be better, we can agree, if P had been able to kill the wrongdoer, A: there seems little doubt about the potential for a defence were P to have done so. But let us stipulate that such a response was impracticable.

[6] A version of necessity has been recognised as a defence in certain (especially, medical) situations when intervention is in the victim's 'best interests': *Re F* [1990] 2 AC 1, 55, 73–76 (Lord Goff). We can take it, however, that it is not in V's best interests to be killed in *Emergency*. Although not the meaning used here, 'necessity' is sometimes also used to refer to duress of circumstances: *Conway* (1989) 88 Cr App R 159, 164; *Colin Martin* (1989) 88 Cr App R 343, 345.

[7] See *Southwark London Borough Council v Williams* [1971] 1 Ch 734, 744 (Lord Denning); compare *Bournewood Community and Mental Health NHS Trust, Ex parte L* [1999] 1 AC 458, 490 (Lord Goff) and *Wawrzyniak* [2017] EWCA Crim 2008, [23]–[24].

[8] *R v Dudley and Stephens* (1884) XIV QBD 273, 287.

[9] GL Williams, *Criminal Law: The General Part*, 2nd edn (London, Stevens, 1961) 740, § 237.

[10] *Re A* [2001] Fam 147, 240 (Brooke LJ). Ward LJ appeared to agree (198), albeit phrasing the issue merely as choosing the lesser of two evils in the circumstances of that case (203).

[11] *R (on the application of Nicklinson and another) v Ministry of Justice* [2014] UKSC 38, [130] (Lord Neuberger); endorsing [2013] EWCA Civ 961, [25].

[12] *Re A* [2001] Fam 147, 225 (Brooke LJ).

By killing V instead, P still acts to uphold and protect the fundamental rights of the schoolchildren not to be killed by others – rights that are legal as well as moral.

We can see in this line of reasoning that there is a natural overlap between necessity and the prevention or avoidance of crime. Later, we shall turn explicitly to the latter justification, as enacted in section 3 of the Criminal Law Act 1967. What is of immediate interest, for now, is the common law regarding such cases *prior to* 1967, which – I claim – in part reflects that overlap. If we look back to *Kenny's Outlines*, we find that there was thought to be a common law defence of some sort for preventing crime, ultimately rooted in a notion of necessity, and that it applied in homicide cases. In the 1964 edition, under the heading of 'Justifiable Homicide' and the subheading of 'The advancement of public justice', Turner wrote:

> Life may be taken with impunity, if it be necessary and reasonable for arresting a felon, or suppressing a felonious riot, or preventing a crime of a 'forcible or atrocious' character. The old books in speaking of 'atrocious and violent crimes' referred to felonious attacks; for in the old days they were capital.[13]

On its terms, the passage from *Kenny's Outlines* does not distinguish between taking the life of the aggressor – what might be considered 'true' prevention of crime – and that of some innocent third party, in which crime is indirectly prevented or avoided. What appears to have mattered more for the common law position was that the threatened attack was a felony. (As will be seen below, it was this dependence on felony that the Criminal Law Act 1967 was intended to remove.) A few pages later, under the subheading of 'Self-defence', Turner continues:

> It has often been stated that a death inflicted by a man in self-defence against an unlawful assailant would be a case of justifiable homicide. But Blackstone pointed out that this was too wide, and based upon misconception; for such a homicide could only be justified when the attack resisted was itself a felonious one and therefore the cases must be classed with those above discussed, as homicides justified by the fact that they were effected in order to prevent a capital felony.[14]

Thus self-defence, and perhaps defence of others, is here too subsumed into the more general defence of prevention of felony. The authority cited for the first passage's claim about prevention of 'forcible or atrocious' crime is Blackstone, who wrote:

> In the next place, such homicide as is committed for the *prevention* of any forcible and atrocious *crime*, is justifiable by the law of nature;[15] and also by the law of

[13] JWC Turner, *Kenny's Outlines of Criminal Law*, 18th edn (Cambridge, Cambridge University Press, 1964) 135, para 96 (citations omitted); a footnote in that passage after 'preventing a crime of a forcible or atrocious character' refers the reader to 4 Bl Comm 180.

[14] Turner (n 13) 137, para 97 (citations omitted).

[15] Blackstone cites here 'Puff. L. of N. l. 2. c. 5', a reference to J Pufendorf, *Of the Law of Nature and Nations* (Oxford, L Lichfield, 1703) book II, ch 5 (74), which deals with self-defence, but which does not discuss our scenario.

> England, as it stood so early as the time of Bracton, and as it is since declared in statute 24 Hen. VIII. c. 5.[16]

The statute of Henry VIII to which Blackstone refers is not, however, in such wide terms[17] as it might appear to be in this passage: it refers only to the killing of an initial aggressor; indeed, all of the examples that Blackstone then cites in the following paragraph are similarly of the killing of the initial aggressor. On the other hand, Blackstone also gives a citation to folio 155 of Bracton, which provides:

> Hence, (as) briefly explained above, if one is slain we must see whether he is wrongfully slain. (He is slain wrongfully) who is slain without right. That is why he who kills a thief, either a day thief or a night thief, is not liable, (that is), if he could not otherwise escape danger; if he could he is liable.[18]

The reference to 'explained above' appears to be a reference to Bracton's earlier discussion of the four kinds of homicide by deed, one of which was through necessity:

> Of necessity, and here we must distinguish whether the necessity was avoidable or not; if avoidable and he could escape without slaying, he will then be guilty of homicide; if unavoidable, since he kills without premeditated hatred but with sorrow of heart, in order to save himself and his family, since he could not otherwise escape (danger), he is not liable to the penalty for homicide.[19]

It is difficult to be more exact. In *Emergency*, it is certainly possible that P kills V 'without premeditated hatred but with sorrow of heart', even though the threat is from A and against someone else.

A proviso is in order. The argument here should not be misunderstood as saying there is nothing problematic about *Emergency*. None of the foregoing is to deny that V is *wronged*, both morally and legally, when P kills him. Simester argues that one of the distinctive features of necessitous action is that it may be justified even though (and unlike cases, say, of self-defence) the victim – who is innocent throughout – is wronged.[20] The unique normative character of necessity arises from the fact that the victim does not bring down the use of force upon himself, by his own conduct. He is simply a victim of circumstance. As such, civil liability might properly arise from P's actions, liability that might fall upon P as well as A. The suggestion is merely that *criminal* liability should fall only upon A.

[16] W Blackstone, *Commentaries on the Laws of England, Book the Fourth* (Oxford, Clarendon Press, 1769) 180.

[17] Textual problems may arise with older statutes: JH Baker, *An Introduction to English Legal History*, 5th edn (Oxford, Oxford University Press, 2019) 216–20; I rely here on the reprint in the *Statutes of the Realm*, vol III (London: 1817) 422.

[18] SE Thorne (ed), *Bracton on the Laws and Customs of England*, vol II (Cambridge, MA, Harvard University Press, 1977) 437–38. The words in parentheses are Thorne's interpolations.

[19] ibid 340. See the discussion in E Papp-Kamali, *Felony and the Guilty Mind in Medieval England* (Cambridge, Cambridge University Press, 2019) 67.

[20] A Simester, *Fundamentals of Criminal Law* (Oxford, Oxford University Press, 2021) ch 18. Ultimately, however, Simester would not extend a justification to cases such as *Emergency*.

II. A Statutory Defence?

Let us turn now to how the use of force is permitted under section 3 of the Criminal Law Act 1967.[21] There was no opportunity to apply section 3 in *Re A*, as Mary was clearly not capable of committing a crime. Clarkson has argued, without discussing section 3 at all, for a unified defence of necessary action,[22] but the advantage of section 3 is that such a considerable reshaping of existing defences is not required, in a context where Parliament has shown no appetite for reform in this area. Further, unlike in *Nicklinson*, the application of section 3 does not require any extension by the courts. But could section 3 supply a defence in *Emergency*? The section is familiar, and currently provides:

> Use of force in making arrest, etc.
>
> (1) A person may use such force as is reasonable in the circumstances in the prevention of crime, or in effecting or assisting in the lawful arrest of offenders or suspected offenders or of persons unlawfully at large.
>
> (2) Subsection (1) above shall replace the rules of the common law on the question when force used for a purpose mentioned in the subsection is justified by that purpose.

Obviously, applying the section to *Emergency* raises some questions of statutory interpretation. To that end, it is useful to start by looking at the origin and purposes of the provision.

The Background to Section 3

The genesis of Part I of the 1967 Act was the *Seventh Report* of the Criminal Law Revision Committee.[23] The *Report* arose from a query from the Home Secretary, Henry Brooke, regarding whether the 'division of indictable offences into felonies and misdemeanours should be retained and, if not, what revision of the law should be made in consequence of its abolition'.[24] The focus of the *Report* was on that distinction between felonies and misdemeanours, and the other reforms suggested were incidental to that.

The Committee was clear that the distinction should be abolished, and its draft Bill set out clauses to do so. One of the main issues dependent on the distinction

[21] This now must be interpreted in light of s 76 of the Criminal Justice and Immigration Act 2008, on which see the discussion in the text at and following n 68.

[22] CMV Clarkson, 'Necessary Action: A New Defence' [2004] *Crim LR* 81. But see J Horder, 'Self-defence, Necessity and Duress: Understanding the Relationship' (1998) XI *Canadian Journal of Law and Jurisprudence* 143.

[23] Criminal Law Revision Committee, *Seventh Report: Felonies and Misdemeanours*, Cmnd 2659 (London, HMSO, 1965). See *R v Jones* [2007] 1 AC 136, 161 (Lord Bingham). As an unsigned editorial ('Criminal Law Act' [1967] Crim LR 495–96) noted, 'the Criminal Law Revision Committee's *Report* itself provides an explanation of the Act which it will be hard to better'.

[24] Hansard vol 692, House of Commons, Thursday 26 March 1964, written answer of Henry Brooke.

was the issue of arrest without warrant, something the Committee found difficult to resolve.[25] One apparent feature of the distinction between felonies and misdemeanours relating to arrest was the use of force. As the *Report* set out:

> There is some old authority for the proposition that, if in order to arrest a person for an offence it is necessary to use extreme or even fatal force, this is allowed only where the offence is a felony. The matter is very obscure. … There is also some old authority, though it is not clear or consistent, that the right to use extreme force in order to prevent the commission of a crime depends on the crime being a felony or a certain kind of felony. (Blackstone in one place relates the right to the prevention of "forcible and atrocious crimes", without making it clear what these are (Comm IV, 180), though elsewhere he appears to limit the rule to capital felonies (p 182).)[26]
>
> We considered at some length whether to recommend the inclusion of a detailed provision setting out rules as to the crimes in relation to which these rights should exist in future and what precisely should be the rights. … The case for doing so is that ideally the law should define clearly the rights of the police and private persons in the situations which might confront them and that, since it is possible that under the present law it would be easier to defend the use of extreme force against a felon than against a misdemeanant, the abolition of the distinction is a suitable occasion to define the law.
>
> But we concluded that it was not necessary or desirable to make any detailed provision. … So far, fortunately, these questions have arisen very rarely, and in general they can safely be left to be determined by the courts when necessary. However, lest it should be argued that some rights will be lost with the disappearance of felonies, we recommend that it should be provided that a person may lawfully use reasonable force in the prevention of crime or in effecting or assisting in the lawful arrest of offenders. The provision is in clause 3.

Clause 3 in the draft Bill attached at the end of the *Report* was consequently in simple terms:

> A person may use reasonable force in the prevention of crime, or in effecting or assisting in the lawful arrest of offenders.

There was no equivalent of what was to be section 3(2), a matter to which we shall return. The Committee considered whether more specificity was generally required, but decided that it was not:

> No doubt if a question arose on clause 3, the court, in considering what was reasonable force, would take into account all the circumstances, including in particular the nature and degree of force used, the seriousness of the evil to be prevented and the possibility of preventing it by other means; but there is no need to specify in the clause the criteria for deciding the question. Since the clause is framed in general terms, it is not limited to arrestable or any other class of offences.[27]

[25] Criminal Law Revision Committee, *Seventh Report* (n 22) 4, para 6.

[26] ibid 7, paras 20–22. A similar explanation was given in Annex 2 to the *Report*, 'Notes on draft Criminal Law Bill', referring back to paras 20–23 of the *Report*: 'This clause [clause 3] allows the use of reasonable force in the prevention of crime or in effecting or assisting in the lawful arrest of offenders. It is included because of the possibility that some of those rights at present depend to some extent on whether the offence is a felony or misdemeanour (paragraphs 20–3).'

[27] ibid 7, para 23.

Thus the clause was deliberately general, setting a standard that has a clear family resemblance to the kind of inquiry required for necessity. Clearly the use of force was intended to be interpreted in line with the pre-existing common law, with just the essential changes required by abolition of the distinction between felonies and misdemeanours. The only envisaged effect of the clause was to extend any pre-existing liberty to use force – in order to prevent felonies – also to misdemeanours. It was not intended to confirm the existence and scope of such liberty. As will be seen, however, whether this matches what was produced in the Act is less clear.

The Introduction of Section 3(2)

The *Report* was generally welcomed by the *Criminal Law Review*, and received perhaps more warily by the *Modern Law Review*;[28] neither publication dwelt at length on the draft clause 3. The draft Bill attached to the *Report* was the basis of the Bill that came to Parliament in 1965, and there was no change to clause 3 between the *Report* and Bill that came to Parliament. The Explanatory Memorandum preceding the Bill, as first introduced in the Commons, did not deal with clause 3 at all, but merely stated:

> [T]he Bill is largely designed to consolidate and clarify the existing law, though with modifications going somewhat beyond the adjustments required by the abolition of the distinction [between felony and misdemeanour]. The provisions of most practical importance are those made by clauses 2, 4 and 5 to replace the present law about arrest for felony, about accessories after the fact to felony and about misprision and compounding of felony.

The Bill was referred in the Commons to the Second Reading Committee, and substantive discussion took place there on 9 February 1966. The speech was given by the then Alice Bacon MP, Minister of State for the Home Office; as she put it:

> The object of this Bill is simple. It is stated very directly and concisely in nine words in the first subsection of Clause 1. It is to abolish all distinctions between felony and misdemeanour. All that follows that simple provision in Clause 1 is no more than consequential. …
>
> Clause 3 allows the use of reasonable force in the prevention of crime or in effecting, or assisting in, the lawful arrest of offenders. It has been included to prevent any argument that the law has been changed by reason of the disappearance of felonies.[29]

[28] The unsigned editorial ('Criminal Law Act' [1967] *Crim LR* 495) proclaimed that 'the Committee deserves praise without stint for its work'. The *Modern Law Review* note, signed 'C', 'Reports of Committee: Criminal Law Revision Committee: Seventh Report' (1965) 28 *MLR* 689, 690, stated: 'though its main proposal, which is the abolition of the distinction between felonies and misdemeanours, will certainly be generally acceptable, some of the others are likely to evoke criticism'. This latter note mentioned clause 3 briefly, as of reassurance to those concerned with the powers of arrest issue.

[29] Hansard (HC Committee Debates, Second Reading Committee, Criminal Law Bill) 9 February 1966, cols 3 and 7.

That Criminal Law Bill, however, lapsed with the dissolution of Parliament, and when Parliament returned, the Criminal Law Bill [*Lords*] was introduced in the House of Lords in substantially the same terms.[30] The Second Reading speech there was by Lord Stonham:

> Clause 3, which makes statutory provision in a field hitherto left to the Common Law, allows the use of reasonable force in the prevention of crime, or in effecting or assisting in the lawful arrest of offenders. I understand that this clause has given rise to a certain amount of concern, and that there is some fear that it may extend the law by giving general sanction for the use of extreme measures to protect land and property. We shall, of course, consider this in more detail in Committee, but I think it may be helpful to say a few words now about what is intended.
>
> The Common Law on the matter is very obscure, but there is reason to think that it allows the use of force, where necessary, to carry out an arrest or to prevent crime, although it is possible that the extent of the existing powers may depend on whether the crime is a felony or a misdemeanour. The clause has been included to prevent any argument that the law has been changed because of the disappearance of felonies. The intention is to place on a statutory basis what is probably the existing law on the matter.[31]

Notably, clause 3(2), which explicitly replaced the common law with the statute, was an addition from the debate in the Lords. During the Second Reading debate in the House of Lords, Viscount Colville had raised the issue of whether clauses 2 and 3 removed common law confusion in the area; it would appear his main concern had been with the potential for resuscitation of an obscure common law ground for arrest. Nevertheless, as he put it:

> The other subsidiary point, which arises, I think, on Clause 2 and on Clause 3, is whether or not this supersedes the Common Law. I am sure that I shall be told by the noble and learned Lord, the Lord Chancellor, that, as a matter of drafting, this is apparently so; even though it does not say so in the Bill. But if we are attempting to replace the existing law of the country in realms where it is extremely dubious with clear statutory provisions, there should be no room left, where a matter does not appear to be covered by the Bill, for a reliance on doubtful cases of Common Law.[32]

The obscurity of the common law prior to clause 3 had been noted both by the *Report* and Lord Stonham in his Second Reading speech.[33] In dealing with Viscount Colville's points, the response from the Lord Chancellor was, perhaps surprisingly, that the 'statutory powers do not supersede the Common Law'; albeit this was seemingly in reference only to clause 2(7)[34] which did not affect clause 3.

[30] Hansard (HC Committee Debates, Second Reading Committee, Criminal Law Bill [*Lords*]) 8 March 1967, cols 4–5.

[31] Hansard (HL Debates) 1 November 1966, cols 510–11.

[32] Hansard (HL Debates) 1 November 1966, cols 518–19.

[33] Hansard (HL Debates) 1 November 1966, col 510.

[34] Hansard (HL Debates) 1 November 1966, col 559. Clause 2(7) read: 'This section shall not affect the operation of any enactment restricting the institution of proceedings for an offence, nor prejudice any power of arrest conferred by law apart from this section.'

In response, noting the Lord Chancellor's reply, Viscount Colville moved in Committee an amendment to clause 3 to make certain of the point:

> Any rule of law which does not accord with the provisions of the last foregoing subsection shall cease to have effect.[35]

Lord Stonham in response replied:

> Our view is that the clause as it stands has the effect of replacing the existing law and that it would be unnecessary to add words saying so. But having said that, we have no objection in principle … to considering before Report whether a suitable Amendment can be drafted; but in our view it would have the effect only of saying again what we believe the clause says already.[36]

Viscount Colville withdrew his amendment on Lord Stonham's undertaking to look at the point again. At the Third Reading, in Lord Stonham's absence, the Lord Chancellor moved the amendment that became section 3(2):

> My Lords, this Amendment meets a point raised by the noble Viscount, Lord Colville of Culross, in Committee. … It makes clear that Clause 3 supersedes the Common Law relating to the use of force in preventing crime or effecting an arrest. It is the Government's view that Clause 3 has that effect without the Amendment, but the Amendment removes any possible doubt. I beg to move.[37]

The amendment was agreed in the House of Lords, and was in the Bill that was introduced then into the Commons. At the Second Reading Committee discussion of the Criminal Law Bill [*Lords*] in the House of Commons there was little discussion of the amended clause 3. Introducing the Bill, after rehearsing the reasons for the abolition of the distinction between felonies and misdemeanours, Dick Taverne MP, a Home Office minister, said of the clause:

> Clause 3 deals with something which was previously left to the common law. Subsection (1) allows the use of such force as is reasonable in the circumstances in the prevention of crime. …
>
> The common law on these matters is very obscure at present. It is possible that the extent of the existing powers depends on whether the crime is a felony or a misdemeanour. This Clause has been included to avoid any argument that any existing power will be lost because felonies have disappeared. The intention is to place on a statutory basis what is probably the existing law on the matter, and subsection (2) makes it clear that the new statutory provisions in this Clause supersede the common law.[38]

This was the only discussion. Moreover, when Standing Committee F met to discuss the Bill, there was no substantive discussion of clause 3.[39] The upshot is

[35] Hansard (HL Debates) 24 November 1966, col 430.

[36] Hansard (HL Debates) 24 November 1966, col 431.

[37] Hansard (HL Debates) 2 February 1967, cols 1069–70.

[38] Hansard (HC Committee Debates, Second Reading Committee, Criminal Law Bill [*Lords*]) 8 March 1967, col 8.

[39] Hansard (HC Committee Debates, Standing Committee F, Criminal Law Bill [*Lords*]) 1 June 1967, col 121.

that clause 3 *confirms* a power to use preventive force against traditional felonies, as well as extending that power to what had been misdemeanours. Of note, of course, is that clause 3 did not, and section 3 does not, specify against whom the force may be used.

Application in the Cases

After some years of use, perhaps the most controversial issues arising under section 3 of the Criminal Law Act 1967 concerned protest cases and the meaning of 'force' in the permission to use 'such force as is reasonable'; and the question of which 'crime' would count in the 'prevention of crime'. In *Jones*, involving prosecutions for (inter alia) criminal damage by protestors against the 2003 invasion of Iraq, Lord Hoffmann did say:

> My Lords, I pass over the question of whether damaging property counts as the use of force within the meaning of section 3 of the 1967 Act. There is much to be said for the view that offences against property have their own provisions for justification, such as 'reasonable excuse' as defined in section 5 of the 1971 Act and that *'force' in section 3 means force against persons committing crimes or escaping arrest.* But I am willing to assume for the sake of argument that chaining oneself to railings or putting sugar into the petrol tanks of lorries involves the use of force for the purposes of section 3 of the 1967 Act.[40]

It is difficult to know how much weight to give to these remarks, in such a different context, especially as, though there may be 'much to be said' for restricting section 3 in the manner contemplated, the arguments themselves went unsaid. Neither were any counterarguments considered. A more permissive gloss was put on the defence in *The Queen v Stratford Magistrates Court* by Simon LJ:

> Although it is not possible to set out all-embracing principles which can be derived from these cases, certain themes emerge. First, the defence under s 3(1) of the CLA 1967 operates as a justification for the use of force rather than an excuse to use force, and is linked to the concept of necessity. There must be an apprehension of a need to use force (or, I would accept for reasons that I will come to, in an appropriate case something less than force) to prevent an imminent or immediate crime; or as expressed in Hale, *Pleas of the Crown* (1778) volume 1 (p 52) 'an actual and inevitable danger'. There must be a clear nexus between the use of force and the prevention of crime. …[41]

Such a gloss could well apply to *Emergency*, albeit these protest cases were not ones where the salient issue was against whom the force was used to prevent or avoid crime.

One less well reported case, however, that provides a step on the way is *Baker and Wilkins*.[42] The slightly complicated facts of this case are set out in the decision

[40] *R v Jones* [2007] 1 AC 136, 173 (emphasis added).
[41] *The Queen v Stratford Magistrates Court* [2017] EWHC 1794 (Admin), [25] (Simon LJ).
[42] The case appears reported only in [1997] Crim LR 497.

of the Court of Appeal (Criminal Division).[43] In 1995, Janet Baker and Carl Wilkins, her then boyfriend, had, amongst other things, been convicted of criminal damage. This had been done in a misguided mission to rescue Janet Baker's daughter, Stephanie, from what Baker and Wilkins took to be false imprisonment, kidnapping or child abduction by Baker's former partner, Wakeling (who was Stephanie's father), and Wakeling's new wife. In 1994, Baker and Wilkins had broken into a house owned by a Mr Wonnacut, where Wakeling was staying with his new wife and the daughter Stephanie. This was the basis of the criminal damage count.

Towards the end of the trial, counsel for Baker argued that Baker's actions had been lawful. One of the arguments was that this was so because of section 3 of the Criminal Law Act 1967: it was argued that Baker and Wilkins had been acting in what they took to be the prevention of a crime when they damaged property belonging to the innocent third party, Wonnacut.

The trial judge summed up to the jury on the basis that an intention to recover the child would not provide a lawful excuse or defence, and refused leave to appeal. At the leave to appeal hearing in 1996 it was, among other things, argued that:

> [A]s section 3 of the Criminal Law Act 1967 makes provision for the lawful use of such force as is reasonable in the circumstances to prevent a crime, it would be strange if damaging property, in circumstances where this was reasonable to prevent a crime, was unlawful.[44]

Noting that 'submissions made by counsel for the applicants raise issues of law which are complex and which are, to a very large extent, not covered by authority', Philips LJ granted leave for the appeal to be heard by the Full Court. The Full Court, however, was able to dispose of the section 3 issue relatively quickly: the father, Wakeling, had not been committing a crime, as he had a defence under the Child Abduction Act 1984. That Baker and Wilkins thought that they were preventing crime was not germane, as there would need to be a crime to be prevented.[45] That being the case, no section 3 issue ultimately arose for decision; but the use of section 3 as defence against damaging the property of innocent third parties was, for what that is worth, not dismissed out of hand.

Baker and Wilkins is, however, no more than faint precedent for the argument put forward, much more compellingly, in *Hichens*.[46] Peter Craig Hichens[47] was

[43] *R v Baker and Wilkins*, Court of Appeal Criminal Division, 95/6372/Z5 and 95/6373/Z5 (Thursday, 17 October 1996).

[44] *R v Baker and Wilkins*, Court of Appeal Criminal Division, 95/6372/Z5 and 95/6373/Z5 (Friday, 19 July 1996).

[45] *Baker and Wilkins* (under the name *Baker v Wilkins*) was followed on this point in the High Court in *Hutchinson v Newbury Magistrates' Court* (2000) 122 ILR 499, 508 (Buxton LJ).

[46] *R v Hichens* (Peter Craig) [2011] EWCA Crim 1626.

[47] It may be that the 'Hichens' of this case is the same as the Peter Craig 'Hitchens' who pleaded guilty to a charge of assault occasioning actual bodily harm in 2001: see *R v Peter Craig Hitchens* [2002] EWCA Crim 20. Hitchens in that case was thirty years old in 2002; Hichens in the main case discussed

living in Kathleen Brown's flat from 29 October 2010. Brown had had a relationship with John Oliver that had ended. Olivier had behaved abusively towards Hichens on the morning of 5 November 2010 and on the previous day. That evening Oliver returned to Brown's flat. Brown wanted to let him in, but she was physically prevented from doing so by Hichens. The defence case was that Hichens had slapped Brown to stop her from opening the door, in order to prevent Oliver assaulting Hichens or causing a breach of the peace.

At trial the judge had directed the jury that the chance that Oliver might commit a crime was not sufficient to give Hichens a defence against the touching of Brown. The main question for the Court of Appeal was whether or not the trial judge was correct in this direction; this required determination of whether there could be a defence under the common law or section 3 of the Criminal Law Act 1967 for the use of force against innocent third parties to prevent a crime by someone else. After consideration, though not after any discussion of Lord Hoffmann's dicta in *Jones*, the Court of Appeal came to a clear decision:

> If and in so far as the judge thought that these defences were not capable of extending to the use of force against an innocent third party, we respectfully disagree .... Although we suspect that the facts capable realistically of giving rise to such a defence will only rarely be encountered, examples can be adduced and two will suffice:
>
> 1. A police constable bundles a passer-by out of the way to get at a man he believes about to shoot with a firearm or detonate an explosive device.
> 2. Y seeks to give Z car keys with Z about to drive. X, believing Z to be unfit drive through drink, knocks the keys out of Y's hands and retains them.
>
> As ever that the defence is capable of being advanced is of course a very different question from that of whether it would succeed.[48]

As the Court put it a few lines later, 'there is no rule of law that violence to an innocent person must, in all cases be unlawful'.[49] The decision makes good sense; indeed, in his commentary on the case in the *Criminal Law Review*, Ashworth wondered whether it might be possible to go further:

> If in the first example the police constable used substantial force on the passer-by, who initially resisted the constable's attempt to push past, might not the constable's actions be a defence to assault occasioning actual bodily harm or worse?[50]

Presumably, Ashworth's question would become one for the jury of the reasonableness of the force used in the prevention of crime, and, at that stage, section 76 of

in the text above was forty in 2011. Hichens, in the main case discussed in the text, was, in the remarks on sentencing at the end, described as having 'had a bad record for violence going back to 1999': [2011] EWCA Crim 1626, [33].

[48] ibid [30]. In the next paragraph the Court went on to warn that 'the question of remoteness remains to be considered. Plainly both the common law and statutory defences have greater scope for operation where it is certain or nearly certain that a crime will be committed immediately if action is not taken.'

[49] ibid [31].

[50] [2011] Crim LR 873, 875.

the Criminal Justice and Immigration Act 2008, which sets out statutory criteria for the reasonableness of the use of force, would need to be considered.

Hichens clearly sets up the use of section 3 against innocent third parties to prevent crime: a threat by A against P, resulting in force by P against V, gives a consequent defence for P under section 3. And, as Ashworth pointed out, this could well be the case even when the force used by P was greater than that in *Hichens* itself. Now compare the facts of *Emergency*: a threat by A against those for whom P is responsible, resulting in (lethal) force against V. When P responds by killing V, P may argue as a defence to a murder charge that she was acting to prevent the (greater) crime, using reasonable force under section 3, in a fashion analogous to *Hichens*.

Of course, one relevant difference is that in *Hichens*, the original perceived aggressor, Oliver, presumably did not pick out the landlady, Brown, to be the subject of force by Hichens, whereas in *Emergency*, D's very purpose is that the eventual victim is picked out. To that extent, *Hichens* appears in relation to *Emergency* much as duress of circumstances appears in relation to duress by threats. Yet, as the Court of Appeal noted in the duress of circumstances case *Martin*, the danger dealt with by the defendant is not changed by the changed nature of the threat:[51] if the response is reasonable, a defence should be provided regardless.

III. Some Objections

What, then, would be the objections to the foregoing arguments? There might be several, and it is time now to address them.

The Challenge of *Howe*

Neither the defence of necessity nor that of preventing crime is directly precluded by *Howe*, which is a decision on the law of duress. At the same time, both defences are dependent upon a finding that the defendant's response was proportionate or reasonable, and there is clearly the potential for an argument to be made about the reasonableness of force in situations like *Emergency*. It may be that, because of the reasonableness criterion, if either defence is correctly applied in *Emergency*-type scenarios, it will not result in unmeritorious acquittals.[52] As such, some of Lord

[51] '[W]e can see no distinction in principle between various threats of death: it matters not whether the risk of death is by murder or by suicide or, indeed, by accident': *Colin Martin* (1989) 88 Cr App R 343, 346 (Simon Brown J).

[52] It may also be worth recalling Lord Hoffmann's comment that 'when law enforcement officers, if called upon, would be in a position to do whatever is necessary, the citizen must leave the use of force to them': *R v Jones* [2007] 1 AC 136, 176.

Hailsham's concerns may still be met, and the principles expressed in *Howe* may not be sidestepped so easily.

The moral justification of killing in these situations is admittedly complex.[53] Undoubtedly in *Emergency*, and *Hichens*, the protagonists are morally responsible: their actions are 'non-involuntary',[54] but, probably in *Emergency*, and possibly in *Hichens*, the protagonists are not culpable, as their actions may on some accounts be justified, or at least excused. The reasoning in *Howe* primarily addresses the possibility that a prima facie murder may be excused: but it does not address the prospect that it may be justified (eg in self-defence or defence of others). In any case, the key argument of this paper is merely that, for necessity and, if the logic of *Hichens* is followed, for section 3, these defences generate a real question that ought to be put to a jury, as opposed to its pre-emptive exclusion seen in *Howe*, even apart from any argument that the numbers involved – far more here than in *Howe* – should allow one to distinguish or set aside *Howe* in the application of the defence of duress itself.

Of course, one might object that the *substantive* arguments underlaying *Howe* apply here regardless. Stark finds three core grounds in *Howe* for the Court's conclusion: what he calls the 'Heroism Argument', the 'Terrorism Argument' and the 'Competence Argument'.[55] The first is perhaps the most famous. As Lord Hailsham put it:

> In general, I must say that I do not at all accept in relation to the defence of [duress in] murder it is either good morals, good policy or good law to suggest … that the ordinary man of reasonable fortitude is not to be supposed to be capable of heroism if he is asked to take an innocent life rather than sacrifice his own.[56]

This argument is exposed to various counter-arguments offered by Stark. In particular, and as I noted earlier, it does not deal with the scenario in *Emergency*, where the threat is not to the protagonist herself but to others for whom the protagonist is responsible. And indeed, in 1977, well before *Howe*, the Law Commission had written:

> [W]here the duress is so compelling that the defendant could not reasonably have been expected to resist it, perhaps being a threat not to the defendant himself but to an innocent hostage dear to him, it would in our view be unjust that the defendant should suffer the stigma of a conviction even for manslaughter. We do not think that any social purpose is served by requiring the law to prescribe such standards of determination and heroism.[57]

[53] See also JJC Smart and B Williams, *Utilitarianism: For and Against* (Cambridge, Cambridge University Press, 1973) 98–99.

[54] Simester (n 20) 189.

[55] Stark (n 5) 309.

[56] *R v Howe* [1987] 1 AC 417, 432.

[57] Law Com No 83, *Criminal Law: Report on Defences of General Application* (London, HMSO, 1977) 15, para 2.43. In the later case of *Hasan* (also known as *Z*) [2005] UKHL 22, [21], Lord Bingham, referring to the Law Commission report quoted in the text, noted that 'The Law Commission has in

The Terrorism Argument, that permitting duress to be a defence to murder would empower terrorists to commit terrible crimes and then have a defence, is similarly open to rebuttal: the voluntary association limitation suffices to meet it.[58] The Competence Argument, of deference by the courts to Parliament in the development of the criminal law, is perhaps the most compelling of these rationales. At its strongest, as Stark writes:

> Given the limits placed on the ability of even the highest appellate courts to canvas and appraise different views on such issues, it is epistemically more appropriate for Parliament to do so. However, there is also a point of principle here: where an issue is particularly controversial, it is fitting for elected representatives, rather than unelected judges, to resolve it.[59]

Parliament, however, has not spoken about the common law. Granted, it has not intervened since *Howe*. Yet neither has it intervened since the ruling in *Re A* that deliberate killings are capable of being justified by necessity. Moreover, the Competence Argument does not apply to a defence based on legislation such as section 3, as this is already the product of Parliament. Application of the latter defence requires only interpretation and application of the legislation passed in 1967.

But Would This Not Abolish (Almost) All of Duress?

What is left of duress once we follow the logic of *Hichens* to allow section 3 to be used this way? Given that, for duress, the threat from A needs to be one of death or serious injury, would not a prevention of crime section 3 defence almost always apply? Perhaps. It is not the burden of this chapter to resolve all of the incoherence of the criminal law of England and Wales, and it is true that under this interpretation, section 3 would often seem to cover ground previously thought of as covered by duress. Of course, the limits of section 3 are familiar: it applies only when 'force' is used, or something akin or preparatory to it, perhaps.[60] And it applies only in prevention of crimes, so, for example, if the putative duressor is under the age of 10, the section will not be applicable. Admittedly these are not, in this context, everyday scenarios. Be that as it may, there may be additional distinctions to be made between the use of 'such force as is reasonable' in section 3, and the question in the second part of the test from *Graham*, whether a 'sober person of reasonable firmness' would not respond by taking part in the crime: the latter may not always

the past … recommended that the defence should be available as a defence to all offences, including murder, and the logic of this argument is irresistible.' Nonetheless, his Lordship (at [22]) was in general disinclined to make the defence more widely applicable.

[58] Stark (n 5) 323.

[59] ibid 325.

[60] See eg *Cousins* [1982] QB 526.

be a reasonable use of force, and to the extent that the defence of duress functions merely as an excuse there is ground between it and the justification in section 3.

Is This What Section 3 Envisages?

This brings us to a central worry about invoking the prevention of crime defence. Is it a permissible interpretation of section 3 that it applies to force, possibly lethal force, against third parties in situations such as *Emergency*? *Hichens* might imply that it is. It is true, of course, that section 3 does not make this expressly clear, but recall that the *Report* had designedly left such matters open, and concluded:

> No doubt if a question arose on clause 3, the court, in considering what was reasonable force, would take into account all the circumstances … but there is no need to specify in the clause the criteria for deciding the question.[61]

While that was presumably directed to the question of whether the amount or kind of force was reasonable, there is no reason why the same should not be true for the question of variations of the object against which the force is aimed. Nevertheless, in making such a claim, the rules governing interpretation of statutes are engaged, and we need to turn to consider whether what seems on its face a straightforward application of section 3 to *Emergency* is permissible.

We may securely take as a guide to interpretation the 2017 Hamlyn Lectures by the then Professor Burrows; from these it appears that recent statutory interpretation has generally adopted a contextual and purposive approach, and, to that extent, some older maxims of interpretation may be of less help than they were.[62] As we have discussed, the purpose of the Bill seems clear from the *Report* and second reading speech: it was to remove the distinction between felonies and misdemeanours in the criminal law.

It should in addition be noted, however, that even if some of the technical rules of interpretation are now less in favour, the principle that penal statutes should be narrowly construed, though it is capable of being outweighed, has relatively recently been reapproved,[63] and there may thus still be scope for what we might consider its corollary:

> Where an enactment provides for relief from a detriment in certain circumstances, the presumption against doubtful penalisation may point towards construing the exception liberally (ie in favour of the subject). If it is doubtful whether an exception to a penalty applies, it is doubtful whether the penalty itself applies.[64]

[61] Criminal Law Revision Committee, *Seventh Report* (n 22) 7, para 23.

[62] A Burrows, *Thinking about Statutes: Interpretation, Interaction, Improvement* (Cambridge, Cambridge University Press, 2018) 6–7.

[63] *R v Dowds* [2012] EWCA Crim 281, [36]–[38]; *R v Copeland* [2020] UKSC 8, [28].

[64] D Bailey, D Feldman, M Anderson, J George and L Norbury, *Bennion, Bailey, and Norbury on Statutory Interpretation*, 8th edn (London, LexisNexis, 2020) para 26.4.

A liberal interpretation would lead to the conclusion that section 3 applies here.

All statutes, however, need to be interpreted in light of their context, generally including that of the common law. As Burrows wrote:

> No doubt those drafting statutes are all too well aware of the necessity of 'reading into' a statute the background common law. It would make the task of drafting almost impossible if no assumptions as to that background could be made.[65]

Here, however, the situation is slightly more complicated, because of the presence of section 3(2):

> Subsection (1) above shall replace the rules of the common law on the question when force used for a purpose mentioned in the subsection is justified by that purpose.

This is not the easiest subsection: its background, as a late amendment to deal with concerns in the House of Lords, was noted earlier. As originally moved by Lord Colville, it may have been intended only to prevent reliance on obscure distinctions between felonies and misdemeanours in arrest. However, as later put forth by the Lord Chancellor, its aim was simply to make it clear that indeed section 3 'supersedes the Common Law relating to the use of force in preventing crime'.

As passed, therefore, Section 3 presents an example of the difficulty of finding the intention of Parliament in enacting a statute which, on the one hand, was originally drafted on one basis – that of the *Report* – but, on the other hand, was amended to remove the common law context presupposed by that *Report*. Nevertheless, as Lord Steyn in *Hinks* noted, quoting Lord Reid:

> We often say that we are looking for the intention of Parliament, but that is not quite accurate. We are seeking the meaning of the words which Parliament used. We are seeking not what Parliament meant but the true meaning of what they said.[66]

On its face then, section 3(2) seems to render much of the prior history redundant when interpreting section 3(1); it certainly seems to push to one side any claim that common law doctrines such as duress and necessity might be thought to have been intended by Parliament to be the sole authority in these factual situations, or perhaps even to be considerations in interpreting section 3(1). Even if section 3(2) were thought to ensure only that section 3(1) replaces the *pre-existing* rules of the common law, it was already thought to be the common law in 1967 that duress was no defence to murder,[67] and so later reiteration of the same point by *Howe*, not being a new development, should have no effect on the

[65] Burrows (n 62) 58.

[66] *Black-Clawson International Ltd v Papierwerke Waldhoff-Anschaffenburg AG* [1975] AC 591, 613 (Lord Reid); quoted in *R v Hinks* [2001] 2 AC 241, 248 (Lord Steyn).

[67] JWC Turner, *Kenny's Outlines of Criminal Law*, 17th edn (Cambridge, Cambridge University Press, 1958) 67, paras 47, and 65, para 46.

operation of section 3(1). Section 3(2) has not, however, attracted much attention, perhaps because common law self-defence has largely been interpreted as coexisting alongside section 3; indeed the later section 76(2)(a) of the Criminal Justice and Immigration Act 2008, which recognises the existence of the common law defence, is some evidence of the intention of Parliament to preserve the common law defence.

What of other statutes? The most obviously relevant is indeed that section 76 of the 2008 Act, designed to provide guidance on the reasonableness of the use of force. This complicated section was originally added to the voluminous 2008 legislation only very late, at the time of the Third Reading.[68] It expressly applies to applications of section 3(1) of the Criminal Law Act 1967,[69] and deals with questions of 'whether the degree of force used by D against a person ("V") was reasonable in the circumstances'.[70] Admittedly, our question is not about the 'degree' of force, as such, so much as about its direction against an innocent third party V at the behest of another: but for what it is worth section 76 does not preclude this possibility.

Section 76 was itself amended by section 43 of the Crime and Courts Act 2013, and by section 148 of the Legal Aid, Sentencing and Punishment of Offenders Act 2012, to distinguish 'householder' cases – essentially, where D is at home when using the relevant force – and to add the common law defence of property as another defence (alongside self-defence and the section 3(1) defence) to which section 76 applies. Although the question remains whether or not D's conduct was reasonable, the householder provisions in the new sections 76(5A) and 76(6) require conduct in householder cases to be regarded as unreasonable if 'grossly disproporptionate', whereas, in non-householder cases, D's conduct is to be regarded as unreasonable if merely 'disproportionate'. The higher threshold of *gross* disproportionality envisaged for householders is expressed in section 76(8A)(a) to apply, however, only to common law self-defence, and thus does not apply in our section 3 Criminal Law Act 1967 examples: the defendant in *Emergency* will be restricted to conduct that is reasonable and proportionate.[71] We may conclude that, given the terms of section 3, the wider context of the common law and statute do not preclude the application of section 3 in *Emergency*.

A subsidiary interpretive question arises of whether extrinsic materials such as the *Report* and Hansard could be consulted by a court in interpreting section 3. Such reports have been considered in the highest courts when interpreting statutes,[72] although sometimes without much enthusiasm: while there was

[68] Hansard (HC Debates) 9 January 2008, col 308; debate on the section is in Hansard (HC Debates) 9 January 2008, col 346.

[69] Criminal Justice and Immigration Act 2008, s 76(2)(b).

[70] ibid s 76(1)(b).

[71] See ibid s 76(8A)(a).

[72] Lord Mustill briefly considered the genesis of the Criminal Law Act 1967 in the *Report* when giving the judgment of the Privy Council in *Moses v The State* [1997] AC 53, 60; Lord Steyn in *R v Hasan*

disagreement in the House of Lords in *DPP v Gomez* on the use of the analogous *Eighth Report*,[73] in *R v Hinks* Lord Steyn held merely that it might 'arguably be relevant as part of the background against which Parliament enacted the Bill' which became the Theft Act 1968.[74] A review of the case law finds almost no discussion of section 3 in the *Seventh Report*, which was considered but briefly in the judgment in *R v Jones*.[75] In any case, as noted above, the *Report*, designed for a section 3 without a section 3(2), is of less utility than might otherwise be hoped. As for Hansard, in *Pepper v Hart*, Lord Browne-Wilkinson famously set out three conditions which allow reference to debates in Parliament where:

> (a) legislation is ambiguous or obscure, or leads to an absurdity; (b) the material relied upon consists of one or more statements by a Minister or other promoter of the Bill together if necessary with such other Parliamentary material as is necessary to understand such statements and their effect; (c) the statements relied upon are clear.[76]

If, on its face, section 3 provides a defence in *Emergency*, does this lead to 'an absurdity'? That might depend on one's view of threshold deontology, the inviolability of rights, and their role as constraints on utilitarian calculations; but it is not necessarily absurd to have a possible defence to put to a jury, surprising as that might be to the defendants and judges in *Howe*.

There is of course a distinction between someone's consulting Hansard as an academic, and whether such materials are admissible in court; any relevant materials may be consulted for the former purpose. In any case, it would appear that there are means for the admission of Hansard other than for *Pepper v Hart* purposes. As *Bennion* puts it:

> There is a growing tendency for courts to rely on legislative debates on a Bill not as an indication of legislative intent in resolving an ambiguity as to the meaning of a particular word or phrase but rather to supply context or identify the nature or extent of the issue at which legislation is aimed.[77]

Admitting the debates for that more general purpose, they do confirm for us that the Lord Chancellor meant what he said that section 3 articulates what Parliament intended, and that the section is therefore to be interpreted as enacted.

(also known as *Z*) [2005] UKHL 22, [53] and [56] considered the *Eleventh Report* of the Criminal Law Revision Committee (but found nothing of relevance).

[73] *DPP v Gomez* [1993] AC 442; compare Lord Keith at 464 with Lord Lowry at 470, 480, 482, 491 and 494.

[74] *R v Hinks* [2001] 2 AC 241, 248.

[75] *R v Jones* [2007] 1 AC 136, 161, Lord Bingham; at 169, Lord Hoffman; the *Report* was also discussed in argument by counsel.

[76] *Pepper v Hart* [1993] AC 593, 640. Although there is the suggestion that these apply mainly when the executive is 'estopped' from diverging from a ministerial statement (N Duxbury, *Elements of Legislation* (Cambridge, Cambridge University Press, 2013) 216), the better view may be that this is not a requirement: Bailey et al (n 64) para 26.4.

[77] ibid para 24.12.

The Human Rights Act?

What else can limit how we interpret the scope of either necessity or the prevention of crime? One possible constraint is in the Human Rights Act 1998, which provides that both legislation and the common law, including legislation passed before the 1998 Act, should as far as possible be interpreted in a way compatible with rights in the European Convention on Human Rights.[78] It is relevant here to note Article 2 of the ECHR, which sets out:

> 1. Everyone's right to life shall be protected by law …
> 2. Deprivation of life shall not be regarded as inflicted in contravention of this Article when it results from the use of force which is no more than absolutely necessary:
>
>   in defence of any person from unlawful violence …

This Article was considered in the High Court in the context of self-defence in *Collins*, a householder case.[79] As Sir Brian Leveson P observed there, in discussion of the householder defence requirements in section 76(5A) and their compatibility with the ECHR, any action taken in self-defence needs to be *reasonable*, rather than *proportionate*, to meet the requirements of the defence:

> For the present purpose, what results from the above is one simple question: does the criminal law of England and Wales effectively deter offences against the person in householder cases?
>
> … [A] householder will only be able to avail himself of the defence if the degree of force he used was reasonable in the circumstances as he believed them to be. In that context, it is not irrelevant that Article 2 … rights of the householder are also engaged.
>
> It is important to note that in this regard, the ECtHR has consistently held that the reasonableness limb of self-defence (in the circumstances as the defendant believed them to be) as applied in state actor cases is compatible with the Article 2(2) requirement of 'absolute necessity'. … On any view, therefore, the test of reasonableness in the circumstances in private party householder cases, even after the minor qualification of s. 76(5A), would not cause a breach of the Article 2(1) positive obligation, which is shorn of strict proportionality.
>
> All of this adds up to there being reasonable safeguards against the commission of offences against the person in householder cases. In the circumstances, I conclude that the criminal law of England and Wales on self-defence in householder cases, taken as a whole, fulfils the framework obligation under Article 2(1).[80]

In substance, the same is true for the defendant in *Emergency*. She will have a defence only when her use of force, in prevention of crime, is reasonable, and indeed, as discussed above, she will not be able to rely on disproportionate force, unlike the householder in *Collins*.

[78] Human Rights Act 1998, s 3(1); and see 3(2)(a) ('legislation … whenever enacted').
[79] *R (on the application of Denby Collins) v The Secretary of State for Justice* [2016] EWHC 33 (Admin).
[80] ibid [62]–[64].

Does it matter that formally the defendant in *Emergency* is acting to prevent a criminal wrong, rather than in defence of someone? (One might contest the claim that P is not acting in defence of life, but let us concede that point *arguendo*.) The European Court of Human Rights has said that prevention of crime is not a valid reason under Article 2(2) for the deprivation of life.[81] But the direct obligation under Article 2 is on the state and state agents: the 'framework' obligation is on the United Kingdom, as party to the Convention, to set up, among other things, a a criminal law that adequately protects the right to life. The judgment in *Collins* implies that, if the system is safe – that is, the use of force is restricted to that which is reasonable – then there is no Article 2(1) violation in the first place and, hence, no need for application of the exceptions in Article 2(2).

Running alongside these specific rights protections from the Convention, the common law provides its own. As Burrows explains it:

> [T]he 'principle of legality' engenders a strong presumption so that fundamental common law rights can be removed only by express words or by necessary implication.[82]

Bennion adds, as a gloss:

> The principle against interference with a person's health may also point towards ensuring that they are not prevented from self-help.[83]

There is no doubt that the right to life is a fundamental common law right, in Burrows's terms, and no doubt that, in *Emergency*, V's right to life is endangered. Does the interpretation of section 3 envisaged in this chapter violate the principle of legality? No: where the force used by P is reasonable, it is indeed a 'necessary implication' from section 3 that it may be used to end life in the prevention of crime, so there is no breach.

IV. Conclusion

The result of this analysis is that it may be possible to claim both some form of common law necessity *and* the section 3 defence in situations such as *Emergency*. Both the criteria endorsed by Brooke LJ in *Re A* and the terms of section 3 apply on their face. Moreover, there is nothing in the extrinsic materials for section 3, as it was eventually passed, which implies that the section should not apply: and section 3(2), if taken seriously, removes any pre-existing common law limitations upon the use of section 3(1) and, hence, upon the use of force in *Emergency*-type scenarios. The intuitive difficulty one might have in reaching this conclusion is

[81] D Harris, E Bates and C Buckley, *Harris, O'Boyle, and Warbrick: Law of the European Convention on Human Rights*, 4th edn (Oxford, Oxford University Press, 2018) 228.
[82] Burrows (n 62) 58.
[83] Bailey et al (n 64) para 27.3.

perhaps due to the looming conceptual shadow cast by duress and *Howe*, but it has been the aim of this chapter to illuminate some ways around that particular precedent, without the need to argue that it is incorrect in its description of the confines of duress.

All of which is not to deny that a wrong to V has been done. However, from the perspective of the criminal law, it may be that the person who ought to be held responsible is A, the person who set up *Emergency* and ordered the killing, not P. It seems appropriate that someone such as P, who has, all things considered, taken the best available option, and used reasonable force, should not face criminal sanction. At the least, the claim in this chapter is that *this very question should be open for the jury to decide*. Endorsing the arguments advanced here regarding the scope of necessity, and regarding the interpretation of section 3, would achieve that end.

PART IV

Criminal Jurisprudence

10

What Does a Conceptual Argument Prove? Sullivan's Presumptive Conduct on Criminal Trial

PAUL ROBERTS*

I. Appreciating Bob, Engaging Sullivan

When I was taking my first baby steps as a law lecturer, Bob Sullivan was already a towering presence in British legal scholarship. I well remember meeting him at an SPTL conference in the mid-1990s, and was both astonished and flushed with pride by his praise for a book review I had recently published. Typically, Bob took an interest and was generous in his encouragement. His own publications have always been wide-ranging and originally conceived, addressing topics beyond the standard criminal law canon[1] and posing jurisprudential questions that would never have occurred to most of us.[2] Bob later told me that he often just wrote about what he found fascinating: an excellent piece of advice for any aspiring academic, and a model of curiosity-driven scholarship all the more inspiring and relevant today in institutions increasingly incapable of making proper time for it (though still styling themselves 'universities'). Nostalgia, regret, admiration and gratitude make fine bar-talk but poor *Festschriften*. So let me turn without ceremony from appreciating Bob as mentor and friend, to serious engagement with GR Sullivan, the criminal law theorist.

In a series of overlapping articles and essays, Sullivan develops an avowedly 'conceptual' argument designed to show that criminal trials are (conceptually) bound to satisfy certain prescriptive criteria. Absent particular constitutive features, institutional arrangements purporting to be criminal trials lack authenticity. They are only faking, simulacra, going through the motions, pale imitations of the

* With thanks to Antje du Bois-Pedain for comments, to Andrew Simester for his indefatigable editorial rigour, and to Bob Sullivan for this latest opportunity.

[1] See e.g. GR Sullivan, 'Ministering Death' (1997) 17 OJLS 123.

[2] One memorable illustration is GR Sullivan and CJ Warbrick, 'Territoriality, Theft and *Atakpu*' [1994] Crim LR 650.

real thing. To call these deficient institutional arrangements 'criminal trials' (as they claim for themselves) is a 'category error'. The type of argument advanced by Sullivan is emphatically *conceptual*, not normative or (merely) semantic. Definitional stipulation, notoriously,[3] does not settle any controversy concerning the nature of the world or human affairs: you can call a cat a fish if you want to, but it still won't swim under water. Conceptual arguments succeed for our purposes only if they carry robust theoretical or practical implications – and Sullivan wants both for his account of criminal trials.

As a general methodological predicate, I am wary of conceptual arguments. They often take a dogmatically 'conceptualist' turn, by which I mean that they illegitimately purport to derive normative (political morality) conclusions by logical derivation from (merely) conceptual analysis. Conceptualist argument is my term designating (conceptually) invalid arguments, a species of fallacious reasoning. Normative (political morality) conclusions can generally be derived only through normative (political morality) argument and reasoning. Conceptual analysis, by contrast, is a tool for *analytical* inquiry and argumentation. Analytical results may be interesting and important. They contribute to the development and clarification of concepts. *Conceptualist* reasoning, however, involves a fundamental (not necessarily *obvious*) methodological error, the fallacy of purporting to derive normative conclusions from conceptual analysis. Rather than settling normative disputes, conceptual analysis typically only repackages them. The fallacy lies in thinking or claiming that a perfectly sound analytical tool is capable of performing a normative job for which it is unsuitable, like trying to drive nails with a saw or cut planks with a hammer.

Does Sullivan's account demonstrate, as he contends, that certain forms of criminal adjudication are, simply, categorically, *conceptually* wrong? Or is Sullivan's position redolent of a more general form of fallacious *conceptualist* argumentation? Section II of this essay first summarises Sullivan's core thesis, which extrapolates claims about criminal procedure from a novel conception of the conceptual limits of substantive criminal law specifically indexed to 'conduct'. This recapitulation identifies significant gaps and pressure points in Sullivan's argument, motivating Section III's excursion into the conceptual heartlands and definitional extremities of 'criminal trial'. With the benefit of back-to-basics conceptual refurbishment, Section IV draws out some practical implications of conceptual argumentation, engaging directly with the constraints on legitimately criminalizable conduct asserted by Sullivan and their suggested implications for English law's presumption of innocence. The essay concludes by burnishing the wisdom of an old philosophical truism about seeking answers to difficult questions: the pilgrimage is often more enlightening than any ultimate revelation.

[3] I Hacking, *The Social Construction of* What? (Cambridge MA, Harvard University Press, 1999); S Haack, *Manifesto of A Passionate Moderate* (Chicago, University of Chicago Press, 1998).

II. Sullivan's Conceptual(ist) Argument

Sullivan presents the most fully elucidated version of his conceptual argument in an essay titled and proposing 'Conduct and Proof of Conduct'[4] as 'two fundamental conditions … prerequisite for any criminal conviction'.[5] Without conduct and proof of conduct, Sullivan insists, there can be no legitimate attribution of responsibility for criminal wrongs; and absent responsibility, criminal liability is 'conceptually untenable'.[6] Tempted by the prospect of cheap and easy fixes for difficult social problems, politicians and policymakers too readily invoke criminal law for tasks that would be better discharged by other, less coercive and condemnatory regulatory techniques or through positive incentives, public information campaigns and moral suasion. There is consequently a modern 'crisis of over-criminalisation',[7] extending criminal prescriptions and punishments into areas of life where they have no business to be, at all or with such intensity. Legislative mission-creep in proliferating criminal prohibitions is not the only culprit. Penal excess is also the inevitable implication, as Sullivan has prominently argued,[8] of interpreting general doctrines of criminal liability to restrict or water down *mens rea* requirements, multiply forms of inchoate liability, and expand liability for accomplices, accessories and conspirators.

Sullivan depicts what is 'essential if the criminal law is to constitute a distinctive domain distinguishable from other forms of coercion that a state may deploy against its citizens'.[9] He is at pains to stress that his two conditions are merely threshold criteria for the legitimacy of criminal conviction: they do not furnish a comprehensive account of normative adequacy or justification. Thus, 'compliance with these two conditions is compatible with a harsh and human rights insensitive criminal law'[10] that would be susceptible to normative criticism on those or other grounds. What the conceptual argument lacks in normative extension, however, is more than compensated by its methodological primacy and purchase. Criminal convictions violating either of the two conditions perpetrate a fundamental 'category error'.[11] They involve an abuse of conceptual language:

[4] GR Sullivan, 'Conduct and Proof of Conduct – Two Fundamental Conditions for the Imposition of Criminal Liability' in KH Kaikobad and M Bohlander (eds), *International Law and Power – Perspectives on Legal Order and Justice: Essays in Honour of Colin Warbrick* (Leiden, Martinus Nijhoff, 2009) 235.

[5] ibid.

[6] ibid.

[7] J Chalmers and F Leverick, 'Tracking the Creation of Criminal Offences' [2013] Crim LR 543, 560. Also see eg D Husak, *Overcriminalization: The Limits of the Criminal Law* (Oxford, Oxford University Press, 2008); A Ashworth, 'Is the Criminal Law A Lost Cause?' (2000) 116 LQR 225.

[8] GR Sullivan, 'Wrongs and Responsibility for Wrongs in Crime and Tort', in M Dyson (ed), *Unravelling Tort and Crime* (Cambridge, Cambridge University Press, 2014); GR Sullivan and I Dennis (eds), *Seeking Security: Pre-Empting the Commission of Criminal Harms* (Oxford, Hart Publishing, 2012).

[9] 'Conduct and Proof of Conduct' (n 4) 235.

[10] ibid.

[11] ibid, 249.

'A criminal trial properly so called requires some issue relating to responsibility to be resolved, otherwise the very language and process of the trial rings false'.[12] Criminal convictions obtained in disregard of the two complementary responsibility conditions are not merely problematic or unjustified in terms of institutional political morality. We are invited to regard them as penal abominations, categorically illegitimate, conceptually wrong. These are powerful claims with intuitive plausibility. Sullivan is building on the compelling thought, elucidated by many contemporary jurists and philosophers,[13] that penal censure is a distinctive form of regulation and that this modality implies certain normative and practical constraints on its appropriate uses. Sledgehammers should not be employed to crack nuts – or heads.[14] From this point of convergence, penal theorists divide on the contentious issues of what, exactly, those constraints are, and what – if any – consequences should flow from failing to observe them in any institutional context or on any particular occasion.

Sullivan's first constraint addresses substantive criteria of criminal liability. His conduct condition embraces both acts and omissions, and with a little bit of further stretching can be made to accommodate many status offences. Sullivan's second, procedural constraint is concerned with *proving* conduct of the required sort in a (contested) criminal trial. Crucially, Sullivan regards these two constraints as intimately related. Substantively, the imposition of criminal censure and punishment must respect 'the "no liability without responsibility" condition'.[15] The proof condition is the procedural counterpart of the substantive condition. From the foundational premiss that 'imposition of criminal liability in the absence of anything done or omitted by D defies the most basic assumptions of the criminal law',[16] Sullivan infers the secondary condition that legitimate criminal convictions demand proof of whatever conduct is proscribed:

> What is necessary is that a finding based at least on the balance of probabilities be made against D in respect of the conduct requirement. If such a finding is not a prerequisite for a conviction, in substance any conduct requirement will be negated. A legislature cannot coherently enact an offence requiring conduct yet waive any need for proof of that conduct.[17]

[12] ibid, 242.

[13] Prominently including A von Hirsch, *Censure and Sanctions* (Oxford, Oxford University Press, 1993); RA Duff, *Punishment, Communication, and Community* (New York, Oxford University Press, 2001); AP Simester and A von Hirsch, *Crimes, Harms and Wrongs* (Oxford, Hart Publishing, 2011).

[14] '[A]s regulatory tools go, the criminal law is a sledgehammer … and its judgments of the accused have a symbolic significance that civil judgments lack. They condemn not merely the defendant's ϕing, but *the defendant for ϕing*': A Simester, *Fundamentals of Criminal Law* (Oxford, Oxford University Press, 2021) 6.

[15] GR Sullivan, 'Parents and their Truanting Children: An English Lesson in Liability without Responsibility' (2010) 12 Otago LR 285, 298.

[16] 'Conduct and Proof of Conduct' (n 4) 238.

[17] ibid. Note that proof 'at least on the balance of probabilities' (correctly) tracks the minimal epistemic threshold for rational belief, and (appropriately) states only an institutional threshold, not an ideal.

And for the avoidance of any residual doubt about the methodological status and ambitions of the argument, Sullivan reiterates that 'the condition is conceptual. The state cannot logically set down the actus reus of an offence whilst waiving the need for proof that D's conduct had brought about the actus reus'.[18]

In the first part of 'Conduct and Proof of Conduct', Sullivan expounds his conduct condition and diagnoses its dilution in offences of strict liability. This leads into a discussion of the presumption of innocence and its doctrinal status under Article 6(2) of the ECHR. Sullivan is disappointed that English courts have resisted the argument that Article 6(2) should bite on substantive criteria of criminal liability. He suggests that 'engagement with the concept of innocence should raise a query whether the issue of guilt and innocence is in any real sense implicated if liability for a state of affairs can be imposed in the absence of proof of any act or omission falling within the control of the defendant'.[19] The doctrinal implication is that '[g]uilt imposed without responsibility should have been castigated as a breach of Article 6(2)':

> [I]f the process of proof makes no connection with anything done or not done by D within the competence of his agency, he is in a very real sense uninvolved, a spectator to his own fate. We are confronted with the simulacrum of a trial, not the real thing. Such a fact finding process, by whatever name called, should be ruled incompatible with Article 6(1), if used to determine criminal guilt.[20]

The second part of 'Conduct and Proof of Conduct' extends the argument, on the procedural side, to reverse onus clauses imposing probative burdens on the accused. The vital nexus between conduct and proof of conduct is reflected in 'a baseline where the presumption of innocence and the minimum conditions for the imposition of criminal liability meet'.[21] Sullivan argues that post-HRA 1998 jurisprudence[22] on the presumption of innocence has fallen into conceptual

[18] ibid. Further underlined ibid, 245: 'we are making a conceptual argument not an argument based on justice'.

[19] ibid, 243.

[20] ibid, 243-4. This passage notably invokes Article 6(1), the general right to a fair trial. Within the Strasbourg system, '[t]he presumption of innocence is one of the elements of a fair criminal trial required by Article 6(1)': *Euro Wines Ltd* v *HM Revenue and Customs* [2018] EWCA Civ 46, [14]. Combining Article 6(1) and Article 6(2) indicates that Sullivan's central argument is directed to the concept of a (fair) trial. Any residual disagreement between us (explored in Part IV, below) cannot (wholly) be attributable to competing conceptions of the presumption of innocence.

[21] 'Conduct and Proof of Conduct' (n 4) 250.

[22] For critical surveys, see P Roberts, 'Criminal Procedure, the Presumption of Innocence and Judicial Reasoning under the Human Rights Act' in H Fenwick, G Phillipson and R Masterman (eds), *Judicial Reasoning under the UK Human Rights Act* (Cambridge, Cambridge University Press, 2007); D Hamer, 'The Presumption of Innocence and Reverse Burdens: A Balancing Act' (2007) 66 CLJ 143; I Dennis, 'Reverse Onuses and the Presumption of Innocence: In Search of Principle' [2005] Crim LR 901; A Stumer, *The Presumption of Innocence: Evidential and Human Rights Perspectives* (Oxford, Hart Publishing, 2010).

incoherence because courts have failed to appreciate the significance of his two conditions and their fateful combination:

> [T]hese are formal constraints with no normative bite on the content of the prohibitory norms of the criminal law. An eccentric, despotic ruler could create a criminal offence consisting of stepping on the cracks between paving stones. What he could not do, faithful with a system of criminal law, is stipulate that anyone found walking the pavements falls under a reasonable suspicion of stepping on the cracks and will be convicted of the offence unless he can prove that he has not transgressed.[23]

Sullivan concludes that English law has sinned in failing to 'insist on conduct as a predicate for criminal liability', but remains hopeful of some redemption courtesy of the jurisprudential latitude afforded to UK judges by the Human Rights Act:

> If the potential of Article 6 of the European Convention – fair trial and the presumption of innocence – were to be fully realised by the judiciary, all offences would be construed as requiring a conduct element and proof of the conduct element by the prosecution. This would improve the conceptual and to some extent the normative condition of English criminal law.[24]

Surveying the potential impact of the ECHR on English criminal law more generally, Sullivan had previously argued that 'Article 6(2) should be interpreted to protect against the imposition of what may be regarded as the ultimate form of strict liability, a liability that may be imposed without proof of anything, either *actus reus* or *mens rea*'.[25] More particularly, 'mere proof that the defendant may be reasonably suspected of such [proscribed] conduct will not satisfy the presumption of innocence guaranteed by Article 6(2)'.[26]

Article 6(2) of the ECHR, in my view, gains no traction on the substantive criminal law. The Conventional presumption of innocence, I have consistently argued,[27] is procedural rather than substantive. This is a *jurisprudential* rather than a philosophical – much less conceptual – claim.[28] Of course, theorists may give the presumption of innocence a substantive spin, and many do.[29] All that is

[23] 'Conduct and Proof of Conduct' (n 4) 250.

[24] ibid, 253. Does tacking on 'to some extent the normative' anticipate this essay's methodological critique? cf Sullivan's clarifications that '[t]he responsibility condition is best understood as a conceptual/logical requirement but not without normative implications'; and 'when liability requires nothing in the way of positive conduct on the part of D, this formal requirement can only be satisfied by reading in a normative element': 'Parents and their Truanting Children' (n 15) 299, 301.

[25] GR Sullivan, 'Strict Liability for Criminal Offences in England and Wales Following Incorporation into English Law of the European Convention on Human Rights' in AP Simester (ed), *Appraising Strict Liability* (Oxford, Oxford University Press, 2005) 211.

[26] ibid, 213.

[27] P Roberts, 'The Presumption of Innocence Brought Home? *Kebilene* Deconstructed' (2002) 118 LQR 41; P Roberts, 'Drug-Dealing and the Presumption of Innocence: The Human Rights Act (Almost) Bites' (2002) 6 International Journal of Evidence & Proof 17.

[28] P Roberts, 'Presumptuous or Pluralistic Presumptions of Innocence? Methodological Diagnosis towards Conceptual Reinvigoration' (2021) 198 Synthese 8901.

[29] See e.g. P Tomlin, 'Extending the Golden Thread? Criminalisation and the Presumption of Innocence' (2013) 21 Journal of Political Philosophy 44; V Tadros and S Tierney, 'The Presumption of Innocence and the Human Rights Act' (2004) 67 MLR 402.

required, conceptually speaking, is to interpret 'innocence' as *moral* innocence, and then it is possible to say that any morally unjustified criminal law violates the presumption of innocence. Even if it is proved to the criminal standard that the accused committed the proscribed conduct with the requisite *mens rea*, if the offence itself is morally decrepit the accused, though legally guilty, is morally innocent. Hence, conviction of an illegitimate criminal law breaches the presumption of innocence. More nuanced versions of the argument attempt to show that only a subset of encroachments on moral innocence infringes the juridical presumption.[30] Sullivan's argument is distinctive, inasmuch as he rejects roving appeals to moral innocence,[31] and agrees with me that 'Article 6(2) has no bearing on the elements of offences or on the provision or denial of defences'.[32] Yet he also insists that '[i]f something short of proof of a fact such as establishing a "reasonable suspicion" suffices for criminal liability then, effectively, the prosecution is relieved of the burden of proof'[33] and Article 6(2) is thereby engaged.

It is important to appreciate how Sullivan's moderated thesis still endows Article 6(2) with jurisdiction over substantive criminal law doctrines, albeit on a narrower doctrinal ('conceptual') footing. An explicit reverse onus provision is properly classified as procedural and *might* breach Article 6(2),[34] but an offence element that (merely) 'effectively' relieves the prosecution of the burden of proof is a creature of substantive law; and the same objection could theoretically be posed to *any* aspect of 'strict liability' in substantive offence definitions or even in the specification of criminal law defences.[35] So Article 6(2) would still purport to arbitrate the scope of states parties' substantive criminal laws, ostensibly as a guardian of trial fairness, even on Sullivan's relatively moderate thesis. Once already on this substantive slope it may be too late to discover just how slippery it could become under adverse environmental conditions. According to my *jurisprudential* analysis, it is necessary to take relevant institutional facts more seriously, prominently including the following four: (1) criminal courts in England and Wales, the House of Lords[36] and – subsequently – the UK Supreme Court[37] have never materially

[30] A notably more cautious restatement is advanced by V Tadros, 'The Ideal of the Presumption of Innocence' (2014) 8 Criminal Law and Philosophy 449.

[31] Thus, Sullivan rejects the argument advanced by Tadros and Tierney: 'Strict Liability for Criminal Offences in England and Wales' (n 25) 211.

[32] ibid, 217.

[33] ibid.

[34] Establishing that Article 6(2) is engaged is only the first analytical step: *Salabiaku* v *France* (1991) 13 EHRR 379, [28]; *Sheldrake* v *DPP; Attorney General's Reference (No 4 of 2002)* [2005] 1 AC 264, [2004] UKHL 43.

[35] One implication would appear to be that English law's refusal to extend the defence of duress to murder breaches Article 6(2). For extended elucidation and critique of this 'functionalist' manoeuvre, see P Roberts, 'Strict Liability and the Presumption of Innocence: An Exposé of Functionalist Assumptions' in A Simester (ed), *Appraising Strict Liability* (Oxford, Oxford University Press, 2005).

[36] *R* v *G* [2009] 1 AC 92, [2008] UKHL 37.

[37] *R (Hallam) v Secretary of State for Justice* [2020] AC 279, [2019] UKSC 2; *Serious Organised Crime Agency v Gale* [2011] 1 WLR 2760, [2011] UKSC 49.

deviated from the proposition that Article 6(2) ECHR is limited to procedural effects; (2) the European Court of Human Rights consistently endorses this view;[38] (3) there is nothing in the *traveaux préparatoires*,[39] the structure of the Convention, or the 'evolutive' teleology of Article 6(2) jurisprudence to suggest a broader jurisdiction; and (4) the ECtHR has no institutional capacity, competence or desire to shoulder the burden of reviewing the entirety of states parties' substantive criminal laws for compliance with Article 6(2).

For the time being at least, the scope of Article 6(2)'s presumption of innocence appears fairly well-settled in Strasbourg jurisprudence and in English law on reverse onus clauses.[40] Theoretical debates meanwhile rumble on without much tangible resolution.[41] Sullivan's imaginative resort to *conceptual* argument, expounding 'two fundamental conditions for the imposition of criminal liability', tantalises with the dual promise of theoretical progress and practical implications for fair trials jurisprudence. If the argument is, in my terms, conceptual*ist*, it will ultimately fail. But final judgement should be reserved pending more methodical appraisal. Focusing principally on Sullivan's second, procedural, 'proof of conduct' condition, it would be helpful to have a clearer picture of what a 'concept of the criminal trial' actually is, and what it does (and doesn't do), before attempting to assess any institutional extrapolations or practical consequences. To say that some instance of institutional performance fails at a threshold conceptual level implies some criterion of success. What are the necessary and sufficient (constituent) conditions qualifying a trial *as* a trial? The next section accordingly takes up Sullivan's implicit challenge to develop a more fully theorised and articulated conceptual understanding of the criminal trial.

[38] See eg *Kangers* v *Latvia* (2020) 70 EHRR 5, [50]: 'Article 6(2) safeguards the right to be presumed innocent until proved guilty according to law. Viewed as a procedural guarantee in the context of a criminal trial itself, the presumption of innocence imposes requirements in respect of, inter alia, the burden of proof; legal presumptions of fact and law; the privilege against self-incrimination; pre-trial publicity; and premature expressions, by the trial court or by other public officials, of a defendant's guilt'; *G* v *United Kingdom* (2011) 53 EHRR SE25, [26]–[27]: 'It is not the Court's role under art.6(1) or (2) to dictate the content of domestic criminal law, including whether or not a blameworthy state of mind should be one of the elements of the offence or whether there should be any particular defence available to the accused'.

[39] G Marston, 'The United Kingdom's Part in the Preparation of the European Convention on Human Rights, 1950' (1993) 42 ICLQ 796.

[40] P Roberts, *Roberts and Zuckerman's Criminal Evidence* 3rd edn (Oxford, Oxford University Press, 2022) ch 6. Article 6(2) has broader procedural applications generating their own controversies: see L Campbell, 'Criminal Labels, the European Convention on Human Rights and the Presumption of Innocence' (2013) 75 MLR 681.

[41] Generally, see P Roberts, 'Presumptuous or Pluralistic Presumptions of Innocence? A Methodological Diagnosis towards Conceptual Reinvigoration' (2021) 198 *Synthese* 8901; F Picinali, 'The Presumption of Innocence: A Deflationary Account' (2021) 84 MLR 708; J Allen, 'Rethinking the Relationship between Reverse Burdens and the Presumption of Innocence' (2021) 25 E & P 115; PR Ferguson, 'The Presumption of Innocence and its Role in the Criminal Process' (2016) 27 Criminal Law Forum 131; RL Lippke, *Taming the Presumption of Innocence* (Oxford, Oxford University Press, 2016); RA Duff, 'Who Must Presume Whom to be Innocent of What?' (2013) 42 Netherlands Journal of Legal Philosophy 170.

III. What's in a Concept of the Criminal Trial?

Conceptual comprehension, analysis and arguments relate to *concepts*. A concept is, roughly, an idea, notion or mental scaffolding for expanding, organising and sharpening thinking, reasoning or perception. As on building-sites, so in philosophical and jurisprudential theorising, robust scaffolding can support more elaborate and impressive constructions. To be a *useful* idea to think with or through, a concept should be functionally well-calibrated to the particular purpose or purposes it is designed or adapted to serve.[42] There are no 'innocent' concepts, devoid of purpose, just as there are no tools without intent.[43] A flint is just a rock until somebody employs it as a scraper. Idle musings or spontaneous mental activity are not concepts until the thinker fashions inchoate thoughts into tools for rational introspection, reflection, analysis, criticism, discourse and argumentation. Given their functional character, concepts cannot be appraised acontextually. Scraping tools are great for scraping, but lousy writing implements and positively dangerous hair combs. It is therefore an elementary methodological error to rate concepts 'good' or 'bad' *tout court*. The inescapably evaluative character of concepts, indexed to their purpose(s), appears to extend even to the most basic concepts invoked by criminal law theorists (and philosophers generally), including agency and rationality.[44]

The goodness of concepts depends on their intended use. Does this constitutive intentionality imply that concepts cannot be objective or – worse – that concepts must be irremediably subjective and 'relativistic' in a pejorative sense? Not at all. Like all linguistic phenomena, concepts could not function in thought or communication unless they were objective, in the sense of having shared conventional meaning and reference. If you are tempted to think that the intentionality of concepts implies some kind of recursive subjectivity verging on solipsism, you are probably in the grip of the wrong concept of objectivity.[45] Contested concepts frequently require definitional clarification, but largely idiosyncratic definitions butter no parsnips in the philosophical kitchen. Unless we have a core agreed understanding of what a criminal trial is, for example, we will not be having any *discussion* about anything. Conceptual incontinence is a recipe for talking at cross-purposes. You say 'trial', I say 'schmile': let's call the whole thing froth.

What kind of concept of 'criminal trial' will serve the present inquiry (as a particular instance of criminal law theorising more generally)? Refined conceptual

[42] Answers to the 'what?', 'why?' and 'how?' of a concept constitute its 'eternal triangle': see P Roberts, 'Interdisciplinarity in Legal Research' in Mike McConville and Wing Hong Cui (eds), *Research Methods for Law* 2nd edn (Edinburgh, Edinburgh University Press, 2017).

[43] On the 'intentional stance' enabling us, for example, to make sense of the idea of non-human animals or even robots 'using tools', see DC Dennett, *Intuition Pumps and Other Tools for Thinking* (London, Penguin, 2014).

[44] See e.g. R Wedgwood, *The Value of Rationality* (Oxford, Oxford University Press, 2017).

[45] For helpful conceptual clarifications, see G Axtell, *Objectivity* (Cambridge, Polity Press, 2016).

analysis builds on ordinary life experience and linguistic competence and can legitimately make theoretical assumptions, 'bracketing' issues that are either beside the present point or agreed[46] by participants in the discussion. Criminal trials are plainly organised, social institutions of significant complexity, but they are not football matches, or general elections, or university lectures on criminal procedure. Criminal trials are a special kind of complex social institution. On a conventional understanding, crimes are public wrongs which disturb social peace, violate protected interests and offend public morality. Criminality consequently calls for appropriate official responses. With this very generalised thought,[47] richly embroidered by rival penal theories down the centuries, we begin to get a grip on the conceptual issue. Social conflict resolution must be integral to the concept of a criminal trial, inasmuch as trials are the contentious remedial mechanism of legal regulation more generally.[48] This is one reason why trial systems (as opposed to individual trials[49]) prize finality so highly. The aim is to *resolve* conflicts, not merely to defer or displace them. Moreover, pacific dispute resolution claims for itself not merely instrumental efficacy but normative *legitimacy*. Social conflicts must be resolved *in the right way*, not any which way that arguably 'works'. Modern democratic governments assume the normative burden of answering for the legitimacy claims of their penal institutions. The manner in which criminal trials are themselves conducted is part – but only part – of the institutional machinery through which governments discharge this burden of public justification.

It is important not to confuse the concept of a criminal *trial* with the related, more capacious and pliable concept of criminal law. The animating purpose(s) and values of criminal law should be continuous with and, to some extent, reflected in criminal adjudication, minimally to avoid self-defeating institutional paralysis or normative incoherence. However, criminal law and criminal trials have distinctive normative structures, neither reducible to the other. If everybody always and reliably admitted their guilt,[50] the purpose(s) of criminal law (whatever they are

[46] Agreement could be *arguendo*, or from conviction. Either way, the methodological objective is to cut the contentious issue down to size and promote more focussed investigation and debate.

[47] Although my way of putting it has an undeniably deontological flavour, utilitarians, welfare economists, and other consequentialists are accommodated, because theorists can define 'public wrong' according to their own normative preferences, in terms of 'harmful conduct', 'disutility', 'inefficiency', or whatever. Likewise, to the extent that nonliberal or authoritarian polities employ criminal adjudication as a distinct mode of social ordering, rather than as ideological camouflage for naked coercion etc., they do so to maintain social peace and in the name of legitimate government (as they see and claim it).

[48] For institutional and jurisprudential elaborations, see e.g. N MacCormick, *Institutions of Law: An Essay in Legal Theory* (Oxford, Oxford University Press, 2007); C Nesson, 'The Evidence or the Event? On Judicial Proof and the Acceptability of Verdicts' (1985) 98 Harvard LR 1357; LL Fuller, 'The Forms and Limits of Adjudication' (1978) 92 Harvard LR 353 ('adjudication should be viewed as a form of social ordering, as a way in which the relations of men to one another are governed and regulated').

[49] cf JD Jackson, 'Managing Uncertainty and Finality: The Function of the Criminal Trial in Legal Inquiry' in A Duff, L Farmer, S Marshall and V Tadros (eds), *The Trial on Trial: Truth and Due Process* (Oxford, Hart Publishing, 2004).

[50] I am simplifying. There are actually multiple preconditions, including: the absence of official impropriety or error in the conduct of criminal investigations and prosecutions; adequate opportunities for

thought to be) might conceivably be implemented without resorting to trials. Indeed, this is essentially the reality of the greater part of modern municipal criminal law, which achieves its aims (to the extent that it does) through a combination of *ex ante* prescription and *ex post facto* managed guilty pleas. Contested trials, when they occur, are *inherently* disputatious in some threshold sense. In the absence of any issue to be tried, there could not be any 'trial of the issue'. Although trials generally focus on factual disputes concerning who did what to whom on designated occasions, criminal trials also sometimes adjudicate social disputes and uncertainties about norms and their contextual applications. At the retail end of the administration of criminal justice, trials play a supplementary role in determining the scope of criminal wrongs and their relative gravity.

Two further conceptual refinements are largely self-evident: not all mechanisms of social conflict resolution are trials, and not all trials are criminal trials. The second contrast engages the familiar jurisprudential task of demarcating criminal law from other regulatory subsystems, including private law and non-criminal public law. Most legal scholars (including Sullivan) insist or assume that it is possible to differentiate criminal law and criminal trials[51] from other kinds of law and their associated trials (or other adjudicative mechanisms), in one or more ways that are both conceptually robust and normatively coherent. It is telling that expositors traditionally demarcated criminal law by ostensive reference to the laws applied by criminal courts, i.e. they began with the tangible institutions of trials and court structures and worked back to the abstractions of substantive criminal law.[52] But I will say no more here about the historical priority of procedure over substance. The condemnatory character of criminal law is a quintessential characteristic on which contemporary theoretical constructions converge. Further reflection on differentiating (criminal) trials from other forms of social dispute resolution will put us on the right track to identifying a core concept of criminal trial.

The Conceptual Core

In the general conceptual neighbourhood of criminal trials we encounter a variety of conflict-resolution mechanisms that are not conventionally regarded as trials. Pertinent institutional arrangements include public inquiries, disciplinary tribunals, coronial inquests, and truth and reconciliation commissions. Such institutional mechanisms generally adopt an 'inquisitorial' method and style, but it

victim participation; and social trust in authoritative pronouncements of guilt, untainted by coercion or improper influence.

[51] See further, *Roberts and Zuckerman's Criminal Evidence* (n 40) §1.2.

[52] See e.g. G Williams, 'The Definition of Crime' (1955) 8 Current Legal Problems 107; J C Smith and B Hogan, *Criminal Law*, 1st edn (London, Butterworths, 1965) ch 2.

cannot be their inquisitorialism (in the comparative lawyer's sense)[53] that places these mechanisms outside the trial concept. A conception of trials restricted to institutions adopting 'adversarial' procedures would push us in the direction of saying that criminal trials have existed only in the common law Anglosphere and its contemporary geopolitical extensions, which is implausibly exclusive. Even the most ardent anglophiles should accept that criminal trials *exist* within the civilian juristic orbit, albeit (by their lights) in debased currency relative to the common law gold-standard. Public inquiries, disciplinary tribunals, and the like are focused on fact-finding – discovering the truth about events of concern – and they adopt an essentially inquisitorial methodology because that is how rational inquiry proceeds, through the identification, organisation, analysis, testing and evaluation of evidence as a basis for inferential reasoning and conclusions.[54] But if these institutional arrangements are calibrated for fact-finding, does this undercut their presumptive classification as dispute-resolution mechanisms? Not at all. For one thing, criminal trials are also centrally concerned with fact-finding, and that epistemic ambition (obviously) does not prevent them from being criminal trials. We will return to this. More significantly for present purposes, institutional fact-finding is largely *in the service of* social conflict management and pacific dispute resolution, sensitive to legal entitlements and more comprehensive (substantive) schemes of justice.[55]

Public inquiries, tribunal hearings and coronial inquests are frequently followed by related criminal proceedings. But even when there is no criminal law sequel, inquiries, hearings and inquests are all, in part, prophylactic social measures that aim to interdict brewing or anticipated troubles and engineer remediation before they escalate into something (much) worse. Consider, for example, how the family of a deceased relative might react if there were no official inquiry into an, even minimally, suspicious death. Or imagine that the survivors of the Grenfell Tower fire[56] or the Manchester Arena bombing[57] (not to mention Bloody Sunday[58]) had been met with an official shrug of the shoulders and sincere wishes

[53] Models of 'adversarial' and 'inquisitorial' procedure are ideal-types with explanatory and cultural power but should not be taken *too* seriously. See further, Máximo Langer, 'The Long Shadow of the Adversarial and Inquisitorial Categories' in MD Dubber and T Hörnle (eds), *The Oxford Handbook of Criminal Law* (Oxford, Oxford University Press, 2014); P Roberts, 'Comparative Criminal Justice Goes Global' (2008) 28 OJLS 369.

[54] P Tillers and D Schum, 'A Theory of Preliminary Fact Investigation' (1991) 24 UC Davis LR 931; D Schum, 'Marshaling Thoughts and Evidence During Fact Investigation' (1999) 40 South Texas LR 401.

[55] To spell this out, pacific dispute resolution does not legitimately shore up social peace irrespective of the (in)justice of background social arrangements. That would be compatible with stable despotism and exploitation. Rather, the point is that any defensible scheme of justice will require pacific dispute resolution for its maintenance and prospective viability.

[56] Grenfell Tower Inquiry, www.grenfelltowerinquiry.org.uk/.

[57] Manchester Arena Inquiry, https://manchesterarenainquiry.org.uk/.

[58] The Bloody Sunday Inquiry, webarchive.nationalarchives.gov.uk/ukgwa/20101017060831/http://report.bloody-sunday-inquiry.org/index.html.

for better luck in future. We don't need imagination to anticipate how people might react if lethal police force went unquestioned[59] or the criminality of particular officers threatened catastrophic loss of trust in the policing response:[60] we need only switch on the news. Less dramatically but far more routinely, non-criminal tribunals resolve disputes between neighbours, in the workplace, on family break-up, when commercial transactions turn sour, when consumers are dissatisfied, when interactions with professionals or public officials become contentious, and so on. The translation of human suffering, frustration and anger into social disruption is surely predictable (and understandable) unless mechanisms are put in place to communicate official recognition and concern, defuse immediate tensions and temptations to self-help, establish a reliable factual record of events (including refuting pernicious falsehoods), and – ideally – provide recompense or social security to victims (consistent with some defensible conception of justice). Jurisdictionally speaking, criminal adjudication is the ultimate non-negotiable[61] mechanism of social conflict resolution in peacetime,[62] but it is only (conceptually) the last in a phalanx of institutional arrangements deployed by modern democracies for maintaining civility and *ordre public*, safeguarding rights, and dispensing justice.

This discussion hints at another important role for concepts of 'trial' in modern jurisprudential and penal discourse. Critics of traditional or orthodox criminal trial practice frequently propose alternative dispute resolution mechanisms, explicitly *not* styled *trials*. Forms of conciliation, mediation, negotiation, reparation and restorative justice, for example, may be characterized as 'diversion' from trial or formal process.[63] Are all of these diversionary processes and mechanisms self-evidently not trials? There is surely room for debate. It seems pretty obvious that, say, restorative cautioning[64] and family mediation[65] are not trials. At the other end of the institutional spectrum, however, a victim-offender mediation or a sentencing circle[66] might easily be regarded as an adjunct to trial,

[59] DB Taylor, 'George Floyd Protests: A Timeline', *New York Times*, 5 November 2021 (noting that '[s]ince the death of Mr. Floyd, protests have erupted in at least 140 cities across the United States, and the National Guard has been activated in at least 21 states').

[60] E Graham-Harrison, 'Police Clash with Mourners at Sarah Everard Vigil in London', *The Observer*, 14 March 2021; H Siddique, 'Sarah Everard Vigil Report further Damages Trust in Met Chief, Say Activists' *The Guardian*, 1 July 2021.

[61] Disposals in particular cases may be 'negotiated', by plea bargain or otherwise: see e.g. N Cowdery, 'Negotiating Justice with Integrity in New South Wales' in J Hunter et al (eds), *The Integrity of Criminal Process* (Oxford, Hart Publishing, 2016). But this is a forced choice between limited alternatives, none of which might be especially palatable to defendants. Opting out entirely is never an option.

[62] Thus, prison represents the final terminus for 'clients' of social intervention, who cannot be refused entry or involuntarily referred on to other agencies not prepared to accept them.

[63] G Dingwall and C Harding, *Diversion in the Criminal Process* (London, Sweet & Maxwell, 1998).

[64] R Young and B Goold, 'Restorative Cautioning in Aylesbury – From Degrading to Reintegrative Shaming Ceremonies?' [1999] Crim LR 126.

[65] J Hudson, A Morris, G Maxwell and B Galaway, *Family Group Conferences: Perspectives on Policy and Practice* (Sydney, Federation Press, 1996).

[66] TS Goldbach, 'Instrumentalizing the Expressive: Transplanting Sentencing Circles into the Canadian Criminal Trial' (2015) 25 Trans L & Contemp Prob 61.

or possibly even as a novel additional component of trials on the conventional model. A trial does not automatically cease to be a trial in consequence of any non-trivial[67] procedural innovation. The related concept of criminal adjudication may be useful here. Adjudication encompasses non-trial case disposals (i.e. dispute resolution), including guilty pleas, as well as trial verdicts. Any criminal process resulting in a formal determination can plausibly be termed an adjudication, including non-judicial final outcomes such as formal cautions administered by police officers.[68] It makes more sense to me to describe criminal proceedings, from (say) charge to final disposal, as an adjudicative process rather than a 'criminal trial process'. Common lawyers tend to regard 'the trial' as a discrete event, and hence can intelligibly refer to 'pre-trial process', 'pre-trial disclosure', 'pre-trial hearings' etc, as antecedent procedural phases or events. Civilians generally conceptualise 'trials' less dichotomously in formal procedural terms,[69] though perhaps share with common lawyers a narrower understanding of 'the trial' as the public courtroom stage of criminal adjudication. On one influential interpretation of the civilian principle of 'immediacy' (or 'orality'),[70] criminal convictions must be based only on evidence presented in a procedurally differentiated public trial. Still, I would not go so far as to say that somebody describing the entirety of criminal proceedings as 'criminal trial process' has made a conceptual error or lapsed into incoherence. To the extent that such usage is non-standard, it would be wise to press this interlocutor on what, exactly, they understand by 'criminal trial process' and why they are deploying that term in preference to any alternative. Is it really *trials* they are interested in, after all? Would a different concept (adjudication, process, proceedings …) not encapsulate their intent with greater perspicacity and precision? It is always advisable to check and coordinate conceptual definitions in any event. Sooner or later the point will be reached where a concept in play, in fair and transparent discussion, may fairly accommodate thicker (more inclusive) or thinner (more parsimonious) usage. Clarity of purpose, effective communication of one's intentions, and mutual understanding are then required to keep the conversation alive and productive, rather than

[67] Some procedural refinements are obviously *de minimis*. Trials would not cease to be trials if barristers and judges abandoned horsehair wigs. More interesting conceptual questions are posed by major or significant procedural reform. A tailless Manx cat is still a cat. What else would it need to lose or gain over evolutionary time to qualify as a new species?.

[68] And, in Scotland, 'fiscal fines': P Duff, 'The Prosecutor Fine and Social Control: The Introduction of the Fiscal Fine to Scotland' (1993) 33 BJ Crim 481.

[69] The European Court of Human Rights encountered no theoretical or conceptual difficulty in extending 'fair trial' rights to the entirety of criminal process: see e.g. *Teixeira de Castro* v *Portugal* (1998) 28 EHRR 101; *Salduz* v *Turkey* (2009) 49 EHRR 19 (GC). The text of Article 6 enumerates rights 'to be informed promptly, in a language which [the accused] understands and in detail, of the nature and cause of the accusation' and to 'adequate time and facilities for the preparation of his defence'.

[70] JD Jackson and T Weigend, 'Witness Evidence in Pre-Trial and Trial Procedure' in K Ambos et al (eds), *Core Concepts in Criminal Law and Criminal Justice – Volume 2* (Cambridge, Cambridge University Press, 2022) 260.

appealing to the limits of conventional terminology in an effort to rule certain applications conceptually off-side and definitively out of bounds.[71]

We have proceeded on the basis that criminal trials comprise a subset of modern society's institutional machinery for pacific dispute resolution. Let us add, as a second conceptual ingredient in the mix, that criminal trials must be epistemically[72] *serious*, that is, they must affirm and enact a threshold commitment to rationalism, evidence-based proof and the logic of inferential reasoning. Epistemological seriousness is not strictly mandated by the concept of a (criminal) trial. As we know from the common law's (pre)history, it is possible to have trial by battle, ordeal or ducking stool.[73] These procedures were designed as *tests* of some kind, and thus share a recognisable etymological root with modern-day criminal trials,[74] but their modus operandi is so far moved from our current understanding of criminal adjudication that it would be a misuse of language, and not merely a controversial extension, to describe them as 'trials' without further (historical) contextual explanation. Imagine that prosecuting and defence counsel turned up to court to be presented with duelling pistols or fencing foils. Or if the presiding judge were to unveil a roulette wheel, or deal out cards for a round of poker. How about a penalty shootout? Although pretty much any game or contest of skill or chance could, in a sense, settle litigated issues by producing a 'result', sports and games are, precisely, not criminal trials; and this is so, irrespective of venue or participants' attire. Although social conventions change over time and are not necessarily determinative of linguistic reference, a post-Enlightenment conception of the criminal trial must be epistemically serious or it is not a serious invocation or application of the concept.

This much is trite. Procedural scholars routinely invoke accurate fact-finding (or 'truth-seeking') as a preeminent concern and objective of criminal adjudication.[75] Even though the epistemic credentials of 'the rationalist tradition

[71] The 'definitional stop' famously denounced by HLA Hart, *Punishment and Responsibility* (Oxford, Clarendon Press, 1968) 5–6.

[72] A synonymous shortening of 'epistemologically' now widely employed in Anglophone Evidence scholarship.

[73] JB Thayer, *A Preliminary Treatise on Evidence at the Common Law* (Boston MA, Little, Brown & Co, 1898), ch 1; M Gaskill, 'Witchcraft and Evidence in Early Modern England' (2008) 198 Past and Present 33; M Damaška, 'Rational and Irrational Proof Revisited' (1997) 5 Cardozo Journal of International and Comparative Law 25.

[74] *OED* definitions of trial include: 'The action of testing or putting to the proof the fitness, truth, strength, or other quality of anything …'; 'A testing of qualifications, attainments, or progress; examination'; 'That which puts one to the test, esp. a painful test of one's endurance, patience, or faith; hence, affliction, trouble, misfortune'; 'A contest in which horses, dogs etc., are put through various tests and assessed on their performance'.

[75] See e.g. T Weigend, 'Should We Search for the Truth, And Who Should Do It?' (2011) 36 North Carolina Journal of International Law and Commercial Regulation 389; HL Ho, *A Philosophy of Evidence Law – Justice in the Search for Truth* (Oxford, Oxford University Press, 2008); MR Damaška, *The Faces of Justice and State Authority* (New Haven CT, Yale University Press, 1986). The point may appear self-evident to non-lawyers: cf L Laudan, *Truth, Error, and Criminal Law: An Essay in Legal Epistemology* (Cambridge, Cambridge University Press, 2006).

of evidence scholarship'[76] are sometimes probed and questioned,[77] nobody to my knowledge – certainly not Sullivan – is arguing for a reversion to pre-Enlightenment irrationalism. If the issue were genuinely open to debate, it would be necessary to deploy *normative* arguments to establish the moral superiority of epistemologically serious forms of trial over their non-serious rivals. Such arguments would show that law's rights, duties and instrumental effectiveness are essentially meaningless in the absence of a strong institutional commitment to factual rectitude.[78] Given broadly-based and enduring consensus on the indispensability of epistemic seriousness, however, it is legitimate to treat epistemic seriousness as a constitutive element and necessary condition of our concept of criminal trial. Somebody who argues, deliberately or otherwise, that criminal trials can or should dispense with epistemic seriousness either doesn't know what a criminal trial is or is actually – possibly unbeknownst to themselves – talking about something else. Conceptual parameters operate to rule out of court (so to speak) particular arguments, deployed on particular occasions, for particular reasons. This is not, ultimately, a question of linguistic meaning or conceptual *possibility* (short of Humpty Dumpty's solipsism). Arguments that are legitimately conceptual in one context might be, or need to be, normative in different circumstances. Somebody who rejects epistemic seriousness in criminal trials is not (necessarily) spouting gibberish, but even when such arguments are intelligible they remain, for all practical purposes, (conceptually) beyond the pale. An analogue in the field of ethics would be an argument that challenged the foundational normative ideal that all human beings are equal in dignity and should be treated with ethical concern and respect. That premiss is logically deniable, and has been denied repeatedly throughout human history,[79] but the argument (as opposed to the people making it) is not jurisprudentially serious. Human equality is a conceptual premiss of post-1945 global political morality.

Criminal trials, we can now say, are epistemically serious mechanisms for the pacific resolution of disputes concerning (alleged) violations of the (jurisdictionally competent) criminal law. One significant implication is that criminal trials involve inquiries into past events: their temporal orientation is fundamentally historical rather than future-predictive. This characteristic differentiates judicial trials from tests of current ability (e.g. trials of strength; endurance trials;

[76] W Twining, 'The Rationalist Tradition of Evidence Scholarship', reprinted in Twining, *Rethinking Evidence* 2nd edn (Cambridge, Cambridge University Press, 2006) ch 3; W Twining, *Theories of Evidence: Bentham & Wigmore* (London, Weidenfeld and Nicolson, 1985) ch 1.

[77] D Nicolson, 'Taking Epistemology Seriously: "Truth, Reason and Justice" Revisited' (2013) 17 International Journal of Evidence & Proof 1; KW Graham Jr, '"There'll Always be an England": The Instrumental Ideology of Evidence' (1987) 85 Michigan LR 1204.

[78] P Roberts, 'The Priority of Procedure and the Neglect of Evidence and Proof: Facing Facts in International Criminal Law' (2015) 13 Journal of International Criminal Justice 479; RJ Allen, 'Laudan, Stein, and the Limits of Theorizing about Juridical Proof' (2010) 29 Law & Philosophy 195.

[79] J Glover, *Humanity: A Moral History of the Twentieth Century* (London, Pimlico, 2001); E Hobsbawm, *The Age of Extremes* (London, Abacus, 1995).

motorcross trials) or of prospective suitability (e.g. trials for sports teams; 'trial runs'; trial periods). Although criminal law assuredly has future-orientated objectives, notably guiding lawful behaviour and deterring criminality, a criminal *trial* is quintessentially backward-looking. To be tried today for what you will[80] do tomorrow or in five years' time is not merely illegitimate, it is a conceptual impossibility – according to our[81] prevailing conceptual understanding. Stated more fully, then, the second constitutive feature of our concept of criminal trial is that it must be an epistemically serious inquiry into (allegations of) past events of a particular kind, namely (alleged) criminal wrongdoing.

A third, independent, conceptual ingredient I now propose is that criminal trials must involve *jeopardy*. The notion of jeopardy most familiar to discussions of criminal adjudication is (thanks to Blackstone[82]) encapsulated in the common law prohibition on *double jeopardy*. The double jeopardy prohibition throws up many conceptual puzzles (and policy controversies) of its own,[83] but for present purposes the essential idea is that criminal trials are, ideally, one-shot affairs with no repeat performances. The state cannot keep retrying the accused for the same offence until the 'right result' – presumptively a conviction[84] – is achieved. What I want to highlight is that a related, but more comprehensive and fundamental, sense of jeopardy attaches to the *first* trial, as well. The accused is always in jeopardy of criminal conviction and punishment. There is also jeopardy for complainants and prosecutors in the prospect of a guilty accused securing an unmerited, or possibly even an unwarranted, acquittal. Fact-finders, too, are exposed to the jeopardy of fateful public decision-making in which they are conscripted participants (willingly or otherwise).[85] Trials, in short, are inherently *risky* events which can misfire in various ways. The specifically *epistemic* dimension of criminal trial jeopardy flows from the inherent uncertainty of contested facts and the pervasive possibility of adjudicative error which trial procedure is designed to mitigate and manage.

[80] Or *might* do? I am unapologetically skating over interminable problems of Determinism: see DC Dennett and GD Caruso, *Just Deserts: Debating Free Will* (London, Wiley, 2021).

[81] Anglophones conceive of 'trial and sentencing' as two distinct phases of criminal adjudication. In legal cultures in which the court deliberates on and pronounces guilt and sentence as an integrated package, the retrospective orientation of criminal trials may be less pronounced. But even sentencing is partly backward-looking. The punishment must 'fit' the crime, and this is an exclusively future-orientated criterion only for monomaniacal consequentialists.

[82] Sir William Backstone, *Commentaries on the Laws of England* (1765-9), Book IV, ch 26, 329-30 ('no man is to be brought into jeopardy of his life, more than once, for the same offence … no man ought to be twice brought in danger of his life for one and the same crime').

[83] I Dennis, 'Quashing Acquittals: Applying the "New and Compelling Evidence" Exception to Double Jeopardy' [2014] Crim LR 247; P Roberts, 'Double Jeopardy Law Reform: A Criminal Justice Commentary' (2002) 65 MLR 393.

[84] Nothing sinister implied. Prosecutors in England and Wales cannot lawfully initiate or continue a prosecution unless they assess that a conviction is more likely than not on the evidence. Prosecutors are thus *ex ante* professionally committed to endorsing a conviction at trial as the (probable) right result (which is not to say that they should *express* such a view, or be hostile to changing their minds in light of new information).

[85] James Q Whitman, *The Origins of Reasonable Doubt: Theological Roots of the Criminal Trial* (New Haven, Yale University Press, 2008).

By conceptual extrapolation, the outcome of a criminal trial can never be, literally, a foregone conclusion.

To be sure, where incriminating evidence is strong and uncontradicted by innocent explanation a conviction may be highly likely and eminently predictable. The prosecutor might be convinced of the accused's guilt. Victims of crime sometimes know that the accused is guilty; though this is far less common than might be imagined, because much acquisitive crime is perpetrated by individuals unknown to the victim and perpetrators' identities are frequently plausibly contested even in relation to offences of interpersonal violence and sexual exploitation. Irrespective of what the victim, police, prosecutor or anybody else might believe (or even know), however, the inherent jeopardy of a criminal trial is that the verdict could always, in principle, go either way. A contested trial is a unique event, and its performance cannot be minutely scripted or foretold. Cases on paper sometimes materialise differently in the flesh. Witnesses fail to show up, or do not 'come up to proof' in the witness-box. Scientific evidence that seemed watertight in an expert's analytical report turns out under cross-examination to be full of questionable assumptions and conjectures.[86] The accused suddenly presents an unanticipated line of defence. Previously undisclosed material contradicts the complainant's narrative.[87] The accused elects to testify in his own defence, but proceeds to perform as the prosecution's best witness. There are innumerable contingencies, with compound effects. Moreover, the way in which the case is argued and presented to the fact-finder in the courtroom is a profoundly human interaction of such dynamism, complexity and emotional intensity that even a full retrial on the same facts and evidence (e.g. where the jury fails to return a verdict) could only be an approximate surrogate, never a completely faithful replica. It is reasonable to surmise that these performance dimensions of the criminal trial are accentuated in cases involving lay jurors or magistrates, but they are not eliminated even in bench trials before professional judges. Truly open-and-shut cases exist only in police procedural fiction.[88] Loss of control over trial outcomes is one reason why many lawyers prefer to negotiate pleas, achieving more or less predictable case disposals, rather than 'roll the dice' in a contested trial.[89] Once a trial is underway, no particular verdict is assured.

[86] Scientific evidence is both highly probative *and* susceptible to a raft of infirmities, errors and misapplications: P Roberts, 'Making Sense of Forensic Science Evidence' in P Roberts and M Stockdale (eds), *Forensic Science Evidence and Expert Witness Testimony: Reliability Through Reform?* (Cheltenham, Edward Elgar, 2018) 27.

[87] Dramatically illustrated by T Smith, 'The "Near Miss" of Liam Allan: Critical Problems in Police Disclosure, Investigation Culture and the Resourcing of Criminal Justice' [2018] Crim LR 711.

[88] '[T]he path of the law is strewn with examples of open and shut cases which, somehow, were not; of unanswerable charges which, in the event, were completely answered; of inexplicable conduct which was fully explained; of fixed and unalterable determinations that, by discussion, suffered a change': *John* v *Rees* [1970] Ch 345, 402 (Megarry J).

[89] Invoking the language of lotteries might be interpreted as an implicit confession of institutional weakness. '[E]ven those who work in the system – lawyers and judges – don't respect it .... But if the outcome of a trial is simply, as those in the system often put it, "a crapshoot", who can blame them for

What if criminal verdicts in contested proceedings[90] *were* literally forgone conclusions, eliminating all (epistemic) jeopardy from criminal trial adjudication? That would be a show trial, a purely symbolic performance that was neither epistemically serious nor orientated to fact-finding (as opposed to announcing, broadcasting or symbolically acting out preordained facts).[91] Linguistic usage is not friendly to conceptual clarity in this instance. When we say 'show trial' we mean 'not a real trial', rather than a trial that was (merely) deficient in its excessive showiness. If a trial is materially flawed, for example because the court lacked jurisdiction or on account of a significant violation of due process, an appellate court might quash the conviction, but it would not say that the accused didn't have a trial. Indeed, fair trial jurisprudence in general is predicated on the assumption that trials may be marred by unfairness, not that unfairness deprives criminal trials of their conceptual identity. An unfair trial is *still a trial*, though flawed. But a show trial is not a flawed trial in any parallel sense. A show trial is not any genuine kind of trial. It would not be enough, I think, to say that a show trial was a legal nullity. Trials found and held to be legal nullities, ex post, never had any legal effect (we now know), but were conceived as valid trials at the time, at least by key participants.[92] Show trials are nullities *ex ante*. Key participants *knew* all along (not merely guessed or predicted) what the final conclusion would be. Observers were intentionally fooled; or their cynicism was disregarded. The proceedings were devoid of all verdict jeopardy, all epistemic seriousness, all fact-finding aspirations. It hardly suffices to characterise such arrangements as flawed trials or trials vulnerable to being declared nullities. Show trials are bad faith parodies of the authentic adjudicative procedure. And just as a Hollywood moon landing is not a moon landing and deep fake photography is not merely a poor likeness, shows trials are not trials, conceptually and constitutively speaking.

The jeopardy in a criminal verdict is not only a question of epistemic uncertainty, but also, from the accused's point of view,[93] a matter of highly consequential

not wanting to gamble when very important issues are at stake?": WT Pizzi, *Trials Without Truth* (New York, New York University Press, 1999) 88. It seems to me, however, that uncertainty is an inherent – conceptual – feature of adjudication, and lawyers (and judges) inevitably cede some of their power to influence trial outcomes once the case is put to the jury.

[90] Caution mandates confining the conceptual necessity of jeopardy to *contested* trials. Even with routine guilty pleas, however, the deal is not sealed until the accused actually pleads guilty, and that plea is accepted by the court: see eg *R* v *NJ* [2022] EWCA Crim 790. For as long as the accused retains the right to a contested trial, some element of verdict jeopardy remains.

[91] J Peterson, 'Unpacking Show Trials: Situating the Trial of Saddam Hussein' (2007) 48 Harvard International LJ 257; G Simpson, 'Objective Responsibility: Show Trials and War Crimes Trials' (2006) 4(1) International Commentary on Evidence, Article 2.

[92] Conversely, acquittals procured through chicanery do not attract the protection of the double jeopardy prohibition, because there was no real jeopardy in the first place: cf Criminal Procedure and Investigations Act 1996, s. 57 ('tainted acquittals'). Proceedings were fixed. These are defence-orchestrated 'show trials'.

[93] As mentioned, there is also jeopardy for complainants, for legal professionals, and for other trial participants, including witnesses and jurors. The verdict jeopardy to which the accused is exposed takes a unique form – the accused is *literally* on trial – but the risks borne by others should not be underestimated.

personal risk. Liberty, amenity, prosperity and reputation are routinely on the line in criminal proceedings. A criminal verdict of guilty may seriously set back the accused's life, or – in some places – even end it. This is bad enough if the accused is actually guilty and deserves conviction and punishment, simply excruciating for those who are innocent (or genuinely believe themselves to be so). Given that the focal point of criminal adjudication is public censure and sanction of the guilty (but only of them, and only of the right charge and in the right way, with epistemic warrant and procedural due process), it seems to be a precondition of criminal trials that there must be an identifiable defendant to hold responsible for proven criminal wrongdoing. Thus, verdicts pronounce 'guilty' or 'not guilty' in relation to one or more named accused.[94] They do not make declarations about past events without attributing those events to some responsible agency. Verdict jeopardy infuses allocations of responsibility in criminal adjudication. Holding to account[95] is the paradigmatic instrumentality of the criminal trial. This poses further questions of criminal capacity, that is, who (or what) qualifies as the type of moral agent who (or which) can be answerable for criminal wrongdoing *and* is 'fit to plead' (i.e. stand trial) on criminal charges. Conceptions of criminal capacity vary across time and place. On the theory of criminal capacity embraced by modern legal systems, a criminal defendant cannot be a non-human animal,[96] a child below the age of criminal responsibility at the material time, or a person suffering from a mental condition incompatible with moral agency. Conversely, corporations, states and some other non-natural persons do possess the right kind of agency to be defendants in criminal trials.

What if the suspected offender has already died? It is conceivable that a trial could still be conducted, with a variety of possible objectives: to vindicate victims, to pursue remedies against the offender's estate, to set the historical record straight, to defuse social tensions, and so forth. It seems to me, however, that the existence (as opposed to physical presence[97]) of a living accused who could be held responsible for public wrongs is an essential component of the jeopardy we expect from our criminal trials, in the English common law tradition. If it is possible symbolically to execute a corpse – as the Restoration Stuarts did with Cromwell – it is possible symbolically to try a corpse: yet we never do. This seldom remarked procedural

[94] An imposter will not do: *R (Bahbahani)* v *Ealing Magistrates' Court* [2020] QB 478, [2019] EWHC 1385 (Admin).

[95] More precisely, I think, than 'calling to account'. Cf RA Duff, *Answering for Crime* (Oxford, Hart Publishing, 2007).

[96] Animal trials were commonplace in medieval Europe, vividly demonstrating the historical relativity of concepts of agency and responsibility: W Ewald, 'Comparative Jurisprudence (I): What Was it Like to Try a Rat?' (1995) 143 *University of Pennsylvania Law Review* 1898; EP Evans, *The Criminal Prosecution and Capital Punishment of Animals: The Lost History of Europe's Animal Trials* (London, Faber & Faber, 1987 [1906]).

[97] Physical availability to stand trial is a normal expectation but not a conceptual precondition. Criminal trials *in absentia* may be vulnerable to principled objections, but their status *as trials* producing valid judgments is settled law. See e.g. *R* v *Jones (Anthony)* [2003] 1 AC 1, [2002] UKHL 1; *Sejdovic* v *Italy*, App no 56581/00, Grand Chamber Judgment, 1 March 2006.

axiom was revisited in *Turk*,[98] where the accused participated in his trial of historic child sexual offences until the jury had retired to deliberate but committed suicide before a verdict could be returned. The jury was deadlocked on certain counts. Not unreasonably, the trial judge thought that the public investment in the proceedings and the victims' expectations and desire for closure militated in favour of hearing the jury's verdicts in relation to those counts on which agreement had already been reached. Verdicts of guilty on ten counts (and acquittals of six others) were duly returned. The Court of Appeal quashed the convictions and reiterated the orthodox common law position:

> [I]n order to preserve the bright line that criminal prosecutions are not pursued against those who have died, there is no discretion as to the course of action then to be taken. As soon as a judge learns that a defendant has died, it is his duty to take no further step in the case against that defendant save for receiving proof of death whereupon the indictment as far as it concerns that defendant must be declared of no effect … We appreciate that, in relation to many of the allegations pursued at trial, complainants may well consider that they had been vindicated and that, by this decision, there was important recognition of their position; so far as the record is concerned, that would be lost. We recognise that entirely understandable view but we repeat that it is critical to maintain an approach to criminal justice that is consistent and even-handed, maintaining a definitive position that the death of a defendant brings any criminal prosecution of that defendant to an end.[99]

Death of the accused automatically concludes trial proceedings against them. This is not a self-evident proposition from an ethical perspective, but it is both normatively defensible and settled English criminal jurisprudence. These institutional facts support the conclusion that a living accused in jeopardy is a conceptual prerequisite of a criminal trial, at least in England and Wales. Inquiries or hearings concerned with the deeds of the dead are not criminal trials,[100] conceptually speaking, because in our procedural tradition[101] verdict jeopardy is confined by mortality. Unless and until we invest our concept of the criminal trial with revised metaphysical assumptions, the class of potentially responsible defendants excludes souls or ghosts impervious to secular justice.

[98] *R* v *Turk* [2017] 1 WLR 2919, [2017] EWCA Crim 391.

[99] ibid, [22], [25].

[100] Criminal *appeals* may be pursued on behalf of deceased appellants by virtue of section 44A of the Criminal Appeal Act 1968. The stigma and pain of wrongful conviction survive the accused's death. The Criminal Cases Review Commission has referred high profile cases involving deceased (indeed, executed) accused back to the Court of Appeal, notably *R* v *Derek Bentley (Deceased)* [2001] 1 Cr App R 307, CA (conviction quashed); and *R* v *Hanratty (Deceased)* [2002] EWCA Crim 1141; [2002] 2 Cr App R 419 (conviction upheld).

[101] And in others: cf *Nölkenbockhoff* v *Germany* (1988) 10 EHRR 163. Besides, juridical concepts are always more or less particularistic according to their intended field(s) of application, making trade-offs between generality and usefulness unavoidable in jurisprudential analysis: W Twining, 'Have Concepts, Will Travel: Analytical Jurisprudence in a Global Context' (2005) 1 International Journal of Law in Context 5.

Conceptual Boundary Work

Discussion to this point has built up a core conception of the criminal trial as an epistemically serious institutional mechanism for pacific dispute resolution with verdict jeopardy (both epistemic and personal). We can further elucidate and test this conception of the concept, and simultaneously develop a deeper understanding of its usefulness and limitations, by probing its conceptual boundaries. Existing institutional practices will almost certainly combine constitutive with contingent features. In fact, when institutional practices are delineated in sufficiently granular detail this will necessarily be so. The colour of judicial robes or the architectural style of courthouses cannot plausibly be conceptual prerequisites of criminal trial. Inverting our perspective, it is illuminating to consider which features of contemporary criminal trial practice are *not* conceptually constitutive. There are plainly many contingent features of criminal adjudication that could be altered, subtracted, augmented or supplemented without stripping a criminal trial of its conceptual identity. Contingency extends to features of criminal adjudication that are widely regarded as very important, notwithstanding their dispensability in strictly conceptual terms.

We have already peremptorily ruled out the notion that a criminal trial must necessarily adopt a party-driven adversarial procedure. Inquisitorialism can be epistemologically serious, indeed it is arguably intuitively more congruent with rational fact-finding than an adversarial contest model of trial.[102] It follows that justifications of adversarial procedure cannot succeed merely on the basis of (conceptualist) appeals to the concept of a criminal trial. Inclusivity and tolerance of jurisdictional variation is a methodological strength of this conceptual analysis. A test of pedigree would not be much use if it failed to recognise and claim uncontroversial tokens of the pertinent type. A viable concept of criminal trial cannot afford to take sides in debates between adversarial and inquisitorial models of adjudication, because it is self-evident that criminal trials are not confined to common law jurisdictions (or jurisdictions importing common law thinking). Adversarial and inquisitorial procedures can alike, in principle, accommodate epistemically serious dispute resolution with verdict jeopardy, three primary conceptual hallmarks of authentic criminal trials.

A parallel analysis disqualifies juries and lay fact-finding more generally as conceptual predicates of criminal trial. Juries are, of course, core features of the common law tradition of criminal adjudication. Whilst some think their

[102] 'The continental system would tend to embrace a paradigm closer to that of scientific investigation': M Damaška, 'Presentation of Evidence and Factfinding Precision' (1975) 123 U Penn LR 1083, 1104–5; M Damaška, *Evaluation of Evidence: Pre-Modern and Modern Approaches* (Cambridge, Cambridge University Press, 2019). Adversarial procedure undeniably has numerous epistemic pressure points as well as practical strengths: cf G van Kessel, 'Adversary Excesses in the American Criminal Trial' (1992) 67 Notre Dame LR 403.

importance exaggerated,[103] others (including me) believe that trial by jury has constitutional significance in England and Wales.[104] Either way, the justification for fact-finding by lay jury cannot rest on conceptualist appeals to the concept of a criminal trial. That would imply that only trials on indictment in the Crown Court are actually trials, whereas instances of adjudication in magistrates' courts – statistically, the vast majority of criminal case disposals – would be … well, I am not sure what we would call them. 'Summary justice'? 'Magisterial adjudications'? The professional discourse of 'summary trial' is not merely a linguistic habit or an implicit admission of lack of terminological imagination. Summary trials are distinctive because they employ summary procedure, not because they fail at being trials. A conceptualist approach cannot be saved by relaxing 'juries' to 'lay participation in fact-finding', because although this would accommodate trials by magistrates in England and Wales and trials involving mixed panels in Continental Europe and further afield, it would still fail to recognise bench trials in common law jurisdictions[105] and criminal adjudication in procedural systems with no lay involvement whatsoever. If your concept of criminal trial implies that there are no criminal trials in the Netherlands[106] or Singapore, or entails that the Diplock system in Northern Ireland involved detention without trial,[107] then your concept is maladapted for service in current controversies and debates. There may be reasons to oppose the introduction in England and Wales of judge-only trials on indictment,[108] and legitimate concerns may be expressed about the quality of justice routinely dispensed by district judges in magistrates' courts,[109] but critics do not suggest that these proceedings are not trials. If such a conceptualist argument were ever mounted or encountered, the most likely reaction

[103] Lord Justice Auld, *Review of the Criminal Courts of England and Wales* (London, TSO, 2001) ch 5; P Darbyshire, 'The Lamp That Shows that Freedom Lives: Is it Worth the Candle?' [1991] Crim LR 740.

[104] 'In this country trial by jury is a hallowed principle of the administration of criminal justice. It is properly identified as a right, available to be exercised by a defendant unless and until the right is amended or circumscribed by express legislation': *R* v *Twomey* [2009] 2 Cr App R 25, [10] (Judge CJ).

[105] S Doran, JD Jackson and ML Seigel, 'Rethinking Adversariness in Nonjury Criminal Trials' (1995) 23 Am J Crim L 1.

[106] The Netherlands stands out as having the most professionalized criminal process in Western Europe: PJP Tak, *The Dutch Criminal Justice System* (Nijmegen, Wolf Legal Publishers, 3/e 2008); P Fennell, C Harding, N Jörg and B Swart (eds), *Criminal Justice in Europe: A Comparative Study* (Oxford, Oxford University Press, 1995). The ECtHR Grand Chamber in *Taxquet* v *Belgium* (2012) 54 EHRR 26, [14], identified fourteen Council of Europe states with no lay involvement in criminal adjudication.

[107] The ECtHR affirmed that 'Diplock courts and the procedures which have evolved in a system where the trial judge is both tribunal of fact and tribunal of law' were ECHR Article 6 compliant: *McKeown* v *United Kingdom* (2012) 54 EHRR 7, [48]. The system of 'Diplock courts' for 'scheduled' (terrorist) offences was abolished by the Justice and Security (Northern Ireland) Act 2007. Generally, see John Jackson and Sean Doran, *Judge Without Jury: Diplock Trials in the Adversary System* (OUP, 1995).

[108] Criminal Justice Act 2003, s.44 introduced a power to order judge only trial to forestall 'a real and present danger that jury tampering would take place'.

[109] cf The Secret Barrister, *Stories of the Law and How It's Broken* (London, Picador, 2019) ch 2 (characterising magistrates' courts as 'The Wild West').

to it would be bemusement rather than opposition or assent. It makes sense to claim that such trials are deficient, either categorically in design or contingently in practice, and normative arguments might then be marshalled and assessed on both sides of the issue. To insist that such procedures are *not trials*, however, is merely a counter-intuitive assertion that begs all the significant normative and policy questions.

If major architectural features of criminal adjudication such as adversarial structure and lay participation in fact-finding are not conceptually constitutive of criminal trials, it must follow (a fortiori, as only lawyers ever say) that more granular details of local criminal procedure are not conceptually decisive, either. For example, whether or not a particular jurisdiction operates an exclusionary rule of evidence attaching to improperly obtained 'fruit of the poisoned tree'[110] or interposes a 'rape shield' against the admission of previous sexual history evidence[111] will not shift conceptual understanding of the criminal trial; still less will idiosyncratic choices of procedural doctrine or institutional design trouble the core concept. Arguments about the underlying rationale for excluding improperly obtained evidence,[112] for example, appeal directly to normative ideals (e.g. moral integrity), instrumental objectives (e.g. safeguarding rights) and institutional incentives (e.g. 'discipling the police'), rather than trading rival concepts. These patterns of argumentation are both mundane and entirely appropriate. Any non-parochial concept of criminal trial must be capable of handling the diverse traditions and major contemporary configurations of cosmopolitan criminal jurisprudence, accommodating stupendous institutional variability at the microscopic level. Neither should procedural evolution and variation over time within a single trial system warrant arbitrary conceptual disqualification.

These strictures do not preclude further conceptual refinements. Consider the normative injunction that fair trials must be 'conducted by an independent and impartial tribunal established by law'.[113] Allowing that a criminal trial is an institutional mechanism governed by the rule of law,[114] this formula's legality requirement seems unproblematic. Criminal trials in liberal democracies must

[110] England and Wales never endorsed such a doctrine: Police and Criminal Evidence Act 1984, s.76(4); *R* v *Twigg* [2019] 1 WLR 6533, [2019] EWCA Crim 1553; *R* v *Warwickshall* (1783) 1 Leach 263.

[111] Youth Justice and Criminal Evidence Act 1999, s.41.

[112] *Roberts and Zuckerman's Criminal Evidence* (n 40) ch 5.

[113] ECHR Art 6(1); ICCPR Art 14. See UN Basic Principles on the Independence of the Judiciary, GA Res 40/32 (29 November 1985) and GA Res 40/146 (13 December 1985), www.ohchr.org/EN/ProfessionalInterest/Pages/IndependenceJudiciary.aspx.

[114] Not necessarily embracing every aspect of the liberal conception: cf J Raz, 'The Rule of Law and its Virtue' (1977) 93 LQR 195; Lord Bingham, 'The Rule of Law' (2007) 66 CLJ 67. For example, bills of attainder contradict the generality requirement of legality, but it is at least a theoretical possibility that, say, Thomas More or Mary Queen of Scots could have received fair *trials*, so long as proceedings against them were epistemically serious and guilty verdicts were not a foregone conclusion. (In reality, bills of attainder might also breach the non-retroactivity norm, but that is a different objection, engaging Sullivan's primary conduct condition.).

satisfy minimum requirements for legitimate exercises of public power. A mafia interrogation preliminary to a punishment beating, or murder, is not a criminal trial, even though it may be (somewhat) epistemologically serious, it might resolve a (mafia) dispute, and could well entail (mortal) jeopardy for those at the sticky end of Don Corleone's suspicions. At the limit, a drumhead court martial can be a trial (only) to the extent that the commanding officer exercises lawful authority to conduct it. Rule of law procedures are not incompatible with official discretion, nor do they necessarily require elaborate rules of procedure for the conduct of hearings, but properly constituted legal authority is conceptually indispensable. Any procedure outside the law, and irrespective of its substantive merits, is not within our modern concept of criminal trial, which seems to presuppose non-delegable public duties.[115]

Turning to the twin criteria of independence and impartiality, a more nuanced analysis is required. Some defects would plausibly be conceptually fatal, others might not be. If we envisage complete abnegation of independence, akin to the old Soviet 'telephone law' tradition of judges calling up prosecutors to ask what their verdicts should be,[116] or complete lack of impartiality – as where the judge is driven by personal animosity to nobble a despised litigant – then I think it would be appropriate to place such procedures beyond the conceptual pale. The process is not epistemologically serious, and there is minimal if any true verdict jeopardy. To the extent that the result is preordained, by complete lack of independence or extreme partiality, we encounter a sham – a show trial/non-trial – rather than the genuine forensic article. By the same token, tribunals can fail to be independent owing to improper influence or lack of (perceived) impartiality falling far short of these extreme (and one would hope, unusual) scenarios. For example, a judge might be a director of an NGO charity which is also an intervener in the case.[117] Or the judge might have received submissions from a prosecutor, in the guise of amicus curiae or advocate general, to which defence counsel has not been able to respond on equal terms, thus creating a *perception* of bias even where there is no lack of impartiality in fact.[118] In these and similar instances, it seems more natural to say that a flawed, unfair trial occurred rather than invoking the more

[115] Hence, adjudicative processes conducted by employers, associations or institutions such as universities are not criminal trials, even when they concern alleged criminal conduct.

[116] K Hendley, '"Telephone Law" and the "Rule of Law": The Russian Case' (2009) 1 Hague Journal on the Rule of Law 241; PH Solomon, Jr, *Soviet Criminal Justice Under Stalin* (Cambridge, Cambridge University Press, 1996) ch 7.

[117] 'If the absolute impartiality of the judiciary is to be maintained, there must be a rule which automatically disqualifies a judge who is involved, whether personally or as a director of a company, in promoting the same causes in the same organisation as is a party to the suit. There is no room for fine distinctions': *R* v *Bow Street Metropolitan Stipendiary Magistrate ex parte Pinochet Ugarte (No 2)* [2000] 1 AC 119, 135, HL (Lord Browne-Wilkinson).

[118] *Borgers* v *Belgium* (1993) 15 EHRR 92; *Reinhardt and Slimane-Kaïd* v *France* (1998) 28 EHRR 59; echoing the common law principle that justice must also be 'seen to be done': *R* v *Breslin* (1985) 80 Cr App R 226, 230, CA; *R* v *Sussex Justices, ex p McCarthy* [1924] 1 KB 256, 259.

extravagant categorical claim that there was never any trial. Inasmuch as the independence and impartiality of the tribunal are constitutive of a fair trial, we might properly categorise such constitutively defective trials as legal nullities. Still, it seems to me that we are here describing the absence of a *fair* trial, rather than the absence of any trial *tout court*. If this impression is correct, then an authentic jurisprudential concept of criminal trial cuts across the institutional (human rights) concept of a fair (criminal) trial – which is an interesting analytical insight, worthy of further contemplation.

Having now admitted institutional criteria, namely compliance with the rule of law, into the conceptual definition of criminal trials, one might wonder at the extent of this normative bridgehead. Might it be argued, for example, that a trial process lacking in procedural integrity or marred by some serious failure of due process forfeits its conceptual identity as a criminal trial? Only at the extremities of normative tolerance. A sound concept of criminal trial will not purport to resolve live controversies through conceptual fiat. Concepts collapse in on themselves when ill-advisedly over-extended. Well-designed conceptual scaffolding should help to frame normative controversies, and thereby assist in clarifying the nature and significance of normative disagreement. It is methodologically inept (or rhetorical legerdemain) to try to circumvent or conceal ethical controversies by gerrymandering concepts. It may tempting, for example, to try to argue that a trial process that fails to uphold standards of procedural propriety or which affords too little weight to procedural safeguards such as the privilege against self-incrimination[119] is a conceptual impossibility, a self-refuting contradiction that cannot logically exist.[120] That style of argument is reminiscent of Kant's attempts to derive ethical duties from a substantive account of rationality,[121] and it is methodologically problematic for much the same reasons that neo-Kantian rationalism seems question-begging or obscure to non-Kantians. To demonstrate that evil deeds are not merely wrong but irrational requires the same, or similar, normative resources as moral argument to establish directly why evil deeds should not be done. You can bundle these arguments up in a capacious conception of rationality if that is your

[119] cf BM Zupančič, 'The Privilege Against Self-Incrimination' [1981] Arizona State Law Journal 1, 25: 'If the privilege against self-incrimination is a logical concomitant of adversary adjudication and if, furthermore, the privilege against self-incrimination cannot exist without the exclusion of evidence obtained in violation of that privilege, then the exclusionary rule itself can be deduced from the postulate of impartial adversary adjudication'.

[120] '[I]n criminal procedure, too, the violation of certain basic rules should affect the substantive outcome of the case …. To put it bluntly, if the constable does blunder, the criminal should go free …. [Violation of the privilege against self-incrimination] covers the pristine Kafkaesque absurd in which the State uses the fraudulent semblance of the legal process to conceal law's precise opposite – the instant regression to anti-law': BM Zupančič, 'The Crown and the Criminal: The Privilege Against Self-Incrimination – Towards General Principles of Criminal Procedure' (1996) 5 Nottingham LJ 32, 45, 50.

[121] O O'Neill, 'Kant', in AR Mele and P Rawling (eds), *The Oxford Handbook of Rationality* (Oxford, Oxford University Press, 2004); J Raz, *Engaging Reason* (Oxford, Oxford University Press, 1999). cf J Gardner and T Macklem, 'Reasons', in JL Coleman, KE Himma and SJ Shapiro (eds), *The Oxford Handbook of Jurisprudence and Philosophy of Law* (Oxford, Oxford University Press, 2002) 440.

theoretical preference, but this conceptualist manoeuvre does not automatically vindicate any normative claim. It simply repackages and restates the question.[122] Likewise, in the criminal procedure context, notions of procedural impropriety and complex jurisprudential doctrines are shot through with normative controversy, extending from the primary threads of ethical principle right down into the dense institutional fabric of legal definitions and doctrinal constructs. Even where the rules themselves are clear and settled, criminal adjudication constantly throws up hard cases where detailed facts and circumstances muddy the waters of general principles and pull in the direction of allowing exceptions (finding reasons to distinguish the precedent, in the common lawyer's lexicon). Thus, cultivation of ethical practice in the administration of criminal justice is not exhausted by conscientious rule-following, it also requires sound judgement in context. It will not do to side-step these controversies simply by proclaiming that anybody who does not (apparently) share your normative preferences is making an elementary conceptual error. Practical reasoning is not axiomatic. Inasmuch as conceptual redefinition announces normatively salient conclusions without putting in the normative legwork or showing its working, conceptualist arguments never truly resolve jurisprudential issues of any moral significance.

We should not foreclose the possibility that some extreme instances of procedural impropriety or failures of due process could be so corrosively delegitimizing that proceedings are cast beyond the conceptual pale of a criminal trial. Such dereliction would imply radical loss of legitimacy in social dispute resolution and forfeiture of normative standing to adjudicate. Most likely, conceptual limits would be reached or breached where the impropriety in question effectively reneges on one or more of the core conceptual commitments previously identified. For example, a criminal trial that was so racist or sectarian that any defendant from a particular pariah group would always be convicted is not epistemically serious and lacks threshold verdict jeopardy. Likewise, if criminal justice officials were systematically[123] corrupt or derelict in their professional duties it is difficult to see how criminal adjudication would be taking evidence, proof or factfinding sufficiently seriously. Other components of the standard specification of fair trial in international human rights law could be warped and stretched to such an extent that procedures officially labelled 'trials' would no longer be trials. For example, the accused could be held on pre-trial remand for such protracted periods that the prospect of reaching a final verdict becomes implausibly remote. Suppose that the

[122] For example, 'Why should I not do evil?', via 'Because evil is irrational', becomes 'Why would it be irrational for me to do evil?'. cf P Unger, *Empty Ideas: A Critique of Analytic Philosophy* (New York, Oxford University Press, 2014) (mercilessly eviscerating conceptual logic-chopping in the realm of metaphysics).

[123] The (fuzzy) thought here is that sporadic or geographically delimited corruption is 'only' a normative problem, not a conceptual existential threat. Trial systems can exist with bad apples, and even tolerate some corrupted barrels, but if the entire orchard is worm-eaten, the harvest is lost – or the business is different to that advertised (producing poison rather than wine, oppression rather than justice).

majority of suspects die in the squalor of remand gaols, or from disease or old age, before their cases are finally resolved by a court. In these circumstances, it seems inadequate to complain that excessive delay renders trial proceedings unfair. The reality is a system of executive justice (or liquidation of social enemies) masquerading as criminal adjudication. These proceedings are not show trials, but no-show trials. The promise of trial is, for the majority, only for show. Either extreme form of institutional bad faith would be sufficient to dissolve the conceptual integrity of a trial.

IV. From Conceptual Analysis to Conceptualist Argument? Implicating the Presumption of Innocence

Inspired by Sullivan's intriguing – if sketchy – 'conceptual' claims regarding proof of conduct as an essential precondition of criminal liability, the foregoing discussion proceeded in two steps. First, I established some general methodological preconditions and expectations for a virtuous concept of criminal trial. Concepts are appropriately formulated, and – by extension – should be judged, relative to context and purpose. There could be different, equally valid, concepts of criminal trial, calibrated to different theoretical or practical tasks (just as chainsaws and hacksaws are both saws, but are far from interchangeable in use – if you want to keep all your fingers). Secondly, I took up the challenge, implicit in Sullivan's exposition, to elucidate a serviceable concept of 'criminal trial', cohering with prevailing jurisprudence, contemporary institutional practices and evolved procedural traditions.

Conceptual analysis precedes or is presupposed by normative evaluation: before we can say whether a criminal trial was 'fair' or achieved justice, for example, we have to be able to identify what a criminal trial is. Distilling the essence of the previous section's analysis, criminal trials may now be conceptualised as (1) institutionalised, formal, and legitimacy-claiming (2) conflict-resolution mechanisms conducted as (3) epistemically serious inquiries into (4) alleged criminal wrongdoing by (5) responsible agents entailing (6) verdict jeopardy. The preceding discussion mostly concentrated on items (2), (3) and (6), with incidental observations on the other three components. The terminology of 'epistemic seriousness' and 'verdict jeopardy', though superficially novel, mainly serves to encapsulate and organise familiar trial-related values and objectives, including rational fact-finding, reliable evidence, proof of guilt, legitimate verdicts, judgement under uncertainty, holding offenders to account, and public censure of criminal wrongdoing. One important set of functions for concepts is diagnostic and remedial. A robust concept of criminal trial should help us identify instances of radical institutional failure, where official shortcomings or misconduct fatally compromise constitutive features of this distinctively penal conflict resolution mechanism. Where perversions of trial process exceed the limits of conceptual tolerance we should say, with Sullivan, that imposing criminal liability in such circumstances would be incoherent and illogical, not 'merely' unfair or unjust.

Conceptual objections claim a certain methodological priority. Contentious normative issues are not even reached where conceptual default pre-empts any further discussion or analysis. With such awesome methodological power comes commensurately great discursive responsibility. Conceptual arguments should be deployed only to close down propositions that are not legitimately arguable. If overextended to debateable controversies, conceptual argument becomes conceptual*ist* – an illegitimate definitional stop. This general methodological principle extrapolates to institutional contexts where, for example, conceptualist claims may be deployed in attempts to choke off doctrinal or jurisprudential propositions meriting further critical examination and considered normative appraisal. The 'presumption of innocence' is, I think, particularly susceptible to such conceptualist assumptions and arguments. Longstanding theoretical and jurisprudential puzzles clouding the presumption's conceptual parameters have been exacerbated in recent decades by a rebarbative[124] post-HRA 1998 jurisprudence on reverse onus clauses. Article 6(2)'s right to be presumed innocent in criminal proceedings is conceptualised as part of the ECHR's more comprehensive Article 6(1) right to a fair trial. Alleged violations of Article 6(2) consequently afford a doctrinal toehold for testing the conceptual limits of (fair) trials.

Sullivan offers few clues regarding the details of *his* conception of the criminal trial, save that it must – on pain of conceptual incoherence – establish proof of proscribed conduct. On a minimalist reading, Sullivan's thesis might be confined to an argument about substantive criminal law, entirely consistent with the conceptual reconstruction of criminal adjudication presented in this essay. That cramped interpretation would, however, trivialise the second of Sullivan's 'two fundamental conditions' for imposing criminal liability. One would be hard-pressed to name any post-Enlightenment jurist, judge or lawyer in the common law tradition[125] who would disagree with the elementary principle that the prosecution must prove the material facts establishing each prescribed element of a criminal offence. Indeed, it is difficult to see how Sullivan could derive conclusions regarding '[a] criminal trial properly so called'[126] or 'the simulacrum of a trial'[127] if the second, proof condition were merely an idle wheel in the argumentative works. On a fair reading, Sullivan appears to be committed to two, more substantial, propositions.

[124] A *mot juste* I owe to Bob Sullivan.

[125] Indeed, the proposition should be uncontroversial in any 'accusatorial' system separating the prosecutorial from the judicial function, encompassing a pan-European procedural heritage: SJ Summers, *Fair Trials: The European Criminal Procedural Tradition and the European Court of Human Rights* (Oxford, Hart Publishing, 2007).

[126] 'Conduct and Proof of Conduct' (n 4) 248.

[127] ibid, 244.

First, his concept of 'conduct' imposes material constraints on the legitimate scope of criminal prohibitions. Second and cumulatively, Sullivan's own illustrations and commentary imply that Article 6(2) ECHR is somehow implicated in satisfying (or not) his 'proof of conduct' precondition. Thus, Sullivan characterises 'proof of conduct as an entailment of the presumption of innocence'.[128] *Entailment* can here mean only logical entailment, consistent with Sullivan's methodological conceptualism and his repeated reassurances that convictions secured by unjust means may still be *conceptually* sound even when normatively illegitimate.[129]

To this extent, and as previously noted in Section II, Sullivan aligns himself with those theorists and legal commentators who want to invest ECHR Article 6(2) with some measure of jurisdiction over state parties' substantive criminal law. This manoeuvre would achieve something of a jurisprudential coup, if it could be executed successfully, since it would open up to collateral attack, via an 'unfair trial' objection, substantive offence definitions that would be doctrinally unimpeachable on ordinary canons of statutory interpretation, presupposing the primacy of literal construction and an orthodox constitutional theory of the separation of powers. This argument, moreover, would be available in domestic criminal proceedings, irrespective of whether the question ever reached Strasbourg. Essential to this manoeuvre is the fusing of substantive and procedural elements of criminal liability, represented, in Sullivan's account, by his 'two fundamental conditions': conduct, and proof of conduct. Without this merging, or conflation, a purely conceptual argument addressed only to the conduct element of criminal offences could not achieve the institutional traction claimed for it. More specifically, the argument would not engage Article 6(2) ECHR if framed in purely substantive law terms. We can try to reconstruct the general argument's somewhat elusive logic through the particular doctrinal and hypothetical examples that Sullivan deploys to vindicate his central conceptual claims.

The offence of possessing otherwise innocent articles for (apparently) terrorist purposes proscribed by section 57 of the Terrorism Act 2000 is the direct statutory descendant of the offence litigated in *Kebilene*,[130] an early authority on the application of Article 6(2) to criminal proceedings in England and Wales. 'This offence', says Sullivan, 'has been defended as a conceptually defensible criminal offence on the basis that the actus reus is possession which gives rise to the reasonable suspicion' of terrorist intent. He continues:

> Apparently, all is well, at least in conceptual terms, provided the prosecution has the burden of proving the possession and the presence of reasonable suspicion. It is submitted that this is a flawed analysis if we insist that minimum standards of responsibility must be satisfied in respect of criminal liability. Conduct giving rise to mere suspicion cannot be characterised as the wrong with which the offence is engaged.[131]

[128] ibid, 248.
[129] ibid, 245.
[130] *R* v *DPP, ex p. Kebilene* [2000] 2 AC 326, DC and HL.
[131] 'Conduct and Proof of Conduct' (n 4) 246.

The section 57 offence, so construed, offends Sullivan's concept of legitimately criminalisable conduct. How so? Sullivan apparently thinks that epistemic standards short of belief are incapable of constituting authentic elements of a criminal offence. Yet that proposition is far from self-evident, and is not grounded in direct doctrinal or broader jurisprudential authority, so far as I can tell. According to Sullivan:

> [A] full reading of *Kebilene* and subsequent authority, together with consideration of the jurisprudence of Article 6(2), establishes that offences which purport to convict on the basis of a reasonable suspicion must be read so as to require proof of the wrong underlying the offence.[132]

Section 57-type offences fall into conceptual dereliction, therefore, when they disregard 'a basic and unyielding principle that conduct which constitutes the underlying wrong must be proved'.[133] After the Human Rights Act, however, ECHR Article 6(2) supposedly empowers judges to restore conceptual rectitude.

For all its theoretical ingenuity and potential strategic utility in criminal litigation, I cannot see how this argument succeeds without presupposing a *normatively* controversial conception of criminal responsibility. Plainly, an epistemic standard *qua* offence element – e.g. a circumstantial element of an offence *actus reus* stipulating 'reasonable suspicion' of legislatively particularised conduct – must not be confused with the standard of proof required to establish that element. In *purely* conceptual terms, there is no difficulty in stipulating that reasonable suspicion, say, must be proved to the criminal standard, requiring the fact-finder to be 'sure' that said conduct *was* reasonably suspected. If this were all that conceptual defensibility entailed, section 57 would not violate the 'basic and unyielding principle' stipulating that 'conduct which constitutes the underlying wrong must be proved'. More emphatically, Sullivan is adamant that '[c]onduct giving rise to mere suspicion cannot be characterised as the wrong with which the offence is engaged'. I agree that there must be *some* conceptual limitations on what can count as a crime, broadly corresponding to legally-defined wrongs for which a moral agent can plausibly be held criminally responsible. For example, one cannot be criminally responsible for events that occurred before one was born, and one cannot – as we have seen – be tried for future deeds or events occurring after one's death (even though one may be said to 'commit a crime' whilst alive that eventuates in a completed criminal wrong only after one's death). The *nullum crimen* principle imposes further conceptual limitations on the scope of criminality, inasmuch as ex post facto criminalisation of past conduct forestalls any possibility of compliance and would reduce the accused to a hapless 'spectator to his own fate' in exactly the way Sullivan laments.[134] Of course, as Sullivan says, imposing criminal

[132] ibid, 247.

[133] ibid.

[134] The *nullum crimen* principle is a constraint on criminal legislation, rather than a fair trial norm. Thus, it relates to Sullivan's first fundamental condition (conduct), rather than the second (proof of conduct) – unless the second is a trivial derivation of the first.

liability for the state of the weather would be absurd;[135] more precisely, because the state of the weather is not something that human agents (absent superhero powers or evil genius technology) can be responsible for orchestrating. Weather events are, in my terms, beyond the cognisable scope of legitimate trial jeopardy.

By virtue of requiring *reasonable* suspicion, however, the section 57 offence isn't conceptually absurd in any equivalent sense. It *would be* absurd if the normative requirement of reasonableness were dropped, so that a person could be convicted on the strength of any far-fetched crazy or prejudiced suspicion that some random onlooker happened to entertain. In that nightmare world, all our lives would be hostage to vicissitudes as unfathomable and uncontrollable as the weather. Back in our world, if the correct doctrinal interpretation of the offence is that (objective) reasonable suspicion pre-empts (subjectively) innocent intent – because, on the correct reading, that's what Parliament did in enacting the offence – then that frames 'the wrong', in positive law, which the offence proscribes. Article 6(2)'s presumption of innocence cannot render practical assistance to revise or countermand that conclusion, any more than direct appeals to authentic moral wrongs or blameless moral innocence (the legal positivist's caricature of natural law) can step in to save the day. These normative arguments are not institutionally cognisable. Those who wish to avoid conviction of the section 57 offence will need to conduct themselves accordingly. They should not hoard large quantities of sodium hydroxide in their cellars, drive across town centres with bootfulls of fertiliser, or download copies of the Al-Qaeda Manual or white supremacist literature on how to start a race riot.[136] Failing that, they had better have some credible exculpatory explanation for their conduct by way of affirmative defence. Those who choose to skate on thin ice are held, at law, *volenti* to the risk of calamity.

On my account, the decisive considerations are jurisprudential and institutional, not conceptual. There is undeniably a problem of inconsistency if a court first identifies some component of a criminal wrong as part of the offence definition and then says, without further rationale or authority, that the prosecutor doesn't have to prove it. In England and Wales, *Woolmington*[137] emphatically dictates otherwise. Post-HRA 1998 reverse onus jurisprudence is admittedly sometimes unhelpfully obscure or self-contradictory, not least in its reliance on the slippery concept of 'gravamen'.[138] Scything through the doctrinal

[135] 'Any attempt to decouple liability for a criminal wrong from any degree of involvement in the wrong will entail straying from the path of the criminal law. Indeed if such a decoupling were made a general principle, the sky would be the limit. One could be made liable for anything and everything, such as the state of the weather': GR Sullivan, 'Parents and their Truanting Children' (n 15) 296.

[136] cf *R* v *Dunleavy* [2021] EWCA Crim 39, [16].

[137] *Woolmington v DPP* 1935] AC 462, HL.

[138] Sullivan, 'Strict Liability for Criminal Offences in England and Wales' (n 25) 213 suggests, by interpolation, that '[f]or Roberts … the gravamen of the [*Kebilene*] offence was proof of possessing an article giving rise to a reasonable suspicion of such connection or use and there was, therefore, no contravention of Article 6(2)'. On my reading, judicial appeals to the 'gravamen' of an offence in reverse

thicket,[139] the question always comes down to this: *what is the pertinent criminal wrong encapsulated in the offence definition*? The answer to that question follows from jurisprudential analysis of relevant institutional materials (statutes, case law precedents, hard-working soft law, canons of statutory interpretation, broader jurisprudential principles, etc) supplemented by institutionally-cognisable normative sources (including comparative law influences and political morality) and general intellectual resources (e.g. logic, reasoning by analogy, rational inference, common sense relevancy). Most of the offences perplexing courts and debated by commentators in relation to Article 6(2) are statutory. Whilst models of statutory interpretation too closely aligned to parliamentary intent are typically reductive and institutionally unrealistic, the literal wording and structural organisation of penal statutes must always command judicial respect and are often decisive. This is the nub of (liberal) law's normative formalism. The question is not what Parliament said, or even what Parliament intended, but what Parliament *did* in enacting a particular offence. What Parliament did is located in the relational institutional space between Parliament's deeds and their authentic interpretation in authoritative rulings by appellate courts.

Excessively broad criminal offences may well be illegitimate as a matter of legislative policy.[140] If sentencing practice enables personal culpability assessments to re-enter the analysis and mitigate the harshness of extravagant liability doctrines,[141] this is welcome. Moreover, English criminal jurisprudence contains well-established principles of statutory interpretation designed to curb legislative overarching. Penal statutes should be interpreted strictly in favour of the accused.[142] In cases of doubt, courts should lean towards reading advertent *mens*

onus clause jurisprudence (see e.g. *R* v *DPP, ex p Kebilene* [2000] 2 AC 326, 344, DC (Lord Bingham); *R* v *S* [2003] 1 Cr App R 35, [2002] EWCA Crim 2558 (Davis J)) are seldom helpful, sometimes obfuscating and generally best avoided. 'Gravamen' can be invoked intelligibly to characterise the core wrong targeted by the prohibition. But this is at most a stepping-stone towards the decisive doctrinal issue, i.e. defining the offence at law. If the *offence*, properly interpreted, criminalises conduct inciting reasonable suspicion, then that's the definition of the offence. Neither 'gravamen' nor Article 6(2) has obvious (let alone decisive) interpretational significance.

[139] To be clear, I don't seek to defend every court decision or passage of judicial analysis addressing reverse onus clauses. When primary materials are not logically reconcilable, the jurist's task is principled reconstruction. Superior judgments include: *R* v *Williams (Orette)* [2013] 1 WLR 1200; [2012] EWCA Crim 2162; *R* v *Wilcocks* [2017] 4 WLR 39, [2016] EWCA Crim 2043; *R* v *K(M)*; *R* v *Gega* [2019] QB 86, [2018] EWCA Crim 667; *R* v *Webster* [2011] 1 Cr App R 16, [2010] EWCA Crim 2819.

[140] cf Roberts (n 27) 67, 66 (castigating the *Kebilene* offence as 'procedurally sound, but substantively bad … a thoroughly bad piece of over-criminalisation … mak[ing] unnecessary in-roads into individuals' personal autonomy').

[141] For creative thinking along these lines, see GR Sullivan, 'Strict Liability for Criminal Offences in England and Wales' (n 25) 214.

[142] *Tuck & Sons* v *Priester* (1887) 19 QBD 629. But this (weak?) presumption is overridden by clear parliamentary intent expressed in literal meaning, as Lord Reid elaborated in *R* v *Ottewell* [1970] AC 642, 649, HL: 'I would never seek to diminish in any way the importance of that principle within its proper sphere. But it only applies where after full inquiry and consideration one is left in real doubt'. Also see e.g. *Isle of Wight Council* v *Platt* [2017] 1 WLR 1441, [2017] UKSC 28, [45].

rea into offence definitions.[143] Reverse onus clauses can be imposed by implication, but there is a strong presumption against it.[144] Where reverse onuses have been imposed, courts should 'read down' the burden to a mere burden of production if a fully probative onus would be incompatible with Article 6(2).[145] But these jurisprudential and broader normative considerations are ancillary to Sullivan's meticulously 'non-normative'[146] central thesis. Violation of the Sullivine responsibility condition is supposedly 'not merely unduly harsh, it is incoherent'.[147] As demonstrated in relation to the section 57 offence, the argument – on pain of circularity – seemingly trades on an undeclared (and therefore undefended) normative stipulation, to the effect that (objectively) suspicious behaviour should never be enough to constitute criminal liability, even when proved to the criminal standard. Even if this normative stipulation were vindicated by explicit doctrinal authority in English criminal law, I cannot see how any jurisprudentially credible interpretation of Article 6(2) can be used to shore it up. Purely conceptual analysis, either of 'conduct' or of 'proof of conduct' (or of both combined), furnishes neither the substantive destination nor a doctrinal vehicle capable of getting there.

V. Conclusion

Compared with the gallons of ink (nowadays, pixels) devoted to jurisprudential reconstruction and doctrinal criticism of criminal procedure law, relatively little has been written on the concept of criminal trial.[148] This essay accepted the challenge implicit in Bob Sullivan's influential writings to develop a more fully articulated conception, at least in preliminary outline. According to Sullivan, 'proof of conduct' is a necessary attribute of a criminal trial properly so-called. But what, exactly, does 'proof of conduct' entail, in either theoretical or practical jurisprudence? It seems entirely plausible that there could be distinctive hallmarks or distinguishing features of criminal trials, some of which may be conceptually essential. Yet Sullivan offers only a few emblematic illustrations and never attempts more systematic analysis. In taking up these suggestive threads, one methodological aim was to demonstrate (with no pretension to be definitive

[143] *Pwr* v *DPP* [2022] 1 WLR 789, [2022] UKSC 2; *Attorney General's Reference (No 1 of 2020)* [2021] QB 441, [2020] EWCA Crim 1665; *DPP* v *Jagnauth* [2019] UKPC 8; *B* v *DPP* [2000] 2 AC 428, HL; *Sweet* v *Parsley* [1970] AC 132, HL.

[144] *R* v *Hunt* [1987] AC 352, HL; *R* v *K(M)*; *R* v *Gega* [2019] QB 86, [2018] EWCA Crim 667.

[145] *Sheldrake* v *DPP* [2005] 1 AC 264, [2004] UKHL 43; *R* v *Lambert* [2002] 2 AC 545, HL; *DPP* v *Wright (Anthony)* [2009] 3 All ER 726, [2009] EWHC 105 (Admin).

[146] GR Sullivan, 'Parents and their Truanting Children' (n 15) 293 (advancing 'a non-normative line of attack' underpinned by 'non-normative critique').

[147] ibid.

[148] cf RA Duff, L Farmer, SE Marshall and V Tadros, *The Trial on Trial: Towards a Normative Theory of the Criminal Trial* (Oxford, Hart Publishing, 2007) (avowedly *normative* ambitions).

or comprehensive[149]) the viability and analytical value of a general conceptual analysis.

Concepts should be judged contextually and relative to their uses. In the context of criminal jurisprudence, a useful concept of the trial must be sufficiently capacious to accommodate a variety of paradigm instances but without becoming conceptually incontinent or vacuously uninformative. On the account developed here, trials are, roughly, epistemically serious institutional mechanisms for (legitimate) dispute resolution with outcome jeopardy. Criminal trials are, by derivation, epistemically serious institutional mechanisms for the legitimate resolution of disputed allegations of criminal wrongdoing by responsible agents, with verdict jeopardy.[150] This conception of the concept of (criminal) trial underscores the importance of rational inquiry and evidential warrant in adjudicative outcomes claiming legitimacy, where pacific dispute resolution demands that criminal verdicts be *demonstrably* justifiable – not merely supported by good reasons. In functional terms, our conceptual reconstruction established criteria for distinguishing constitutive from merely contingent features of trial practice (which do *not* map neatly onto the most emblematic or celebrated aspects of procedural traditions), clarified why show trials are not trials, and yielded some non-obvious analytical results, including identifying an intriguing (and still largely unexplored) intersection between the theoretical concept of a criminal trial and the human rights law concept of a fair trial. The concept of a trial, we saw, also partly incorporates rule of law values. However, this normative component must be strictly policed to avoid pre-empting legitimate arguments or foreclosing live controversies in criminal law theory, policy or practice. 'Criminal trial', then, is a Goldilocks concept: it must be calibrated at just the right level of generality, neither too broad nor too narrow, to serve its intended purposes.

Sullivan and I are substantially in agreement about the basic tenets of liberal criminal law.[151] We both think that criminal liability should be reserved for responsible agents who deserve condemnation for (serious) wrongdoing. We agree that 'wrongdoing' of the relevant kind must be confined to forms of conduct for which an agent can properly be held (criminally) responsible, and this stipulation rules out liability for many things (including involuntary behaviour, future conduct, and the weather). On the procedural side, we agree that criminal liability should not

[149] One respect in which the foregoing account is somewhat vague and non-committal concerns the distinction between the constitutive elements of a concept of criminal trial, and its necessary preconditions or assumptions. I hope to clarify this in future work.

[150] More precisely, I proposed that criminal trials are (1) institutionalised, formal, and legitimacy-claiming (2) conflict-resolution mechanisms conducted as (3) epistemically serious inquiries into (4) alleged criminal wrongdoing by (5) responsible agents entailing (6) verdict jeopardy. Note, however, that greater precision increases complexity, and does not necessarily enhance intelligibility of core claims.

[151] P Roberts, 'Criminal Law Theory and the Limits of Liberalism' in AP Simester, A du Bois-Pedain and U Neumann (eds), *Liberal Criminal Theory: Essays for Andreas von Hirsch* (Oxford, Hart Publishing, 2014).

be imposed without proof of each element of the offence. Diagnosis of lingering disagreement converged on three issues: (1) the rigour of the 'conduct' requirement in its application to particular offences; (2) the competent jurisdiction of ECHR Article 6(2)'s presumption of innocence; and (3) the scope, in English law or otherwise, for invoking purely conceptual objections to excessively broad criminal liability. Proceeding chiefly along the third, methodological axis, this essay directly engaged with Sullivan's central thesis proposing 'conduct' and 'proof of conduct' as two conceptual preconditions of legitimate criminal convictions and authentic criminal trials.

Conceptual analysis is an essential tool in the jurist's toolkit and a staple of legal doctrinal method. Just about any notable concept can benefit from conceptual elucidation.[152] Sullivan's attempt to leverage conceptual analysis into an argument about the scope of the substantive criminal law and the institutional purchase of the presumption of innocence is a typically bold and imaginative methodological gambit. Compared with Sullivan's apparently muscular contrivance, however, my concept of the trial is relatively thin, abstract and ill-equipped for doctrinal heavy-lifting. It could not bear the weight of the jurisprudential and institutional conclusions that Sullivan wants to claim for his conceptual preferences. Though it is possible to envisage very extreme scenarios in which violations of the presumption of innocence would undercut the status of a criminal trial (e.g because they would destroy epistemic seriousness and/or verdict jeopardy), such thought experiments are very far removed from the real-life litigated cases thrown up by post-HRA 1998 jurisprudence. When it moves from abstract theoretical speculation to concrete illustrations, Sullivan's conceptual argument becomes, in my terms, *conceptualist*: a form of argumentation trading on the false promise to deliver through peremptory conceptual analysis what can only be obtained by more extended normative (political morality) argument and institutional (jurisprudential and doctrinal) reasoning.

In reflective mood, Sullivan muses that 'conceptual critique [may] have as little effect on legislators and policy makers as the more familiar normative critiques'.[153] My hunch, for what it is worth, inverts this rhetorical priority: if the argument for liberal criminal law fails to carry the day through direct appeal to political morality and jurisprudential tradition,[154] informing policymakers that their opposition is incoherent, illogical or a categorical impossibility is unlikely to shift opinion. Likewise, if judges cannot be persuaded to utilise the familiar interpretative tools at their disposal in order to tether criminal offence definitions to cohere with – or

[152] For the ultimate proof, see HG Frankfurt, *The Importance of What We Care About: Philosophical Essays* (Cambridge, Cambridge University Press, 1988) ch 10 ('On Bullshit').

[153] Sullivan, 'Parents and their Truanting Children' (n 15) 303.

[154] Sullivan, 'Strict Liability for Criminal Offences in England and Wales' (n 25) 213 succinctly encapsulates several of the best arguments: 'It would be a flagrant breach of the harm principle to penalize persons merely suspected of being associated with an immediate or more remote harm …. It is an essential safeguard of liberal democracy that persons merely under suspicion should not be obliged, on pain of conviction and punishment, to clear their name'.

at least better approximate – judgements of moral culpability for conduct, I cannot see how appealing to a conception of 'conduct' with minimal doctrinal recognition is going to exert any additional institutional pressure. Right and wrong can be debated; conceptual incoherence is a conversational guillotine inviting forensic stalemate.

Being wrong is an occupational hazard of theoretical work. On a clear-eyed view, most of the philosophical giants of the Enlightenment made major theoretical errors. Kant: wrong about the rigour of deontological ethics; Hume: wrong about the limits of reason; Bentham: promiscuously wrong on diverse subjects, at inordinate length, in spidery handwriting. In contrast to legal doctrinal analysis, where being right is at a premium (few clients or judges award style points for wrong advice or faulty legal submissions), the best theoretical work may be valued for its imagination, innovation, pioneering exploration, provocation to engagement, potential for development, fecundity in spawning research programmes, productive error, or glorious failure. Is it better to be right or interesting in theorising criminal law, if you can't be both? That could be an intriguing topic for another round of conceptual analysis, but the question could only be settled by normative argument.

11

Why Fraud Prevention is Relevant to Criminal Law Theorists

JENNIFER COLLINS*

A volume on modern criminal law is an opportunity to probe and explore the boundaries of the criminal law. Which phenomena do we have an inadequate understanding of? How can principle be brought to bear on them?

The focus of this chapter is on fraud – one part of the larger issue of 'economic crime'.[1] Fraud is now the highest volume crime in England and Wales: its incidence in the first half of 2021 was described by UK Finance as a 'national security threat'.[2] Fresh study of fraud by criminal law theorists should inform a new strategic response to fraud in England and Wales. The chapter scrutinises an emerging key focus on pre-empting and preventing fraud. Rather than classifying these as non-coercive regulatory measures, I argue that these measures have created a complex preventive interface, one deserving of attention from criminal law theorists. Limits need to be placed on the preventive role entrusted to public–private partnerships in particular, and upon their use of emerging technologies, to prevent fraud.

In what follows, section I puts fraud in focus, identifying recent changes in the volume, nature and complexity of fraud. Section II identifies an emergent focus on fraud-prevention, illustrated most clearly in the *Economic Crime Plan 2019 to 2022*. It argues that this new fraud-prevention interface has been supported by two under-theorised developments: (1) a strong push towards public–private partnerships to prevent fraud, and (2) the use of artificial intelligence (AI) and machine learning (ML) technologies. Section III unpacks the complexity of this interface,

* Funding for this work was received from AHRC AH/V014781/1. Thanks to Andrew Simester for incisive comments on a draft, and to Bonnie Venter for research assistance.

[1] Which includes money laundering, bribery, corruption and illicit financing. HM Treasury, *Economic Crime Plan 2019 to 2022*, www.gov.uk/government/publications/economic-crime-plan-2019-to-2022/economic-crime-plan-2019-to-2022-accessible-version (accessed 16 March 2022).

[2] UK Finance, 'Government-coordinated Action Needed as Fraud Losses Rise by 30 Percent' (22 September 2021) www.ukfinance.org.uk/press/press-releases/government-coordinated-action-needed-fraud-losses-rise-30-cent (accessed 16 March 2022).

shedding light on what is at stake for criminal law theorists. AI technologies, and public–private partnerships, are rapidly facilitating a new 'fraud-prevention' infrastructure, without clear limits on their interaction with the criminal law and criminal justice system. Section IV enumerates key principles, arguing that privacy, transparency and explainability must be respected. Section V argues that analysis of real-world examples about fraud prevention can lead a criminal law theorist to a richer theoretical account about the nature of fraud in England and Wales.

I. Fraud in Focus

It is fitting in a volume dedicated to Professor Sullivan's work that attention is given to the topic of fraud. He is responsible for multiple forward-looking analyses of the topic which have informed fraud criminalisation and governance in England and Wales.[3] His meticulous theoretical work with Andrew Simester developed my own interest in dishonesty offences as a graduate student in Oxford.[4] The next generation of criminal law scholars should aspire to emulate Professor Sullivan's ability to weave together focus on criminal law theory with firm sight of necessary practical applications. Few will do so as successfully as Professor Sullivan. I offer the present chapter in this spirit.

Why reprioritise the study of fraud now? Statistics show that fraud is on the rise. Fraud now makes up 42 percent of crimes against individuals in England.[5] When combined with cybercrime, it accounts for over 50 percent of all reported crime in England and Wales.[6] There were 4.6 million fraud offences recorded in the year ending March 2021.[7] Early indicators are that fraud represents the largest volume of crime emerging from the COVID-19 crisis, targeting both the public and private sectors. Action Fraud (the UK's National Fraud and Cyber Crime Reporting Centre) reported a 36 percent rise in fraud offences between June 2020 and June 2021.[8] Overall, between June 2019 and June 2021, there was a 43 percent increase in fraud and computer misuse.[9] Estimated losses incurred as a result of

[3] GR Sullivan, 'Reforming the Substantive Law of Fraud' (1988) 52 *Journal of Criminal Law* 288; GR Sullivan, 'Framing an Acceptable General Offence of Fraud' (1989) 53 *Journal of Criminal Law* 92; GR Sullivan and AP Simester, 'Judging Dishonesty' (2020) 136 *LQR* 523.

[4] AP Simester and GR Sullivan, 'On the Nature and Rationale of Property Offences' in RA Duff and S Green (eds), *Defining Crimes: Essays on The Special Part of Criminal Law* (Oxford, Oxford University Press, 2005).

[5] *Crime in England and Wales: Year Ending September 2021*, Table A2, www.ons.gov.uk/peoplepopulationandcommunity/crimeandjustice/datasets/crimeinenglandandwalesappendixtable (accessed 16 March 2022).

[6] ibid.

[7] UK Finance, *Fraud – The Facts 2021* (2021) www.ukfinance.org.uk/policy-and-guidance/reports-publications/fraud-facts-2021 (accessed 16 March 2022).

[8] National Crime Agency, *Money Laundering and Illicit Finance*, www.nationalcrimeagency.gov.uk/what-we-do/crime-threats/money-laundering-and-illicit-finance (accessed 16 March 2022) 23.

[9] HM Treasury (n 1) [12].

fraud are significant. UK Finance estimates that in the first half of 2021 alone, £753.9 million was stolen through fraud,[10] an increase of 30 percent compared with the first half of 2020. Modelling predicts that fraud costs the UK economy at least £4.7 billion per year.[11] The government is estimated to have lost £4.9 billion to fraud through the COVID-19 Bounce Back Loan Scheme alone.[12]

Against this background of prevalence, the nature of fraud is rapidly changing. The majority of fraud is now cyber-enabled, a trend accelerated by the COVID-19 pandemic.[13] A global health pandemic and resulting restrictions has made direct access to individuals and businesses readily available online. This has enabled fraudsters to adapt and to develop fraudulent schemes for the online environment, making use of emerging technologies in support.[14] Authorised push payment fraud involves pressuring individuals to transfer money into electronic accounts that are not legitimate:[15] it is now the most prevalent form of reported cyber-enabled fraud.[16] There have also been significant increases in reported advance fee scams, romance scams, investment scams and impersonation scams.[17] Across these forms of fraudulent wrongdoing, there have been notable increases in the losses caused.[18] The pandemic has led to new vulnerabilities to fraud, in some instances linked to isolation or economic uncertainty.[19] Individuals who are unfamiliar with online technologies have been particular targets.[20] Some of the most predictable examples of this have been linked to fraudsters preying on fears created by the pandemic. (Cifas notes the example of a phishing campaign using Microsoft's Office 365 software.[21] The campaign offered information about the COVID-19 pandemic, requiring individuals to provide personal details in exchange.) Businesses and organisations have also experienced vulnerability to fraud in new ways. Phishing schemes have been prevalent, and so has dishonest conduct linked to remote and hybrid working arrangements.[22] Fraudulent scams

[10] UK Finance (n 2).

[11] National Crime Agency, *National Strategic Assessment of Serious and Organised Crime 2021*, https://nationalcrimeagency.gov.uk/who-we-are/publications/533-national-strategic-assessment-of-serious-and-organised-crime-2021/file (accessed 16 March 2022).

[12] Report by the Comptroller and Auditor General, 'The Bounce Back Scheme: An Update' HC 861 (2021–22) (3 December 2021) 4.

[13] HC 145 Treasury Committee, *Economic Crime* (2 February 2022) [18], [62].

[14] Cifas, *Fraudscape 2022* (April 2022).

[15] Lloyds Bank, 'Fighting Fraud in the Age of AI' (2018) www.lloydsbankcardnet.com/insight-series/innovation-in-payments/ai-and-the-future-of-fraud-prevention.html (accessed 16 March 2022).

[16] UK Finance (n 7).

[17] Treasury Committee (n 13) [18], drawing on statistics from UK Finance (n 7).

[18] ibid.

[19] M Levi and RG Smith, 'Fraud and its Relationship to Pandemics and Economic Crises: From Spanish Flu to Covid-19' Australian Institute of Criminology Research Report No 19 (2021) www.aic.gov.au/publications/rr/rr19 (accessed 16 March 2022).

[20] Cifas (n 14).

[21] Financier Worldwide, 'Q and A: Fraud Risk and Enforcement in the UK' (July 2020) www.financierworldwide.com/qa-fraud-risk-and-enforcement-in-the-uk#.YlA0GOlKi4k (accessed 16 March 2022).

[22] Cifas (n 14).

involving cryptocurrencies and cryptoassets have increased, as have online scams linked to the pandemic involving personal protective equipment (PPE) and false vaccination information.[23]

Adding to this picture is a complex and pressured fraud governance structure in England and Wales. There are well-known difficulties with resource. Despite its scale, currently only 1 percent of police spending goes on fraud.[24] Processing fraud cases through the criminal justice system has been particularly problematic, something exacerbated by the pandemic. The government's *Economic Crime Plan 2019 to 2022* committed to launching a flagship Economic Crime Court in central London by 2026, but its funding has not yet been confirmed.[25] The substantial number of bodies involved in fraud governance has been strongly criticised as 'bewildering', and has led to calls for a single agency to lead in building a strategic response to fraud.[26]

The future trajectory of fraud governance is uncertain. Of the fifty-two action points set out in the *Economic Crime Plan 2019 to 2022*, only seven relate to fraud. There is a pressing need for a new iteration of an economic crime plan that addresses fraud in a strategic way beyond 2022. As yet, none is forthcoming.[27] The Joint Fraud Taskforce was relaunched in October 2021 but has been criticised for meeting infrequently. It is not a stretch to question the political will for strategic governance. The estimated £4.9 billion loss incurred through the COVID-19 Bounce Back Loan Scheme was swiftly written-off.[28] Lord Agnew, the Joint Treasury and Cabinet Office Minister for Efficiency and Transformation, resigned as a result. He argued that 'the government machine has failed spectacularly … for allowing such dysfunctionality to continue on such a colossal scale'.[29] Alongside governance failures, there are questions whether existing criminal law measures are sufficient to target fraud.[30] It is seen as politically important to criminalise fraud, as well as imperative to recover the proceeds of crime. This can lead to fraud becoming a site of reactionary legislation.

Fraud sits front and centre as a criminal law issue that requires systematic analysis by criminal law theorists. Which principles should inform fraud

[23] C McGinn, 'Travel: Fraud' (UK Parliament: Written question 24 May 2021) UIN 6343, https://questions-statements.parliament.uk/written-questions/detail/2021-05-24/6343/ (accessed 16 March 2022).

[24] HC 145 Treasury Committee (n 13) [19], [38], and [53].

[25] HM Treasury (n 1) [5.7], [5.23]–[5.24]; O Bennett and A Shalchi, *Economic Crime in the UK: A Multi-billion Pound Problem*, HC Library No Cb 9013 (6 April 2022).

[26] HC 145 Treasury Committee (n 13) [50], [56]; K Beioley, 'MPs Call for Single Agency to Fight Fraud and Economic Crime', *Financial Times*, 2 February 2022.

[27] HC 145 Treasury Committee (n 13) 3, recommends that the current Plan be adapted and renewed for a further three years.

[28] T Agnew, 'Fraud Is Rampant – And No One in Government Is Paying Attention', *Financial Times*, 24 January 2022.

[29] ibid.

[30] eg Online Safety Bill, https://bills.parliament.uk/bills/3137 (accessed 16 March 2022); Economic Crime (Transparency and Enforcement) Act 2022, https://bills.parliament.uk/bills/3120 (accessed 7 April 2022).

criminalisation and governance as we emerge from the COVID-19 pandemic, to meet the challenges of a digital age and a stretched criminal justice system? In this chapter I take the view that forming a strategic and principled response to fraud is not simply about whether existing criminal law offences are sufficient. What lies on the periphery of the criminal law in terms of fraud prevention must be guided by principle too.

II. Preventing Fraud with Public–Private Partnerships and AI/ML Technologies

Alongside discussion of new coercive measures to penalise fraud is a recent strong emphasis on *fraud prevention*. This is evident in some of the *Economic Crime Plan 2019 to 22*'s priority areas.[31] A context of 'ontological insecurity'[32] underlies a strong push towards fraud prevention, using a range of actors in this preventive task. The destabilizing impact of fraud on a system of property rights is of wider public concern, as well as having significant impact on victims.[33] The rationale that fraud should be prevented before it reaches the criminal law is clear, and capable of attracting support from both public and private sectors.

In this section, I highlight two under-theorised means of preventing fraud.[34] First, the private sector has been quickly enlisted through public–private partnerships. Second, fraud prevention is being facilitated by use of AI and ML technologies. Both represent areas of rapid change, with swift real-world implementation. Transparency in identifying these preventive means is a key first step for criminal law theory. Notably, neither development was discussed in the Treasury Committee's February 2022 report on *Economic Crime*.[35]

Public–Private Partnerships

The government has pushed to formalise and strengthen collaboration to prevent fraud through public–private partnerships. The current *Economic Crime Plan* identifies such partnerships as the future of fighting fraud in England and Wales,

[31] HM Treasury (n 1); Home Office, 'Economic Crime Plan: Statement of Progress July 2019–February 2021' (April 2021) www.gov.uk/government/publications/economic-crime-plan-2019-to-2022, [1.11] (accessed 16 March 2022).

[32] A concept used by A Giddens, *The Consequences of Modernity* (Cambridge, Polity Press 1990) 92, to explain lack of confidence in oneself, as well as in 'the constancy of the surrounding social and material environments of action'.

[33] See House of Lords Fraud Act 2006 and Digital Fraud Committee, *Select Committee with Joe Lycett* (7 April 2022).

[34] These are illustrative examples rather than exhaustive.

[35] HM Treasury (n 1).

a position endorsed by the Joint Fraud Taskforce.[36] The Treasury Committee's report on *Economic Crime* is emphatic that 'a public–private partnership approach is needed' and that partnerships should be a key feature of a new iteration of an Economic Crime Plan.[37] Public–private partnerships signal a move away from public enforcement of fraud-related measures, instead giving the private sector a 'reactive market-fixing role' via regulation.[38] They formalise relationships in which value is created through supporting shared aims. In the case of fraud prevention, these lie in ensuring stability in the marketplace and protection for individuals operating therein. Gatekeeper responsibility is placed on the private sector, which comes under a positive duty to advance the shared aims.

There are efficiency gains for the criminal justice system in using data and intelligence held, or accessible, by the private sector to prevent fraud, given the latter's access to resources for surveillance, data collection and intelligence about suspicious transactions. For example, there is particular enthusiasm to expand the role of public–private partnerships in preventing online fraud, because the private sector has access to information about how online platforms are being used.[39] In relation to the Bounce Back Loans scheme, referred to in section I above, public-sector data was used alongside 'syndicated adverse intelligence from the private sector' to identify several million pounds worth of fraudulent loans.[40] Bodies responsible for fraud prevention have highlighted the untapped potential of partnerships in preventing fraud. UK Finance notes that a number of commercial and not-for-profit entities 'hold cross-sector adverse intelligence' about fraud, with current data-sharing partnerships under review by the Cabinet Office.[41] It argues boldly that:

> The opportunity for collaboration across so many more public and private sector bodies could yield incredible results if only we could develop the appropriate eco-system to facilitate this. The technology is available now to support this collaboration, it is all our responsibility to remove the remaining barriers.[42]

Public–private partnerships are already widely used as means of preventing money laundering.[43] The Joint Money Laundering Intelligence Task Force (JMLIT)

[36] HM Treasury (n 1) strategic priority 4; T Prenzler and R Sarre, 'Public–Private Crime Prevention Partnerships' in T Prenzler (ed), *Policing and Security in Practice: Challenges and Achievements* (New York, Palgrave Macmillan, 2012) 149–67.

[37] HC 145 Treasury Committee (n 13) [103]–[105].

[38] A Keller, 'The Public Role of Banks – A New Narrative Born?' (2022) 37 *Journal of International Banking Law and Regulation* 4.

[39] Cifas (n 14).

[40] UK Finance, 'Public/Private Collaboration: Why Is it So Hard to Get Right?' (September 2021) www.ukfinance.org.uk/news-and-insight/blogs/public-private-collaboration-why-it-so-hard-get-right (accessed 16 March 2022).

[41] ibid.

[42] ibid.

[43] RUSI and The Future of Financial Information Sharing, 'Five Years of Growth in Public–Private Partnerships to Fight Financial Crimes' (August 2020) www.future-fis.com/uploads/3/7/9/4/3794525/

was launched in 2015. It is a collaboration between banks, the National Crime Agency and the Financial Conduct Authority (FCA). By June 2020, JMLIT investigations had led to closure of 3400 bank accounts, seizure of £56 million in assets and 210 arrests.[44]

Two key questions immediately present. First, what is information gleaned from public–private partnerships used for? On the one hand, partnerships can allow for 'strategic intelligence sharing'.[45] This involves the creation of a knowledge product about a particular fraud threat. It could, for example, involve identifying behavioural flags for potentially fraudulent conduct.[46] Strategic intelligence sharing does not tend to involve confidential information that could aid identification of 'specific suspects or entities, or individual clients or customers of financial institutions'.[47] In most circumstances it does not require regulation using regulatory frameworks. The results could be available to non-partners (eg online), or 'released through non-public distribution channels to regulated entities (such as in the United Kingdom or Hong Kong)'.[48] On the other hand, and more controversially, public–private partnerships can allow for 'tactical information sharing' with law enforcement or intelligence agencies; this does require compliance with regulatory frameworks. Information sharing in this instance is more targeted. In England and Wales, sensitive information can be shared with law enforcement through the Suspicious Activity Reports (SARs) system.[49] Depending on the details of the partnership, Keller notes that sensitive information can also be shared 'dynamically within the partnership'.[50]

The second question follows: how are public–private partnerships governed? It is a strategic priority in the *Economic Crime Plan 2019 to 2022* to 'promote information-sharing between public and private sectors for the purposes of preventing fraud'.[51] However, there are privacy and confidentiality concerns where potentially sensitive datasets are collected and/or shared by public–private partnerships. In many cases this will require more than voluntary charters to ensure adequate regulation. For example, there may need to be privacy controls where tactical information is shared. This is of current relevance: the Treasury Committee's February 2022 report highlighted that it was concerned to 'ensure that regulators and law

five_years_of_growth_of_public-private_partnerships_to_fight_financial_crime_-_18_aug_2020.pdf (accessed 16 March 2022) 48.

[44] UK Finance, 'Information Fusion in the Fight Against Financial Crime' (March 2021) www.ukfinance.org.uk/news-and-insight/blogs/information-fusion-fight-against-financial-crime (accessed 16 March 2022).

[45] Keller (n 38).

[46] ibid 13.

[47] ibid 13.

[48] ibid 13.

[49] The Suspicious Activity Reports system, ibid 13. The UK Fraud Intelligence Unit (UKFIU) receives intelligence gathered from SARs, in some cases passing on to law enforcement or other approved agencies for further analysis.

[50] Keller (n 38) 13.

[51] HM Treasury (n 1) strategic priority 2 (supported by action point 10).

enforcement agencies have the powers they need to ensure that online companies provide them with information and comply with regulatory requirements'.[52] As things stand, emerging technologies have the potential to enable collaboration without banks 'risking statutory data privacy infringement and the long-standing duty of confidentiality to their customers'.[53] Yet that benefit is not unequivocal; it is not without downsides. As I argue below, the utility of information gleaned by technological developments in countering fraud cannot ipso facto provide justification for its use. There must be careful engagement with the interests at stake, enumerating how those interests will be protected.

AI and ML Technologies

In addition to the development of public–private relationships, another key trend in recent years is linked to increases in cyberfraud during, and emerging from, the COVID-19 pandemic. This is the rapid turn by the private sector to AI and ML technologies to detect and prevent fraud.[54] The AI sector is burgeoning in the United Kingdom – there are an estimated 1300 AI companies in operation.[55] The adoption of AI across the private sector is set to grow significantly, given that emerging technologies have become more accessible as costs have come down.[56] A 2019 Bank of England survey found that two-thirds of financial institutions surveyed used some form of ML, covering a number of tasks already undertaken in banks.[57] For example, UK Finance currently uses 'AI and machine learning to track and detect economic crimes going on in the UK, specifically fraud, money laundering and mule accounts'.[58] The Australian government uses AI and ML to detect fraudulent schemes related to economic stimulus programmes.[59] A key benefit is the preventive potential in relation to fraud. Technologies can prevent fraud before it happens.

This preventive turn using technology is closely linked to the push towards public–private partnerships outlined above. AI and ML technologies are key to the way in which the private sector is collecting data, to pass on to its partners in the public sector. For example, the National Crime Security Centre has contracts with private-sector companies to collect intelligence from online traffic

[52] HC 145 Treasury Committee (n 13) [103]–[105].

[53] Keller (n 38).

[54] Bank of England, 'The AI Public–Private Forum: Final Report' (2022) 11.

[55] Talent Nation Applied AI, 'The UK and Artificial Intelligence: What's Next?', https://technation.io/news/talent-key-to-helping-ai-sector-unlock-huge-opportunity/ (accessed 16 March 2022).

[56] Department for Digital, Culture, Media and Sport, 'AI Activity in UK Businesses' (January 2022) 3, estimates an increase in adoption rate of AI from '15.1% in 2020 to 22.7% in 2025, with an additional 267,000 businesses using AI in their operations'. This is in the report's modelling of the 'central scenario'.

[57] GB Buchanan and D Wright, 'The Impact of Machine Learning on UK Financial Services' (2021) 37 *Oxford Review of Economic Policy* 527.

[58] HC 145 Treasury Committee (n 13) [50].

[59] Levi and Smith (n 19) 51.

to support pre-emption work of the National Economic Crime Centre (NECC). Public–private partnerships have come together to develop 'shared data platforms, reporting protocols and feedback loops' to detect and prevent fraud.[60] Beyond these existing practices, there are ambitions for more extensive use of AI and ML by the *public* sector. The *Economic Crime Plan to 2019 to 2022* sets out to invest £48 million into tackling economic crime, including by 'establishing the National Data Exploitation Capability (NDEC) in the NCA, which will harness analytics, automation, machine learning, bulk data ingestion and algorithms to improve our exploitation of data'.[61]

Several questions arise. Amongst them, what is meant by AI and ML? And how is information collected by emerging technologies then used to prevent fraud?

On the former question, AI is a rapidly evolving umbrella term. It includes the 'use of advanced statistical techniques with large computational and data needs'.[62] At minimum, a 'non-natural entity' is involved in making 'choices by an evaluative process'.[63] The choices made from this process could be supervised (by human input) or unsupervised (without human input).[64] For example, a non-natural entity could use 'statistics to find patterns in large amounts of data'.[65] Or a non-natural entity could develop the 'ability' to perform repetitive tasks with data without the need for constant human guidance'.[66]

ML is a subset of AI. It sits alongside non-traditional data and automation as subcategories of AI. ML involves 'development of AI systems that are able to perform tasks as a result of a "learning" process that relies on data'.[67] Some uses of ML simply automate traditional statistical methods. For example, it can be used for what is called 'traditional data analysis': that is, for detection tasks where there is precedent for using data in this way.[68] The ML in this context is 'focused on identifying the occurrence of phenomena of interest, often through the detection of outliers or anomalies in data'.[69] This usage has already been effective in the fields of fraud and money-laundering.[70] At the other end of the spectrum, signifying new

[60] L Quest et al, 'The Risks and Benefits of Using AI to Detect Crime', *Harvard Business Review*, August 2018, https://hbr.org/2018/08/the-risks-and-benefits-of-using-ai-to-detect-crime (accessed 16 March 2022).

[61] HM Treasury (n 1).

[62] Bank of England (n 54) 10.

[63] J Turner, *Robot Rules: Regulating Artificial Intelligence* (London, Palgrave Macmillan 2019) 16.

[64] International Public Sector Fraud Forum, 'The Use of Artificial Intelligence to Combat Public Sector Fraud: Professional Guidance' (February 2020) https://assets.publishing.service.gov.uk/government/uploads/system/uploads/attachment_data/file/865721/Artificial_intelligence_13_Feb.pdf (accessed 16 March 2022) 9.

[65] ibid 9.

[66] ibid 9.

[67] Alan Turing Institute, 'AI in Financial Services' (2021) www.turing.ac.uk/sites/default/files/2021-06/ati_ai_in_financial_services_lores.pdf (accessed 16 March 2022) [2.2].

[68] ibid [2.3].

[69] ibid [2.3].

[70] ibid [2.2.2.1]. For example, see M Jullum et al, 'Detecting Money Laundering Transactions with Machine Learning' (2020) 23 *Journal of Money Laundering Control* 173.

innovation, is the use of supervised and unsupervised ML as a means of detecting fraud.[71] Machine learning systems (MLSs) can use computer algorithms that 'learn' patterns in databases containing large amounts of data, bringing together information from different 'silos'. This enables prediction and/or detection of potentially fraudulent transactions or scenarios in real-time. 'Supervised MLS can be used when the company knows which data is fraudulent and the MLS then attempts to learn the patterns in this data.'[72] By contrast, unsupervised MLSs work with previously unconnected datasets, where there is not yet recognition of fraudulent patterns in data at the point at which the ML is deployed. Unsupervised MLSs are used in the context of fraud and money-laundering to 'learn' what amounts to a suspicious transaction by analysing datasets and attaching labels to suspicious conduct. Updates to the accuracy of labels attached allows the ML systems to improve their accuracy over time.[73] The predictive element to this technology raises novel ethical issues for criminal lawyers.

Typically, ML systems are designed to prevent fraud by combining aspects of both supervised and unsupervised systems. For example, ML is widely used as a means of detecting credit-card fraud.[74] Using historical data about previous suspicious transactions, algorithms are programmed to highlight suspicious activity in real-time. AI, such as Mastercard's VocaLink technology, is used to detect mule accounts[75] Lloyds Banking Group uses Pindrops Phoneprinting™ technology. It enables the bank to analyse 147 features from calls received, using these features to produce 'audio fingerprints'.[76] 'Audio fingerprints' are then linked to a risk score for fraud.[77] AI technologies are advancing with rapidity, allowing for more invasive interventions. For example, several banks are looking at using 'behaviour biometrics' to identify fraud. This involves using AI technology which 'monitors the ways in which consumers type and swipe on their devices or how they hold their device in terms of grip, when logged into banking apps'.[78] If the technology identifies irregular changes in behaviour, the transaction will be flagged by the bank.[79]

[71] Alan Turing Institute (n 67) [2.2.2].

[72] ibid.

[73] Databricks, 'Detecting Financial Fraud at Scale with Machine Learning' (7 August 2019) https://databricks.com/session_eu19/detecting-financial-fraud-at-scale-with-machine-learning (accessed 16 March 2022).

[74] 'The Power of Data: How PayPal Leverages Machine Learning to Tackle Fraud' (22 December 2022) www.paypal.com/us/brc/article/enterprise-solutions-paypal-machine-learning-stop-fraud (accessed 16 March 2022).

[75] ICAEW, 'Fighting Fraud With AI' (March 2021) www.icaew.com/insights/viewpoints-on-the-news/2021/mar-2021/fighting-fraud-with-artificial-intelligence (accessed 16 March 2022). Mule accounts are a means of rapidly transferring illegally acquired money, often facilitated by bots.

[76] Lloyds Bank, 'AI and the Future of Fraud Prevention' (October 2018) www.lloydsbankcardnet.com/assets/content/pdf/lloyds_ai_fraud_whitepaper.pdf (accessed 16 March 2022) 3.

[77] ibid.

[78] UK Finance, *Fraud – The Facts 2021* (n 7) 15.

[79] ibid. See also Bank of England and FCA, 'Machine Learning in UK Financial Services' (2019) 28–29.

The second question follows: what is information collected by AI and ML technologies then used to do? For financial institutions such as banks, information gleaned can affect onboarding or de-risking decisions. Onboarding concerns whether to take on a customer in the first place.[80] De-risking involves a financial institution ending a relationship with a customer because it deems that that customer poses too high a risk of economic crime.[81] Financial institutions can flag potentially fraudulent conduct using emerging technologies, passing the signal on to the criminal justice system through the SARs system.[82] Suspicious activity is evaluated by specialist fraud teams at the UK Fraud Intelligence Unit (UKFIU), who in most cases send information on to law enforcement or other approved bodies for investigation.[83]

It is important to emphasise that not all information gleaned using emerging technologies is shared. The Chairperson of the Fraud Advisory Panel has recently lamented that: 'There is technology available to identify [online fraud] and the big tech companies do not use it. They keep the data, but they do not show you it. They take down stuff. … Technology could be switched on tomorrow to protect the customer.'[84] Prevention-minded concerns such as these feed into a strong push by law enforcement to 'better harness and enable the use of technology to detect, disrupt and deter crime'.[85] We could, and it is urged should, do more. A number of bodies are currently looking into this.[86] But should we do *all* that we can? In what follows, I argue that principles are needed to regulate fraud-prevention measures, to control some of potential costs that they impose upon individuals and the wider community.

III. Why Fraud Prevention Is Relevant to Criminal Law Theorists

Public–private partnerships, using AI and ML technologies, are rapidly facilitating a new 'fraud-prevention' infrastructure, without clear limits to its interactions with the criminal law and criminal justice system. Two underexplored interactions are highlighted in this section. Underlying the concerns identified here is the in-principle point that 'fraud-prevention' measures cannot simply be theorised

[80] S Nandi. 'Fraud and Financial Crime Reduction in Banking with AI' (December 2020) www.rtinsights.com/fraud-and-financial-crime-reduction-in-banking-with-ai/ (accessed 16 March 2022).

[81] HC 145 Treasury Committee (n 13) [180].

[82] National Crime Agency, *Suspicious Activity Reports*, www.nationalcrimeagency.gov.uk/what-we-do/crime-threats/money-laundering-and-illicit-finance/suspicious-activity-reports (accessed 16 March 2022).

[83] HC 145 Treasury Committee (n 13) [50]. The SARs regime is currently undergoing reform (see action 30 of the *Economic Crime Plan* (n 1)).

[84] HC 145 Treasury Committee (n 13) [135].

[85] ibid 5.

[86] Bank of England (n 54) 13, for discussion of the *UK National AI Strategy* (September 2021).

as non-coercive, 'regulatory' measures. The boundary between 'regulatory' and criminal law measures has become more porous with private-sector involvement and technological advancement.

How Suspected 'Fraud' Is Identified: The Need for Consistency

A first concern involves consistency of approach in identifying suspected fraud. The involvement of the private sector in this task via public–private partnerships is not neutral. Complex incentive and disincentive structures motivate private-sector involvement. In turn, this affects when and if suspected fraud is identified. On the incentive side, the private sector stands to profit through 'information production' by flagging suspected fraud.[87] Keller notes that this has created a growth industry in fraud detection, particularly for large firms which can benefit from economies of scale in setting up fraud-detection systems. However, public–private partnerships are susceptible to policy capture, which can reduce incentives towards fraud reporting in certain circumstances.[88] For example, private-sector entities such as banks may hold obligations to law enforcement through the establishment of partnerships, but they also operate under obligations of loyalty to their customers as well as to their shareholders, and these obligations may conflict.[89] This is of concern because there are significant exclusionary or stigmatic effects for individuals where suspected fraud is identified and/or passed on via SARs. In order to be sure that there is consistency of approach in suspected fraud identification, one challenge for criminal law theorists is to push for exploration of 'exactly what functions are being privatized', and of how public–private partnerships are incentivised.[90] The extent and duties of the private sector's 'responsibilisation' for fraud detection should be addressed in a new iteration of an Economic Crime Plan.

Another consistency concern arises about how suspected fraud is identified. A central issue here lies in ensuring the accuracy of AI and/or ML technologies in identifying fraud, and their potential to replicate bias.[91] This carries significant implications for individuals, such as through barring them from loan or mortgage access because of AI identifying potential fraud. A recent example is seen in relation to an algorithm applied to identify benefit fraud. The Department for Work and Pensions was asked to explain how 'cutting-edge artificial intelligence',

[87] Keller (n 38) 9.
[88] ibid 12.
[89] ibid 8–9.
[90] J Gilsinan et al, 'The Role of Private Sector Organizations in the Control and Policing of Serious Financial Crime and Abuse' (2008) *Journal of Financial Crime* 111, 122–23.
[91] See 'How Can Algorithms Be Biased?' (8 April 2022) https://philosophicaldisquisitions.blogspot.com/2022/04/how-can-algorithms-be-biased.html (accessed 8 April 2022).

used to identify suspected fraud, had the effect of targeting an unusually large number of individuals with disabilities.[92] The government department refused to explain how the algorithm worked. Charity groups appealed on the basis that certain groups had been disproportionately targeted by the algorithm.[93] Where algorithms are involved, there is always the risk of false positives. This leads to concerns surrounding consistency, accuracy and transparency in using emerging technologies for fraud detection. Of course, inconsistency and inaccuracy are risks that existed prior to the introduction of AI and ML. However, they become significantly more troubling when algorithms introduce them on a much larger and more systematic scale.

Governance of Data Collection and Storage Regarding Suspected Fraud and 'Feed-Into' the Criminal Law/Criminal Justice System

A second concern relates to how information that is collected and stored by public–private partnerships, facilitated by emerging technologies, is then passed onto law enforcement.

There is a pressing need for criminal lawyers to take interest in the coercive consequences of widespread surveillance and data collection. Public–private partnerships can collect a large amount of information specific to individuals in attempts to prevent fraud. This triggers concern about the extent to which individual privacy rights should be sacrificed to disrupt fraud, for the benefit of the collective. It is not only cases where an individual has been suspected of fraud which are of concern, but the wider issues of 'surveillance capitalism', data exploitation and profiling of citizens.[94] In recent times, widespread surveillance using live facial recognition software has led to breaches of the Data Protection Act 2018 and Article 8 of the European Convention on Human Rights.[95] The increasingly pervasive phenomenon of private providers using AI to collect and hold biometrics data carries implications for individuals,[96] and has already led to restrictions on movement for some individuals, without due process having been respected.[97]

[92] 'DWP Urged to Reveal Algorithm That "Targets" Disabled for Benefit Fraud' (21 November 2021) www.theguardian.com/society/2021/nov/21/dwp-urged-to-reveal-algorithm-that-targets-disabled-for-benefit (accessed 16 March 2022).

[93] ibid.

[94] S Zuboff, *The Age of Surveillance Capitalism: The Fight for a Human Future at the New Frontier of Power* (New York, Public Affairs, 2019), which involves collecting information about individual experiences, without payment, so as to create knowledge products.

[95] *R (Bridges) v SWP* [2020] EWCA Civ 1058, breach of DPA 2018, s 64(3)(b)(c).

[96] D Baker and PH Robinson (eds), *Artificial Intelligence and the Law: Cybercrime and Criminal Liability* (Oxford and New York, Routledge, 2021) 7–8.

[97] ibid.

In the case of fraud prevention, individuals' access to essential services may be at stake.[98]

Another potential worry is the extent to which organisations in a partnership are sharing data, and the level and clarity of regulation involved. As explained above, public–private partnership models allow for information sharing between different entities. The aim is to bring together information from discrete areas ('silos'), so as to enable the public and private sectors to have a better understanding of potential fraud threats.[99] This can involve sharing strategic or tactical information. 'Information fusion' of this kind, between multiple sources in the financial services industry and law enforcement, allows for predictive modelling, with the aim of providing more nuanced assessments of fraud threats.[100] Giving its wide-ranging scope, limits have already been placed upon some 'information fusion' models. For example, federated ML systems permit organisations to data-share to create joint predictive models without sharing data specific to individuals.[101] There is regulation of such public-sector data sharing by the Data Protection Act 2018, the General Data Protection Regulation (GDPR) and the Digital Economy Act 2017.[102] However, even within the limits of federated ML, there are concerns about the extent to which data privacy and the GDPR are respected.[103] At the time of writing, a government response to a consultation on reform of the data protection regime in England and Wales is pending. Of key relevance is a reform tabled in the consultation document to facilitate increased sharing of information from public–private sector partnerships to law enforcement.[104] Concerns have been raised that the proposed reforms do not take due account of privacy concerns, and that the current framework for data sharing for fraud prevention is unduly complex.[105]

Recently, there have been strong pushes by the financial sector for government to expand information-sharing powers, in a way that exceeds current data protection laws. For example, UK Finance has argued that the fraud-prevention industry is 'fighting fraud with one arm tied behind it at the moment' because of limits to information-sharing between banks, regulators and law enforcement.[106] It has advocated enhanced powers to 'enable banks to share information in situations

[98] International Public Sector Fraud Forum (n 64).

[99] UK Finance, 'Fighting Financial Crime in a Complex Landscape for Information Sharing' (May 2021) www.ukfinance.org.uk/news-and-insight/blogs/fighting-financial-crime-complex-landscape-information-sharing (accessed 16 March 2022).

[100] ibid.

[101] ibid.

[102] UK Parliament Research Briefing No 664, 'Sharing Public Sector Data', https://researchbriefings.files.parliament.uk/documents/POST-PN-0664/POST-PN-0664.pdf (accessed 16 March 2022) box 1.

[103] UK Finance (n 99).

[104] DCMS, *Data: A New Direction* (2021).

[105] ibid 4 (box 3); S Gautam and H. Jahankhani, 'Balancing Privacy and Public Benefit to Detect and Prevent Fraud' in H Jahankhani et al (eds), *Strategy, Leadership, and AI in the Cyber Ecosystem: The Role of Digital Societies in Information Governance and Decision Maing* (London, Academic Press, 2021).

[106] ICAEW (n 75).

where there is reasonable suspicion of illegal activity'.[107] Indeed, proposals to lower the threshold to below 'reasonable suspicion' in the context of money laundering may well spill over into the fraud-prevention infrastructure. A witness to the Treasury Committee's February 2022's report argued that 'banks should share information with the NCA even in cases where the current legal requirement of a reasonable suspicion may not be met'.[108] The witness argued that if the bar were to be reduced, banks would be able to provide more detailed risk-assessment reports. From this follows a push to reform the current legal framework in order 'to enable more of that [data sharing] to happen'.[109]

Any lowering of the bar for information sharing should be accompanied by scrutiny of the principles at stake. It is not the case that pressure to increase information sharing between the private sector, tech industry and law enforcement is an unmitigated good. Increased powers to share reports of suspected fraud with law enforcement must be subject to proportionate threshold access to data. The exclusionary effects for individuals suspected of fraud need to be considered.[110]

It matters what data shared via public–private partnerships is then used to do. In 2019, the Treasury Committee wrote that de-risking practices, including freezing accounts, had 'become too widespread and were having a detrimental effect on innocent businesses and consumers'.[111] The report emphasised the need for transparency and proportionality, as well as scrutiny of the AI involved in making de-risking decisions. The same warning carries through to the Treasury Committee's February 2022 report. There is a clear need for enhanced and proactive monitoring of de-risking decisions by the financial services industry. Such monitoring should include annual reports on the volume of de-risking decisions, considering effects upon individuals in terms of fairness and access to key services such as banking.[112] In relation to money laundering, there is an acknowledged need for 'clear processes and standards for deconflicting criminal and regulatory investigations'.[113] Scrutiny is needed of these issues in relation to fraud prevention, too. The need for delineating the powers given to partnerships is all the greater given the complex governance structure of fraud in England and Wales. Clear limits need to be developed by criminal lawyers on when suspected fraud is reported and why. Key to building a principled response is a fast-track review body which audits de-risking decisions in relation to suspected fraud, and considers how information necessary for criminal investigations is handled.

[107] ibid.

[108] HC 145 Treasury Committee (n 13) [135].

[109] ibid. Action 9 of the *Economic Crime Plan* (n 1) outlines a focus on improving information-sharing between AML/CTF supervisors and law enforcement.

[110] Baker and Robinson (n 96) 17 for discussion of pressure on the private sector using AI to 'build backdoors' to give law enforcement agencies access to encrypted data to fight cybercrime.

[111] HC 248 Treasury Committee, 'Economic Crime: Consumer View' (November 2019).

[112] HC 145 Treasury Committee (n 13) [180] ff.

[113] *Economic Crime Plan 2019 to 2022* (n 1) action 9 para 3.18, sets out the aim of improving information-sharing between AML/CTF supervisors and law enforcement.

IV. Developing Principles

One implication of a rapidly developing 'fraud-prevention' infrastructure is the importance of developing restraining principles at the periphery of preventive criminalisation. This is especially important where regulatory measures carry coercive consequences and/or exclusionary features, or where they involve widespread surveillance and data collection. Although it is impossible to be exhaustive in an exploratory chapter of this kind, several key principles should be emphasised by criminal law theorists to inform the future trajectory of fraud prevention.

First, analysis of the role of the private sector, and its use of AI and ML technologies, needs to be integrated into mainstream discussion of the special part of the criminal law. These are not tangential issues that lie on the perimeter of criminal law theory. Rapid integration of surveillance tools via public–private partnerships, which carry the potential for exclusion from core services, imports rule of law concerns. The limits of these tools must be clear and advertised ex ante. There has already been some progress in acknowledging the need for analysis of AI technologies by criminal law theorists. The AI Council has boldly written that 'the UK will only feel the full benefits of AI if all parts of society have full confidence in the science and the technologies, and in the governance and regulation that enable them'.[114] The Ada Lovelace Institute – an independent research institute into data and AI – notes that there cannot be a 'cross-cutting approach to UK AI regulation'.[115] Regulatory frameworks must be industry specific and nuanced to the challenges of each context. For the criminal law, this will require a focus on respecting first principles which are sensitive to the justice system – the specific environment in which AI and ML technologies are deployed.

Secondly, the high-risk nature of identifying suspected fraud needs to inform decision-making by public–private partnerships, in some instances facilitated by AI and/or ML technologies. It is high-risk because of the significant personal and collective interests at stake. Individuals and businesses are at risk of financial exclusion through onboarding and de-risking decision-making. They also risk harm to their reputations and to personal data rights.[116] There are not yet clear protocols for how information about suspected fraud is fed into the criminal justice system, and this adds to risk for individuals.[117] There is some recognition of the risks involved in flagging suspected fraud within the European Commission's 2021 report on the use of AI systems.[118] In analysing how AI systems appraise

[114] AI Council, *AI Roadmap, UK Government* (2021).

[115] Ada Lovelace Institute, 'Regulate to Innovate' (2021) www.adalovelaceinstitute.org/report/regulate-innovate/ (accessed 16 March 2022).

[116] ibid, see Annex 1 on 'use cases'.

[117] Gautam and Jahankhani (n 105).

[118] European Commission, 'Proposal for a Regulation Laying Down Harmonised Rules on Artificial Intelligence' (April 2021) https://digital-strategy.ec.europa.eu/en/library/proposal-regulation-laying-down-harmonised-rules-artificial-intelligence (accessed 16 March 2021).

creditworthiness, the report argues that AI systems used for this task should be classified as 'high-risk'. This is because resulting classifications either permit or bar entry to financial services across a range of sectors.[119] The Commission's reasoning should be integrated into theorising the current impetus towards fraud prevention. The classification of suspected fraud is itself high risk.

Alongside the effects upon individuals of classifying suspected fraud using emerging technologies, there are also risks embedded in the use of AI technologies themselves. Using emerging technologies as the means of identifying suspected fraud always carries the risk of false positives. AI systems can impose harm, even when deployed to prevent fraud. There is an argument that, so long as the potential harm caused by the system does not outweigh the harm is seeks to prevent, it is justified. But this 'lesser evils' rationale nevertheless poses threats to individuals where transactions are incorrectly flagged as atypical. It also threatens collective interests protected by a criminal justice system if suspected fraud is incorrectly labelled or flagged. The Law Society noted in 2019 that 'uncritical reliance on technology could lead to wrong decisions that threaten human rights and undermine public trust in the justice system'.[120] The requirement that suspected fraud be 'linked with provable accuracy' must be maintained, despite the involvement of 'partial automaton or augmentation of a decision-making process by an AI tool'.[121] There must therefore be continual testing and human monitoring of the risks carried by AI and ML systems.[122] It is also important to highlight risks inherent in the use of public–private partnerships for fraud detection. In section II above, I argued that partnerships are underpinned by complex incentive and disincentive structures. The commodification of personal data poses a threat insofar as some transactions are incorrectly flagged as fraudulent to meet targets. It also follows that public–private partnerships must also be informed by a robust risk management system, which operates from the first principle that it is harmful for individuals when a transaction is incorrectly suspected to be fraudulent.

It follows from the nature of these risks that a developing 'fraud-prevention' infrastructure which interfaces with the criminal law must be informed by transparency and a clear ability to explain how suspected fraud is identified. There is precedent for a focus on transparency and 'explainability' in the growing literature on regulation of AI and ML technologies.[123] Transparency and explanation of how AI technologies are used helps to 'ensure that people understand AI-based outcomes and can challenge them'.[124] Mechanisms must be in place to facilitate this type of scrutiny.

[119] ibid: 'high-risk and high-impact AI models will require more due diligence'.

[120] The Law Society of England and Wales, *Algorithms in the Criminal Justice System* (London, HMSO, 2019).

[121] International Public Sector Fraud Forum (n 64) 11.

[122] European Commission (n 118) [29].

[123] Ada Lovelace Institute (n 115).

[124] Organisation for Economic Co-operation and Development, *OECD Principles on Artificial Intelligence* (2019).

A third principle highlights particular challenges for building transparency and explainability in the fraud-prevention context. Too much transparency as to how fraud detection mechanisms work may be exploited by fraudsters, allowing circumvention of fraud-detection systems.[125] In relation to AI and ML technologies, it is useful to disaggregate the need for transparency about the *substance* of the systems at play in fraud-detection from transparency about the *process* deployed for doing so. There ought to be scrutiny of both aspects. However, there may be a stronger case for transparency in relation to process, given that transparency here is less likely to be exploited by fraudsters. Such transparency facilitates opportunities for individuals to challenge given outputs and to seek legal redress. There is also a case for disaggregating explanation of how systems work at an 'individual' and 'societal' level.[126] Individuals must have enough information to be able to understand 'whether a given output is justified, and whether they should seek a remedy through the courts'.[153] At the societal level, this requires 'explanation facilities designed to allow broader internal and external scrutiny, such as over the general logics, functioning, behavior and impact of the models'.[127] Challenges for transparency are different in relation to public–private partnerships. Here there is a compelling case for transparency both in relation to how partnerships specific to fraud-prevention operate in practice, as well as in relation to the details of their regulatory oversight: for example, can we be confident that there is appropriate supervision of the competing incentive structures in place?

Fraud can be detected using several different ML approaches. Some systems use a combination of supervised and unsupervised learning to detect fraud. Unsupervised systems carry added risk because there is no human oversight. Literature on ML notes that unsupervised systems may be more difficult to explain.[128] The ability to explain the methodology should be prioritised wherever unsupervised ML is used to prevent fraud. These systems pose a greater threat to the rule of law, insofar as their outputs can be unforeseen and closer scrutiny of their outputs is necessary.[129]

A fourth principle argues that criminal law theorists need to advocate testing of AI and ML systems, as well as public–private partnerships, for accuracy

[125] Bank of England (n 54).

[126] European Commission (n 118) 65.

[127] ibid 66.

[128] OECD Business and Finance Outlook 2021, *Trends and Policy Frameworks for AI in Finance* (2021) www.oecd-ilibrary.org/sites/cbc9d1af-en/index.html?itemId=/content/component/cbc9d1af-en (accessed 16 March 2022).

[129] Mirroring Article 22 GDPR's 'right to an explanation' which requires companies using automated decision-making to give individuals information about how data is processed and providing a process for appeal. See Information Commissioner's Office, 'Rights Related to Automated Decision-Making Including Profiling', https://ico.org.uk/for-organisations/guide-to-data-protection/guide-to-the-general-data-protection-regulation-gdpr/individual-rights/rights-related-to-automated-decision-making-including-profiling/ (accessed 16 March 2022).

and against bias. Accuracy and protecting against bias are two clear goals that are emerging for AI governance.[130] There is especial need for rigorous pursuit of these goals in the justice context where there are exclusionary or intrusive effects. For example, the International Public Sector Fraud Forum suggests that, before AI tools are deployed, they 'should be tested against independent and well understood data for accuracy'.[131] They should also be kept under regular review post-deployment, and 'tested and trained using quality, unbiased data'.[132] There are useful applications of AI systems themselves being used to review other operating AI systems for bias. For example, major tech companies such as IBM, Microsoft and Google are involved in developing means of testing algorithms for bias. IBM has released software which visually represents an algorithm's application to a set of facts, with the aim of enhancing accuracy and improving transparency.[133] The Ada Lovelace Institute has recently developed a proposal for a first Algorithmic Impact Assessment in a different context – healthcare – that aims to promote good governance around application of algorithms to public-sector data, enhancing outcomes for affected groups and to ensure the prevention of bias in process and outcomes.[134] Similar impact assessments ought to be undertaken regarding the use of AI and ML technologies to prevent fraud.

V. Implications for Theorising Fraud Criminalisation

We have seen a strong push towards fraud prevention in England and Wales, using public–private partnerships with AI and ML technologies in support. What are the implications for theorising fraud criminalisation? I argue that theorising a flatter regulatory structure ought to be the future trajectory for analysis of fraud criminalisation in England and Wales. The rapid integration of the private sector, using AI, into fraud prevention signifies a change in the dynamics of fraud regulation. Coercive consequences exist across the regulatory landscape – through exclusions resulting from data sharing, surveillance and data retention, as well as through coercive criminal law measures. Rather than giving an expanded role to fraud as a paradigm dishonesty offence as the threat of fraud intensifies, a 'flatter' regulatory structure is the future trajectory for fraud governance in England and Wales. This mirrors the changing nature of fraud itself. The way in which fraud is being perpetrated has shifted. The paradigm is now technology-driven and cyber-enabled. A response in kind involves the grafting of technology onto the mainstay of fraud

[130] OECD Business and Finance Outlook (n 128).
[131] International Public Sector Fraud Forum (n 64) 13.
[132] ibid 13.
[133] International Public Sector Fraud Forum (n 64) 12.
[134] Ada Lovelace Institute, *Algorithmic Impact Assessment: A Case Study in Healthcare* (February 2022) www.adalovelaceinstitute.org/report/algorithmic-impact-assessment-case-study-healthcare/ (accessed 16 March 2022).

regulation. It involves the need to draw upon expertise of those familiar with new technologies, and with the resources available to access them. This signifies a change in the dynamics of regulation. There is greater fluidity between criminal law and regulatory measures in relation to fraud in an AI-propelled world.

One effect of this is that it requires regulatory preventive measures to be brought into our field of vision, alongside criminal law interventions.[135] As is well known, criminal law measures must be clearly justified given their coercive features. But regulatory measures at the periphery of the criminal law may also have coercive features and/or consequences, and therefore must also be informed by clear principles of the kinds identified above in section IV. Criminal law theory is needed to elaborate principles at the periphery of fraud criminalisation, as well as the core, along the lines elaborated in section IV above.

It also follows that criminal law measures cannot be theorised as detached from the wider regulatory landscape of fraud governance. A 'flatter' regulatory structure encourages us to look not only at the (multiple) interests at stake that fraud offences seek to protect, but also to theorise fraud interventions from an approach which looks at the importance of the techniques used. Lindsey Farmer has examined aspects of this problem in his forward-looking monograph, *Making the Modern Criminal Law*. Farmer hypothesises an expanding role for the criminal law's dishonesty offences. He argues that there is a risk of an open-door criminalisation policy if the criminal law is used 'as a backstop to systems of credit', accompanied by reliance on dishonesty as the key fault requirement.[136] This would allocate an 'unduly expansive role' to the criminal law.[137]

By contrast, a focus on the rapid development of a fraud-prevention infrastructure identifies another shift. Given the dominance of regulatory measures, there may be a lesser role for the criminal law as a backstop to wide-ranging preventive regulatory measures assisted by AI technologies. Analysis of the means used, as well as the aims pursued, enables theorists to consider the strengths and weaknesses of a move away from top-down criminalisation of fraud. The merits and demerits of a shared-governance approach can be scrutinised, resisting simple-minded bids to classify measures as non-coercive regulatory measures rather than coercive criminal law measures.

It is imperative that the aims of the range of interventions represented in a flatter regulatory structure are interrogated and tested. One aim of fraud prevention, evident in current policy discussions and highlighted in this chapter, is to protect the security of the market. 'Ontological insecurity' from the threat of fraud encourages a move to non-coercive regulatory measures backed up by

[135] L Farmer, 'The "Market" in Criminal Law Theory' (2022) *MLR* 435: '*Market* crimes, such as insider dealing or market manipulations, are a niche area of interest, viewed as a form of "regulatory" criminal law, and not regarded as either practically or normatively significant for the wider criminal law.'

[136] L Farmer, *Making the Modern Criminal Law: Criminalization and Civil Order* (Oxford, Oxford University Press, 2016) 233.

[137] ibid 233.

coercive measures.[138] A similar emphasis can be tracked in relation to the state's responses to terrorism. Andrew Ashworth and Lucia Zedner identify a sense of 'unprecedented threats to security' as providing a strong 'sociopolitical context for the rise of the Preventive State'.[139] This led, in the terrorism context, to reliance on a 'new penology' focused on actuarial justice – a desire 'to prevent future harms by calculating aggregate risks to minimize their probability and reduce their severity'.[140]

A parallel shift has been noted in relation to dishonesty offences in England and Wales. Here there has been a drift away from an individualised harm-based model, towards a more inchoate model, criminalising 'the risk of harm to the enjoyment or security of property interests posed by dishonest acquisitive conduct'.[141] On this model, 'trust in the security of property' is paramount, and individuals have 'responsibility not to act towards the property of others in a way which' would 'undermine trust in the security of property'.[142] This marks a movement away from preventing action that harms individuals towards *preventing disruption* to a system of property interests. The new approach could easily become expansionist if applied to a flatter fraud-regulation structure. There must be limits to the aims of a more participatory mode of fraud governance in England and Wales.

These trends raise important questions about the role of private actors. What is the role of an increasingly dominant private sector in preventing fraud, and how does this interact with criminal law interventions? A focus on 'responsibilisation' has emerged, as contrasted with law enforcement.[143] 'Responsibilisation' permits the state to continue in a 'steering role' while everyday implementation of its policies 'is increasingly delegated to the civil society'.[144] This shifting of accountability onto individuals and organisations can be seen in recent discussions regarding responsibilisation of those operating online forums in the Online Safety Bill. There are important normative questions about how far an idea of 'responsibilisation' should extend. For example, are there equivalent public law controls operating in the 'civil society' sphere? A focus on the collective interest in preventing fraud, for example, could come at the expense of individual privacy rights through widespread surveillance facilitated by AI. Incentive and disincentive structures in public–private partnerships must be unpacked, as well as the limits of an increasingly prevalent surveillance culture.

[138] For example, a corporate failure to prevent economic crime offence, see Law Commission, *Corporate Criminal Liability: An Options Paper* (London, HMSO, June 2022).
[139] A Ashworth and L Zedner, 'The Rise and Restraint of the Preventive State' [2019] *Annual Review of Criminology* 429, 434.
[140] ibid 435.
[141] Farmer (n 136) 223.
[142] ibid 229.
[143] D Garland, 'The Limits of the Sovereign State: Strategies of Crime Control in Contemporary Society' (1996) 36 *British Journal of Criminology* 445.
[144] L Pasculli, 'Coronavirus and Fraud in the UK: From the Responsibilisation of the Civil Society to the Deresponsibilisation of the State' (2020) 25(2) *Coventry Law Journal* 3.

The private sector's interaction with the criminal law should also be analysed. Ironically, increased responsibilisation through an expanded regulatory and civil liability structure does not always reduce criminal law involvement. It is not necessarily the case that when regulation waxes, criminalisation wanes. Pasculli argues that we see this dichotomy in the *Economic Crime Plan 2019 to 2022*, with a reassertion of 'punitive power' sitting alongside collaborative exercises.[145] An emphasis on collaborative public–private partnerships through improving information sharing between the public and private sectors is followed by calls to enhance 'powers, procedures, tools and capabilities' of law enforcement and the justice system. This highlights the importance for theorists of interrogating the power structures that underlie AI and the involvement of the private sector. Fraud prevention is a key site for analysing how power is distributed in a society, considering what dynamics have become entrenched and why.[146]

VI. Conclusion

This chapter has made the case for criminal law theorists to engage with what is happening on the periphery of fraud criminalisation. While much current focus is on whether current criminal law measures are sufficient to respond to the pullulating problem of fraud, I have interrogated a new form and function to regulatory preventive measures in response to fraud.[147] Two such measures – public–private partnerships, and the use of AI and ML technologies – are under-theorised by criminal law theorists. These developments carry weighty implications for due process and privacy. Against a backdrop of rapid development and implementation, we need guiding principles to inform the limits of these preventive measures.

Currently the Economic Crime Strategic Board is formulating an anti-fraud plan for the United Kingdom. It is fitting in a volume dedicated to Professor Sullivan's work that a call for input from criminal law theorists is made and taken up. Among the variety of stakeholders who must input should be those who are concerned with the implications of non-coercive preventive measures. These carry important implications for privacy and due process. It matters not only what prevention of fraud looks like using AI within the criminal justice system, but also outside of that system, and the interaction between the two. This sets a new research trajectory for modern criminal law.

[145] ibid.

[146] M Hidebrandt and K De Vries (eds), *Privacy, Due Process and the Computational Turn: The Philosophy of Law Meets the Philosophy of Technology* (Oxford and New York, Routledge, 2015); Alan Turing Institute, *Privacy, Agency and Trust in Human-AI Ecosystem* (December 2021) 19–20.

[147] eg The House of Lords Fraud Act 2006 and Digital Fraud Committee's call for evidence closed in April 2022, https://committees.parliament.uk/call-for-evidence/2578/ (accessed 16 March 2022).

12

Precedent in English Criminal Law

GRANT LAMOND*

The aim of this chapter is to consider the Supreme Court's decision in *Ivey v Genting Casinos*[1] and the subsequent decision of the Court of Appeal in *Barton*[2] from the perspective of the English practice of precedent, particularly as it applies to criminal law. Like other commentators, my conclusion will be that *Ivey* and *Barton* involve problematic departures from the doctrine of precedent. This chapter will seek to deepen earlier critiques by assessing *Ivey* and *Barton* in terms of the established approach to case law reasoning, and the applicable norms of judicial law-making, in the common law. The chapter will proceed as follows. In the first section I will quickly sketch the standard view of the doctrine of precedent in English criminal law, before considering the decision in *Ivey*, and how that decision was treated in *Barton*. I will also consider the reliance placed by the Court of Appeal in *Barton* on the earlier decisions in *Holley*[3] and *James*.[4] In the second section I will discuss the distinction between ratio decidendi and obiter dictum, and the standard view on why the former is binding whereas the latter is not. In the third section I will discuss the rationales for the doctrine of precedent, and the orthodox view of how it operates and how it may be modified. In the fourth section I will reconsider the above four decisions in the light of the previous two sections. Finally, in the fifth section, I will argue that the doctrine of precedent, and other aspects of case law, are both forms of customary law within the common law. To be more precise, precedent and case law are forms of customary law *in foro*: that is, legally binding customary practices of officials. This form of law is subject to legal

* I would like to thank the participants at the Legal Theory workshop at the National University of Singapore for their discussion of a draft of this chapter, and I would especially like to thank Andrew Simester for his very helpful written comments on that draft. I am also very grateful to Peter Mirfield for his comments on the penultimate draft. This chapter takes up some of the issues raised by Bob Sullivan's incisive comments (coauthored with Andrew Simester) in 'Judging Dishonesty' (2020) 136 *LQR* 523.

[1] *Ivey v Genting Casinos (UK) Ltd (trading as Crockfords Club)* [2017] UKSC 67, [2018] AC 391. (Hereafter *Ivey*.)

[2] *R v Barton* [2020] EWCA Crim 575, [2021] QB 685. (Hereafter *Barton*.)

[3] *Attorney General for Jersey v Holley* [2005] UKPC 23, [2005] 2 AC 580. (Hereafter *Holley*.)

[4] *R v James* [2006] EWCA Crim 14, [2006] QB 588. (Hereafter *James*.)

alteration, through the standard forms of law-making that exist in the common law, but is otherwise legally binding on officials, including the Supreme Court.

Before embarking on this discussion, I should address a thought that some readers of this chapter might have. The thought goes along these lines: whatever the criticisms of *Barton*, *Ivey*, *James* and *Holley* over their treatment of precedent, this is just a technical quibble, and represents an unrealistic academic concern with what are ultimately practical questions of adjudication. I am mindful of such reservations, and in the case of *James* and *Holley*, despite their unorthodox features, I might be tempted to agree. But a culture of legality is a central feature of a well-functioning legal system, and the judiciary should exhibit an exemplary commitment to legality. On its own, *James* might be thought to be harmless enough. But *James* provided the justification for *Barton*, and it is unclear what further departures from the operation of precedent *James* and *Barton* will be cited to justify. The rule of law requires scrupulous official conformity to the law, which includes the doctrine of precedent, even when such conformity makes the achievement of certain desirable ends more difficult than would otherwise be the case. Of course, the heavens will not fall because of decisions such as *Ivey* and *Barton* in themselves. But a certain carelessness about how and when various aspects of the doctrine of precedent can be modified, particularly in the context of criminal law, is an unattractive feature of a legal system committed to the rule of law.

I. The Rules on Precedent in English Criminal Law

The basic position on precedent in English criminal law is well known:

1. The Court of Appeal (Criminal Division) and lower courts are strictly bound by decisions of the Supreme Court (and its predecessor, the House of Lords); that is, courts below the Supreme Court can distinguish Supreme Court decisions, but cannot depart from them.
2. Courts below the Court of Appeal are strictly bound by decisions of the Court of Appeal (Criminal Division) (and its predecessor, the Court of Criminal Appeal).
3. The Supreme Court is presumptively bound by its own decisions (and those of its predecessor, the House of Lords), but in conformity with the *Practice Statement* may overrule or depart from its own decisions (or decisions of the House of Lords) in appropriate cases.[5]
4. The Court of Appeal (Criminal Division) is strictly bound by its own earlier decisions (and the decisions of its predecessor the Court of Criminal Appeal), subject to the three exceptions recognised by the Court of Appeal in *Young*

[5] *Practice Statement (Judicial Precedents)* [1966] 1 WLR 1234; see now *Supreme Court of the United Kingdom: Practice Direction 4: Notice of Appeal*, § 4.2.4.

v Bristol Aeroplane,[6] and certain further exceptions, in particular where the court concludes that the law has been misunderstood or misapplied.[7]

5. The Supreme Court and the Court of Appeal (Criminal Division) are not bound by decisions of the Judicial Committee of the Privy Council, though those decisions are persuasive where there is no contrary binding authority.[8]

In addition, courts are only bound by the ratio decidendi of a precedent, not by obiter dicta.

Set against this background, the decisions in *Ivey* and *Barton* are anomalous. In *Ivey* the Supreme Court had to decide whether the claimant was entitled to his winnings at a casino, or whether he had committed the offence of 'cheating' under section 42 of the Gambling Act 2005, by virtue of his practice of 'edge-sorting'. If he had cheated, he was not entitled to his winnings. One issue that was raised in the appeal was whether cheating under section 42 required that a defendant be 'dishonest' in law. The Supreme Court held that the offence does not require a defendant to have been dishonest.[9] Having determined this issue, and concluded that given the trial court's findings Ivey was not entitled to his winnings, the Court went on to provide a lengthy discussion of the nature of 'dishonesty' in the law.[10] It concluded that the test that had been used for the previous thirty-five years (the *Ghosh* test[11]) was mistaken:

> These several considerations provide convincing grounds for holding that the second leg of the test propounded in *R v Ghosh* [1982] QB 1053 does not correctly represent the law and that directions based upon it ought no longer to be given.[12]

The discussion of the *Ghosh* test, and the conclusion reached in the judgment were, therefore, obiter dicta. The Court had concluded that cheating did not require that the defendant was 'dishonest' in law, and so the discussion was not part of the reasoning to the conclusion in the appeal.

In *Barton*, the Court of Appeal had to decide what to do with the conflict between *Ivey* and the earlier binding decision in *Ghosh*.[13] The Court of Appeal concluded that the Supreme Court, in *Ivey*,

> altered the established common law approach to precedent in the criminal courts by stating that test for dishonesty they identified, albeit strictly contained in obiter dicta, should be followed in preference to an otherwise binding authority of the Court of

[6] *Young* v *Bristol Aeroplane Company, Limited* [1944] KB 718 (CA).

[7] *R v Taylor* [1950] 2 KB 368 (CCA) and *R v Gould* [1968] 2 QB 65 (CA); see also *R v Simpson* [2003] EWCA Crim 1499, [2004] QB 118.

[8] An important exception to (5)—*Willers v Joyce (No 2)* [2016] UKSC 44, [2018] AC 843 – will be discussed below.

[9] *Ivey* [48]–[50].

[10] *Ivey* [52]–[75].

[11] *R v Ghosh* [1982] QB 1053 (CA).

[12] *Ivey* [74].

[13] *Barton* [93].

> Appeal. As in *James* [2006] QB 533 we do not consider that it is for this court to conclude that it was beyond their powers to act in this way.[14]

The Court of Appeal went on:

> We conclude that where the Supreme Court itself directs that an otherwise binding decision of the Court of Appeal should no longer be followed and proposes an alternative test that it says must be adopted, the Court of Appeal is bound to follow what amounts to a direction from the Supreme Court even though it is strictly obiter. To that limited extent the ordinary rules of precedent (or stare decisis) have been modified. We emphasise that this limited modification is confined to cases in which all the judges in the appeal in question in the Supreme Court agree that to be the effect of the decision. Such was a necessary condition before adjusting the rules of precedent accepted by this court in *R v James* in relation to the Privy Council. Had the minority of the Privy Council in *Holley* not agreed that the effect of the judgment was to state definitively the law in England, it would not have been accepted as such by this court. The same approach is necessary here because it forms the foundation for the conclusion that the result is considered by the Supreme Court to be definitive, with the consequence that a further appeal would be a foregone conclusion, and binding on lower courts.[15]

As is clear from these quotations, the Court of Appeal relied heavily on the authority of *James* in reaching this conclusion.[16] That earlier case had arisen from the Privy Council decision in *Holley*, which decided (by majority) that the House of Lords decision in *Smith*,[17] on the proper understanding of the characteristics to be attributed to the 'reasonable man' under section 57 of the Homicide Act 1957 for the purposes of the then partial defence of provocation, had been wrongly decided. The Privy Council instead preferred the Committee's earlier decision in *Luc Thiet Thuan*,[18] which was in accord with the English law of provocation prior to the decision in *Smith*. The Privy Council had sat in an enlarged panel of nine, comprised entirely of Law Lords from the House of Lords. The majority stated in the first paragraph of their judgment:

> This appeal, being heard by an enlarged board of nine members, is concerned to resolve this conflict [between *Smith* and *Luc Thiet Thuan*] and clarify definitively the present state of English law, and hence Jersey law, on this important subject.[19]

Two of the dissentients observed: 'We must however accept that the effect of the majority decision is as stated in para 1 of the majority judgment.'[20] The third dissentient stated that he agreed with the other dissentients' judgment and their conclusions.[21]

[14] ibid [102].
[15] ibid [104].
[16] The court said that it was in a 'strongly analogous' position to the court in *James* [102].
[17] *R v Smith (Morgan)* [2001] 1 AC 146 (HL).
[18] *Luc Thiet Thuan v The Queen* [1997] AC 131 (PC).
[19] *Holley* [1].
[20] ibid [68] (Lord Bingham and Lord Hoffmann).
[21] ibid [69] (Lord Carswell).

In *James*, the Court of Appeal had to decide whether to follow the Privy Council's decision in *Holley* or the House of Lords' decision in *Smith*. It concluded that it should follow *Holley*. The discussion was as follows:

> 40. … (i) How do we justify disregarding very well established rules of precedent? And (ii) what principles do we put in place of those that we are disregarding? The two questions are obviously interrelated.
>
> 41. As to the first question, it is not this court, but the Lords of Appeal in Ordinary who have altered the established approach to precedent. There are possible constitutional issues in postulating that a Board of the Privy Council, however numerous or distinguished, is in a position on an appeal from Jersey to displace and replace a decision of the Appellate Committee on an issue of English law. Our principles in relation to precedent are, however, common law principles. Putting on one side the position of the European Court of Justice, the Lords of Appeal in Ordinary have never hitherto accepted that any other tribunal could overrule a decision of the Appellate Committee. Uniquely a majority of the Law Lords have on this occasion decided that they could do so and have done so in their capacity as members of the Judicial Committee of the Privy Council. We do not consider that it is for this court to rule that it was beyond their powers to alter the common law rules of precedent in this way.
>
> 42. The rule that this court must always follow a decision of the House of Lords and, indeed, one of its own decisions rather than a decision of the Privy Council is one that was established at a time when no tribunal other than the House of Lords itself could rule that a previous decision of the House of Lords was no longer good law. Once one postulates that there are circumstances in which a decision of the Judicial Committee of the Privy Council can take precedence over a decision of the House of Lords, it seems to us that this court must be bound in those circumstances to prefer the decision of the Privy Council to the prior decision of the House of Lords. That, so it seems to us, is the position that has been reached in the case of these appeals.
>
> 43. What are the exceptional features in this case which justify our preferring the decision in *Holley's* case to that in the *Morgan Smith* case? We identify the following. (i) All nine of the Lords of Appeal in Ordinary sitting in Holley's case agreed in the course of their judgments that the result reached by the majority clarified definitively English law on the issue in question. (ii) The majority in *Holley's* case constituted half the Appellate Committee of the House of Lords. We do not know whether there would have been agreement that the result was definitive had the members of the Board divided five/four. (iii) In the circumstances, the result of any appeal on the issue to the House of Lords is a foregone conclusion.
>
> 44. We doubt whether this court will often, if ever again, be presented with the circumstances that we have described above. It is those circumstances which we consider justify the course that we have decided to take, and our decision should not be taken as a licence to decline to follow a decision of the House of Lords in any other circumstances.

How was this authority of assistance in *Barton*? The Court of Appeal regarded its position vis-à-vis *Ivey* to be 'strongly analogous' to that of *James* vis-à-vis *Holley*.[22]

[22] *Barton* [102].

It might be thought, on the other hand, that the disanalogies, rather than the analogies, were more striking. Consider some points of difference:

(a) The issue of the proper understanding of the 'reasonable man' in the law of provocation under the then law was the central question in *Holley*; it formed part of the ratio decidendi of the decision, whereas the statements on dishonesty were clearly obiter dicta and were not central to the dispute in *Ivey*.
(b) *Holley* was a case concerned with the criminal law, whereas *Ivey* was a case concerning liability in private law.
(c) *Holley* had been decided by an expanded panel of nine Law Lords, specially assembled to consider the correctness of *Smith*, whereas *Ivey* was decided by a standard panel of five judges of the Supreme Court to decide the question of the content of the offence of 'cheating'.
(d) Given that nine Law Lords had heard the *Holley* appeal, and that the six in the majority represented a majority of all the Law Lords, it was a 'foregone conclusion' that the House of Lords would decide the issue in the same way, whereas the five judges in *Ivey* did not constitute a majority of Supreme Court, and it was far from a 'foregone conclusion' that an expanded panel of the Supreme Court, hearing full argument on the merits of *Ghosh*, would have followed the dicta in *Ivey*.
(e) Although the Law Lords in *Holley* and the judges in *Ivey* had been unanimous in their view of the result of the case, the Law Lords in *Holley* represented the overwhelming majority of all Law Lords, whereas the panel in *Ivey* did not represent a majority of judges of the Supreme Court.

The analogy to *James* seems to rest, instead, on the dictum that in neither case was the Court of Appeal willing to consider whether it was beyond the power of the Lords of Appeal in Ordinary sitting on the Privy Council, or a panel of the Supreme Court, to alter the rules of precedent. But again, the disanalogy seems stronger than the analogy. In *Holley*, the Law Lords sitting in the Privy Council had held that the Privy Council could rule that a decision of the House of Lords was wrongly decided. Presumably the Law Lords accepted that such a decision was (presumptively) binding on the House of Lords, and, thus, that – contrary to point (5) in the standard view of precedent outlined above – the House of Lords was not the only arbiter of the correctness of its own decisions. And indeed this view was confirmed by the Supreme Court in *Willers v Joyce (No 2)* in 2016, which held that in certain circumstances the Privy Council could determine the correctness of a precedent of the Supreme Court (or Court of Appeal).[23] So the Law Lords in *Holley*, and the Supreme Court judges in *Willers v Joyce (No 2)*, were effectively altering the rules of precedent for the House of Lords/Supreme Court. This, a fortiori, had a knock-on effect for the treatment of House of Lords and Supreme Court decisions by the Court of Appeal. *Barton*, by contrast, attributed to *Ivey* a

[23] *Willers v Joyce (No 2)* [2016] UKSC 44, [2018] AC 843, [19]–[21]. (Hereafter *Willers v Joyce (No 2)*.).

decision to alter the settled doctrines on which parts of a judgment can be binding on lower courts.

II. Ratio Decidendi and Obiter Dictum

It is a well-established part of the common law that it is the rationes decidendi of precedents that are binding on other courts, not obiter dicta. What is the rationale for this distinction? Essentially, it reflects the difference between judicial law-making and legislative law-making. Courts, of course, often make law when they decide cases. But it has traditionally been supposed that the way that courts make law, and the type of law they make, is different to the way that Parliament (and delegated legislative bodies) make law, and different to the type of law that legislative bodies make. In particular, it has been thought that the law-making of the courts is far more constrained than that of a legislature.

The fundamental way in which judicial law-making differs from legislative law-making is that courts make law by applying a legal ruling to the facts of a concrete case before them in order to settle the case. Why is this? The principal function of courts is an adjudicative one: courts exist to apply the law to the parties in proceedings before it. The court issues an authoritative determination of the legal issues that have been raised by the parties in order to resolve the case. It will at times be necessary, in order to resolve a case, to settle a legal issue disputed by the parties that has not previously been conclusively determined by another law-maker (legislative or judicial). Courts are thus at times called upon to make law in order to reach a conclusion in a case, and this is the context for judicial law-making.

Because the ruling on an issue is relied upon by the court to resolve a case, such a decision commits the law to a certain position, and as a matter of consistency it commits the law to deciding the same way in future cases. To do otherwise would be to treat parties inconsistently. Of course, as a matter of consistency the law has two options: (i) to follow the ruling, or (ii) to disavow it. But unless the law disavows a previous decision, it should be followed in later cases. By contrast, if the court did *not* rely on some view of the law to resolve the case before it, the law is not committed, as a matter of consistency, to adopting that view in later cases. This reflects the basic distinction between ratio decidendi and obiter dicta.

There is a second central feature of judicial law-making. Courts are expected to give *reasons* for their decisions: that is, to provide a justification for the outcomes they reach. Trial courts are expected to explain the view that was taken of the facts and evidence in reaching its conclusion. Similarly, courts are expected to justify the rulings of law that they make. Often this will be simple enough: there will be an applicable statute or binding precedent to be applied. But where there is no such source, courts must explain the view they have taken of the law, and why they have ruled as they have. A judgment, then, is not equivalent to a statute. A valid statute constitutes a decision of the legislature that must be followed by the courts. The legislature has the authority to make such decisions, and does not need to justify these decisions to the courts. Courts lack the type of political legitimacy that legislatures are presumed to enjoy. As such, they must provide reasons for creating new law.

The obligation to give reasons is linked to a third feature of judicial law-making. Judicial law-making is not done de novo: it is guided by existing law. A legislature can decide to start afresh on a subject within its power, but courts must show that their decisions, whilst making new law, are guided by existing law. Judicial decisions, therefore, must establish a degree of continuity with the law as it is. Most rulings of law are nested within an existing body of doctrine. Even the recognition of a novel cause of action or a novel remedy must demonstrate that it is coherent with the existing law and its underlying principles. Here we see a further constraint on judicial law-making. Courts must resolve an issue that has been raised by the parties. They aim to reach the best decision within the context of the rest of the law. The rest of the law may be far from ideal: it may be that the court would change it if it could. But that is not within the court's power. So the resolution of the issue will not always constitute what would be ideal if the rest of the law could also be altered at the same time: this is sometimes called the problem of 'partial reform'.[24] Courts must often settle for doing the best they can in the circumstances of the existing law.

So the ratio versus obiter distinction rests on the deeper foundations of the nature of judicial law-making. But there are also sound practical reasons for respecting the distinction, and for not treating obiter dicta as binding. Firstly, as a general matter, courts are not well suited to address broad issues of law reform. They lack the resources to engage in a wide-ranging analysis of the merits of changing the law. They have limited personnel, limited time and limited expertise to deal with the broader impact of proposed changes to the law.[25] Of course courts must make law: they have no choice if they are to settle disputes that are not already determined by existing law.[26] And some issues, such as very specific technical legal questions within private law, may be comfortably within the expertise of lawyers to determine. But the more general limitations of courts mentioned here favour treating only those rulings that the court relied upon to reach their conclusions as making law, and not their expressions of views on issues that did not have to be resolved to make the decision.

Secondly, the distinction between ratio and obiter reflects the fact that courts do not have the authority simply to choose to make law at their own initiative: they

[24] Joseph Raz's terminology: see 'Law and Value in Adjudication' in *The Authority of Law*, 2nd edn (Oxford, Oxford University Press, 2009) 199–201 and 'The Inner Logic of Law' in *Ethics in the Public Domain*, rev edn (Oxford, Oxford University Press, 1995) 240–41.

[25] See the discussion by the US Federal Second Circuit Court of Appeals judge PN Leval in 'Judging under the Constitution: *Dicta* about *Dictum*' in N Dorsen (ed), *The Embattled Constitution* (New York, NYU Press, 2013) 146.

[26] Some legal systems, such as the French system, do not have an official doctrine of precedent, and thus court decisions do not create law beyond the case in question. But even in such systems cases operate as a de facto source of law, albeit one that is not binding in the same way as in the common law.

only have the authority to make law that is pertinent to resolving the case before them. Courts are of course at liberty to express their views on other questions of law in the course of their judgments. But if obiter dicta were binding, it would confer an authority to make law at will, whenever the court thought it appropriate to do so. And the ability to make law in this way might well encourage some courts to express views on unrelated matters, and thus to adopt a more legislative role in taking the opportunity of a case to make law.

Thirdly, courts rely on the arguments of the parties before them to reach their decisions, and those arguments are focused on persuading the court to adopt the view on an issue favourable to their client, not on creating the best law in the circumstances. In particular, litigants will not press arguments on collateral issues that are incidental to their case, and so the court will generally not have the benefit of the presentation of arguments for and against matters that are obiter.[27]

Fourthly, given how difficult it is to change the law once it is settled by an appellate court – that is, given the fact that it is normally thought that a later court's disagreement with the ruling made in an earlier case is not sufficient to depart from an existing precedent – there are good reasons to be wary of treating dicta as binding. This is particularly true in light of the first three points discussed here.

Finally, it is simply unnecessary to treat obiter dicta as legally binding. Later courts do not ignore the dicta from earlier cases. In particular, if an appellate court expresses a seriously considered view about some legal doctrine, where the court has had the benefit of full argument from the parties about the doctrine, that carries considerable persuasive weight with lower courts and with the same court in later cases. If the question is unsettled, it strongly supports the view, whilst providing a later court the opportunity to examine the issue for itself and reach its own conclusion. If the question is one on which the courts have previously ruled, it signals to lawyers and other courts that the issue is ripe for reconsideration in an appropriate case. So obiter dicta play a significant role in legal reasoning without having binding force: treating them, as courts do, as having persuasive force might be thought to strike the appropriate balance between courts having influence over other decisions, and later decision-makers having the opportunity to test the strength of the arguments for themselves before committing the law to that view.

III. The Doctrine of Precedent

The doctrine of precedent as it applies in English criminal law was outlined earlier. In this section I will consider the rationale for the doctrine. In essence, the doctrine of precedent requires lower courts to follow the decisions of higher courts, and requires courts to follow (at least presumptively) their own earlier decisions.

[27] Leval (n 25) 147. Of course, sometimes an issue will have been fully argued before the court, but it will decide the case on other grounds.

What is the reason for this? The first and most prominent reason is the need for consistency in the application of the law.[28] Judges disagree about the merits of some decisions. If courts were at liberty to decide each case as they thought fit, irrespective of earlier decisions, it is very likely that the same issue would be determined differently by different courts. A hierarchical system of courts allocates the responsibility for settling the law to appellate courts, on the basis that those courts are better situated to reach decisions that are sound. Appellate courts have various advantages over trial courts: they are generally composed of the most able judges; they sit in benches that can pool their assessments; they are able to examine the existing analysis of the trial court; and they are presented with arguments by counsel over the soundness of the trial court's decision. A hierarchical system of courts seeks to promote the consistent application of legal doctrines, while subjecting those doctrines to critical review.

The concern for consistency is related to a second important value promoted by precedent: predictability. That lower courts are bound to follow the rulings of higher courts, and that courts are presumptively bound to follow their own decisions, means that those to whom the law applies can more reliably predict what law is applicable to them.[29] This has the further consequence that it facilitates reliance on the part of those to whom the law applies in organising their affairs, both in the short term and in the longer term. It also facilitates ex post facto decision-making: it enables parties to make better-informed decisions about how to resolve a legal dispute over past conduct, for example, by settling a claim or pleading guilty to a charge.

On the other hand, the fact that some courts are only presumptively bound by their own decisions, and that higher courts are not bound by decisions of lower courts, permits the courts to alter established law. This strikes a balance between undue rigidity in the operation of case law and excessive flexibility in its development. On this basis, (some) courts are permitted to overrule or depart from earlier decisions. The courts tend to be wary of overruling or departing from their own decisions, and also cautious in doing the same to lower court decisions that have been followed for a lengthy period of time. There are two main reasons for this. The first, as noted above, is that on many legal issues, different judges will assess the merits of a ruling in different ways. Some will think it correct, others will think it should be modified, and others again will think it is, on balance, mistaken. If every precedent were subject to being challenged and reassessed by different benches of judges, without any presumption in favour of following the precedent, there is a risk that the law will be altered too frequently, thereby undermining the consistency, predictability and reliability of case law.[30]

[28] Not that precedent, in isolation, can achieve this. The precedential rulings must also be relatively clear, sufficiently precise, and consistent with other laws. But I will assume that these other desiderata are satisfied by the rulings in question.

[29] And even if many ordinary citizens cannot make this prediction, their legal advisers can.

[30] There is also the risk that far more cases would be taken on appeal, straining the resources of the appellate system to deal with the workload.

The other reason for the courts' being cautious about overruling precedents is the retroactive effect of such overruling. In the common law, where an earlier decision is overruled, the new decision becomes the law not just from the time of the new decision, but for the past as well.[31] Overruling does not just potentially frustrate other parties' expectations and reliance for the *future*: their past arrangements may be jeopardised by an unexpected alteration in the law. This is a particularly pressing issue for indictable offences in English criminal law.[32] Private law operates a system of limitation periods that require legal actions to be brought within a certain (relatively short) time from the event that is the subject of the case. But there are no equivalent limitation periods for serious criminal offences in England. If the law is altered, the new law will apply to all past cases except those that have already been the subject of acquittal or conviction in earlier proceedings.[33] Where, in particular, the law is modified in a way that is disadvantageous to the defendant, defendants who were previously not charged or tried may find themselves subject to conviction for actions that were, at the time they acted, not criminal.

There is a further aspect to the doctrine of precedent that should be noted. The doctrine of precedent promotes consistency, predictability and reliance by requiring courts to follow the decisions of higher and coordinate courts. But these values also rely on the doctrine of precedent *itself* being sufficiently clear, predictable and consistent in its operation. The rules governing how cases make law – especially, when courts are bound, and when they are permitted to depart from earlier decisions – need to be stable in order for the values of a system of precedent to be promoted.[34] Furthermore, judicial development of the rules of precedent needs to conform to the requirements of judicial law-making discussed in the previous section. The decision to alter the rules of precedent should form part of the ratio of a judgment; it should be reasoned; and it should be grounded in pre-existing law.

IV. The Cases on Precedent Reconsidered

In the light of the discussion above, how do the decisions in *Holley*, *James*, *Ivey* and *Barton* fare? Let me consider each in turn. *Holley* was a decision of the Privy Council. At the time it was decided there was clear authority that (a) the Privy

[31] See *In re Spectrum* [2005] UKHL 41, [2005] 2 AC 680, [7]. Some other common law jurisdictions such as the United States and India recognise exceptional circumstances for prospective overruling; and *In re Spectrum* did not rule out the possibility in English law. Either way, prospective overruling is very rare.

[32] By contrast, proceedings in summary offences must generally be brought within six months of the offence being committed: Magistrates' Court Act 1980, s 127.

[33] Under the doctrine of *autrefois acquit* and *autrefois convict*. Note, though, that *autrefois acquit* is subject to the exceptions on double jeopardy in English law: see Part 10 of the Criminal Justice Act 2003.

[34] Raz makes a similar point about the making of particular legal rulings in 'The Rule of Law and its Virtue' in *The Authority of Law* (n 26) 215–16.

Council should follow decisions of the House of Lords on English law, and that (b) Privy Council decisions were not binding within the English legal system.[35] Nonetheless, the Privy Council announced that it was sitting as an enlarged panel and that it would clarify, definitively, the law of England as well as the law of Jersey (the jurisdiction from which the appeal originated).[36] Such a decision was clearly contrary to the established rules of precedent, yet no reference was made to the authorities recognising those rules, and no justification was offered for the novel approach. Neither were any comments made to indicate the limits of the departure involved.

In *James*, the Court of Appeal was left in the invidious position of reconciling *Holley* with the existing rules on precedent.[37] The Court of Appeal was clearly bound by the House of Lords decision in *Smith*, and yet *Holley* had disapproved of the decision in *Smith* and declared that it was not good law. The Court acknowledged the difficulty of its position and confronted the conflict between *Holley* and the existing law. But its arguments and conclusions are not easy to follow. On the conflict between *Holley* and the existing rules of precedent, the Court observed that a majority of Law Lords, albeit sitting in the Privy Council, had decided to do so, and opined that: 'We do not consider that it is for this court to rule that it was beyond their powers to alter the common law rules of precedent in this way.'[38] But the Law Lords, when sitting in the Privy Council, do not constitute the House of Lords, so it was the Privy Council that was presuming to alter the relationship between the Privy Council and the House of Lords, and doing so in the face of clear authority to the contrary that was not considered. Neither did the Law Lords, acting in this way, explain *when* such a decision would override a House of Lords precedent. *James* ruled that the Court of Appeal was bound to follow a decision of the Privy Council in preference to a binding decision of the House of Lords when: (i) all Law Lords hearing the case agreed that this was the effect of the decision; (ii) the majority in the Privy Council represented a majority of the Law Lords as a whole; and consequently (iii) 'the result of any appeal on the issue to the House of Lords is a foregone conclusion'.[39] The Court of Appeal did not explain the rationale for this set of conditions. The closest it came was in point (iii), that the result of an appeal to the House of Lords would be a foregone conclusion.

As already noted, the anomaly of *Holley* and *James* was alleviated to some extent by the decision of the Supreme Court in *Willers v Joyce (No 2)*.[40] *Willers v Joyce (No 2)* followed on from the decision of the Supreme Court in *Willers v Joyce (No 1)*,[41] which recognised that a claim for malicious prosecution in tort existed in

[35] *Tai Hing Cotton Mill Ltd v Liu Chong Hing Bank Ltd* [1986] AC 80 (PC).
[36] *Holley* [1].
[37] For a helpful discussion of *James*, see J Elvin, 'The Doctrine of Precedent and the Provocation Defence' (2006) 69 *MLR* 819.
[38] *James* [42].
[39] ibid [43].
[40] *Willers v Joyce (No 2)* [2016] UKSC 44, [2018] AC 843.
[41] *Willers v Joyce (No 1)* [2016] UKSC 43, [2018] AC 779.

the case of civil as well as criminal proceedings. At first instance the trial court had been confronted by a conflict between the view expressed by the House of Lords in *Gregory v Portsmouth City Council*[42] and the decision of the Privy Council in *Crawford Adjusters (Cayman) v Sagicor General Insurance (Cayman)*.[43] The trial judge concluded that she should follow the carefully considered dicta in *Gregory* rejecting the extension of the tort to civil proceedings rather than the majority's decision in *Crawford* recognising such an action, on the basis that it was not a 'foregone conclusion' that the Privy Council's majority decision in *Crawford* would be adopted by the Supreme Court in preference to the considered view expressed in *Gregory*.[44] On (leapfrog) appeal to the Supreme Court[45] a bench of nine judges held five to four that the tort of malicious prosecution should be recognised as extending to civil proceedings.[46] Because the trial judge had accepted the argument that a Privy Council decision was to be preferred to a Supreme Court decision if it were a 'foregone conclusion' that the Supreme Court would adopt the Privy Council view, the Supreme Court turned to this issue in a companion judgment. It restated the orthodox view that the courts in England are bound by the decisions of the Supreme Court and Court of Appeal, even if these conflict with a later decision of the Privy Council. In particular, the Supreme Court expressly rejected the view that a Privy Council decision should be preferred to a binding Supreme Court decision if it was a 'foregone conclusion' that the Supreme Court would follow the Privy Council's view.[47] But near the end of its discussion, the Supreme Court adopted the unorthodox view that it would nonetheless be 'convenient' and 'sensible' to permit parties to challenge House of Lords, Supreme Court, and Court of Appeal decisions on questions of English law before the Privy Council. The President of the Privy Council (who is also the President of the Supreme Court), could select an appropriate panel to hear the case, and 'the members of that panel can, if they think it appropriate, not only decide that the earlier decision of the House of Lords or Supreme Court, or of the Court of Appeal, was wrong, but also can expressly direct that domestic courts should treat the decision of the JCPC as representing the law of England and Wales'.[48] The Supreme Court conceded that this

> may, in terms of strict logic, be inconsistent with the above analysis [of the relationship between the Privy Council and English Courts], but is plainly sensible in practice and justified by experience (and is therefore consistent with Oliver Wendell Holmes's view of the common law (Wendell Holmes, *The Common Law* (1881)).[49]

[42] *Gregory v Portsmouth City Council* [2000] 1 AC 419 (HL).

[43] *Crawford Adjusters (Cayman) Ltd v Sagicor General Insurance (Cayman) Ltd* [2013] UKPC 17, [2014] AC 366 (PC).

[44] *Willers v Gubay* [2015] EWHC 1315 (Ch), [69]–[72].

[45] Under ss 12 and 13 of the Administration of Justice Act 1969.

[46] *Willers v Joyce (No 1)* [2016] UKSC 43, [2018] AC 779.

[47] *Willers v Joyce (No 2)*, [17]–[18].

[48] ibid [21].

[49] ibid [19].

The decision had earlier acknowledged that the Privy Council is not a court of the United Kingdom 'at all',[50] and that existing authorities of both the Privy Council and the House of Lords were clear that the courts in England were not bound by decisions of the Privy Council.[51] *Willers v Joyce (No 2)* was clearly decided on the basis of careful and thorough arguments from counsel[52] before a bench of nine Supreme Court judges especially empanelled to consider the relationship between the decisions in *Gregory* and *Crawford*, and reasons were given for adopting a novel approach in future cases before the Privy Council. Of course the merits of the exception may be questioned.[53] For one thing, Oliver Wendell Holmes was not suggesting in *The Common Law* that the common law is illogical, or that illogicality is an acceptable feature of the law: his point was that the content and operation of the law cannot be derived logically, like a mathematical proof, from certain self-evident axioms.[54] Neither is the position of the Privy Council vis-à-vis the courts of England a matter of 'logic': it is a matter of its constitutional status. The Privy Council is a foreign court for the purposes of English law, and so its decisions (absent statutory authority) are constitutionally not binding on courts in England and Wales. Neither the Senior Courts Act 1981 nor the Constitutional Reform Act 2005 confers a general role on the Privy Council in determining English law.[55]

Turning now to *Ivey* and its treatment of the question of 'dishonesty', it is clear from the judgment in *Ivey* that its discussion of *Ghosh* was obiter. Nonetheless, the Supreme Court went on to assert that there were 'convincing grounds for holding that the second leg of the test propounded in *R v Ghosh* [1982] QB 1053 does not correctly represent the law and that directions based upon it ought no longer to be given'.[56] It is not clear what the Supreme Court intended the legal effect of this statement to be. Was it meant to be binding on lower courts?[57] There is no common law authority for the Supreme Court's having the power to direct a lower court to follow its obiter dicta, and (if that was meant to be the effect of the

[50] ibid [12]. See further *Halsbury's Laws of England*, 5th edn (LexisNexis, 2019) vol 24A, §§ 78–91 ('Privy Council').

[51] *Willers v Joyce (No 2)* [12]–[14]. See *Tai Hing Cotton Mill Ltd v Liu Chong Hing Bank* [1986] AC 80 (PC) and *In re Spectrum* [2005] UKHL 41, [2005] 2 AC 680.

[52] See *Willers v Joyce (No 2)* [2018] AC 843, 847–50.

[53] See P Mirfield, 'A Novel Theory of Privy Council Precedent' (2017) 133 *LQR* 1. The judgment is also unclear on whether the Privy Council must agree unanimously that its decision alters domestic English law. Such a requirement is itself a judicial innovation.

[54] OW Holmes, *The Common Law* (Boston, Macmillan, 1887) ch 1.

[55] Whereas the Privy Council does have statutory authority to hear cases in some specialised matters, eg appeals from the High Court when it is acting as a prize court: see Senior Courts Act 1981, s 16(2), or claims that a person purporting to be a member of the House of Commons is disqualified: House of Commons Disqualification Act 1975, s 7. See generally *Halsbury's Laws of England* (n 50) vol 24A, §§ 86–90 ('Privy Council').

[56] *Ivey* [74].

[57] At an earlier point in the judgment (*Ivey* [63]), it was said that: 'there is some doubt about the freedom of that court [the Court of Appeal] to depart from *R v Ghosh* [1982] QB 1053 in the absence of a decision from this court'.

decision) no justification was offered for having such a power in *Ivey*. The statement in *Ivey* satisfied none of the desiderata of judicial law-making. It was not relied upon in reaching the decision in the case; no reasons were given to justify the departure from the practice of precedent; and it was not grounded in existing law. Alternatively, were the comments on *Ghosh* merely meant to be *obiter* and thus not binding on lower courts? Speaking extra-judicially between the decision in *Ivey* and the Court of Appeal decision in *Barton*, the President of the Supreme Court, Lady Hale, who had been a party to the decision in *Ivey*, observed that some judges were already applying *Ivey* rather than *Ghosh*. She observed that: 'Convicted defendants may appeal on the basis that *Ghosh* was right and we were wrong. The Court of Appeal does not have to agree with us.'[58]

Either way, the discussion of *Ghosh* in *Ivey* demonstrates some of the practical reasons why the common law does not treat obiter dicta as binding. The merits of retaining *Ghosh* as the test of dishonesty in property offences were not canvassed before the court by counsel taking opposing views, since the point had not needed to be settled. As commentators have noted, none of the arguments in favour of retaining the *Ghosh* decision, which had been the law for thirty-five years, was mentioned in the judgment, and it is not clear whether the Supreme Court was aware of these arguments, or whether it would have made any difference to the Court's view.[59] Neither was any attention given to the issue of 'partial reform'. One of the arguments in favour of retention of the *Ghosh* test was to compensate for the extremely wide characterisation that the House of Lords has given to the concept of 'appropriation' in the law of theft. Essentially, any transfer of property,[60] and any interference with any property right,[61] even with the owner's consent,[62] amounts to an 'appropriation' in the law of theft. Perhaps *Ivey* is a better test than *Ghosh* given a narrower characterisation of appropriation; but perhaps *Ghosh* is a better test than *Ivey* given the existing characterisation of appropriation.[63]

So what was the effect of these Supreme Court dicta on *Ghosh*? In *Barton* the Court of Appeal held that the Supreme Court had altered the rules of precedent.[64] The Court did not explain how the Supreme Court had done so, since the Supreme Court had offered no explanation of what it had done. All the Court of Appeal

[58] B Hale, 'Dishonesty' (Bristol Alumni Lecture 2018) (2019) 48 *Common Law World Review* 3, 12.

[59] See GR Sullivan and AP Simester, 'Judging Dishonesty' (2020) 136 *LQR* 523; M Dyson and P Jarvis, 'Poison Ivey or Herbal Leaf Tea?' (2018) 134 *LQR* 198; K Laird, 'Dishonesty' [2020] *Crim LR* 1065; and D Ormerod and K Laird, '*Ivey v Genting Casinos*: Much Ado about Nothing?' (2018) 9 *UK Supreme Court Yearbook* 380. The Fraud Act 2006, for instance, was enacted by Parliament on the presupposition that the test for dishonesty in fraud would be that in *Ghosh*: see Dyson and Jarvis, 201.

[60] *R v Hinks* [2001] 2 AC 241 (HL).

[61] *R v Morris* [1984] AC 320 (HL).

[62] *Lawrence v Metropolitan Police Commissioner* [1972] AC 626 (HL).

[63] See JR Spencer, 'Two Cases on the Law of Theft: A Concertina Movement?' [2018] *Archbold Review* 4.

[64] *Barton* [102].

could offer was that (relying on *James*) 'we do not consider that it is for this court to conclude that it was beyond their powers to act in this way'.[65] The basis of this novel power went unexplained; neither was it explained why it was beyond the Court of Appeal's authority to question such a departure from the settled practice of the common law.

The Court of Appeal held that 'where the Supreme Court itself directs that an otherwise binding decision of the Court of Appeal should no longer be followed and proposes an alternative test that it says must be adopted, the Court of Appeal is bound to follow what amounts to a direction from the Supreme Court even though it is strictly obiter'.[66] The Court of Appeal added that this was only the case where the 'direction' was unanimous, since 'a further appeal would be a foregone conclusion',[67] again relying on the discussion in *James*. But as noted earlier, the argument in *James* had been that, since the majority in *Holley* constituted a majority of the Law Lords as a whole, a challenge to the correctness of *Holley* would inevitably fail. The panel in *Ivey*, on the other hand, did not constitute a majority of the judges of the Supreme Court. Furthermore, the Court's attention was not drawn to the discussion in *Willers v Joyce (No 2)*, which had expressly rejected the idea that a binding decision could be disregarded if it was a 'foregone conclusion' that it would not be followed.[68] Finally, it was the Court of Appeal itself that glossed the statements in *Ivey* as 'directions' to the Court of Appeal. The Supreme Court merely stated that the second leg of the test in *Ghosh* 'ought no longer to be given':[69] the effect of that statement was not made clear.

It should also be noted that a more orthodox route to the Court of Appeal's departure from *Ghosh* existed. There was clear authority from the Court of Criminal Appeal and the Criminal Division of the Court of Appeal that the Court was free to depart from one of its earlier decisions if that decision had misunderstood or misapplied the law.[70] The discussion in *Ivey* clearly provided grounds for considering whether *Ghosh* had misunderstood the law. Although the Court of Appeal considered this argument, it concluded that the earlier authorities 'are not directly concerned with the circumstances in these appeals, which involve an instruction from the Supreme Court'.[71] The Court of Appeal considered itself compelled to decide *Barton* on the precedent point.[72]

[65] ibid.

[66] ibid [104].

[67] ibid [104].

[68] *Willers v Joyce (No 2)* [17]–[18]. Strictly speaking, the decision related to preferring Privy Council decisions to those of the Supreme Court or Court of Appeal, but the reasons given (essentially, that it was better to have a clear, simple rule that did not require argument to apply) are equally applicable to other courts.

[69] *Ivey* [74].

[70] *Taylor* [1950] 2 KB 368 (CCA) and *Gould* [1968] 2 QB 65 (CA).

[71] *Barton* [96].

[72] The Court added that it was not following *Ivey* reluctantly, as the analysis in *Ivey* was 'compelling' (*Barton* [106]); but it did not explain why the analysis was compelling, or discuss any of the substantive criticisms of *Ivey*.

V. The Legal Nature of Case Law

One underlying issue that touches on the cases considered in this chapter concerns the nature and status of case law. Legal practice naturally foregrounds the statutes and cases that courts use to determine the rights and duties of those subject to the jurisdiction of the courts. But in the background are the doctrines and practices that give those materials their status as law. Case law (as opposed to statutory law) has the following four features:

(a) The decisions of superior courts of record[73] can create law.
(b) The binding law created by (a) is restricted to the ratio decidendi of the case: that is, to the rulings on points of law that were relied upon by the court in reaching its decision in the case.
(c) Other statements about the law made in the course of a decision (obiter dicta) do not create binding law. (They can, nonetheless, have legal relevance, both in interpreting (b) and in providing persuasive authority for a view of the law.)
(d) Some courts can overrule and depart from (or modify) earlier decisions – that is, they can extinguish or alter the binding law made in an earlier case.

For ease of discussion, let me call features (a)–(d) 'the doctrines of case law'. The doctrines of case law are normally regarded as legally binding on courts, in that courts have a legal obligation to follow them. But how should their legal status be understood? These features do not rest on a statutory footing: case law isn't binding because of a 'Doctrines of Case Law Act'. But neither could case law be binding because of a precedent establishing that it is binding. Precedents are only binding in the first place because of the doctrines of case law, so precedent can't be what makes the doctrines themselves binding.

What then (if anything) does give case law its legal status? The preceding points are often deflected by speaking of the *practice* of precedent. It is said, for example, that 'courts in this country have long adopted the practice of treating decisions on a point of law as precedents for the future',[74] and that the 'rules of precedent reflect the practices of the courts'.[75] The same thought underlies the 'Practice Statement' of 1966 which spoke of the House of Lords proposing to 'modify their present practice'.[76] A more philosophical account of case law holds that precedent is part of the 'rule of recognition' of a legal system: a fundamental social practice followed and endorsed by officials in their official roles.[77]

[73] On superior courts of record, see *R v Chancellor of St Edmundsbury and Ipswich Diocese: ex p White* [1948] 1 KB 195 (CA).
[74] *In re Spectrum* [2005] UKHL 41, [2005] 2 AC 680, [5].
[75] *R v Simpson* [2003] EWCA Crim 1499, [27].
[76] *Practice Statement (Judicial Precedents)* [1966] 1 WLR 1234.
[77] HLA Hart, *The Concept of Law*, 3rd edn (Oxford, Oxford University Press, 2012) 94–110.

There is good sense in these views. Clearly the doctrines of case law are followed by the courts (and other officials) in their official practices. But these are not *just* social practices that the courts and others uphold: they are not equivalent to other social practices that courts might follow and endorse, such as a concern for efficiency and for decorum in judges' dealings with each other. Instead, the doctrines of case law such as precedent are regarded as legally binding on judges and officials. A trial judge who fails to follow a binding precedent makes a legal mistake, as does a judge who treats as ratio what is merely obiter in a judgment. But what sort of law could this be, if it is neither statutory nor based on precedent? The answer is that the doctrines of case law are part of the *customary* law of the legal system (or more specifically what is sometimes called 'customary law *in foro*').[78] Lawyers are most familiar with a different type of customary law, though it plays only a marginal role in contemporary domestic law. This is customary law *in pays*: the customs of legal subjects that are given legal effect by the law. If fishermen have for many generations dried their nets along a stretch of beach unchallenged, and done so in the belief that they have a right to do so, that right may be(come) legally valid, despite the lack of any statutory authorisation or judicial decision establishing such a right.[79] If the system has some existing criteria by which officials can identify certain customs of its *subjects* as legally valid, then it recognises customary law *in pays*.[80] The second type of customary law, less frequently discussed, is customary law *in foro*: customary law of the *officials themselves*.[81] These are standards that are not validated by any other legal source, but are treated as legally binding by officials in their official roles. In the common law, the most obvious example of customary law *in foro* is the Royal Prerogative – prerogative rights and powers of the Crown that have been long established as parts of the laws of England, such as the power to enter treaties and issue passports,[82] but which rest on neither statute nor precedent.[83] From this perspective, the doctrines of case law can also be understood as a form of customary law *in foro*.

The hallmark of customary law *in foro* is that officials treat those standards as *authoritative* for officials in their official roles, despite the fact that these standards

[78] The term was coined by Bentham: J Bentham, *A Comment on the Commentaries*, ed JH Burns and HLA Hart (Oxford, Oxford University Press, 1977) 182–84.

[79] *Mercer v Denne* [1904] 2 Ch 534, esp 551–52.

[80] This is the only sort of customary law that Hart explicitly discusses in *The Concept of Law* (n 77) 44–48, 100, 101.

[81] A more detailed discussion of customary law *in foro* can be found in G Lamond, 'The Doctrine of Precedent and the Rule of Recognition' in TAO Endicott, H Kristjánsson, and S Lewis (eds), *Philosophical Foundations of Precedent* (Oxford, Oxford University Press, 2023). It is possible, of course, that there might be a custom *in pays* of officials, which satisfied the same criteria of identification as customs of non-officials. Customary law *in foro*, by contrast, relates to the practices of officials in performing their official roles.

[82] See D Feldman (ed), *English Public Law*, 2nd edn (Oxford, Oxford University Press, 2009) 181–86.

[83] As the British Ministry of Justice commented in *The Governance of Britain: Review of the Executive Royal Prerogative Powers: Final Report* (London, Ministry of Justice, 2009) 7 (§ 27): 'there are many prerogative powers for which there is no recent judicial authority and sometimes no judicial authority at all'.

are not validated by another legal source (such as statute). What does this mean? A standard is treated as authoritative when it is regarded as a standard that must be followed independently of the officials' views about the *merits* of the standard. So whether or not an official thinks that a standard is a desirable one, they regard it as a standard that they and other officials are obliged to follow. And this is precisely how the doctrines of case law are treated by the courts.

The fact that the doctrines of case law amount to customary law *in foro* does not mean, however, that (i) the doctrines are immutable, or that (ii) they can only be altered by changes in courts' customary practices. Customary law *in foro* can, in principle, be overridden by both statutory law and case law.[84] This is shown clearly by the case of the Royal Prerogative, which has been altered by both legislation[85] and precedent.[86] But if customary law *in foro* is to be altered deliberately, that should be done through appropriate law-making procedures. This is one of the reasons that the House of Lords' *Practice Statement* on precedent was controversial.[87] Commentators accepted the desirability of the House of Lords embracing the power that other ultimate appellate courts in the common law world had long since acknowledged to overrule their own decisions. But some were critical of the method adopted to do so. The House of Lords had ruled in *London Street Tramways*[88] that it was strictly bound by its own decisions. This was binding law. Practice statements normally deal with matters of court procedure. A more orthodox approach would have been to rely on the inherent jurisdiction of the House of Lords to reconsider *London Street Tramways* in an appropriate case and hold that it had been wrongly decided, or was no longer good law, for the sorts of reasons that were outlined in the *Practice Statement*. Of course, the *Practice Statement* has been accepted by officials and is regarded as authoritative, but it represented a departure from standard methods of law creation.

So the concern with *Holley* and *Ivey* (or, more precisely, *Ivey* as interpreted by *Barton*) is not that modifying the doctrines of case law is per se impermissible. It is simply that the two cases are *judicial* law-making in only the thinnest sense of the term: that they are merely law made by the judiciary. They do not accord with the norms of judicial law-making, which require that: (i) an issue is relied upon by the court in reaching its decision;[89] (ii) that reasons are given for the resolution settled upon, which also involves the issue having been properly canvassed with the parties and fully argued by opposing counsel; and (iii) that the reasons relied upon are grounded in existing law and provide a compelling justification for the

[84] Although there may be some customary law *in foro* that cannot be altered by the courts, eg, the doctrine of Parliamentary supremacy.

[85] eg Civil Contingencies Act 2004.

[86] eg *Council of Civil Service Unions v Minister for the Civil Service* [1985] AC 374 (HL).

[87] See eg J Stone, '1066 and All That! Loosening the Chains of Precedent' (1969) 69 *Columbia Law Review* 1162.

[88] *London Street Tramways Company Limited v London County Council* [1898] AC 375 (HL).

[89] Or was relied upon by the lower court from which the appeal is being heard, as in *Willers v Joyce (No 2)*.

departure from existing law. The justification should also be commensurate with the seriousness of the issue and the extent of the departure from settled law. By these standards the two decisions fall short. *James* and *Barton* fare better on scores (i) and (ii), but fall short on score (iii), as the rationale for accepting the Privy Council's and Supreme Court's actions are far from persuasive.[90]

It should be noted that *Ivey* (as interpreted by *Barton*) represents the most striking departure from the norms of common law judicial law-making. According to *Barton*, *Ivey* claimed that lower courts should follow certain obiter dicta from the Supreme Court in preference to binding authority of the Court of Appeal. This claim was itself obiter, since it was not part of the ratio of the decision. The ratio decidendi–obiter dictum distinction is one of the most fundamental distinctions in the common law. That only rationes bind is one of the cornerstones of case law doctrines, for important reasons of both principle and practice. To assert that it can be overridden without argument or reasoning is a remarkable position to attribute to the Supreme Court.

It is interesting to contrast the approaches in *Holley* and *Ivey* with the approach taken by the House of Lords in *In re Spectrum*.[91] The latter was a civil case dealing with the characterisation of floating charges, where the issue was raised whether the House of Lords should overrule a long-standing lower court decision prospectively, contrary to established doctrine that decisions of the courts have retrospective as well as prospective effect. An enlarged bench of seven Law Lords was convened to hear the case, the issue of prospective overruling was carefully argued by counsel, and three substantive speeches were delivered, all of which offered lengthy views on the propriety of prospective overruling.[92] The ratio–obiter distinction is no less fundamental to case law as is suspending the retroactive effect of precedents; indeed, it is arguably a more fundamental aspect of case law. If it is to be altered, it merits at least the same degree of attention.

VI. Conclusion

This chapter has argued that the Privy Council, the House of Lords, the Supreme Court and the Court of Appeal have at times been too casual in their treatment of the basic doctrines of case law. Of course, it might be said, in response to the preceding criticisms, that the decisions discussed above were sensible solutions to practical problems. As I noted at the beginning, I have some sympathy with this view vis-à-vis *Holley*. But I do not think this is true of *Ivey* and *Barton*.

[90] By these standards, *Willers v Joyce (No 2)* [2016] UKSC 44, [2018] AC 843 fares better, apart from the reasons given for the Privy Council ([19]–[21]) to be exceptionally permitted to overrule appellate decisions of English courts.

[91] *In re Spectrum* [2005] UKHL 41, [2005] 2 AC 680. And indeed with the approach taken in *Willers v Joyce (No 2)*.

[92] per Lord Nicholls [4]–[43], Lord Hope [65]–[74] and Lord Scott [121]–[127].

There are two fundamental issues here. The first concerns the settled doctrines of case law that are binding law for the courts. The second concerns the alteration of such doctrines through judicial law-making. All courts are bound by the settled doctrines of case law, and should comply with them unless they have the power to alter them and make a deliberate decision to do so. In particular, the ratio–obiter distinction respects the principled reasons why judicial law-making is restricted to the ratio decidendi of a decision, and draws a coherent line between what is binding and what is merely persuasive in a judgment. It also makes good sense given the courts' limited resources for assessing legal changes, and the limitations of the adversarial system as a method for general legal change. Moreover, it reflects the limited political legitimacy that courts enjoy to make new law. Similarly, the doctrine of precedent should be consistent with the constitutional status and role of the courts whose decisions are held to bind other courts.

The ultimate rationale for compliance with the doctrines of case law and judicial law-making is the rule of law. The rule of law depends upon a culture of legality: a scrupulous concern by officials (both judicial and non-judicial) to abide by and be guided by the law. The courts play a special role in maintaining the rule of law. They rightly uphold the rights of individuals against private parties and against other instrumentalities of the state. And they rightly criticise failings by other officials to adhere to the law. Yet this also means that it is incumbent on the courts to set an example in the way in which they follow and uphold the law. The rule of law comes at a price. It would often be easier and more convenient for officials to deviate from legal requirements in order to secure some good or to promote some valuable end. But part of the discipline of the rule of law involves attaching great importance to *how* things are done, not just to what is done. From this perspective it matters how the courts treat the doctrines of case law and judicial law-making: they require just as much, if not more, consideration and concern as any other part of the law.

GR SULLIVAN: LIST OF PUBLICATIONS

Books

AP Simester and GR Sullivan, *Criminal Law: Theory and Doctrine* (Oxford, Hart Publishing, 2000) lxix, 695pp.

Second edition, 2003; lxiv, 697pp. Third edition, 2007; lxxiii, 791pp. Fourth edition (with JR Spencer and GJ Virgo), 2010; lxxxiii, 868pp. Fifth edition, 2013; lxxxvi, 893pp. Sixth edition (with JR Spencer, F Stark, and GJ Virgo), 2016; lxxxvi, 891pp. Seventh edition, 2019; xcii, 964pp (with JR Spencer, F Stark, and GJ Virgo).

Edited Books

GR Sullivan and I Dennis (eds), *Seeking Security: Pre-empting the Commission of Criminal Harms* (Oxford, Hart Publishing, 2012) xxviii, 341pp.

Articles and Essays

'Consent in Modern Criminal law' (2023) 54 *Victoria University of Wellington Law Review* 351 (with AP Simester).

'Causation, Fault and Responsibility' in Reed and Bohlander (eds), *Fault in Criminal Law: Domestic and Comparative Perspectives* (Farnham, Ashgate, 2021) 67 (with AP Simester).

'Loss of Self-Control in the Appellate Courts' [2021] *Northern Ireland Legal Quarterly* 200 (with HS Crombag and JJ Child).

'Defending the Delusional, the Irrational and the Dangerous' [2020] *Criminal Law Review* 306 (with JJ Child and HS Crombag).

'Drunk Dangerous and Delusional: How Legal Concept Creep Risks Overcriminalisation' [2020] *Addiction* (with HS Crombag and JJ Child).

'Workplace Welfare and State Coercion' in Bogg, Collins, Freedland and Herring (eds), *Criminality at Work* (Oxford, Oxford University Press, 2020) 35.

'Law Reform and the Supreme Court: The Abolition of Joint Enterprise Liability?' in Krebs (ed), *Accessorial Liability after Jogee* (Oxford, Hart Publishing, 2019) 7.

'Restitution or Confiscation/Forfeiture? Private Rights versus Public Values' in Green and Bogg (eds), *Illegality after Patel v Mirza* (Oxford, Hart Publishing, 2018) 61.

'The Current State of Murder in English Criminal Law: A Critique, Wrong Turns and All' in Reed and Bohlander (eds), *Homicide: Domestic and Comparative Perspectives* (Abingdon, Routledge, 2018) 62 (with J Child).

'Deciding to Die and Help with Dying: What Can and Cannot be Done in England and Wales' in Reed and Bohlander (eds), *Consent: Domestic and Comparative Perspectives* (Abingdon, Routledge, 2017) 147.

'Avoiding Criminal Liability and Excessive Punishment for Persons who Lack Culpability: What Can and Should Be Done?' in Reed and Bohlander (eds), *General Defences: Domestic and Comparative Perspectives* (Farnham, Ashgate, 2014) 25.

'Wrongs and Responsibility for Wrongs in Tort and Crime' in Dyson (ed), *Unravelling Tort and Crime* (Cambridge, Cambridge University Press, 2014) 82.

'Professing Criminal Law' (2014) 12 *Ohio Journal of Criminal Law* 267.

'When Does the Insanity Defence Arise?' [2014] *Criminal Law Review* 787 (with JJ Child).

'Accomplices and Principals after *Gnango*' in Reed and Bohlander (eds), *Participating in Crime: Domestic, Comparative and International Perspectives* (Farnham, Ashgate 2013) 37.

'Reformulating Bribery – A Legal Critique of the Bribery Act 2010' in Horder and Alldridge, *Modern Bribery Law* (Cambridge, Cambridge University Press, 2013) 13.

'Seeking Security – An Introduction' in Sullivan and Dennis (eds), *Seeking Security: Pre-empting the Commission of Criminal Harms* (Oxford, Hart Publishing, 2012) 1 (with I Dennis).

'The Hard Treatment of Innocent Persons in State Responses to the Threat of Large Scale and Imminent Terrorist Violence' in Sullivan and Dennis (eds), *Seeking Security: Pre-empting the Commission of Criminal Harms* (Oxford, Hart Publishing, 2012) 293.

'Causation without Limits: Causing Death While Driving Without a Licence, While Disqualified, or Without Insurance' [2012] *Criminal Law Review* 753 (with AP Simester).

'Doing Without Complicity' [2012] *Journal of Commonwealth Criminal Law* 199.

'The Bribery Act 2010 – An Overview' [2011] *Criminal Law Review* 87.

'Copyright, Licences and Statutory Fraud' (2011) 3 *Journal of Media Law* 289 (with R Deazley).

'The Conduct Element of offences' in Chan, Wright and Yeo (eds), *Codification, Macaulay, and the Indian Penal Code* (Farnham, Ashgate, 2011) 87.

'Parents and their Truanting Children – An English Lesson in Liability Without Responsibility' (2010) 12 *Otago Law Review* 285.

'Conduct and Proof of Conduct: Two Fundamental Conditions of Criminal Liability' in Kaikobad and Bohlander (eds), *International Law and Power, Perspectives on legal Order and Justice: Essays in Honour of Colin Warbrick* (Leiden, Koninklijke Brill, 2009) 235.

'Liberalism and Constraining Choice: The Cases of Death and Serious Bodily Harm' in Smith and Deazley (eds), *The Legal, Medical and Cultural Regulation of the Body: Transformation and Transgression* (Farnham, Ashgate, 2009) 205.

'Corporate Criminal Liability' in Cane and Conaghan (eds), *The New Oxford Companion to Law* (Oxford University Press, 2008) 232.

'First Degree Murder and Complicity – Parity of Culpability between Principal and Accomplice' (2008) 1 *Journal of Criminal Law and Philosophy* 271.

'Participating in Crime' [2008] *Criminal Law Review* 19.

'Conduct and Complicity: Liability Based on Omission and Risk' [2008] 39 *Cambrian Law Review* 60.

'Bribery outside England and Wales: Corporate Liability, Defences and Consent to Prosecution' [2008] *Criminal Law Review* 687.

'Complicity for First Degree Murder and Complicity in an Unlawful Killing' [2006] *Criminal Law Review* 502.

'Inchoate Liability for Assisting and Encouraging Crime' [2006] *Criminal Law Review* 1047.

'The Nature and Rationale of Property Offences' (with AP Simester) in Duff and Green (eds), *Criminal Law: Doctrines of the Special Part* (Oxford, Oxford University Press, 2004) 169.

'Strict Liability for Criminal Offences in England and Wales Following Incorporation into English Law of the European Convention for Human Rights' in Simester (ed), *Appraising Strict Liability* (Oxford, Oxford University Press, 2004) 195.

'Private Commercial Bribery: The Legal Response in England and Wales' in Heine, Huber and Rose (eds), *Private Commercial Bribery* (Freiburg, Max Planck Institute for Foreign and International Criminal Law, 2003) 55.

'La Riposta Legislativa all Corruzione in Inghliterra' in Acquaroli and Foffani (eds), *La Corruzione Tra Privati* (Milan, Guiffre Editore, 2003) 157 (trans C Bardelli).

'Fraud – The Latest Law Commission Proposals' [2003] 67 *Journal of Criminal Law* 139.

'The Legal Response to Corruption in England and Wales' in Huber (ed), *Combating Corruption in the European Union* (Trier, Academy of European Law, 2002) 81.

'Is Criminal Law Possible?' (2002) 22 *Oxford Journal of Legal Studies* 747.

'Knowledge, Belief and Culpability' in Shute and Simester (eds), *Criminal Law Theory: Doctrines of the General Part* (Oxford, Oxford University Press, 2001) 207.

'Corporate Killing – Some Government Proposals' [2001] *Criminal Law Review* 31.

'Proscribing Corruption – Some Comments on the Law Commission Report' [1998] *Criminal Law Review* 547.

'Reformulating the Corruption Laws' [1997] *Criminal Law Review* 730.

'Ministering Death' (1997) 17 *Oxford Journal of Legal Studies* 123.

'The Attribution of Culpability to Limited Companies' (1996) *Cambridge Law Journal* 515.

'Making Excuses' in Simester and Smith (eds), *Harm and Culpability* (Oxford, Oxford University Press, 1996) 131.

'The Particularity of Serious Fraud' in Birks (ed), *Pressing Problems of the Law* (Oxford, Oxford University Press, 1995) 99.

'Expressing Corporate Guilt' (1995) 15 *Oxford Journal of Legal Studies* 281.

'Territoriality Theft and *Atakpu*' [1994] *Criminal Law Review* 650 (with CJ Warbrick).

'Territorial Jurisdiction' (1994) 43 *International and Comparative Law Quarterly* 460 (with CJ Warbrick).

'Intoxicants and Diminished Responsibility' [1994] *Criminal Law Review* 156.

'Fault Elements and Joint Enterprise' [1994] *Criminal Law Review* 252.

'Anger and Excuse: Reassessing Provocation' (1993) 13 *Oxford Journal of Legal Studies* 421.

'Cause and Contemporaneity of Actus Reus and Mens Rea' (1993) 52 *Cambridge Law Journal* 487.

'The Confiscation of the Proceeds of Crime in England' in Fisse et al (eds), *The Money Trail* (Sydney, Law Book Company, 1992) 305.

'Finality and Fair-Hearing' [1992] *Criminal Law Review* 346 (with CJ Warbrick).

'Intent, Subjective Recklessness and Culpability' (1992) 12 *Oxford Journal of Legal Studies* 380.

'Bad Thoughts and Bad Acts' [1990] *Criminal Law Review* 567.

'Framing an Acceptable General Offence of Fraud' (1989) 53 *Journal of Criminal Law* 92.

'The Need for a Crime of Sexual Assault' [1989] *Criminal Law Review* 340.

'Intent, Purpose and Complicity' [1988] *Criminal Law Review* 641.

'Reforming the Substantive Law of Fraud' (1988) 52 *Journal of Criminal Law* 288.

'Fraud and the Efficacy of the Criminal Law' [1985] *Criminal Law Review* 616.

'Restating the Scope of the Derivative Action' (1985) *Cambridge Law Journal* 236.

'Company Controllers and Theft – A Reply' [1984] *Criminal Law Review* 405.

'Ship Routeing Schemes and the Criminal Liability of the Master' [1983] *Lloyd's Commercial Law Quarterly* 23 (with CJ Warbrick).

'Company Controllers, Company Cheques and Theft' [1983] *Criminal Law Review* 512.

'The Liability of Promoters on Pre-Incorporation Contracts' (1983) 47 *Conveyancer and Property Lawyer* (NS) 119.

'The Committee on the Future of Broadcasting' (1977) 40 *Modern Law Review* 460 (with C Munro).

'The Relationship between the Board of Directors and the General Meeting' (1977) 93 *Law Quarterly Review* 569.

'The Minority Shareholder – Another Advance' (1977) 41 *Conveyancer and Property Lawyer* (NS) 169.

'The Defence of Intoxication' [1970] *Journal of Association of Law Teachers* 9.

Shorter Articles and Notes

'Deadly Whisky' (2022) 138 *Law Quarterly Review* 11 (with AP Simester).
'Omissions, Duties, Causation and Time' (2021) 137 *Law Quarterly Review* 358 (with AP Simester).
'Judging Dishonesty' (2020) 136 *Law Quarterly Review* 523 (with AP Simester).
'Causing Euthanasia' (2019) 135 *Law Quarterly Review* 21 (with AP Simester).
'Causation as Fault' (2014) *Cambridge Law Journal* 14 (with AP Simester).
'Being There' (2012) *Cambridge Law Journal* 21 (with AP Simester).
'The Presumption of Incapacity' (1994) 49 *The Criminal Lawyer* 1.
'Recent Developments in the Control of Commercial Fraud' (1987) 5 *Company Law Digest* 60.
'Recovery of Payments Made Prior to the Revelation of Recipient's Misconduct' (1987) 5 *Company Law Digest* 42.
'Assisting Fraudulent Conduct as a Basis for Constructive Trusteeship' (1983) 5 *Company Lawyer* 242.
'Fraudulent Trading and Credit' (1983) 5 *Company Lawyer* 186.
'Mergers, Ministerial Discretion and Judicial Review' (1983) 4 *Company Lawyer* 125.
'Violent Self Help' (1983) 46 *Modern Law Review* 78.
'Challenging the Accounts by Personal and Derivative Actions' (1982) 3 *Company Lawyer* 261.
'Offences Against the Person – Remaining Elements of Constructive Liability' (1980) 130 *New Law Journal* 901.
'Going it Alone' (1979) 42 *Modern Law Review* 711.
'Crossing the Rubicon in Miami' (1978) 41 *Modern Law Review* 215.
'Duress and First-Degree Murder' (1977) 127 *New Law Journal* 407.
'Aiding and Abetting the Commission of Non-existent Offences' (1976) 39 *Modern Law Review* 350.
'Constructive Manslaughter' (1976) 39 *Modern Law Review* 727.
'Self-induced and Recurring Automatism' (1973) 23 *New Law Journal* 1093.

INDEX

www.ingramcontent.com/pod-product-compliance
Ingram Content Group UK Ltd.
Pitfield, Milton Keynes, MK11 3LW, UK
UKHW020239290926
15470UKWH00002B/619

9 781509 956142